Software Reuse
and Reverse Engineering
in Practice

UNICOM Applied Information Technology

Each book in the series is based upon papers given at a seminar organized by UNICOM Seminars Ltd. The reports cover subjects at the forefront of information technology, and the contributors are all authorities in the subject on which they are invited to write, either as researchers or as practitioners.

Software Reuse and Reverse Engineering in Practice

UNICOM

APPLIED INFORMATION TECHNOLOGY 12

Edited by **P. A. V. Hall**

Professor of Computing, the Open University, Milton Keynes, UK

CHAPMAN & HALL

LONDON · NEW YORK · TOKYO · MELBOURNE · MADRAS

Published by Chapman & Hall, 2–6 Boundary Row, London SE1 8HN

Chapman & Hall, 2–6 Boundary Row, London SE1 8HN, UK

Van Nostrand Reinhold, 115 5th Avenue, New York NY10003, USA

Chapman & Hall Japan, Thomson Publishing Japan, Hirakawacho Nemoto Building, 7F, 1–7–11 Hirakawa-cho, Chiyoda-ku, Tokyo 102, Japan

Chapman & Hall Australia, Thomas Nelson Australia, 102 Dodds Street, South Melbourne, Victoria 3205, Australia

Chapman & Hall India, R. Seshadri, 32 Second Main Road, CIT East, Madras 600 035, India

First edition 1992

© 1992 UNICOM and contributors

Printed and bound in Great Britain by T J Press (Padstow) Ltd, Cornwall

ISBN 0 412 39980 6   0 442 31409 4 (USA)

A catalogue record for this book is available from the British Library

Library of Congress Cataloging-in Publication data available

CONTENTS

CONTRIBUTORS

H. Albrechtsen
CRI/AS
Bregnerodvej 144
DK – 3460 Birkerod
Denmark

J. Barchan
Intasoft Limited
60 Portland Street
Exeter
Devon

M. Bardiaux
Plant Genetic Systems
UCMB Laboratories
ULB CP160
B1050 Brussels
Belgium

C. Boldyreff
Dept of Computer Science
Brunel University
Uxbridge
Middlesex

F. Bott
Department of Computer Science
University College of Wales
The Old College
King Street
Aberysthwyth
Dyfed

M. Brorsson
Telesoft AB
Malmoa
Sweden

P. D. Carroll
Royal Air Force

D. Catton
AI Limited
Watford
Herts

P. Delhaise
Plant Genetic Systems
UCMB Laboratories
ULB CP160
B1050 Brussels
Belgium

D. Francis
Programmes Know-How Ltd
121 Salusbury Road
London

A. Frazer
The Institute of Software Engineers
30 Island St
Belfast
Northern Ireland

S. J. Goldsack
Dept of Computer Science
Imperial College of Science,
Technology and Medicine
South Kensington
London

J. Grumann
Daten-Kommunikation GmbH
Wingertsbergweg 16
6380 Bad Homburg v.d.h.
Germany

P. A. V. Hall
Dept of Computer Science
The Open University
Milton Keynes

R. Hodgson
Interactive Development
Environments Ltd
Surrey Technology Centre
The Surrey Research Park
Guildford
Surrey

S. Holloway
DCE Information Management
Consultancy
Chester House
Chertsey Road
Woking
Surrey

late R. Jones
Software Development Monitor

R. Kenning
Centre for Software Maintenance
University of Durham
Old Shire Hall
Durham

J. Kramer
Dept of Computing
Imperial College of Science,
Technology and Medicine
South Kensington
London

I. Kruzela
Telesoft AB
Malmoa
Sweden

M. Lamb
Intasoft Limited
60 Portland Street
Exeter
Devon

M. K. O. Lee
Information Technology Research
Unit
BP Research Centre
Chertsey Road
Sunbury-on-Thames
Middlesex

R. McGill
ADPAC Software Ltd
Station House
Wembley
Middlesex

C. Minkowitz
STC Technology Ltd
Cophall House
Nelson Place
Newcastle under Lyme

M. Munro
Centre for Software Maintenance
University of Durham
Old Shire Hall
Durham

T. Orme
AEG (UK) Ltd
Engineering Division
Winnersh
Wokingham
Berkshire

M. Ratcliffe
Dept of Computer Science
University College of Wales
The Old College
King Street
Aberysthwyth
Dyfed

A. G. Sutcliffe
Dept of Business Computing
School of Informatics
City University
Northampton Square
London

A. Tilbury
Yard Software Systems
Avonbridge House
Bath Road
Chippenham
Wiltshire

P. Walton
Logica CES Ltd
64 Newman Street
London

R. Warden
K3 Group Ltd
Severn House
Prescott Drive
Worcestershire

P. J. Welch
Daten-Kommunikation GmbH
Wingertsbergweg 16
6380 Bad Homburg v.d.h.
Germany

S. Whalley
BT Research Labs
Martlesham Heath
Ipswich

J. Zhang
Dept of Computer Science
Brunel University
Uxbridge
Middlesex

EDITORIAL INTRODUCTION

P. A. V. Hall

The collection of papers included here were given at two seminars organized by Unicom in central London, from 29 November to 1 December 1989, and on 3 and 4 December 1990. They address a set of very topical important, inter-related, issues:

- software reuse, the use of software in applications other than that for which it was originally built;
- reverse engineering, the extraction of documentation and higher-level descriptions of software from the code itself;
- re-engineering, the improvement of software through restructuring and similar, typically through a process of reverse engineering followed by conventional forward development preserving as much of the original code as possible;
- maintenance, the repair and evolution of software to extend its life, using the above processes, and others like configuration management;
- object-oriented approaches, which are claimed to be a solution to all these issues.

The papers in this collection vary from the highly focused academic paper by Boldyreff and Zhang on reverse engineering, to the highly commerical like those of McGill, Francis, Lamb and Barchan, and Richard Warden. Most of the papers fall solidly in between, demonstrating sound industrial application of the methods, like those of Walton, Kramer, and Kruzela. Taken together they provide a view of the spectrum of activity current in this important branch of software engineering.

The first part of the volume is given to an extended **tutorial**, *Software Reuse, Reverse Engineering, and Re-engineering,* which covers the various issues that are important to the successful reuse of software, its reverse engineering and re-engineering. Of course we have always reused code and reverse engineered it, either informally through modifying some existing routine to meet some new purpose, or more formally through the use of programming languages and libraries. In software reuse we are looking to go beyond that, to ensure that suitable software that already exists can be readily found. In reverse engineering we are hoping to be able to recover some of our investment in existing software, and in re-engineering we are hoping to extend its life. Solutions to most of the problems raised in this overview are taken up by other papers in the collection.

The second part of the volume then looks in more detail at **software reuse**. The concerns about the importance of non-technical issues raised by me in the tutorial are confirmed in *Reuse and Design* by Frank Bott and Mark Ratcliffe, who emphasize the importance of reusing things other than just code. They stress the importance of reusing designs.

What should be reused is taken further by the two papers: *Reuse and Ada* by Tony Orme and *Generalized Components and Application Modelling* by Cydney Minkowitz. Orme argues for the reuse of code components in Ada, showing what has been achieved so far, emphasizing the need for large libraries, where Booch (cited by Orme) has made a start. By contrast, Minkowitz argues for a different focus for reuse, through application-oriented languages and platforms, and not through a library of parts. But are these approaches that are different? Both involve parts and methods for the interconnection of those parts to form new systems – in Orme's paper the emphasis is on the library, with Ada as the interconnection language, with Minkowitz the emphasis is on the language and the complete set of 'components' that enable us to put together applications. Then Cornelia Boldyreff in *Design Methods for Integrating System Components* shows how these might be reconciled through architectural frameworks, standard high-level designs for systems into which components can be fitted to solve particular problems. Sutcliffe by contrast discusses the importance of identifying similarities between systems in *Analogy in Software Reuse*.

The objects of reuse must be organized in a library to that they can be found when required, and in the paper *Software Information Systems: Information Retrieval Techniques*, Hanne Albrechtsen reviews the common approaches to this based on information retrieval techniques. The retrieval of components for reuse requires the ability to compare two components descriptions. While the Information Retrieval approach achieves this through keyword matching, a deeper method using analogy is discussed in the paper *Analogy in Software Reuse* by Alistair Sutcliffe.

Object-oriented methods have become very fashionable, and it is frequently argued [e.g. Brad Cox 1986] that these methods solve reuse problems. The two papers *How Applicable is the Object-Oriented Approach to the IS Environment?* by Russell Jones, and *The Impact of Software Reuse on Object-Oriented Methods* by Ralph Hodgson debate the issues, the extent to which object-oriented approaches really do live up to the claims made about them.

Where do our reusable components come from? We could start again, and produce the libraries in anticipation of new developments – as was implicit in the papers by Orme and Minkowitz. But we could look for them in existing code, using the methods of **reverse engineering**. Given a large volume of code, all too frequently it is very difficult to understand, there may be no documentation, and the code itself is unnecessarily complex and difficult to understand. It has been estimated that around half the time spent making a change to software, is spent understanding the software before the change is made. Reverse engineering helps us create that understanding, as is shown in the survey paper by Alan Frazer, *Reverse Engineering – Hype, Hope or Here?* The paper *from Recursion Extraction to Automated Commenting*, by Cornelia Boldyreff and Jian Zhang, shows one research investigation into transforming Pascal programs to make them more understandable and extract useful components. Later papers in this volume refer to other approaches, and yet more approaches are covered in the special issue of *IEEE Software*.

Having reverse-engineered a piece of software (and possibly re-engineered it), it is important to maintain the improvements thereafter, as argued by *Reverse Engineering – Not Yet?* by Rod McGill.

Of course, reverse engineering is not only intended for such use – its primary function is as a support for maintenance through a process of **re-engineering**. Typically re-engineering involves a process of reverse engineering, before forward engineering to a new or modified implementation (it is clearly more than the code to code transformation implied by Munro). The paper *Re-engineering Business Systems to use the Next Generation of Software* by Simon Holloway is mostly concerned with reverse engineering, arguing that higher levels of abstraction are the most important, and are the hardest. He notes that current tools are in their infancy.

Nevertheless re-engineering is currently possible, as described in *Re-engineering – a Practical Methodology with Commerical Applications*, by Richard Warden. The application of a rich set of methods and tools to a COBOL system is described, with some impressive results (e.g. code size reduced by 30% and efficiency improved by 15%). A contrasting study of Fortran is given in *Step-by-step Transition from Dusty-deck Fortan to Object-oriented Programming* by Michel Bardiaux and Philippe Delhaise, where the move was to an object-oriented flavour of Fortran, staying with Fortran because of its established hold in scientific computing, but regretting that a move to a fully object-oriented language was not possible. Any tools that help us understand the code are welcome, and the paper *A Graph Method for Technical Documentation and Re-engineering of DP-applications* by Jens Grumann and Philippa J. Welch shows how various flow diagrams can be extracted from C to aid software understanding.

Re-engineering frequently involves the move to a new language (as was done in effect by Bardiaux and Delhaise) or a new hardware platform. The parallelism that is now possible in hardware can appear very attractive, and much re-engineering effort has been aimed at **reuse and re-engineering for parallel or distributed hardware**. In *Re-engineering Software for Distributed Execution* by S. J. Goldsack, the production of Ada software for distributed execution is examined, based on the concept of a 'virtual node'. While most of the paper discusses new software, there is a short discussion of the conversion of existing software. The potential benefit is large, particularly for scientific software written in Fortran, as shown by *Converting Sequential Applications Software for Parallel Execution with Strand88 Harnesses* by David Catton, where adding more parallelism can reduce execution time to a third (though the pure sequential baseline was not given). The real issue here is how to re-engineer from a sequential form of the program to a form exploiting parallelism to the full. In general we would have to reverse engineer back to an expression of the problem where the parallelism is explicit – and we don't really yet know how to do that for new problems.

Given a set of components for a distributed system, these can be reconfigured into new systems to solve new problems, rather like the architectural frameworks approach discussed by Boldyreff. The paper *Configuration Programming: Exploiting Component Reuse in Distributed Systems* by Jeff Kramer shows a very well worked out system for doing this, the Conic system. This is possible because Conic includes a module interconnection language – these arose in the mid-1970s, and have well been surveyed by Prieto-Diaz and Neighbors [1986].

A lot of the rhetoric supporting reuse, reverse engineering, and re-engineering, is that it provides support for maintenance. But does it really provide that support? In the paper *Introduction of Maintenance Concepts at the Requirement Stage and their Relationship to Re-engineering Strategy*, Peter Carroll argues that the engineering changes that arise during operation and maintenance should be anticipated during requirements analysis, to ensure that these changes will be easy to implement. What we do with existing software is not discussed – 're-engineering' to Carroll appears to mean 'engineering changes'. The possible benefits of re-engineering as defined by Warden, is described as a short anecdote in *Re-engineering as an Opportunity to Reduce the Maintenance Workload* by Derek Francis. An RPG system is re-engineered to the application generator Genesis V which gave more general-purpose flexibility (as required by Carroll) to continue to evolve the software.

During maintenance and change, a major concern is with the tracking of versions and consistent configurations of those versions. The basic ideas here are described in *SMS – A Software Management System* by Malindi Lamb and Jonathan Barchan. This is a system very much in the Unix tradition of SCCS and RCS [e.g. Tichy, 1985]. A more sophisticated aspect of the support for versions and change is given in *Analysis Tools to Support Software Maintenance* by Alistair Tilbury. A feature of a proprietary system for configuration management is described – this enables the automatic analysis of the impact of a proposed change, and the notification of the 'owners' of other affected modules, giving them a chance to vote on the proposed change. Software needs to enter the configuration management system by some procedure, and the PISCES system described in *PISCES – An Inverse Configuration Management System* by Rachel Kenning and Malcolm Munro shows one method – a form of reverse engineering (the term 'inverse engineering' is used by the team writing this paper, but is not used elsewhere).

Clearly maintenance can benefit from tools for reuse, reverse engineering, and re-engineering, but there is also a need for other tools as well, notably configuration management tools and test tools. It is claimed that if we were to start again, we would not get into the current mess and need these reverse engineering tools – but would we be perfect next time round?

Software reuse, reverse engineering, and re-engineering all seem obvious ideas – and yet do not get adopted in practice. Why not? Clearly there are other **management and business issues** which drive this. Possible solutions are discussed by *The Management of Reuse* by Paul Walton. *Human Aspects and Organizational Issues of Software Reuse* by Ivan Kruzela and M. Brorsson looks at the steps necessary for a company to introduce a reuse program, and the problems associated with this. The paper *Reuse Directions in British Telecom* by Steve Whalley shows how British Telecom is systematically introducing reuse into its practices, and in *The Business Case for Re-engineering* by Richard Warden, the business argument for reuse is taken up. Clearly reuse will not be adopted into wide practice until the issues raised here are addressed, and the solutions proposed or others adopted.

Reverse engineering does create legal problems – is reverse engineering breach of copyright or some other legal infringement? The invited paper *The Legal Position of Reverse Engineering in the UK* by Matthew K. O. Lee gives the current position of this important aspect of reverse engineering and reuse.

References

1. Chikofsky, Elliot J. and James H. Cross II. Reverse Engineering and Design Recovery: A Taxonomy. *IEEE Software* January 1990, pp. 13–17.
2. Cox, Brad J., *Object Oriented Programming. An Evolutionary Approach*, Addison Wesley 1986.
3. *IEEE Software*, 1990. Maintenance, Reverse Engineering, and Design Recovery, special issue, vol. 7, no. 1, January 1990.
4. Prieto-Diaz, Ruben and James Neighbors, Module Interconnection Languages, *Journal of System Sciences*, vol. 6, no. 4, November 1986, pp. 307–334.
5. Tichy, Walter F. 1985. RCS – A System for Version Control, *Software Practice and Experience*, vol. 15, no. 7, July 1985, pp. 637–654.

Part One

Tutorial Overview

1 Software reuse, reverse engineering, and re-engineering

P.A.V. Hall

Brunel University

1.1 INTRODUCTION

The development of computer-based systems is now dominated by the cost of developing the software. The real cost of hardware has fallen, and the increase in hardware capability has led to ever more ambitious development projects, while qualified and experienced software development staff are in short supply. How can we keep up with this demand for ever more software? We must improve productivity significantly, while maintaining or improving quality.

One method proposed for making a significant improvement in productivity and quality is software reuse. This is the use of a given piece of software in the solution of more than one problem. Frequently this is taken to mean the reuse of program components like library subroutines in more than one application. However, reuse can also be applied much more broadly, to include the redeployment of designs, ideas, or even the skills and experience of people.

Within the development of software, some 60% to 70% of total lifecycle costs are spent on 'maintenance' – the activities undertaken after the first delivery of the software to sustain it in service, through repairing defects, and enhancing the software to meet new or changing requirements. This has been shown by a number of surveys of the industry, e.g. Swanson and Beath (1989). In order to make changes, we have to first understand the software and, as has been shown by Parikh and Zvegintzov (1983), this could involve around from 47% to 60% of the maintenance effort – because documentation of the software is inadequate and all the maintainer can rely on is the code itself. This means that some 30-35% of total lifecycle costs are consumed in trying to understand software after it has been delivered, in order to make changes. Anything that we can do to alleviate this situation must save a lot of money. Tools and methods are desperately needed, and these are known generically as reverse engineering.

Having reverse engineered a complete system, it may be appropriate to then tidy up the software, restructuring it to meet current standards, or even re-implementing it in a newer version of the programming language, or some other language (for example, in moving from C to C++), and possibly on new hardware and operating systems. This complete cycle of reverse engineering followed by re-implementation is called re-engineering.

Re-engineering can be used to help reuse. For reuse we need to assemble a repository of useful components – and where better to look for them than in systems that have been developed previously. Of course we would not simply use them as we find them, but re-engineer them to the quality standards that we would now expect.

In this article I will review both Software Reuse and then Reverse Engineering and Re-engineering from a technical viewpoint, and then move to more general non-technical issues that influence whether and how the reuse and reverse engineering technology is used.

1.2 SOFTWARE REUSE

The reuse of software has been with us from the beginning through the publication of algorithms, the use of high-level programming languages, and the use of packages, as has been pointed out by many people (e.g. Standish 1984) as well as myself (Hall 1987).

Reuse through the publication of algorithms and designs has been very important for the development of computing. The presence of standard textbooks in an area is an indication of the maturity of that area, and is an important vehicle through which the reuse of ideas takes place. Similarly, the procurement of standard packages is an important example of reuse, and the availability of a wide range of products is again an indicator of the maturity of an area of technology. Capers Jones (1984) makes a thorough appraisal of both these areas.

However, it is the consideration of high-level programming languages as examples of reuse that is the most illuminating. In high-level languages, many frequently used combinations of instructions at the assembly level (e.g. for subroutine entry and exit with parameter passing), have been packaged into single constructs at the higher level. The high-level language thus gives a notation for selecting these generic constructs, instantiating them with the appropriate parameters, and then composing them to build software systems. Facilities are provided so that user-created components at the higher level can be stored and incorporated, for example by subroutines and macros. This is not the usual way of viewing programming languages and compilers which are usually seen as 'tools' rather than as the engineering foundations of software production. This view of programming languages emphasizes the unique nature of software, the great diversity that its components might take, and the very flexible way they might be interconnected. We will see all these ingredients in the recent approaches directed specifically at reuse.

Packages have also been an important aspect of the reuse of software. Packages which are rigidly defined are seldom useful – some flexibility is essential.

This flexibility is provided through a range of capabilities, from simple parameterization, through configuration following some elaborate build script (as is usually done for operating systems), through to the modification of the package at the source level.

Packages may be thought of as a form of software component. The idea of software components as such was promoted in 1968 by McIlroy (only published in 1976). Since then many of the other aspects of software reuse outlined above have been subsumed under other software engineering activities. We will interpret the term 'component' very widely, to include not only executable code, but also more abstract objects such as designs, specifications, and requirements.

1.2.1 The Process of Reuse

We can add in the possibility of software reuse to the traditional lifecycle model of software development, invoking a library of reusable software components including not only code, but also specifications and designs and algorithms.

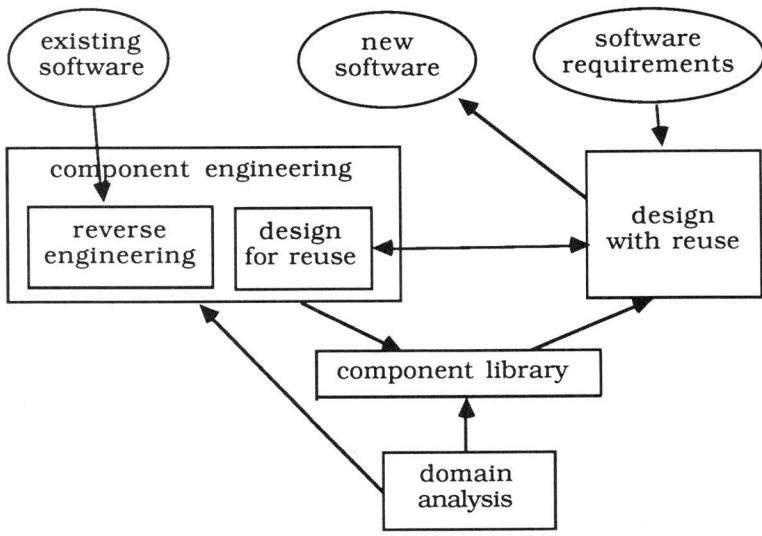

Fig. 1.1   The reuse process.

To be able to reuse software components, we need:

- a building-up phase when reusable software is identified and brought together into a library (shown on the left side of Fig. 1.1), sometimes called 'component engineering';

- and a design phase when reusable software is selected from the library on the basis of system requirements and reused in the construction of a new software system (shown on the right side of Fig. 1.1). New components may be designed for this system, and be added into the library.

There is also a need to consider more general knowledge about the area or domain of application of the components, as shown at the bottom of Fig. 1.1: this helps us identify suitable components, and to structure the component library to aid retrieval (for example, with an index or a thesaurus).

Integration of reuse within the traditional lifecycle of software development is required. In analysing and designing new systems, the possibility of reuse needs to be considered, and the appropriate library components incorporated; new elements of software that are needed should also be considered as candidates for the library and added to it.

1.2.2 Domain Analysis

When addressing a new application area, we need to understand the area – this process of acquiring the understanding is frequently termed domain analysis. To do this we need to identify the major concepts of the area, and identify the relationships between these concepts. The importance of this was first identified in the DRACO project (Freeman 1987, Prieto-Diaz and Freeman 1987).

The notations used for domain analysis could be conceptual dependencies (Schank 1972) or similar, or simply some form of data analysis using entity-relationship models (e.g. Teory and Fry 1982, Nijssen and Halpin 1989). They could even be thesauri (e.g. Aitchison and Gilchrist 1971, Townley and Gee, 1980), and object-oriented methods have also been proposed.

The process of domain analysis has much in common with knowledge acquisition, but needs a lot of further development (e.g. Simos 1988, Prieto-Diaz 1990).

1.2.3 Component Engineering

Domain analysis guides us towards the components which we should produce that will prove useful in the particular application area. Each reusable component should be given a clear specification, and statement of the principles and concepts underlying the component independent of any particular implementation. Quality information should be recorded, for example the levels of inspection or proof undertaken, and for code, the level of testing carried out. Other administrative information would also be recorded, such as who produced the component and when, and its revision history.

Where the component is extracted from existing software, reverse engineering should be used to identify the component and to abstract the specification (see section 1.3 below). Alternatively, we could create reusable software when developing new software, in the process called 'design for reuse' in Fig. 1.1. We would focus extra effort on developing the new reusable parts, to maximize the cost and quality benefits derivable from the reuse of these parts.

In all cases it is essential to create as general a component as possible, while avoiding over-generalization which could make specific uses difficult to specialize, and inefficient in operation. This requires that generalizations and inductions are made over several more specific components, a process for which no general guidance is available as yet. The general-purpose component would be suitably parameterized, so that particular uses are easily specialized from the generic part.

Object-oriented methods are seen as important for reuse (e.g. Booch 1987, Cox 1986): the objects are the components, providing the encapsulation that is necessary, while inheritance structures provide the contexts for reuse to take place – see section 2.4.

An important issue is the size of the components – are they small like in a scientific subroutine library, or large, as packages? Clearly there is a place for both, but the requirements for description and storage may be very different. With large components, the collection may be quite small, and amenable to searching by hand.

1.2.4 Storing and Retrieving Reusable Software

Having identified software which is potentially reusable and described it in such a way that anyone wishing to reuse it would be able to do so, the problem arises as to how to organize the total collection of all such software and related descriptions. Such a library can be structured by classifying the reusable software in various ways. A good system of classification not only provides the basis for cataloguing the software, but it also provides a means for finding a particular piece of software held in the library. Large collections of software present similar problems of classification to those of Information Retrieval (e.g. Salton and McGill 1983).

Frakes and Nejmeh (1985) and Prieto-Diaz and Freeman (1987) have applied library classification methods to software component libraries, with Prieto-Diaz and Freeman using a faceted classification method. By contrast, Wood and Sommerville (1988) take an approach based on Schank's (1972) view of natural language. Albrechtson (1990) surveys the field.

So far software libraries have been very small – typically only a few hundred components, though some special cases like Ada and Smalltalk have a few thousand. With such small collections, the pursuit of sophisticated library search facilities must be in question.

1.2.5   Designing Software with Reusable Parts

Given a statement of requirements or detailed specification or even a high-level design, we will need to match this with the reusable software held in a library. We could:

- find a single component which fully, or almost fully, satisfies our requirement;

- find a collection of components which when suitably interconnected could satisfy the requirement.

The first case is already a common problem in package selection, though this important part of commercial software practice is almost entirely ignored by system development methodologies. What we have to do here is match the requirements or specification against the specifications in the library, using the retrieval mechanisms described above. Exact matching of precise (formal) specifications will in general be undecidable, and therefore we must necessarily reduce our descriptions for search purposes, accepting that we can only ever find near matches. Further, even if we could match precisely, we need to recognize that if we get no exact match we can always customize through the addition of extra software 'shells'. Thus we would be quite content to accept partial or approximate matches, with some further manual process required to vet the retrieved components to find the most suitable.

In the second case, only some combination of several components could satisfy our requirements. We therefore need to decompose our requirements in some way. One way is clearly an extension of the first, looking for some submatch of library components to the requirements, in the manner of searching strings for substrings or graphs for subgraphs.

Alternatively, we could first of all decompose the requirements into parts, and then search for these in the library – we first do a high-level design.   One way to do this would be to use stereotypical designs, often called frameworks, such as those used in some approaches to object-oriented design (Wirfs-Brock and Johnson 1990) and described for the ESPRIT Practitioner project (Hall *et al*. 1990).

Having selected a component (or set of components) for reuse, it remains to adapt the component for its intended use, and to compose it with other components and new software to achieve the desired results.   Adaptation or specialization could vary from modification of sources through to the provision of parameter values to a generic package to instantiate it for a particular use, as in Ada (e.g. Ledgard 1981) or in fully polymorphic languages such as ML (e.g. Wikstrom 1987).   The modification of sources, sometimes known as white-box reuse, is an approach of last resort, for this could compromise the quality of the component, and quality was one of the main motivations for software reuse.

To compose components we need a language for building systems.   This could be the simple linkage mechanisms of the programming language, or could be mechanisms available at the command language level, such as pipes in the UNIX shell. However, the language for system building could be developed specifically for module interconnection, either as part of a larger programming system such as Conic (Sloman *et al*. 1985) or C/MESA (Lauer *et al*. 1979), or could even be an independent language, such as INTERCOL (Tichy 1980).   These module interconnection languages enable the consistency of interconnection to be checked by strong typing: a good survey has been given by Prieto-Diaz and Neighbours (1986).

The available code components when specialized and connected together will probably be insufficient to meet the full requirements, and other original code may be necessary, perhaps to transform the outputs from one component to the required form of inputs to another, or perhaps to add other functions not available from the component library.

At higher levels of abstraction, the same general principles apply. Components might be generic, being instantiated and then connected together, as in the system LIL proposed by Goguen (1986). The components here are not modified other than through instantiation; in other approaches the components might be treated as 'source' and adapted to the particular needs, then connected together with extra material to meet the particular need.

1.3   REVERSE ENGINEERING AND RE-ENGINEERING

Reverse Engineering is a general area that embraces several subtly different ideas. We have already seen it as a process for identifying what the components of a system are and what the interrelationships are. In doing so we will create a representation of this system at some higher level of abstraction, say in data flow diagrams, or perhaps in some more precise notation. The issue for January 1990 of the journal SOFTWARE, published by IEEE, is devoted to software maintenance and reverse engineering. My use of the term is consistent with that given by Chikofsky (1990). But reverse engineering is also sometimes called re-documentation, or design recovery.

Focusing on these activities we see that reverse engineering is just what we have always been doing. It is that part of system analysis which describes the current system. But what is different now is that the current system is a computer system, and descriptions of it are available in machine-readable form, in particular the source code. We could in principle use computer tools to assist us in this conventional system analysis phase, of describing the current system. This is reverse engineering.

When interfacing one piece of software to another through an interface, we need to know in great detail the representation of the data that crosses the interface, and what it means in terms of the functions that are undertaken on it. Frequently the supplier's documentation is inadequate, and we resort to the software itself: we try critical test cases to probe the interface, and in the last resort may have to look at the code itself. Again, this is reverse engineering.

1.3.1   Current Solutions

At any exhibition of tools to support the development software, one will discover many suppliers offering reverse engineering tools. Rosemary Rock-Evans has given a very comprehensive survey of these tools (1990). What are the real capabilities of these tools?

Many tools are really very simple, helping us outline the functions of the software, or helping us follow up cross-references between different parts of the program text. Many of these tools have been use for many decades, and it is surprising to see these being offered now as if they were new.

Outlining tools would list the functions contained within the software, giving the function names, arguments and data types and possibly the key data structures manipulated. Perhaps leading comments which describe the function, suitably identified, would also be abstracted. The internal operation of the procedures may also be condensed in the form of a flow diagram to show its essential structure.

Cross-references between modules may also be abstracted, perhaps showing which procedures call which other procedures and use which data structures. Data structures would distinguish defining occurrences and places where the data structure is used. All of this may be put together in some pictorial diagrammatic form. New offerings of tools may also apply hypertext technology to marshal all the information, enabling one to follow the cross-references between modules and hence navigate through the software and its description.

There are, however, tools available which are aimed specifically at reverse engineering. One such set is Catalyst, developed to support the maintenance of COBOL, and consisting of two parts, PATH SCORE, and RETROFIT. PATH SCORE is a static analysis tool which produces two metrics, a 'complexity' metric, and another independent metric, 'structuredness'. PATH SCORE classifies the COBOL procedures into high and low regions of these two metrics, and this score is then used to guide the application of the second RETROFIT tool. RETROFIT reduces the code to standard constructs and structures so that it can be much more readily understood. In some cases the advice may be to completely recode a piece of software.

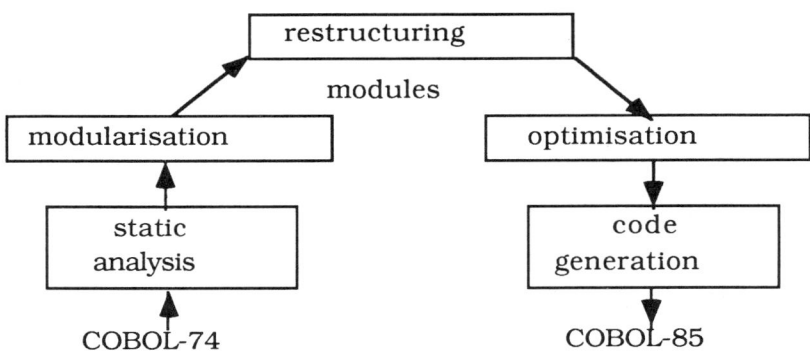

Fig. 1.2 The Sneed and Jandrasics approach.

Also available from Catalyst is a tool called MASCOT, which enables one to go from assembler to structured COBOL. However, the suppliers recommend a considerable application of expertise in this process since the reverse engineering of assembler to COBOL is a very difficult process.

More recently Sneed and Jandrasics (1987) have developed a system re-engineering COBOL-74 into COBOL-85 (see Fig. 1.2).   As with Catalyst, a static analysis is first undertaken, and this is used to identify the modules within the code. These modules are then restructured and the new structured modules are modified (adapted) to optimize their performance.   This optimized module code is then put through the COBOL-85 compiler to generate the new system. This new system might of course execute on a new hardware.

Neither the Catalyst nor the Sneed approaches address data. In the Bachman approach, files of data can be analysed and their structure in terms of entity and relationships abstracted.   Data models rather more complex than the usual models can be produced. This system can be used for the reverse engineering of old systems as a step in the production of new systems, for example in the migration from IDMS to DB2.   It is understood that Bachman will be producing tools which also work upon the functions of the data processing system.

Many other systems are also available. All of these systems have limitations. Many of them are simply the repackaging of old techniques, exploiting the capabilities and power of current hardware, using bit-map graphics and hypertext technology. They all only work on code, either function code or the code description of data. Most of them are aimed at COBOL, though newer systems are also addressing other languages. Typically they only look locally at the structure of the software and do not undertake any global analysis.   There are reservations about performance loss when these tools are used as part of a process of re-engineering, though it should be noted that optimization and performance considerations are part of the Sneed system. Of course performance is not of immediate concern to reverse engineering, since here the intention is to understand the code, not necessarily to replace the code.

1.3.2   Research and Development

The development of new tools is being pursued by a number of CASE vendors, and research into reverse engineering is an active part of several research programmes both in the USA and in Europe.

A couple of projects, funded in or in association with the European Esprit programme, are looking at the use of formal methods. These projects seek to move from code, possibly Assembler, all the way to formal specifications, typically in Z (e.g. Spivey 1989). One example of this is the work of Martin Ward (1988), who transforms the code into an intermediate 'wide-spectrum-language' and then from this transforms the code into Z. A similar system using a different intermediate language is under development by Breuer and Lano (1989) as part of the REDO project. Both these approaches simply work on the code, and give the impression of paraphrasing the software in Z without any real process of abstraction and movement towards higher level concepts either of software or application.

```
#include <stdio.h>
#include "h001.h"
#include "h002.h"
#include "h003.h"
f001(a001)
        unsigned int a001;
        {
        unsigned int i001;
        f002(g005,d001,d002);
        f002(a001,d003,d002);
        f003(g001[a001].s001,g001[a0001].s002);
        g006 = a001;
        i001 = g001[a001].s003;
        if (!f004(i001)&&(g002->g003)[i001].soo4==d004)
            f005(i001);
        }
```

Fig. 1.3   Biggerstaff's example - a machine-eye view of code.   (Reproduced by kind permission of the Institution of Electrical and Electronic Engineers.)

Problems with these formal approaches have been identified by Boldyreff and Zhang (1989), as part of the Practitioner project.   In looking to the insertion of recursion into code as part of the process of understanding what it does, they ran into the problem of what do you call components, once they have been isolated.   While they looked at a typical small 'computer science' problem, that of sorting, this was sufficient to pinpoint a key problem to approaches based entirely upon code.

```
#include <stdio.h>
#include "proc.h"
#include "window.h"
#include "globdefs.h"
change_window(nw)
        unsigned int nw;
        {
        unsigned int pn;
        border_attribute(cwin,NORM,INV);
        border_attribute (nw,NORMHLIT,INV);
        move_cursor(wintbl[nw].crow,wintbl[nw].ccol);
        cwin = nw;
        pn = wintbl[nw].pnumb;
        if (!outrange(pn)&&(g>proctbl)[pn].procstate ==SUSPENDED)  resume(pn);
        }
```

Fig. 1.4   Biggerstaff's example – the human-eye view of the code
– meaningful identifiers added.

The importance of other information in the reverse engineering of code has been pointed out by Ted Biggerstaff (1989).   Figure 1.3 shows an example given by Biggerstaff in which he has replaced all the identifiers that we would normally expect by meaningless numbers and letters, and also stripped out all the comments.   What we get is the machine-eye view of the code.   To us this is incomprehensible.   Figure 1.4 shows the code with the identifiers re-inserted – much more understandable.   From the chosen identifiers we can immediately see this has something to do with window management and can guess something about the structure of the code and the way it operates.   What we are doing is use a higher level of understanding of the problem domain being addressed, in coming to understand the code.   With the comments replaced we would find ourselves even better placed to understand what is happening.

While Biggerstaff in his paper does not explain how he intends to use the informal information contained within the identifiers and comments, he has described this to me in conversation.   The application domain of window management has been described in a form of semantic net, following a domain analysis.   The code itself is described by the essential 'terms' or fragments of words that are contained within it. The problem of relating the terms within the code with the concepts within the application domain of windows is then being bridged using neutral network technology. This will enable a rough description of the code to be generated showing what concepts in the domain it relates to.   Biggerstaff then envisages using the more detailed techniques available in other projects, to be described later in this paper.

From these examples we see that we are concerned with two dimensions of analysis. On the one hand there is the traditional technical dimension which goes from the application through a generic view of computing problems to the methods we use for the architectural description and design of software, through to the particular construct we use in programme code.   Application domain constructs are things like steel-rolling mills, personnel records, pay-rolls, and so on.   Generic problem domain concepts are things like windows, screens, and order-entry systems.   Architecture concepts are components like stacks, files, pipes, processes, and similar.   Design concepts are more detailed things of a similar nature.   Code concepts are assignment statements, declarations, case statements and similar.

On the other hand we are also concerned with degrees of formality of representation, from the very formal descriptions associated with programme code and the newly emerging formal description techniques, to the other extreme of very informal representations of knowledge contained within people's heads.   And in between lie various levels of representation from diagrams through to domain-specific languages. We can draw a two-dimensional grid as shown in Fig. 1.5 and on this place the various languages, formalisms, and notations that we use. The reverse engineering problem is then one of marshalling this information and moving from the bottom left of the area through towards the top left.

So, to reverse engineer we must migrate between levels of language bringing to bear whatever information is available, as shown in Fig. 1.5. Possible components or concepts to be looked for are determined by the higher-level domain analysis, and the software (code, design description, or whatever) is searched to identify parts of the software which could be components. Having identified potential components these will be transformed and generalized and compared against a base of already discovered components, until a candidate component has been demonstrated. We can then abstract to the higher level of description and replace the component discovered by the higher-level concept. The demonstration that a component is present could be very formal involving proof techniques, or it could involve access to a human to get confirmation, or it could involve the execution of code against some critical test case which will confirm or refute the hypothesis. This continues by finding and confirming/discarding.

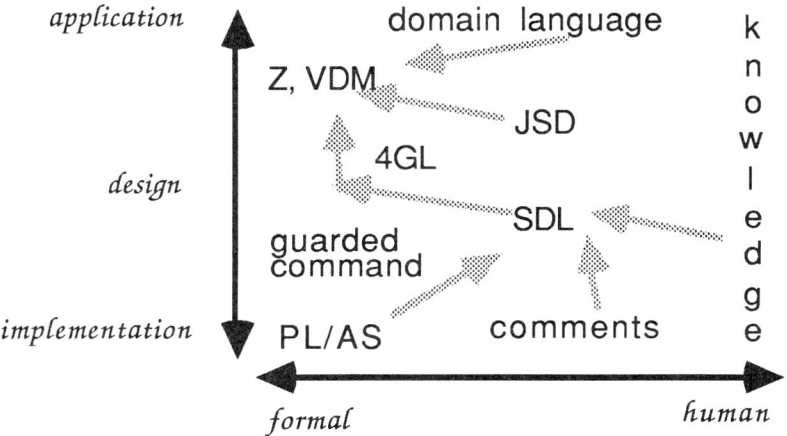

Fig. 1.5   Two dimensions of the problem.

An important part of the whole process is that of relating the code to known domain concepts in a library.   This means storing patterns (also called schemas, or templates, and 'cliches') and then matching these patterns against the code, searching for some approximate form of match within the code.   The whole process could be quite complicated since in matching several things we could get overlapping matches and have to make decisions about which match to accept.   This is the approach taken by the apprentice programmers at MIT (e.g. Rich and Wells, 1990), and that at Arthur Anderson in the University of Illinois (Harandi and Ning, 1990).   We are also investigating this approach in our work at Brunel, both within the Practitioner project, and within a separate study with IBM.

1.4.   NON-TECHNICAL ISSUES IN SOFTWARE REUSE

In order to promote reuse, it is not sufficient to establish the correct technical environment, we must also address other non-technical issues, such as managerial practices and the legal constraints of a particular community.

People who work in software production like producing software, and will develop software rather than look for existing ideas, algorithms, or code.   They use all sorts of personally persuasive arguments:

- 'Reinventing software is fun!'

- 'Why buy when you can build?'

- 'Having seen the commercial product, I know I could build it better.'

- 'If somebody else built it, could you really trust it?'

- 'In acquiring software from outside, there is always some compromise required, it never does exactly what is wanted.'

- 'If you build it yourself, you can control its future development – it will always do what you want.'

The ability to build software yourself, be it by an individual software engineer, by a project, or by the organization as a whole, is an enormous barrier to reuse. Contrast this with electronic engineering, where the cost of designing and fabricating your own microprocessor is so enormous, and requires such specialized equipment, that it is only undertaken in very special circumstances: the margin between buying and building is very many orders of magnitude. The margins between buying and building software are not so great, except in the large volume micro-computer marketplace: a first-shot development could be as cheap as acquiring the software from elsewhere.

For the individual the cost of acquisition consists of the effort of finding the requisite software, and we can address this through the various technical measures discussed above, as well as by the continued training and education of the individual so that more abstract entities will also be reused.

It is the ratio of cost-to-benefit that counts, and as well as reducing the cost, we could also increase the benefit. If reuse does enhance productivity, then at least at the project and company levels there are pay-offs. But what about the individual? What extra benefit does he get from reuse?

Here an idea attributed to the Japanese is worth considering – changing the monetary and status rewards for individuals. Firstly, those who provide software for others to reuse could receive some form of royalty for this reuse. This would encourage both the production of general purpose elements suitably proven and packaged to encourage their reuse, but also encourage the promotion of the element's availability. The actual reuse should be encouraged, perhaps through piecework where the reward for the job was assessed without reuse in mind, or perhaps through a royalty on reuse for the user as well as the supplier. The status of people who succeed in reuse could be enhanced, possibly with the position of manager of the library of reusable components being made a highly rewarded and sought-after post.   This status and reward should be comparable with systems architects and database administrators which are highly sought-after and respected jobs and are very similar in their intent.

There is no doubt that some form of cultural shift is necessary, with people's and institutional attitudes changing, if reuse is to be successful.

The payoff for reuse occurs only after the item's initial production.   Projects are usually established simply to look after the initial development of a software system, with their performance being judged solely by the costs and timescales of the project. Frequently there are quality problems resulting from this practice, for the consequences of low quality are often picked by the follow-on maintenance project – somebody else foots the bill.   This management practice does encourage reuse, to reduce project costs, but does not encourage the production of reusable components for other projects, for where is the pay-off?   Again, some form of royalty payable to the project might be appropriate, if company accounting practices could handle this. Alternatively the Reusable Components Manager could be given a budget to invest in the production of components, either to subsidize their production on projects or to create them speculatively.

A preliminary economic analysis appropriate to individual organizations has been given by Lubars (1986) and taken further forward by Wolff (1990): more work is required here.

Software reuse between organizations, both nationally and internationally, clearly does currently take place through the production and sale of packages.   The experience of the software packages industry is important in understanding how the reuse industry could be expanded to include reusable components.

Illegal copying of software is a problem (e.g. Suhler *et al*. 1986). Copyright protection of software is emerging, but clearly needs to be practised internationally, and much more could be done there. Many producers of software appear to accept this situation, and seek to earn revenue from their software in other ways, by selling manuals or books about using it, or by selling training services. But the problem is more subtle than that.

The ability to reverse engineering software brings about conflicts concerning the market for software products. On the one hand, the suppliers of software products should be protected against their products being illegally copied, not just at the level of software piracy, but also at the level of rival products developed from theirs. With reverse engineering it is perfectly possible to work back from executable code to design descriptions of exactly how the software works, and then to re-engineer the software with selected additions to form the rival product. Clearly this ought to be made illegal.

However, we also want an open market so that third-party suppliers of software can provide products that connect to those of others, particularly the big suppliers. To do this public interfaces will be used, and in principle these should be adequately documented – but in practice are not. All too frequently to adequately interfaced two pieces of software, some level of reverse engineering needs to be undertaken – and this seems to be a legitimate activity in the interests of open markets.

So we have a legal dilemma, which is still under discussion.

Frequently software is acquired on the basis of futures, and if the software is bought, its future development may not turn out to be the way you wanted it. If you build it in-house, you are in total control over its development. This argument ignores all sorts of other costs. Maintenance of in-house software is likely to be more expensive; the software is likely to be less robust, it may be subject to uncontrolled voluntary 'improvements' that are not required and add to cost.

To maintain competitive advantage, some parts of a company's software may always be proprietary. The proprietary software may not even be particularly sophisticated, but comparable to the way application-specific integrated circuits are used in hardware designs to make designs difficult to reproduce from inspection of an example. We must always expect some level of non-reuse.

Software is not a commodity. It does not become an asset of a company that purchases it. Software may be written off in its year of purchase, whereas hardware may be written off over 3 to 5 years or more. Software may not be allowed to be sold on, a computer manufacturer has required that purchasers of second-hand hardware relicense the software. There is no market in second-hand software: indeed the very idea seems mildly ridiculous. Could this be changed? One could envisage some legal remedies to remove what amount to restrictive and monopolistic practices. Could we get as far as enabling third-party maintenance of software?

Preparing software for reuse as a component does require extra effort. This extra effort needs to be rewarded. In the open market this reward would be some form of royalty or licence fee. There may be problems in enforcing these payments, and disputes within the industry are frequent. However, one person has produced a set of Ada components, and is selling these (Booch 1987).

It is clear that to avoid some of these problems, a software components industry should be high-volume and low-cost, producing robust and stable products with low or zero maintenance costs.

1.5 CONCLUSIONS

We have surveyed software reuse, reverse engineering, and re-engineering. Reuse is concerned with accumulating libraries of components, which could be designs, specifications, as well as code. Reverse engineering is one method for obtaining components, but has its major application in maintenance, to assist in the understanding of code before making changes. A complete system could be reverse engineered as part of preventative maintenance, and then could be re-engineered to improve it or to port it to some new operational environment.

In all these areas there are a number of problems that still need to be solved, and research programmes are addressing these, though commercial activity may also solve them where the market is sufficiently large, as for COBOL and for Ada. In reuse the major problem is in component description and matching and adaptation, and in reverse engineering the major problems are in the use if informal natural language information embedded in comments and documentation, and in the systematic use of testing.

There are also social and legal problems to be overcome. The reuse of components is inhibited within a single organization by social factors like 'not invented here', but these can be overcome through organizing the reward structure differently. Between organizations, however, there remain serious legal problems concerned with copyright and accounting practices that will need to be resolved at the level of national and international government. Reverse engineering has also been the subject of legal activity, to resolve the conflict of interests between the protection of the intellectual property rights of software producers and the need for a free market enabling the unfetterred interconnection of software from different suppliers.

REFERENCES

Aitchison, J. and Gilchrist, A. Thesaurus Construction. A practical manual. Aslib 1971.

Albrechtson (1990) Software Information Systems: Information Retrieval Techniques, in Software reuse and reverse engineering in practice, Unicom seminar, December 1990.

Arnold, R.S. Tutorial on Software Restructuring, IEEE Computer Society, 1986.

Biggerstaff, T.J. Design Recovery for Maintenance and Reuse. IEEE Computer, July 1989.

Boldyreff, C. and Zhang, J. From Recursion Abstraction to Automated Commenting – A transformational approach towards Reverse Engineering of Software to Support Reusability. PRACTITIONER. Working Paper, Department of Computer Science, Brunel University, December 1989.

Booch, G. Software Components with Ada, Structures, Tools and Subsystems, Benjamin/Cummings Publishing Company, 1987.

Chikovsky, E.J. and Cross, J.H. II Reverse Engineering and Design Recovery: A Taxonomy. IEEE Software, January 1990.

Cox, B.J. Object-Oriented Programming, Addison-Wesley, 1986.

Dulay, N., Kramer, J., Magee, J., Sloman, M., Twiddle, K. The Conic Configuration Language, Version 1.3, Imperial College London, Research Report DOC 84/20, August 1985.

Frakes, W.B. and Nejmeh, B.A. Software Reuse Through Information Retrieval, SIGIR Forum 1986-87 (21):1-2.

Freeman, P.A. Conceptual Analysis of the Draco Approach to Constructing Software Systems, in IEEE Transactions on Software Engineering, 1987 and included in IEEE Tutorial: Software Reusability, 1987.

Goguen, J.A. Reusing and Interconnecting Software Components, IEEE Computer, February 1986, pp. 16-28.

Goldberg, A. and Robson, D. Smalltalk-80: The Language and Its Implementation, Addison-Wesley, 1983.

Hall, P.A.V. Software components reuse – getting more out of your code, in Information and Software Technology, Butterworths, January/February 1987. Reprinted in IEEE Tutorial, Software Reuse: Emerging Technology, editor Will Tracz, IEEE Computer Society, 1988.

Hall, P., Boldyreff, C., Elzer, P., Keilmann, J., Olsen, L. and Witt, J. PRACTITIONER: Pragmatic Support for the Reuse of Concepts in Existing Software, ancillary papers at ESPRIT week, November 1990.

Harandi, M.T. and Ning, J.Q. Knowledge-Based Program Analysis. IEEE Software. January 1990.

Ichbiah, Jean D. On the Design of Ada, in Information Processing 83, Editor R. Mason, 1983.

IEEE Transactions on Software Engineering. Special Issue on Software Reusability, vol. SE-10, no. 5, September 84.

Kramer, J. and Magee, J. Dynamic Configuration for Distributed Systems, IEEE Trans. on Software Engineering, SE-11, 4, April 1985, pp. 424-436.

Jones, T. Capers Reusability in Programming: A Survey of the State of the Art, in (IEEE 1984), pp. 488-494.

Kazaczynski, W. and Ning, J.Q. SRE: A Knowledge-based Environment for Large-Scale Software Re-engineering Activities.   Proc. Int'l Conf. Software Eng. IEEE CS Press, 1989.

Lanergan, R.G. and Grasso, C.A. Software Engineering with Reusable Designs and Code, in (IEEE 1984), pp. 498-501.

Lano, K. and Breuer P.T. From Programs to Z Specifications, Z User's Meeting, December 1989.

Lauer, H.C. and Satterthwaite, E.H. The Impact of MESA on system design, Proceedings of the 4th International Conference on Software Engineering, Munich, Germany. September 1979, pp. 174-182.

Ledgard, H. ADA An Introduction. Ada Reference Manual (July 1980), Springer-Verlag, 1981.

Lehman, M.M. and Stenning, N.V. Concepts of an Integrated Project Support Environment, Data Processing, vol. 27, no. 3, April 1985.

Littlewood, B. Software reliability model for modular program structure, IEEE Trans. Reliability, R-28, 1979, pp. 241-246.

Lubars, M.D. Affording Higher Software Reliability Through Software Reusability, ACM SIGSOFT Software Engineering Notes, vol. 11, no. 5, October 1986.

McIllroy, M.D. Mass-Produced Software Components in Software Engineering Concepts and Techniques, Petrocelli/Charter, Belgium, 1976, pp. 88-98.

McWilliams, G. Users see a CASE Advance in Reverse Engineering Tools, Datamation, 1 February, 1988, pp. 30-36.

Moineau, Th. J., Rames, A.E. Towards a generic and extensible reuse environment, in Proceedings of SE90 Conference, Editor P.A.V. Hall, Cambridge University Press, July 1990.

Neighbors, J. The Draco Approach to Constructing Software from Reusable Components, in (IEEE 1984).

Nijssen, G.M. and Halpin, T.A. Conceptual Schema and Relational Database Design, Prentice-Hall 1989.

Prieto-Diaz, R. and Freeman, P. Classifying Software for Reusability, IEEE Software, January 1987.

Prieto-Diaz, R., Domain Analysis: An Introduction, Software Engineering Notes, vol. 15, no. 2, April 1990, pp. 47-54.

Prieto-Diaz, R. and Neighbors, J. Module Interconnection Languages, Journal of System Sciences, vol. 6, no. 4, November 1986, pp. 307-334.

Rich, C. and Wills, L.M. Recognizing a Program's Design: A Graph-Parsing Approach, IEEE Software, January 1990.

Rock-Evans, R. and Hales, K. Reverse Engineering: Markets, Methods and Tools, Ovum 1990.

Salton and McGill, M. Introduction to Modern Information Retrieval, McGraw-Hill, 1983.

Schank, R.C. Conceptual Dependency: a theory of natural language understanding, Cognitive Psychology, vol. 3, pp. 552-631, 1972.

Simos, M.A. 1988, Position Paper for the Workshop on Tools and Environments for Reuse, Bass Harbor, Main, June 1988.

Sloman, M., Kramer and Magee, J. The Conic Toolkit for Building Distributed Systems, 6th IFAC Distributed Computer Control Systems Workshop, Monterey, California. Pergamon Press, May 1985..

Sneed, H. and Jandrasics, G. Software recycling, Software Maintenance Conference, Austin 1987.

Sneed, H.M. and Jandrasics, G. Inverse Transformation from Code to Specification, in Software Tools '89, Blenheim Online, 1989.

Spivey, M. The Z Notation, Prentice-Hall, 1989.

Standish, T.A. An Essay on Software Reuse, in (IEEE 1984), pp. 494-497.

Suhler, P.A., Nader Bagherzadeh, N., Malek, M. and Iscoe, N. Software Authorization Systems, IEEE Software, January 1986, pp. 34 et seq.

Swanson, E.B. and Beath, C.M. Maintaining Information Systems in Organisations, Wiley 1989.

Swift, J. Software maintenance: defusing the time-bomb, in Managing large projects, On-Line Software Tools, 1987.

Teory, T.J. and Fry, J.P. Design of Database Structures, Prentice-Hall, 1982.

Tichy, W.F. Software Development Control Based on Module Interconnection, in Proceedings of the 4th International Software Engineering Conference, Munich, September 1979, pp. 29-41.

Tichy, W.F. Software Development Control Based on Systems Structure Description, Ph.D. thesis, Carnegie-Mellon University, Computer Science Department, January 1980.

Townley, H.M. and Gee, R.D. Thesaurus Making. Grow you own word-stock, Andrè Deutsch, 1980.

Ward, M. Transforming a Program into a Specification, Computer Science Technical Report 88/1, University of Durham, January 1988.

Waters, R.C. Program Translation via Abstraction and Reimplementation, IEEE Transactions on Software Engineering, vol. 14, no. 8, August 1988, pp. 1207-1228.

Wegner, P. Capital-Intensive Software Technology, IEEE Software, July 1984.

Wikstrom, A. Functional Programming using ML, Prentice-Hall, 1987.

Wirfs-Brock, R.J. and Johnson, R.E. Surveying Current Research into Object-Oriented Design, Comm ACM, vol. 33, no. 9, September 1990, pp. 104-124.

Wolff, F. Long-term Controlling of Software Reuse, PRACTITIONER working paper BrU-0100, Brunel University, September 1990.

Wood, M. and Sommerville, I. An information retrieval system for software components, in Software Engineering Journal, September 1988, pp. 199-207.

Yatsumoto, Y., Sasaki, O., Nakajima, S., Takezawa, K., Yamamoto, S., and Tanaka, T. SWB System: a Software Factory, in Software Engineering Environments, Editor Huenke, North-Holland, 1980, pp. 305-318.

Part Two

Software Reuse

2 Reuse and design

F. Bott and M. Ratcliffe

University College of Wales

2.1 INTRODUCTION

Software reuse is widely regarded as offering great potential for improving the software production process. Not only is it expected to lead to substantial increases in productivity but it is also likely to lead to software systems which are more robust and more reliable. Indeed, it is widely believed that a massive increase in software reuse is the most promising way of overcoming the software crisis. Not surprisingly, therefore, significant research effort is beginning to be deployed on developing tools to facilitate the reuse of software and on solving the technical problems which are seen as inhibiting it at present.

The problem of software reuse must not be viewed solely in purely technical terms. There are a large number of non-technical factors that militate against the effective reuse of software; the cumulative effect of these factors is almost certainly a greater obstacle to widespread software reuse than are the technical problems.

The term 'software reuse' is susceptible to a number of definitions. The most straightforward is the use of programming language source text or compiled code in a context other than that for which it was originally written. If we restrict ourselves to the reuse of code, however, we shall certainly not reap all the potential benefits of reuse; requirements specifications, designs, test plans and many other products of the development process are capable of being reused.

There is some doubt whether the term software reuse should be interpreted as including reuse with modification or whether it should be restricted to cover only reuse without change. If we allow modification, then the occasions on which we can practise reuse will be much more numerous but we shall not gain the advantages of reliability which come from reusing proven or well tested components unchanged. In this paper we shall normally allow reuse to include reuse with modification.

2.2 EXISTING PRACTICE

To most people, software reuse means the reuse of code. Two types of code reuse have been widely and commonly practised for many years. Subroutine libraries were introduced on the Edsac in the early 1950s (Wilkes 1953) and have proved particularly successful in scientific and engineering computing. System software, such as real time executives, programming support environments or database management systems, is inherently designed as software to be reused and has grown steadily and rapidly in importance.

Subroutine libraries usually consist of a fairly large number of comparatively unrelated components, each of which has a fairly simple but widely required function. Because of this, they can be developed incrementally, with only limited initial planning, and are fairly cheap to produce; new components are often acquired as a result of development for a specific problem.

The development of the idea of the abstract data type and the advent of Ada as a language to support the concept has revitalized the idea of a subroutine library. It is now practicable to build libraries of parameterizable abstract data types which can be reused easily and securely; such libraries have a very wide range of potential applicability precisely because they provide implementations of the basic constructs of computer science. At least one company in the USA is now marketing such a library on a commercial basis (Margono 1987).

System software denotes large items of software such as operating systems, database management systems, sort/merge generators, real time executives, compilers and fourth generation language processors, etc. Such systems are comparatively independent of specific applications. They were traditionally supplied by computer manufacturers but, since the movement to unbundling in the early 1970s, have increasingly been supplied by specialist software houses, particularly in the areas of database management systems and transaction processing monitors.

Much of the use of system software amounts to software reuse. Twenty years ago transaction processing monitors and real time executives would be tailor made for a specific application system and an organization would feel itself very fortunate if it were able to reuse them on a subsequent project. They are now typically bought off the shelf from a specialist supplier.

In contrast to subroutine libraries, system software typically consists of a single component (at least from the users' point of view) which provides a set of closely related and fairly sophisticated functions. It is usually costly to produce and requires substantial effort in the specification and design phases. It is inherently designed to be reusable because this is the only way in which its development can be economically justified; for the same reason, the potential market needs to be fairly large.

The example of system software points up a useful distinction between what we shall call software components and meta-components. A reusable component is a piece of software, such as a subroutine or real time executive, which forms part of the running target system which we aim to produce; a meta-component is a piece of software which generates such components, a parser generator, for example.

Meta-components have been the mechanism through which software reuse has been successfully achieved in the field of data processing. Sort/merge generators and report program generators have a long history; more recently, other types of application generator have become available, merging into the so-called fourth generation languages (4GLs).

2.3   REUSE OF DESIGN AND REQUIREMENTS

Design information is widely reused in an informal and unstructured way; designers carry the expertise developed on one project over to their next project. Indeed, such reuse constitutes the stock in trade of the experienced analyst and designer. It often happens that successive projects are so closely related that very specific design expertise is reused in this way. It is, however, much rarer for design documentation to be reused.

The potential savings from the reuse of design information are probably greater than those obtainable from code reuse. The design process consumes substantial resources of staff time, usually of high quality, expensive staff who are difficult to recruit; the cost of errors in the design phase is much higher than the cost of errors in the coding phase. Both of these facts point to substantial benefits to be derived from the reuse of design information.

So long as design remained an unstructured process with informal documentation, the reuse of design information was bound to be equally informal. The development of structured design methods with more formal documentation stored on a computer offers the opportunity of putting the reuse of design information on to a more organized basis, although there is little evidence of this being done.

2.4 REUSE OF SPECIFICATIONS

In contrast to the reuse of code, which is comparatively widespread in certain areas, there is little evidence that the reuse of specifications is widely practised. As with the reuse of design, however, it is likely that a lot of specification material is reused in a very informal manner.

Where a specification has the force of a standard, whether de facto or de jure, it is likely, of course, to be very widely reused. Typical examples are the definition of the X25 interface and the UNIX system calls. However, the potential benefits of such specification reuse are limited by lack of precision in the specifications; improvements in the techniques of formal specification and their more widespread use (e.g. the formal specification of PCTE) can be expected to alleviate this difficulty. Two obvious benefits are:

- a formal specification is more likely to be complete, consistent and unambiguous (indeed, tools may be available to support checking of these properties) and so can be more reliably implemented;

- it is easier to modify a formal specification safely because checks for completeness and consistency of the revised specification will usually detect oversights in the revision process.

2.5 WHAT ATTRIBUTES MAKE A COMPONENT REUSABLE?

It will be apparent from what has already been said that a unit of software reuse can be as small as a single subprogram to carry out a comparatively trivial task or as large as a database management system. Almost any piece of software is capable of being reused but it may be so specific to the environment for which it was first written that it is unlikely to be reused elsewhere or it may be so designed that it can only be included in other systems with the greatest of difficulty; the term reusability denotes the characteristics which are likely to lead to its being reused regularly and easily.

This notion of reusability as applied to software components is difficult to define precisely. Rather than regard it as a Boolean attribute of a component, one should think of it as being described by several variables, each of which can take a number of values (if not a continuum). In this section, we identify these variables and explain their relevance to reusability. In what follows we describe the attributes under three headings: the functionality which a component provides; the environment in which a component may be used; and the quality of the component.

2.6   FUNCTIONALITY

2.6.1   Applicability

The applicability of a component is a measure of the likelihood that, given a randomly chosen application, a design exists which uses the component. Clearly this depends on how wide or narrow is the field from which the application is chosen, but it also depends upon the nature and function of the component: an implementation of a string as an abstract data type is more widely applicable than a function for testing whether an aircraft's flaps are fully extended.

The applicability of a component may be widened by optimising certain other attributes which we discuss below, but wide applicability should not necessarily be a goal in the design of a component. Many authors, perhaps most notably Neighbours (Neighbours 1986), feel that component reuse works best within well-defined application domains.

2.6.2   Generality

The more general a component, the more reusable it is. For example, a stack of items of arbitrary type is clearly more reusable than a stack of integers and a sine routine which calculates the sine of floating-point numbers of arbitrary precision is more reusable than one which works only on numbers of some fixed precision.

Although generality and applicability are very similar concepts, separating them helps to identify the dangers of excessive generality. The notion of applicability should be used to limit the amount of generality in a component. Improvements to the generality of a component should be aimed at making the component more reusable within its domain, rather than simply widening that domain.

Parameterization is one of the main ways in which generality can be improved. For example, a stack component parameterized by the maximum depth of a stack is more general than one with a fixed maximum depth (but not noticeably more widely applicable). Again excessive parameterization is to be avoided, although new languages and techniques for defaulting may help here (Ratcliffe 1989).

2.6.3 Completeness

The term completeness describes in a component an intuitive degree of adequacy and self-consistency. Unfortunately, attempts at a more formal, mathematical definition of this quality do not seem promising. Such a definition would involve something like every state of the data type being reachable from every other state using the operations provided. For example, a stack abstract data type without a POP operation would clearly be incomplete in this sense. However, most users of such a component would expect other operations on a stack (DEPTH, for example) which are not needed in the formal definition of completeness. Similarly, a component providing an integer data type without multiplication or division operators would normally be regarded as inadequate, even though it satisfies the formal definition of completeness.

2.6.4   Cohesion and Coupling

It is commonly said that reusable components should exhibit high cohesion and low coupling; in other words, the interface which a component presents to the outside world should have a high degree of conceptual unity and the dependence on other components should be small. These are in fact attributes which the modules in any good design decomposition should have, regardless of what part, if any, the desire to generate reusable components may play.

If the interface which a component presents exhibits low cohesion, then it may well be possible to factor the interface into a combination of simpler interfaces with little coupling between them; this in turn makes it more likely that the simpler components will be reused.

The term coupling can be used in two senses: it may denote the number of other components on which the given component depends or it may denote the 'bandwith' (e.g. number of parameters in a subprogram call). High coupling in the first sense discourages designers from reusing a component because of the need to incorporate into the design all the components on which it depends; this often leads to problems of memory occupancy and execution speed – certainly it leads to a loss of control over these things. High coupling in the second sense discourages reuse because specifying large numbers of parameters – many of which are likely to be fixed for a given application – is tedious and conducive to errors; again, it can lead to problems of memory occupancy and execution speed.

2.7   ENVIRONMENT

2.7.1   Portability

The term portability originally applied to the ease with which a piece of software could be made to run on hardware other than that for which it was originally designed. More recently the term has been used to describe the ability to use a piece of software unchanged in an environment other than that for which it was originally designed, where the environment comprises software as well as hardware components. Typical examples of this kind of portability are packages which run under either UNIX or VAX/VMS. A component's potential for being reused is clearly enhanced if the code constituting the component is portable.

Other aspects of portability include the ability of a component designed for a single-threaded environment to be used in a multi-threaded one, and the ability of a component designed for use in a single processor configuration to be used more than once in a multiprocessor system.

2.8 QUALITY

Clearly a component will not be reused if it is not considered to be of sufficiently high quality. Components should have readily demonstrable reliability and robustness, perhaps by means of test data, validation results or formal proofs. The availability of testing support for a component will simplify regression testing following an enhancement of a component.

In order to select a component, the potential reuser must be able to find out what the component does, and to some extent model the behaviour of the component in the intended application. Good (formal) specifications and other documentation are invaluable here; the most widely applicable, general, reliable component in the world will not be reused if its documentation is so poor that it is never selected from a catalogue.

Particular attention should be paid to the maintainability of a reusable component. Reuse is not always simply a case of taking a component and supplying some parameters; often, it is necessary to modify the component, to suit it to an application which the original designer did not foresee. The ease with which a component may be modified, its maintainability, therefore affects its reusability. It is particularly important in this context that repeated modification of the component should not degrade its quality.

2.9   REUSE AND DESIGN METHODS

'Structured' design methods and software reuse interact in two ways. On the one hand, we may ask to what extent the products of a design method, anything from entity life histories to source code, can be expected to be reusable while, on the other hand, we may ask what encouragement the design method gives to the designer to reuse existing components. In other words we must recognize the distinction between design for reuse and design with reuse.

The increased formality and uniformity which design methods introduce might be expected to increase the potential reusability of their products. If all systems produced by an organization require dataflow diagrams drawn according to a fixed convention, then it is more likely that a designer will be able to take an existing diagram from a similar system and modify it to suit the one on which he is currently working. There is anecdotal evidence to suggest that this does indeed happen, but we know of no organization in which there is an established policy, with supporting infrastructure, to encourage it. IPSEs (integrated project support environments) will certainly provide an infrastructure to support this type of reuse, if they are configured appropriately.

Hierarchical decomposition, in one form or another, is a major element in most design methods. On the face of it, this process is inimical to software reuse, since it encourages the designer to decompose the system without regard for what components are available for reuse; indeed, if such considerations are taken into account early in the development process, they are often stigmatized as 'premature design'. In practice, we do not believe that this difficulty is serious. A designer who knows that he must use a particular database management system or a particular type of terminal is well able to design with such constraints in mind. In the same way, if the need to maximize reuse is specified as part of the non-functional requirements for a system, there seems no reason to believe that designers will not be able to accommodate it.

2.10 NON-TECHNICAL ISSUES

2.10.1 Organization and Motivation

Software reuse will not happen merely because the technical means of achieving it become available. Nor will it be applied successfully within an organization merely because it becomes official policy. Project managers and software development staff must be convinced that it is in their interests to reuse software; if the organization intends to produce reusable software as a by-product of other developments, project teams must also be convinced that it is in their interests to develop software in such a way as to produce reusable components.

The most widely recognized obstacle at this level is usually known as the the NIH ('not invented here') syndrome. Technical staff are reluctant to believe that software from another source will be as efficient, effective or reliable as the software they could write themselves; this feeling is often reinforced by bad experiences with imported software. It is easy, however, to overestimate the magnitude of this problem. While some suppliers of embedded systems cling to their own special purpose real time executives, many more have adopted proprietary products very successfully. Provided that the quality of the software being reused meets the reasonable expectations of the developers, there seems to be no reason why it should not be adopted equally successfully.

The NIH syndrome is however likely to prove a serious obstacle to software reuse if the attitudes it represents are reinforced by other organizational obstacles to reuse. Large contracting companies are usually organized in a number of almost autonomous divisions. Contact between the divisions is very restricted and they may even see each other as competitors. In such circumstances, it is clearly difficult for software produced in one division to be reused by another. Indeed, the authors are aware of one case where a perfectly adequate set of software tools for version control and system building had been produced and used by one division of such a company, while other divisions were purchasing inferior tools to do the same job from outside suppliers. The chances of achieving significant reuse of application software across divisions in such an environment are clearly minimal.

The notion of individual profit centres and the project manager's responsibility for the profitability of his project constitute serious motivational and organizational obstacles to software reuse. On the one hand, cross-charging arrangements tend to be arcane and the treatment of fixed costs usually leads to one or other side feeling unfairly treated when a product developed by one profit centre is used by another. On the other hand, the development of reusable software produces benefits in the long term rather than in the short term but individual profit centres and projects are usually judged on short-term criteria, even where the organization as a whole is committed to long-term growth.

Whether reusable software is produced as a by-product of other development activities (and it is not clear that this is technically wise) or as a separate development activity, it must be emphasized that to implement an effective software reuse strategy at corporate level will require substantial investment and the pay-back period will be long. In the absence of firm cost/benefit figures, an act of faith is required on the part of the financial management if such investment is to be made.

The difficulties described in this subsection are more easily surmounted if the aim is to achieve reuse of software within a single group of developers. The benefits are more readily apparent to the staff involved and it is easier to achieve the right psychological atmosphere. It is suggested that the best strategy for an organization wishing to achieve a substantial level of software reuse is to start by planning for reuse at this level. The demonstrable benefits achieved can then be used to support the case for investment in a reuse strategy on a larger scale and as a lever to achieve the organizational changes likely to be necessary before it can be achieved on a wider scale.

2.10.2 Commercial and Contractual Issues

Straightforward cost-plus contracts do not directly encourage software reuse – or, indeed, any other practices aimed at improving the productivity of software developers. Nevertheless, the availability of a repository of relevant reusable software ought to give the bidder a substantial competitive advantage during the tendering stage, because the use of the appropriate reusable software should reduce the overall cost to the customer. It will, however, change the nature of the contract, since charging arrangements and ownership of rights will need modifying. This will require a change of attitude on the part of many customers; there are encouraging signs that such a change is already on its way – many large customers already insist that their suppliers adopt sound software engineering practices and software reuse is just one more example.

It is in bidding for fixed price contracts that the greatest benefits of software reuse should be apparent. The availability of appropriate reusable software, and tools and design methods for exploiting, should allow an organization to keep the price of its bid low and so improve its competitive position.

2.11 THE SOFTWARE COMPONENTS INDUSTRY

The emphasis in the previous subsections of this paper has been on the reuse of software which has been developed within the organization which is reusing it. An alternative paradigm is based on the idea of a 'software components industry', supplying components to suppliers of complete software systems, in the same way as the electronics components industry supplies electronics components to the builders of complete electronically-based systems. This idea seems to have been first conceived by McIlroy (McIlroy 1969); a splendidly fanciful version is to be found at the end of Barnes' book on Ada (Barnes 1982).

There is now at least one company in the USA which is marketing a set of reusable components in this way. The components implement commonly used data structures. They are provided in source form and are made available on the basis of a site licence which allows them to be copied and used freely on that site; furthermore, the components can be incorporated into complete systems and sold on without any royalty being due to the component supplier. What the licensee cannot do is copy the components themselves and pass them on to an unlicensed site. The components are guaranteed so that any defect reported will be rectified free of charge; there is therefore no maintenance charge, although support may be purchased if required.

Because the range of computer applications is still growing steadily, the number of areas for which application specific sets of components might usefully be provided is, for practical purposes, unlimited. The largest of these areas – data processing and scientific calculation – are already well provided for by other means such as fourth-generation languages and the various scientific subroutine libraries. There remains, however, a very large range of application areas which can be addressed. In some of these, such as avionics or digital telephony, the potential benefits from a set of reusable components are very great indeed.

But there are two difficulties. The market for a set of components for a given application area is comparatively small and, in many cases, the expertise to identify and produce suitable components lies in the application development organizations rather than in the component suppliers. If such sets of components are produced and marketed (and it is far from obvious that this will ever take place), whether by the software industry or by organizations working in the application area, it seems unlikely that they will be made available on the liberal licensing terms which at present apply to general purpose components. In particular, rather than allowing free replication in products in which the components are incorporated, it will probably be necessary to charge substantial royalties.

2.12 CONCLUSIONS

It is the authors' belief that, while technical advances can do a great deal to make software reuse easier to achieve, the present state of software technology is quite adequate to allow reuse to be exploited profitably; lack of tools and techniques should not be used as an excuse for postponing investment in reuse. The examples of successful reuse cited earlier should be sufficient to demonstrate this.

The essential problems are organizational. The benefits to be gained from increased reuse of software will only be achieved if there is a strong organizational commitment to achieving it, backed up by adequate resources and sufficient patience. The benefits cannot be achieved overnight. In the same way that the production of high quality software requires the development of a 'quality culture' so the exploitation of software reuse requires the development of a 'reuse culture', in which the search for existing components instinctively precedes any attempt to design new ones.

The industry is still far from being organized in such a way as to exploit reuse to the full. The structural changes needed in large organizations in order to achieve the necessary cooperation between individual sub-units will be very difficult to achieve.

The development of a strategy for software reuse should start at the level of a well integrated and coherent unit within the organization. At this level, some of the organizational problems can be avoided and hard financial evidence of the costs and benefits can be accumulated; this evidence can then be used to justify extending the strategy to larger units.

It is important to ensure that the organization's commitment to reuse is not seen to be compromised by administrative obstacles. Contract negotiating staff must also be made aware of the issues to be addressed and should be encouraged to have appropriate forms of wording available. Sales and marketing staff need to be made alive to the benefits of software reuse. It will fall to them to educate and persuade customers that they stand to benefit from it and so make them willing to accept appropriate contractual provisions.

An attempt should be made to change the performance criteria by which individual staff and project groups are assessed so as to encourage the reuse of software and the development of reusable components. At the same time, a group should be established to act as curators for the reusable software and to develop the ideas coming from the individual project teams. Where appropriate the group would also procure and look after such relevant sets of reusable components as might be commercially available.

Finally, it must not be assumed that investment in reuse is bound to be justified. The examples of successful reuse which have been cited depend for their success on the organization expecting to make a long-term investment.

REFERENCES

1.   Barnes, J.G.P.: Programming in Ada. Addison-Wesley, Wokingham, UK, 1982.

2.   Margono, J. & Berard, E.V.: 'A Modified Booch's Taxonomy for Ada Generic Data Structure Components and Their Implementation', in Tafvelin, S. (Ed.): Ada Components, Libraries and Tools, pp. 61-74. Ada Companion Series, Cambridge University Press, UK, 1987.

3.   McIlroy, M.D.: 'Mass Produced Software Components', in Naur, P., Randell, B. & Buxton, J.N. (Eds.):   Proceedings of NATO Conference on Software Engineering, pp. 88-98. Petrocelli/Charter, New York, 1969.

4.   Neighbours, J.M. & Prieto-Diaz, R.: 'Module Interconnection Language', Journal of Systems and Software, 6(4), 1986.

5.   Ratcliffe, M.: 'Prototyping through the Reuse of Existing Components', PhD. Thesis, University of Wales, 1989.

6.   Wilkes, Wheeler & Gill.: Programming for a Digital Computer. Addison-Wesley, Wokingham, UK, 1953.

3 Reuse and Ada

T. Orme

AEG (UK) Ltd

3.1 INTRODUCTION

By this point in the conference, I expect most of you are rather tired of hearing the repetition of McIlroy's famous analogy (1) of software components being mass-manufactured just like hardware components in a factory. In reality, reuse has proved to be more difficult than predicted, and we shall examine the reasons why. We shall look at why we attempt reuse in the first place, at the work currently being done, and the results achieved. From the latter we can derive enough of an insight into the reuse process to decide whether Ada, which was designed amongst other things for reusability, meets our criteria for a suitable implementation language.

3.2 WHAT IS THE POINT OF REUSE ?

3.2.1 Reduction of Effort

This is the point that is most readily appreciated by senior management. Now that software is very expensive, anything that potentially reduces the cost is greeted with enthusiasm. It is frequently possible to obtain funds from one's organization to set up reusable libraries, etc., as an investment in the future. More difficult to obtain, perhaps, is permission to spend effort and money, in a project under budget and time constraints, in order to make some of the contracted-for software more reusable on other projects.

3.2.2   Increase in Reliability

Generally speaking, when a new version of an existing product comes out, then, provided that cost cutting was not the main impetus for the change, the new version is superior to the preceding one, whether in terms of functionality, maintainability or (particularly) reliability. The reason is that we learn from doing, and from seeing, other people's (and our own) mistakes. After all, the main motivation for coming to a conference such as this must be to hear of the experience of others and reuse some of the more successful ideas. Therefore, in reusing software, we save the effort of not re-inventing the wheel; but, if the reused software has been maintained, then we may also reasonably expect to incorporate material of a higher standard than if we started from scratch.

3.3   DIFFICULTIES OF REUSE

3.3.1   Retrieval

Finding a component that fits the bill turns out to be a non-trival task. Various taxonomies have been proposed for reusable components (e.g. (2) and (3)), but classification is still a problem area. Furthermore, if developers do not imagine that the component might already exist, they will not spend time searching for it, so there has to be a discipline regularly to examine the reusable libraries in the light of current activities.

3.3.2   Ownership

Ownership of the original software is liable to be an issue, as discussed in the previous paper by Paul Walton (4).

3.3.3   Scepticism

Faced with a component of any size, any competent software engineer will consider, 'Does this really work?' If there is doubt, and time has to be taken to make it work, then no-one under milestone pressure will take the risk. The only solution is to make reusable software carry a guarantee – it has to be maintained.

3.3.4   Insufficient Functionality

The competent software engineer next asks, 'Does it do all I need it to do?' Because of this, some writers on the subject have proposed that all components should be written in the most general way possible (see, for example, (5)). This promptly falls foul of:

3.3.5   Excessive Functionality

Generality, apart from the cost of providing it, causes two big problems: inefficiency and complication. The latter's effect is insidious: 'How long will it take me to understand all the software's functions?'

The solutions to the problems of insufficient/oversufficient functionality have to be: clear documentation, highly cohesive modules, reasonable but not officious generality, publication of specimen performance figures, and readable code for the last resort.

3.3.6   The Granularity Problem

It is easy to reuse tiny pieces of software – we do it daily with, e.g. square root and trig routines. It gets much more difficult as the size scale is ascended, because firstly the reused component becomes a bigger part of the design, and secondly some tailoring is normally required. Thus there are further requirements for reusability: the component design must be held together as well as the code, with a means of tracing between the two.

3.3.7 Psychological Factors

There are a number of psychological factors that inhibit reuse, discussed in (6). Further discussion of them is outside the scope of this paper.

3.4 LANGUAGE FACTORS THAT PROMOTE REUSE

3.4.1 Library Support

As will be seen in a later section, reusable libraries must be built up and thereafter constantly maintained. Language support for a library mechanism, and maintainability, are thus important factors for reuse.

3.4.2 Modularity

It goes without saying that ease of encapsulation is important.

3.4.3 Templates

A means of writing software templates is desirable, such that, for example, the same sort routine could sort alphabetically or numerically.

3.4.4 Portability

Portability is radically improved by strict standardization of source language (and by certain other measures such as minimizing machine dependence).

3.4.5 Typing

Strong typing is required to reduce bugs creeping in at the point of reuse. Support for abstract data types (instances of which are often referred to as 'objects') is also needed.

3.5 DOES ADA MEET THE REQUIREMENT ?

Having discussed in the last two sections the characteristics necessary to overcome the difficulties and promote reuse, let us examine how well Ada helps.

3.5.1 Reasonable Generality

Achieving this is a function of experience and language-independent.

3.5.2 Regular Review of Reusable Libraries, Clear Documentation, Publication of Performance Data, and Capture of Design Data Together with Source Code

All of these matters should be dealt with by standards and operating procedures.

3.5.3 Maintainability

This has turned out to be a key issue in keeping libraries, and Ada is highly maintainable (7).

3.5.4 Library Support

Ada has the concept of a program library whose units may be referenced by different applications. Strict compilation order rules minimize integration problems.

3.5.5 Modularity

Modularity and information-hiding are supported in Ada through the package construct. The package spec contains items visible outside the package, concealing implementation details.

3.5.6   Generics

Ada has a template mechanism, the generic, which allows functions, procedures and packages to be written in a general way, and instantiated for different types.

3.5.7   High Cohesion

Cohesion is a measure of how well related the components of a module are, and as such is a design issue.

3.5.8   Readability

In (7) it is found that most sites using Ada believe it more readable than other high-level languages, and none of the 19 sites investigated believed that it was less readable.

3.5.9   Typing

Ada provides the needed strong typing and support for abstract data types.

3.5.10   'Reasonable' Generality

How much generality is reasonable depends on many factors, and experience has been shown to be important in determining this issue. However, whatever the answer may be in any given case, Ada will support it. Evidence for this can be found for example in (2), which contains some very general and abstract types.

3.5.11   Standardization

Ada is unusual in that the language standard appeared before the first implementation. No subsets or supersets of the language are permitted for compilers (although software engineers of course are not obliged to make use of every feature). The rules are strictly enforced through regular rigorous validation of compilers. Portability is found to be an order of magnitude better than in other languages (7).

3.5.12 Widespread Usage

Last but not least, Ada is the programming language used (reused?) in the most important reuse initiatives, to be described in the next section. The results of these initiatives are starting to become available.

3.6 CURRENT AND RECENT WORK

Reusability, often associated with Ada, is a major research topic at many academic and industrial organizations throughout the world. A full list is given in (8). A less comprehensive, but more up-to-date, survey is contained in (9).

Guidelines for reusability appear in (5), (10), (11), (12) and (13).

3.6.1 Reusable Libraries

Tracz (8) has surveyed the work done on reusability by sixteen different organizations. The problems, particularly of obtaining suitable components, are discussed. In other work, Tracz reinforces the current wisdom that reusable components must be designed for reuse, otherwise either a redesign will occur or reuse will not take place.

Ted Biggerstaff has produced two Rules of Three:

1)   The costs of creating and maintaining a component will not be recovered until the component is reused three times;

2)   The creation of a reusable software component to perform a given function is unlikely to succeed until the design incorporates the experience from three previous pieces of software doing the same thing.

The management of reusable libraries was investigated in (14):

Reusability has to be managed to work well, but the rewards can be a considerable increase to effective productivity in the organization. Larger projects may be able to justify a reusable library on their own.

A problem is to identify components for reuse. Some sites formally examine at the design stage for reusability, but at most places it is left to the individual to propose. Experience is found helpful to generalize a design. Excellent documentation is essential before submission to any library.

It is difficult to maintain a reusable library without resources. There must be a formal system for reporting and fixing bugs, otherwise configuration control becomes unmanageable when everyone keeps private versions of public files.

As well as classification of components, it is also important to record any relationships between them. Firesmith (15) reports that some libraries have alternative implementations for some modules, e.g. a package spec with two bodies to choose from, one optimized for time efficiency and the other for memory.

(2) contains a useful summary of the duties of the librarian on page 573, including elimination of unnecessary duplication and ensuring that everyone is kept informed of accessions to the library.

Hitachi ensures that all programmers have to obtain at least some experience of the library: the company sets an exercise, once a month, which is most easily solved by reusing components from it (16).

3.6.2 Domain Analysis

Domain analysis is currently the hottest topic in research into reusability. A manageable application area ('domain') is selected and a team of application experts is assembled. The domain is analysed to determine the common capabilities and features of current systems, as well as of future systems. Alternatives are assessed and a set of components can be constructed. Holibaugh *et al.* (17) give a description of the process. According to (18), about 25-75 useful abstractions are all that are found to be needed in a carefully defined domain (abstractions, of course, are not the same as components).

An advantage of domain analysis is that the library classification can be derived from the analysis results, so that the location and incorporation of components should be easier. A difficulty is that the domain analysis must be maintained – after all, few domains are static. Consequently, and remembering Biggerstaff's first Rule of Three, there is a danger that the up-front effort in domain analysis will outweigh the eventual gains. Domains must be chosen with an eye to potential returns; otherwise domain analysis will more resemble early requirements modelling than genuine reuse.

3.7 CONCLUSION

We have discussed some of the benefits and problems of reusability. Little real reusability seems to have been achieved, compared with the potential (6). The projections of achievable gain from reuse are still valid, so what is stopping us? There appear to be three major problem areas.

3.7.1 Legal/Commercial Issues

These have been referred to and are outside the scope of this paper.

3.7.2 Lack of Large Libraries

It is a truism that software libraries cannot be used until there is material there to reuse. The minimum amount needed to earn the respect of the average software engineer may have been seriously underestimated. The larger the library, the more (formal or informal) pressure there will be on designers to design in reusable components. There is a problem here which harks back to legal/commercial issues: there is incentive to take out of the library, but not to give to it in the first place. The advantages and economies of scale would make industry-wide libraries ideal, but no-one will contribute software that might confer or negate a competitive advantage.

A number of public reusable libraries have been set up in the U.S. (9). One, the Ada Software Repository, is virtually free (19), but the standard is highly variable. Other libraries vary in their openness and charges. The U.S. Army seem to be achieving considerable benefits from reusability; it is to be hoped that smaller organizations will quickly learn to organize themselves to achieve the same ends.

3.7.3   The Technology of Reuse

For a number of reasons referred to in section 3, software reuse is difficult. It will need some organizations to achieve a high sustained level of reuse in order for the rest of us to understand the process better and follow the example. The Japanese apparently understand this well and have set up Software Factories designed, amongst other things, to achieve advances in productivity and quality through reusability (18), (20). Perhaps the threat of competition will spur us to greater activity, as did their Fifth Generation project.

As regards actions you can take in the near-term, two appear very important. One is to obtain management commitment to software reusability. The other is to use a highly standardized language, designed for reusability, and which already carries a very large amount of available reusable software – Ada.

ACKNOWLEDGEMENTS

The author wishes to thank Robert Holibaugh and John Foreman of the SEI, and especially Will Tracz of IBM, for opinions and information during the writing of this paper.

REFERENCES

1. McIlroy, M.D. (1968) 'Mass Produced Software Components' in Software Engineering, P. Naur & B. Randell (eds), NATO Science Committee, Garmisch, Germany.

2. Booch, G. (1987)   Software Components with Ada, Benjamin-Cummings, Menlo Park, Calif.

3. Freeman, P. (1987) 'A Conceptual Analysis of the Draco Approach to Constructing Software Systems', IEEE Transactions on Software Engineering, vol. SE13, no. 7, pages 830-843.

4. Walton, P. (1989) 'The Management of Reuse', Seminar on Reuse, Maintenance and Reverse Engineering of Software, Dec 1st, 1989, Unicom Ltd, Uxbridge, Middlesex.

5. Bott, M.F., A. Elliott, R.J. Gautier (1986) Ada Reuse Guidelines – Report, ECLIPSE report ECLIPSE/REUSE/ADA_GUIDE/RP, available from Software Sciences Ltd, Farnborough, Hampshire.

6. Tracz, W. (1987) 'Software Reuse: Motivators and Inhibitors', Proceedings of Compcon, Feb. 23-27 1987, IEEE Press. Republished in [21].

7. Orme, T. (1989), 'Project Management Experience of Ada in the Maintenance Phase', Supplement to Ada User, vol. 10, October 1989.

8. Tracz, W. (1987) 'Ada Reusability Efforts: A Survey of the State of the Practice', Proceedings of the 5th Annual Joint Conference on Ada Technology, Washington, D.C. Republished in [21]. [9] Ada Information Clearing House Newsletters, December 1988 and March 1989, 1211 S Fern, C-107, The Pentagon, Washington D.C. 20301-3081.

9.   Ada Information Clearing House Newsletters, December 1988 and March 1989, 1211 S. Fern, C-107, The Pentagon, Washington D.C. 20301-3081.

10.   Braun, C.L, J.B. Goodenough, R.S. Eanes (1985), Ada Reusability Guidelines, Softech technical report no. 3285-2-208/2.

11.   St Dennis, R. (1986), Guidebook for Writing Reusable Source Code in Ada, Honeywell technical report.

12.   Wald, E.E. *et al.*, STARS Reusability Guidebook, Naval Research Lab, Washington D.C.

13.   Berard, E.V. (1986), 'Creating Reusable Ada Software', Proceedings of the National Conference on Software Reusability & Maintainability, National Institute for Software Quality and Productivity, U.S., Sept. 10-11, 1986.

14.   Orme, T. (1986), 'Project Management Experience of Ada', Proceedings of Ada U.K. Conference in Ada User, vol. 7, no. 2, May 1986.

15.   Firesmith, D.G. (1987), Ada Project Management, presentation in London, Nov. 1987.

16.   Tajima, D., T. Matsubara (1984) 'Inside the Japanese Software Industry', IEEE Computer, March 1984, pp. 34-43.

17.   Holibaugh, R., S. Cohen, K. Kang, S. Peterson (1989) 'Reuse: Where to Begin and Why', Proceedings of Tri-Ada, Pittsburgh, Penn, Oct. 1989.

18.   Tracz, W. (1988) 'Software Reuse Maxims', Proceedings of the National Symposium and Workshop on Software Reusability, Washington, D.C., April 1988.

19.   Conn, R. (1986) The Ada Software Repository and the Defense Data Network: A Resource Handbook, New York Zoetrope Inc, New York.

20.   Matsumoto, Y. (1984) 'Management of Industrial Software Production', IEEE Computer, Feb. 1984, pp. 59-70.

21.   Tracz, W. (1988) Software Reuse: Emerging Technology, IEEE Press.

4 Generalized components and application modelling

C. Minkowitz

STC Technology Ltd

4.1 INTRODUCTION

There has been much criticism about the lack of software reuse to improve programming productivity. This article argues that software reuse is indeed being practised in the form of generalized components which address the needs of specialized programming tasks. We compare the generalized components approach to software reuse with the 'warehouse of parts' approach. We also present our view of what constitutes a generalized component, as well as what the problems are that inhibit their use. We conclude with some thoughts on where the future lies in building applications using these components.

4.2 ABSTRACTION vs. NUTS AND BOLTS PROGRAMMING

How often have we heard complaints about the lost opportunity for improving programming productivity caused by the lack of software reuse? Some of us wonder what the fuss is about. After all, we reuse software all the time. Look at the way we reuse operating systems and compilers. It is likely that the criticism arises from comparisons drawn between the way in which software programs are constructed and the way in which hardware products are manufactured. Hardware manufacturing has become, in many cases, an automatic process whereby products are assembled from standard hardware parts, which can either be found in the manufacturers' own warehouses or obtained from external suppliers. So why, the critics ask, is it not possible to manufacture software programs by collecting and bolting together standard software components in the same efficient way?

There is a stock answer to that question too. Because software is soft, a program is expected to be able to fit the specific needs of the users, and it is difficult to find a configuration of software components that contains the exact functionality required to meet those needs.

Although the softness of software makes reuse difficult in the above sense, it does possess one capability that makes it more amenable to reuse in another sense. That capability is abstraction, which is the ability to model software objects and operations at a high level without having to worry about how they are implemented at a lower level. With appropriate abstractions one can provide a tool with generic capabilities that provide direct support for specific application tasks.

Thus the success we have found in reusing an operating system is not because it is a standard part fulfilling a particular function, as in the case of a hardware component, but because it is a generalized component that provides a set of functional capabilities which relieve the programmer of low-level system administrative tasks, such as file management, so that he or she can concentrate on the programming task at hand.

A high-level language is another example of a generalized component that enables a programmer to engineer software with complex data structures, functions and procedures. Other examples of generalized components are spreadsheet packages, fourth-generation languages and Artificial Intelligence development toolkits, which provide programming support for particular types of application. Some generalized components provide very high-level programming support for end-users by encapsulating knowledge about specific application domains. For example, there are a number of software packages that can be used in this way to construct programs that perform specific business tasks, such as accounting or forecasting.

We can think of a generalized component as a platform that embodies a particular abstraction, or set of abstractions. Often a tower of platforms supports a particular application, as Fig. 4.1 illustrates. Each platform in the tower provides support for the platform directly above it. There might be many combinations of levels of platform. Reuse occurs when different applications are supported by the same platform.

This layered approach to program development is an alternative approach to the one which suggests that programs be assembled from parts. At the core of the approach is the use of abstraction to raise the level of the programming medium to one that is more suited to the application task. This results in generalized software components which, like their hardware counterparts, are generic and standard in the sense that they are capable of performing certain functions, but which are soft and malleable in the sense that they can be used in a variety of programming contexts and are thus open to more opportunities for reuse.

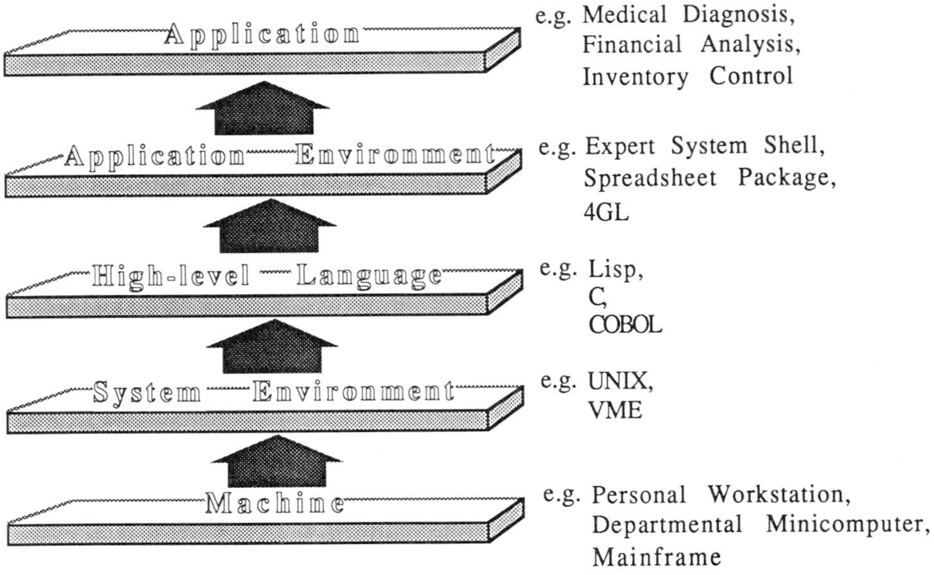

Application	e.g. Medical Diagnosis, Financial Analysis, Inventory Control
Application Environment	e.g. Expert System Shell, Spreadsheet Package, 4GL
High-level Language	e.g. Lisp, C, COBOL
System Environment	e.g. UNIX, VME
Machine	e.g. Personal Workstation, Departmental Minicomputer, Mainframe

Fig. 4.1   Tower of platforms.

4.3   HOW TO RECOGNIZE A GENERALIZED COMPONENT

We will now discuss what it is, in our opinion, that classifies a software tool as a generalized component in the sense described above. By now it should be apparent why system environments and high-level languages can be classified as such, so we shall concentrate the discussion on components at the level of the application environment which support both programmers and end-users in their application tasks.

There are some generalized components that have been in widespread use by end-users. We are thinking here of such packages as word processors, graphics tools, statistics packages and spreadsheets. Over the years, these packages have offered more and more advanced features to support the end-users in their day-to-day tasks.

They have been redesigned to work with today's sophisticated WIMP user interfaces so that they are easier to operate. The individual packages have been made to work together in an integrated way so that users have the ability to operate in an open environment where they can 'cut and paste' between applications.

All these packages encapsulate particular abstractions. Take, for example, the spreadsheet. With a spreadsheet an application is modelled as an array of decision variables whose values are related to each other according to defined functions. This abstraction is complemented in a spreadsheet package by two paradigms, namely a computational paradigm, which is a simple kind of constraint propagation with the characteristic that when the value of one variable changes the values of variables dependent on it are updated to reflect the change, and an HCI paradigm, which provides tabular input and output of data. Users have found that these paradigms are extremely well suited to the kinds of decision making and analysis tasks they need to perform.

Although these packages are intended to help users perform one-off tasks, some of them do provide facilities for automating recurring tasks. For example, most spreadsheet packages enable users to write macros which perform standard functions and procedures. However, these sorts of packages are not regarded as program development tools, at least not in the same sense as programming languages, say.

Another kind of generalized component does assist programming development in certain application areas. We will refer to these components as application-oriented languages. The main objective of an application-oriented language is to make it easier to describe application tasks by stating what it is they are to accomplish, rather than giving instructions on how they should be executed by a computer. To make it even easier for the programmer, the primitives and constructs of an application-oriented language are abstractions of familiar concepts of the application domain. How these abstractions are implemented is known only to the application-oriented language and is not a concern of the programmer.

A good example of an application-oriented language is a fourth-generation language (4GL), which assists with the development of database applications by providing a language for information update and retrieval which hides details about how the information is stored. A simulation language is another classic example of an application-oriented language which provides primitives and constructs for describing a simulation model in terms of real-world entities and events.

Another objective of application-oriented languages is to enable iterative and incremental development, opening up the opportunity for rapid prototyping and simple, maintainable code. An added advantage of these languages is that they are accessible to end-users.

The use of an application-oriented language is restricted to a given application domain. There are other generalized components which assist with more general programming tasks. We refer to these as advanced application environments. These environments are epitomized by the AI, or knowledge-based, development toolkits. An example of an AI toolkit is an expert system shell, which is used to build an expert system for a given application domain. Other examples are tools which are used to develop intelligent planning or scheduling applications.

These environments use abstraction as a way of controlling the complexity which is an inherent characteristic of the applications they aim to support. It has become a reflex action in AI programming, when confronted with a difficult problem, to first find an appropriate medium to describe its solution. Many of the attempts to find such mediums have culminated in the discovery of the general usefulness of certain programming paradigms, such as rule-based, functional, object-oriented and constraint-based programming. The AI toolkits promote the reuse of these paradigms by embedding them within their language environment. Some AI environments package a number of these paradigms together in such a way that they can be mixed and matched to the particular programming tasks at hand.

These toolkits also promote the practice of layering applications using abstractions to reduce the perceived distance between familiar concepts and their implementations. The top layer of an application often resembles an application-oriented language and can be used as such by an end-user to enter new application knowledge. The intermediate layers can often be reused in the development of other applications.

A main objective of these environments is to enable design exploration. Thus, they are used very much as modelling and rapid prototyping tools. Their use is primarily in the programmer's province, although there is usually some provision which enables end-users to maintain programs.

What we have identified here are three classes of components which differ with respect to their intended use. The first class of components are the packages, which embody a single abstraction that supports the end-user in performing one-off tasks. The second class are the application-oriented languages, which provide high-level programming support by encapsulating knowledge about specific application domains. The third class are the advanced programming languages, which provide powerful abstraction mechanisms to control complexity.

Although the components of these three classes are different in nature, there is no reason why they cannot be used together, apart from the fact that the technology is not completely in place yet to facilitate this. In theory, though, a knowledge-based tool could, for example, retrieve information from a database package using the querying facilities of a 4GL, or it could employ a spreadsheet package for number crunching and data formatting purposes.

We end this discussion with a list of features which we believe are common to these components.

- Support for a particular abstraction or set of abstractions. This is what we feel is at the core of these components, whether it be support for a particular kind of application task, as in the case of the spreadsheet, or support for abstractions about an application domain, as in the case of application-oriented languages, or support for the integration of multiple programming paradigms and the layering of abstractions, as in the case of advanced programming environments.

- Sophisticated environment. The components come with environments which provide powerful development aids, such as structure editing, debugging aids, tools for building user interfaces, and other general help facilities.

- Library of functions and procedures. These are standard functions of and procedures which are rather like the reusable hardware parts that we talked about in the first section, except that they tend to be highly parameterized so that they can be used in different contexts.

- Support for further levels of abstraction. This is more a feature of the advanced application environments. However, facilities do exist for this in other types of components. For example, most components provide some kind of macro facility for creating user-defined functions and procedures. Another means of abstraction which is used in spreadsheet and word processing packages is the creation of templates for standard spreadsheets or documents.

- Adoption of standards. The use of standards is important for reasons of portability and usability. Many of the components have adopted a common base upon which to build, so that applications developed using them can be ported to different platforms. For example, a number of AI development toolkits are adopting

Common Lisp as a standard base. Similarly, 4GLs are adopting standard database query languages. The adoption of a common HCI advantageous for increasing a component's usability. This has been proved by the popularity of the software packages designed for the Macintosh, which all use the familiar desktop interface style.

- Communication with external tools. This is the least common feature amongst the components. However, it is a feature that is now being realized due to the influence it can make on a component gaining widespread acceptability.

4.4 SOFTWARE REUSE IS ALIVE, BUT IS IT KICKING?

We now examine how successful these generalized components have been in their strive for software reuse. If we look at the base components, such as the system environments, we have certainly seen some success stories with the likes of UNIX and the Macintosh desktop environment. Also, no one could refute the success of high-level languages, and even, at least in some application areas, the success of declarative languages. Looking at the application environments, the success of the spreadsheet has been phenomenal. Not only are they used widely in their own right, there is also a major secondary industry that has grown out of them to develop spreadsheet templates catering for a wide range of applications.

Unfortunately, though, there has been a slow uptake of some of the other application environments we have mentioned, for example the 4GLs and the AI development toolkits. If they are used at all it tends to be on small projects, or only for prototyping purposes and not for serious software development.

There are a number of factors that limit the extent of reuse of these components. To begin with, there is the problem of platform dependency. Some applications built on a particular platform are bound to that platform. This becomes a serious problem in supplier/customer relationships if there is no common ground on which software can be both developed and delivered. Often the platforms supporting these components are non-standard, or they use standards that are in a continual state of flux. This makes it difficult even to compromise on common grounds.

Another factor limiting the use of some components has to do with their relative lack of maturity. Software development managers are reluctant to take the risk of producing poor quality or inefficient code by using untried development tools.

Inefficiency is a problem with many of the components we have talked about. In fact these tools have deliberately sacrificed efficiency for the sake of usability and maintainability. Sometimes this sacrifice cannot be justified even if there are enormous productivity and quality improvements to be gained.

Many of the components are more attuned to prototyping than production. A finish has to be put on the outputs of these components in order to produce hardened products. The effort that goes into this finishing process sometimes diminishes the benefits gained by using the components in the first instance.

Another impediment to the use of these components is the investment that must be made in tools acquisition and training. This investment can bite very heavily into the budget allocated to a software development project.

One thing that the users of the components complain about is the way they can impinge on design decisions because they are not flexible enough to cope with them. Because they are oriented to specific application areas, their use is restricted to predefined situations and, because they hide implementation details from the programmer, it is difficult to adapt them to cater for unforeseen situations.

The complaint about lack of flexibility is sometimes used as an excuse by some software professionals to conceal a 'not invented here' attitude. This attitude is itself a major reason why these components fail to be taken up.

Finally, some software development managers are loath to take up these components because their worth as productivity improvers has not been fully measured. We find this attitude counter-productive. It is just as sensible to rely on one's intuitions about the value of something as it is to rely on measurements, which in many cases turn out to be inexact and just as subjective. After all, the world did not wait for stringent productivity measurements to be made on high-level languages before it realized their potential.

4.5   THE ROAD AHEAD

How can we overcome the problems that inhibit the use of these components. Or are the problems more apparent than real. The efficiency arguments can be answered by promises of improved hardware processing power. The inflexibility complaints can be confronted by dispelling programmers' prejudices and preconceptions.

There is one serious problem that does limit the extent of reuse of these components. We can illustrate the problem better by returning to our tower-of-platforms analogy. We said that reuse occurs when different applications are supported by the same platform. Realistically though, the reuse is universal only if the platform dependency is in both directions. In other words, if an application built using one platform cannot be ported directly onto another platform, then the advantages of reusing the first platform will be overshadowed by the effort involved in recoding. This is a problem we have witnessed with 4GLs. Often the COBOL code generated by a 4GL can only run in its original environment, and it has to be altered in order to port it onto another COBOL environment. The generated code tends to be obscure in places, and sometimes it is more difficult to alter the code than it is to rewrite the code from scratch.

To a large extent, this problem is being addressed by a number of initiatives which are looking at ways to standardize on platforms, by promoting database and programming language standards, for example. There are also initiatives afoot to promote standards for interconnection, which will enable applications that have been developed independently of one another to work together via commonly defined interfaces for the exchange of data. Examples of interconnection standards are ASCII data, CCITT protocols such as X25, and the ISO seven-layer model. Initiatives, such as OSI for networking and X/OPEN for UNIX-based operating systems, seek to facilitate reuse across a large group of independent suppliers. The dominant applications supporter, IBM, is promoting its own set of platforms and interconnection standards via SAA.

Working to and promoting standards is one way to improve the profile of existing generalized components. We can also look at ways to accommodate emerging components. One way to approach this is to investigate technologies that facilitate abstraction. All programming languages can cater for some form of abstraction. However, there are some languages which are more ideally suited to it. For example, it is very easy to build abstractions using some dialects of Lisp, because there are no ad hoc restrictions on the way in which the basic concepts of the underlying language can be applied or combined [1]. Object-oriented languages provide powerful mechanisms for creating and reusing abstractions which closely mirror application objects [4].

Whilst we are investigating the infrastructure that surrounds these components, we can also try to repeat some of our past successes in discovering computational and HCI paradigms that suit new application areas. We do have reason to suspect that some of these successes, like the success of the spreadsheet package, are difficult acts to follow. After all, we do not know how much of the original design of the spreadsheet package was due to careful thought and how much of it was due to inspiration or luck.

Another idea we can explore is training for reuse. Software engineers are taught the power of abstraction as a tool for controlling complexity. What they are not taught is how to make the most use of abstractions once they have been discovered. Of course, one thing that must be tackled before this can be done successfully is the elitist attitude that some software practitioners have towards programming. To these engineers programming is a skill that they have been proud to master. The thought of life being made easy for them by reusing someone else's software is anathema to them. The thing to do there is to convince them that adapting software to suit the particular needs of an application is a skill in itself. After all, the customized car designer is just as skilled in some ways as the original car designer.

Of course, it could be argued that the ultimate success of generalized components will come when we manage to dispense with the need for professional programmers altogether, and can leave programming development entirely in the hands of the end-users. But this state of affairs is a long way off, especially when one considers how many application areas there are which we have not yet considered, let alone supported.

So it will be a long time before end-users rule the day. Until then there will continue to be a need for software engineers to develop components to support new application areas. There is a case, though, for involving end-users more in this process, to work with the software engineers in discovering the appropriate abstractions. We are seeing a move in this direction with the promotion of methods which seek to analyse users' processes and requirements. Perhaps in time, if we are lucky, we will see these initiatives bear fruit, with the arrival of new components that will be as successful in their time as spreadsheet packages have been in our time.

REFERENCES

1.   Abelson, H. and Sussman, G.J., Lisp: A Language for Stratified Design. In BYTE February 1988, pp. 207-218.

2.   Bobrow, D.G. and Stefik, M.J., Perspectives on Artificial Intelligence Programming. In Readings in Artificial Intelligence and Software Engineering, eds. Rich, C. and Waters, R.C., 1986, pp. 581-587.

3.   Horowitz, E. and Munson J.B., An Expansive View of Reusable Software. In IEEE Transactions on Software Engineering, vol. 10, no. 5, September 1984, pp. 477-487.

4.   Meyer, B., Reusability: the Case for Object-Oriented Design. In IEEE Software, vol. 4, no. 2, March 1987, pp. 50-64.

5.   Sprague, R.H., Jr and McNurlin, B.C., Chapter 9: New Application Development Tools and Approaches. In Information Systems Management in Practice, Canning Publications Inc., 1986, pp. 231-257.

5 Design methods for integrating system components

C. Boldyreff

Brunel University

5.1 INTRODUCTION

A new approach to design is needed to gain the full benefits of software reuse. Here a review is made of developments that make reuse possible: software components and interconnection languages. An examination is made of the requirements that design approaches must meet to support reuse. An argument is advanced that a new view of design is required to take advantage of the rich variety of software components and their interconnection methods; the approach proposed argues that for reuse in the large, these need to be related within design frameworks. Design frameworks are a means of capturing generic architectures for classes of applications and a vehicle for reusing them in future system developments.

Research on the Reuse of Software (Freeman 1987a, Tracz 1988a, Biggerstaff 1989a) has been closely allied with the recognition of software development as an engineering discipline. McIlroy's visionary paper on *Mass Produced Software Components* was delivered at the first conference on Software Engineering in

Garmisch. The high cost and unreliable nature of software products have been key problems in what since then has been identified as the **software crisis**.

One means of lowering the cost of system development resulting in increased productivity of staff is to reuse proven software. Through reuse of software, designs and implementations are developed once, and then used in the solution of many application requirements thus enhancing productivity. It has been estimated that as much as 60% of software systems is unnecessarily redeveloped, and could be standardized and reused (Lanergan 1984a). In the development of applications packages, we are constantly reinventing concepts that should be available from standard references (Jones 1984a). A consideration of the economic benefits of reusing software and the organizational control required to realize these benefits can be found in Wolff (1990a).

The improvement of software quality through reuse is equally important as it has the result of lowering significantly the subsequent software maintenance costs. The extra effort required to verify and test the reusable software can be amortized over a number of uses (Lubars 1986a). Software that is reused can also improve through being refined in the light of usage; and its reliability can be demonstrably proven in practice.

However, the engineering of large systems by interconnecting reusable software components from diverse sources in a systems integration activity remains problematic; not only is it difficult to do, it is difficult to do well as such systems often encounter problems of interworking. Although the technology for large system construction exists (viz. standard frameworks and generic application generators), there are few well developed methods which address the engineering of large integrated systems.

5.2 SOFTWARE COMPONENTS

The idea of commodity software dates from McIlroy's vision of *Mass Produced Software Components* (McIlroy 1969a). Developments in software engineering and improved language technology have made McIlroy's vision a reality; for example, specialized mathematical function libraries such as the NAG library (Ford 1979a) and the publication of a collection of Ada components by Booch (Booch 1987a).

The UNIX shell and software tools provide another well-known example of a widely used collection of software components supporting reuse (Kernighan 1976a, Kernighan 1984a). Within UNIX, the shell interpreter and command language provide a uniform mechanism for tool invocation and interconnection. Using the shell, several tools may be connected together in a pipeline to accomplish a more complex function. In the UNIX software tools approach, each reusable component, i.e. basic tool, has a well-defined and limited function and a uniform interface. Because the components all employ very simple byte stream interfaces, their interconnection is conceptually quite simple, and technically straightforward.

Larger software tools associated with the UNIX system, such as compilers, visual editors, mail systems, source code control systems, are not so easily combined together into integrated systems because the uniformity of interfaces no longer holds. In part this is because the complex data objects processed by these tools are quite diverse; in place of uniform byte streams, these components operate upon programs, textfiles, mail messages, documents and their change histories. Some simple integration of more complex UNIX tools has been achieved; for example, the EMACS editor and various compilers have been integrated by means of a common data item, the line. Provided a compiler produces error messages in a standard format identifying the line number of the source code where the error occurred, it may be combined with EMACS. In the case of compilers who do not produce their error messages in the standard format, a transformer component – called a filter in UNIX terminology – may be introduced to transform the error message into the format which EMACS requires.

What is lacking is a richer conceptual framework within which these larger components can be related. Some systems have provided such a framework to support the interworking of application packages; for example, MacApp on the Apple Macintosh (Schmucker 1986a). In other cases, the developer integrating a number of component packages such as a wordprocessor, a spreadsheet, a database, etc. must provide the framework within which these components are interconnected. Whatever the mechanism used to effect interconnection of components, in order to understand the whole system realized out of components, a means is required to describe such a composition; and interconnection languages reviewed below provide one means of describing systems composed of interconnected components.

5.3   INTERCONNECTION LANGUAGES

The composition of systems from existing components through a process of interconnection was first explicitly addressed by DeRemer and Kron (DeRemer 1976a) in the mid-seventies with their formulation of the basic principles of a module interconnection language (MIL) and their recognition that such a language allowed large systems to be programmed by means of specifying the interconnection of their parts independent of the programming of their parts, that is, modules. DeRemer and Kron characterized this distinction as Programming-in-the-large versus Programming-in-the-small. Programming in the large requires more than the separation of specification of module interfaces from their corresponding module implementation as provided in several languages developed in the the late seventies, notably Wirth's Modula and the Ada language. In addition it requires a means of separately specifying the system architecture, that is the interconnections or structure of modules to form a composite system.

A related concern in the development of systems is their effective configuration; this led to the development of configuration systems such as Feldman's pioneering make tool which enables regeneration of software systems from separately compiled modules (Feldman 1979a). Tichy extended MIL principles and brought them together with developments in configuration management and version control techniques (Tichy 1980a); this work has been the basis for various support tools developed as part of IPSE projects: the Gandalf project at CMU (1985a), the Adele project at LGI, Grenoble (Estublier 1984a) and the ECLIPSE project in the UK (Sommerville 1986a).

The major contribution of MILs is that they provide a means of expressing the architectural design of a system and can be used to control the configuration of specific system implementations. A good survey of work on modular interconnection languages is given in (Prieto-Diaz 1986a).

A development of MIL principles has been to propose the use of MILs not only to assemble code components, but also to assemble modularized formal specifications of components (Goguen 1986a). Goguen has made an important distinction between horizontal and vertical composition. MILs address horizontal composition of systems, that is connection of components at a given level; vertical composition is concerned with moving between levels of abstraction, say from the system design to its implementation. Goguen's insight has been to integrate transformational design, that is vertical composition, with horizontal structuring. Hereby transformational design, we mean the view of programming as a series of linguistic transformations (Lehman 1984a) from a high-level specification to an executable form.

5.4 CURRENT APPROACHES TO DESIGN WITH REUSE

There are two important aspects of reuse which must be expressible in a reuse design method: reuse of software conceptualization principles via generic system models; and reuse of software theories via generic components. It is assumed that any reuse design method will support the reuse of specific system models and specific components.

For example, when we build a compiler, we can reuse the established principles of compiler construction and these give us a variety of models or design frameworks of compilers into which various components such as the lexer, the parser, code generator, optimizer, etc. may be slotted. These components may also be pre-existing i.e. reusable components. In the case of a particular component, say the parser, it may have been automatically derived as a result of well understood theory, in this case, that of parser generation. So what we want to define is a means of specifying generic system models and deriving the framework for a specific system from a generic model as well as the derivation of specific components from generic components which have well understood theories (these are examples of what Goguen calls vertical composition); and specifying the composition of specific reusable components within specific frameworks (Goguen's horizontal composition) to form the system.

A simpler example illustrating these two aspects of reuse is that of producing the research report. The generic framework of such a document is defined by the research project's documentation standard. The components of a report include its frontis pages, table of contents, report body, references, appendices; these may all be represented generically by skeleton text files. In this simpler case, a macro processing language is sufficient to support the vertical composition of a document whilst simple concatenation of text achieves its horizontal composition.

One design approach that supports the reuse of software components is the object-oriented approach. This approach to software design as advocated by Meyer

(Meyer 1982a, Meyer 1987a, Meyer 1987b, Meyer 1988a) and others (Booch 1986a, Cox 1986a, Morrison 1987a) relies on object-based decomposition of software. Like earlier approaches of Parnas (1972a) and Myers (1975a) it focuses on using data i.e. objects rather than functions or processes, as its primary criterion in describing decomposition. Its underlying theory is that of abstract data types (Liskov 1974a, Guttag 1977a).

The reuse of software components has been enhanced by programming language abstractions such as parameterization and the use of abstract data types, classes and inheritance. Object-oriented approaches underlie much of the popular advocacy of software component reuse, but they offer little help with the reuse of overall structural or architectural designs of systems. More is required to encapsulate system architecture leading to reuse in the large – that is the reuse of design principles relating to the overall conceptualization of systems.

5.5   THE FRAMEWORK METHOD OF DESIGN

In our reuse research on the Practitioner project, we have found it helpful to distinguish between the reuse of generalized software components and the reuse of architectural designs or models of systems (Boldyreff 1989a). Such reuse lies at the heart of our proposed framework method of design. Earlier on, current system design practice employs informal architectural sketches to describe the overall structure of the proposed system; and then once the main components have been identified within this context, detailed design or reuse of existing software components may proceed. More than the decompositional approaches to design discussed above are needed to support the designer at this early stage of design if reuse is to take place at this stage. This is where the engineer would benefit from a library of design sketches made for existing systems and, to be useful, these sketches should give the designer insight into why they were chosen. At the most abstract, such insight will take the form of design principles; at a less abstract level, perhaps only guidelines will be available. To support design reuse at this level, software engineers might do well to learn from the example of civil engineers. The Architecture and Engineering Performance Information Center was established at the University of Maryland to maintain a database of structural design experience and material usage experience (these are the analogues of architectural designs and software components for civil engineering). Interestingly this database aims to record failures rather than successes (Petroski 1985a).

This does not mean that libraries of components are unimportant. They have a role, but much later on in the design process. If the engineer sketches the design and then looks for components, by this time through poor initial decomposition, it may be too late to help. Randell has argued that poor design structuring, i.e. decomposition, can doom a system (Randell 1986a). Most design techniques rely on the designer's ability to decompose. If we can support the designer at this stage, by offering a library of known decompositions and give the benefit of other's experience through annotations giving principles or simply guidelines, then the chances of a better structured design are increased. Another way of considering this approach is to consider that in order to stock the library with reusable components, existing systems were analysed and decomposed in order to identify suitable reusable components. Rather than throw away the results of such analysis, we should make it available for reuse. And if a designer chooses to reuse a known decomposition, then its candidate component parts will be known and also available for reuse.

One source of reusable design sketches is existing data from software development projects. For example, system modelling techniques and tools such as Harel's STATEMATE (Harel 1988a) allow the system architecture to be described graphically. It has been suggested that a neglected aspect of the design process is that few methods provide a means of recording design issues and their resolutions although there are research developments such as gIBIS (Potts 1989a) and KAPTUR (Bailin 1990a) have shown how this could be accomplished. The importance of having historical records of architectural sketches and associated design decisions is that without these, the designer must fall back on the very limited resources of her/his individual experience and, in large projects, such information may simply be lost.

The historical design records that provide the basis for the design frameworks will necessarily reflect specific system designs and also the historical development of the design. Such raw data is simply the starting point for the develop- ment of general purpose design frameworks. To get to the heart of a design, it is often necessary to rationalize the original design by examining the designs of several related systems. Parnas has given good pointers on how to get started with this task (Parnas 1986a). The possibility of abstracting out the architecture of a system from its existing realization has also been described by Henderson (1989a) although general principles of the process of abstraction are required so that it may be applied to classes of similar applications. Current work on reverse engineering is too narrowly focused on individual systems, see for example Sneed (1987a); a more expansive approach is required to identify common patterns and design principles applicable to classes of information systems (Zhang 1990a).

Moreover, to support reuse of generic design sketches underlying the informal use of graphics to sketch architectural designs, a more formal method of description is required to express and support abstraction within the design's architecture. The level of abstraction used to describe design frameworks must allow the generic framework of classes of common applications to be expressed; it must also be possible to express possible interconnections and dependencies among the various parts of the application. The description of interconnections and dependencies is covered by existing MIL developments. More importantly is the possibility of expressing options and calculating the impact of their selection on the overall design. For example, many designs are scalable over an application; and this might provide the guideline for selecting one option over another. A specific example might be a transaction processing system design with an optional communications processor subsystem that is included only where speed or security are required. This requires a simple extension to MILs to allow options to be described and associated guidelines for selecting amongst the particular options given in a design framework.

The framework method requires that fieldwork is undertaken to record design sketches and decisions, these once captured are the raw material out of which the design frameworks will be abstracted. On the Practitioner project, we developed a questionnaire that allows software concepts (at the highest level these include applications) to be described; this has been used to study applications in the domain of steel production (Boldyreff 1990a). It was possible to formulate a generic model of an industrial control system that was useful to production engineers responding to calls for tender on new developments. The questionnaire has undergone continuous development since its inception; and within the project, we intend to develop it further to better support the capture of design sketches and related design issues, options and decisions.

Already, the importance of identifying options has been noted; these may have been reflected in design decisions. Bailin has suggested that where established practice makes use of standard designs, any deviation requires justification (Bailin 1990a). In the design frameworks method such deviations are a source of possible options, and while it is important to understand why they have been introduced into the design, they should also be recognized as potentially important signs of design innovation. While every change is not necessarily a change for the better, without change, there can be no progress. This principle of evolution holds for systems in general.

What is new here is that we are looking at abstraction of designs in the large and proposing the design framework as a means of capturing such architectural designs and as the vehicle for employing them in future system developments.

5.6 CONCLUSION

Design with reusable components presents new challenges to those attempting to support the design process. This paper has reviewed the ideas of software components and the means of expressing the interconnection of components such as MILs. There are additional problems in the design of systems built using components; transformer components may be required to ensure data integration, see for example (Mamrak 1989a).

Large-scale reuse requires a larger view of design than that supporting component reuse; it is necessary to incorporate reuse of architectural designs of systems. We have outlined a methodology based on the reuse of design frameworks to address this aspect of system design.

ACKNOWLEDGEMENTS

The work described in this paper has been carried out with the support of the CEC under the ESPRIT programme, Project 1094, Practitioner. Brunel's collaborators in this project are Asea Brown Boveri AG (ABB), Computer Resources International and PCS Computer Systeme GmbH.

REFERENCES

1.   1985a. The Gandalf Project, Journal of Systems and Software, vol. 5, no. 2, May 1985.

2.   Bailin 1990a. Sidney C. Bailin and J. Mike Moore, Kaptur: Knowledge Acquisition for Preservation of Tradeoffs and Underlying Rationales, in Third Annual Workshop: Methods and Tools for Reuse, CASE Center, Syracuse University, June 13-15, 1990.

3. Biggerstaff 1989a. Ted J. Biggerstaff and Alan J. Perlis (editors), Software Reusability, 1 and 2, ACM Press and Addison-Wesley, 1989.

4. Boldyreff1989a. Cornelia Boldyreff, Reuse, Software Concepts, Descriptive Methods and the Practitioner Project, ACM SIGSOFT Software Engineering Notes, vol. 14, no. 2, April 1989.

5. Boldyreff 1990a. C. Boldyreff, P. Elzer, P. Hall, U. Kaaber, J. Keilmann, and J. Witt, PRACTITIONER: Pragmatic Support for the Reuse of Concepts in Existing Software, in Proceedings of Software Engineering 1990, Brighton, UK, Cambridge University Press, 1990.

6. Booch1986a. Grady Booch, Object-Oriented Development, IEEE Transactions on Software Engineering, vol. SE-12, no. 2, February 1986.

7. Booch 1987a. Grady Booch, Software Components with Ada: Structure, Tools and Subsystems, Benjamin Cummings Publishing Company, 1987.

8. Cox 1986a. Brad J. Cox, Object Oriented Programming, An Evolutionary Approach, Addison-Wesley, 1986.

9. DeRemer 1976a. F. DeRemer and H. Kron, Programming-in-the-Large versus Programming-in-the-Small, IEEE Transactions on Software Engineering, June 1976.

10. Estublier 1984a. J. Estublier, S. Ghoul, and S. Krakowiak, Preliminary Experience with a Configuration Control System for Modular Programs, in Proceedings of the ACM SIGSOFT/SIGPLAN Software Engineering Symposium on Practical Software Development Environments, April 1984.

11. Feldman 1979a. S. I. Feldman, Make – A Program for Maintaining Computer Programs, Software - Practice and Experience, vol. 9, no. 4, April 1979.

12. Ford 1979a. B. Ford, J. Bentley, J.J. du Croz, and S.J. Hague, The NAG Library 'Machine', Software Practice and Experience, vol. 9, 1979.

13. Freeman 1987a. Peter Freeman (editor), IEEE Tutorial: Software Reusability, IEEE Computer Society, 1987.

14. Goguen 1986a. Joseph A. Goguen, Reusing and Interconnecting Software Components, IEEE Computer, February 1986.

15. Guttag 1977a. John V. Guttag, Abstract Data Types and the Development of Data Structures, CACM, vol. 20, no. 6, June 1977.

16. Harel 1988a. David Harel, On Visual Formalisms, Communications of the ACM, vol. 31, no. 5, May 1988.

17. Henderson 1989a. P. Henderson and B. Warboys, An architectural framework for systems, ICL Journal, May 1989.

18. Jones 1984a. T. C. Jones, Reusability in Programming: A Survey of the State of the Art, IEEE Transactions on Software Engineering, Special Issue on Software Reusability, vol. SE-10, no. 5, September 1984.

19. Kernighan 1976a. Brian W. Kernighan and P. J. Plauger, Software Tools, Addison-Wesley, 1976.

20. Kernighan 1984a. B. W. Kernighan, The UNIX System and Software Reusability, IEEE Transactions on Software Engineering, Special Issue on Software Reusability, vol. SE-10, no. 5, September 1984.

21.	Lanergan 1984a. R. G. Lanergan and C. A. Grasso, Software engineering with reusable designs and code, IEEE Transactions on Software Engineering, Special Issue on Software Reusablilty, vol. SE-10, no. 5, September 1984.

22.	Lehman 1984a. M. M. Lehman, V. Stenning, and W. Turski, Another Look at Software Design Methodology, ACM SIGSOFT Software Engineering Notes, vol. 9, no. 2, April 1984.

23.	Liskov 1974a. Barbara Liskov and Stephen Zilles, Programming with Abstract Data Types, SIGPLAN Notices, vol. 9, no. 4, April 1974.

24.	Lubars 1986a. Mitchell D. Lubars, Affording Higher Reliability Through Software Reusability, ACM SIGSOFT Software Engineering Notes, vol. 11, no. 5, October 1986.

25.	Mamrak 1989a. Sandra A. Mamrak, Michael J. Kaelbling, Charles K. Nicholas, and Michael Share, Chameleon: A System for Solving the Data-Translation Problem, IEEE Transactions on Software Engineering, vol. 15, no. 9, September 1989.

26.	McIlroy 1969a. M.D. McIlroy, Mass Produced Software Components, in Proceedings of NATO Conference on Software Engineering, ed. Naur, Randell and Buxton, Petrocelli/Charter, 1969.

27.	Meyer 1982a. Bertrand Meyer, Principles of Package Design, Communications of the ACM, vol. 25, no. 7, July 1982.

28.	Meyer 1987a. Bertrand Meyer, Reusability: the Case for Object-Oriented Design, IEEE Software, vol. 4, no. 2, March 1987.

29. Meyer1987b. Bertrand Meyer, Eiffel: Programming for Reusability and Extendability, SIGPLAN Notices, vol. 22, no. 2, February 1987.

30. Meyer1988a. Bertrand Meyer, Object-oriented Software Construction, Prentice-Hall, 1988.

31. Morrison 1987a. R. Morrison, A. L. Brown, R. Carrick, R. C. H. Connor, A. Dearle, and M. Atkinson, Polymorphism, persistence and software reuse in a strongly typed object-oriented environment, Software Engineering Journal, vol. 2, no. 6, November 1987.

32. Myers 1975a. Glenford J. Myers, Reliable Software through Composite Design, van Nostrand Reinhold, 1975.

33. Parnas 1972a. David Lorge Parnas, On the Criteria to be Used in Decomposing Systems into Modules, Communications of the ACM, vol. 5, no. 12, pp. 1053-1058, December 1972.

34. Parnas 1986a. David Lorge Parnas and Paul C. Clements, A Rational Design Process: How and Why to Fake It, IEEE Transactions on Software Engineering, vol. SE-12, no. 2, February 1986.

35. Petroski 1985a. Henry Petroski, To Engineer is Human: The Role of Failure in Successful Design, Macmillan, London, 1985. (First published in the U.S.A. in 1982.)

36. Potts 1989a. Colin Potts, A Generic Model for the Representing Design Methods, in Proceedings of 11th International Conference on Software Engineering, May 15-18, 1989, Pittsburgh, Pennsylvania, IEEE Computer Society Press, 1989.

37.   Prieto-Diaz 1986a. Ruben Prieto-Diaz and James Neighbours, Module Interconnection Languages, Journal of System Sciences, vol. 6, no. 4, pp. 307-334, November 1986.

38.   Randell 1986a. Brian Randell, System Design and Structuring, The Computer Journal, vol. 29, no. 4, 1986.

39.   Schmucker 1986a. K. Schmucker, MacApp: An Application Framework, Byte, August 1986.

40.   Sneed 1987a. Harry M. Sneed and Gabor Jandrasics, Software Recycling, in Proceedings from the IEEE Conference on Software Maintenance, Austin, Texas, 1987.

41.   Sommerville1986a. I. Sommerville and R. Thomson, The ECLIPSE System Structure Language, in Proceedings of the 19th Annual Hawaii International Conference on System Sciences, 1986.

42.   Tichy 1980a. W.F. Tichy, Software Development Control Based on Systems Structure Description, Carnegie-Mellon University, Computer Science Department, January 1980. PhD Thesis.

43.   Tracz 1988a. Will Tracz, Software Reuse: Emerging Technology, pp. 1-60, Computer Society Press, Washington, D.C., USA, 1988. Tutorial, Part 1, Overview.

44.   Wolff 1990a. Frank Wolff, Long-Term Controlling of Software Reuse, Brunel University, Uxbridge, Middlesex, UK, 1990. Practitioner Working Paper P1094-Bru-FW-0100.

45. Zhang 1990a. Jian Zhang, Knowledge Based Reverse Engineering, 9 September 1990. Practitioner Project Report P1094- Bru-0101/02.

6 Software information systems: information retrieval techniques

H. Albrechtsen

CRI, Denmark

6.1 INTRODUCTION

A significant problem in software reuse is the lack of appropriate Software Information Systems, comprising methods and tools for representing and retrieving reusable software (Information Retrieval Techniques).

Currently, there are various approaches for building Software Information Systems (Frakes & Gandel, 1990; Albrechtsen, 1990). Most of them are prototype systems, designed by project teams working on national or international R&D programmes in Software Technology, for instance the European ESPRIT programme. Commercial Software Information Systems are still rare.

This paper discusses the advantages and drawbacks of these approaches, exemplified by the different Information Retrieval Techniques that have been proposed and implemented in prototype or commercial Software Information Systems.

In the conclusion, the approaches will be viewed in the perspective of a new paradigm for Information Retrieval Systems (IR-systems), where R&D in intelligent retrieval systems has resulted in a rapidly increasing interest in developing user-friendly IR-systems.

6.2   SOFTWARE INFORMATION SYSTEMS: CONCEPTS, METHODS AND TOOLS

The major issues to be faced in building Software Information Systems are:

1.   Representation of reusable software items; that is, semantic and syntactic conventions for describing them

2.   Retrieval of reusable software, covering user-system interaction and methods for query formulation

3.   Identification and development of technology for representation and retrieval of reusable software.

Issues 1-2 are, of course, interconnected, as the purpose of representations for software is to provide a basis for comparing and matching these with the queries of users in reuse situations.

Consider this abstract model for Information Retrieval (IR) of software (Fig. 6.1), based on the generic IR-models by Ingwersen (1987) and Belkin & Croft (1987).

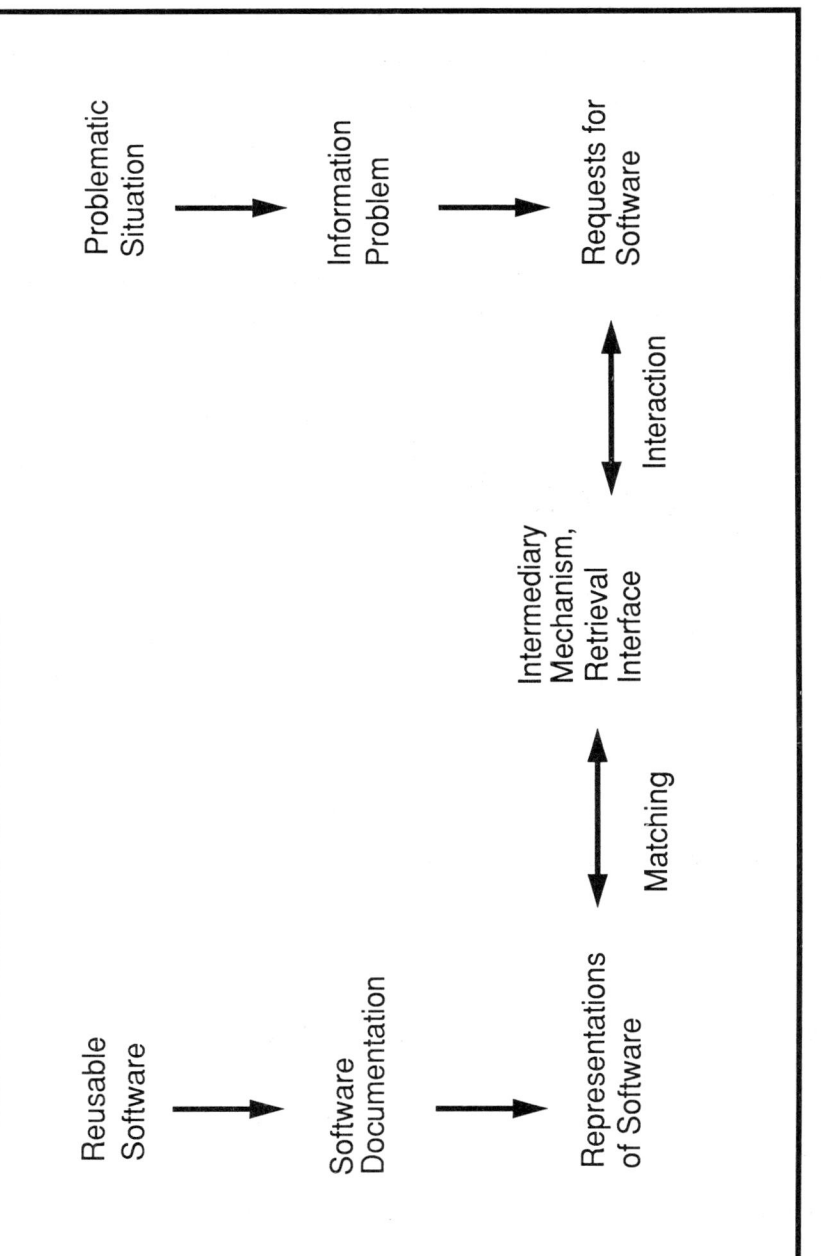

Fig. 6.1 *Abstract model of an IR situation for software reuse.*

At the right side of this model, a user, for instance a software engineer, finds herself in a problematic situation in her system design work. She realizes that for getting further, she needs some information. This she may obtain from talking with colleagues or experts in the field, of course, but she may also choose to investigate previous solutions to her problem, for instance existing software design and code.

In the centre of the model is an intermediary mechanism, human or mechanized, with capabilities of interaction with the user. The software engineer states her information problem in a request to the intermediary, who transforms the request to a query, which matches representations of reusable software. The intermediary then presents the retrieved information for evaluation by the user. If the user is not satisfied with the results, the user/intermediary interaction recycles.

To the left is the information source area, consisting of, e.g., a collection of reusable software and design descriptions (documentation). Each item in the collection is represented with one or more predicates, assigned according to conventions for describing their subject information.

This model exposes an ideal situation, where the user is able to specify her problem, the intermediary is capable of assisting the user, and the representations of reusable software are standardized.

Regrettably, there are no standard methods for representing or retrieving reusable software, but there are currently two different kinds of approaches.

The first approach applies IR-methods, comprising various Indexing and Retrieval Techniques developed in Library and Information Science. These techniques will be discussed in section 6.3: Indexing Methods for Software.

Representation Method	Tool	Generator(s)/ Organisation
Free Text Indexing	IRS-System (Catalog)	AT & T Bell Labs., USA
Enumerated Classification	Several (Printed and Automated)	IBM (IBM-Share), Booch (Ada)
Faceted Classificcation	RDB-System	Prieto-Diaz, USA
Thesaurus	ORACLE + Free-Text	PRACTITIONER (ESPRIT)
Knowledge Representation	Case Frames	ECLIPSE, UK, University of Karlsruhe

Table 6.1   Software information systems: overview of approaches.

The second approach relies on AI-methods, comprising Knowledge Representation Techniques and Methods for Natural Language Understanding and will be discussed in section 4: Knowledge Representation Techniques for Software.

Cf. Table 6.1 for an overview of the approaches, arranged according to subject representation method, the tool that is applied and the generator(s) of the approach.

6.3   INDEXING METHODS FOR SOFTWARE

In Library and Information Science, subject information in documents such as books, proceedings and journal articles, is provided by means of indexing systems.

Indexing systems are often classified according to the type of vocabulary or indexing language that is applied for representation (Foskett, 1982; Lancaster, 1986):

1.   Uncontrolled vocabularies are applied in free-text systems, e.g. relying on the terminology that is applied in the document text, or in keyword systems, where the subject information of the document is expressed in natural language terms by an indexer.

2.   Controlled vocabularies, which may comprise semantic rules for categorization, and sometimes syntactic rules for combining the elements in the vocabularies (formal indexing languages). The elements may be in verbal form (terms from natural languages) or they have symbolic notations (classification symbols).

A taxonomy of indexing vocabularies is provided in Fig. 6.2.

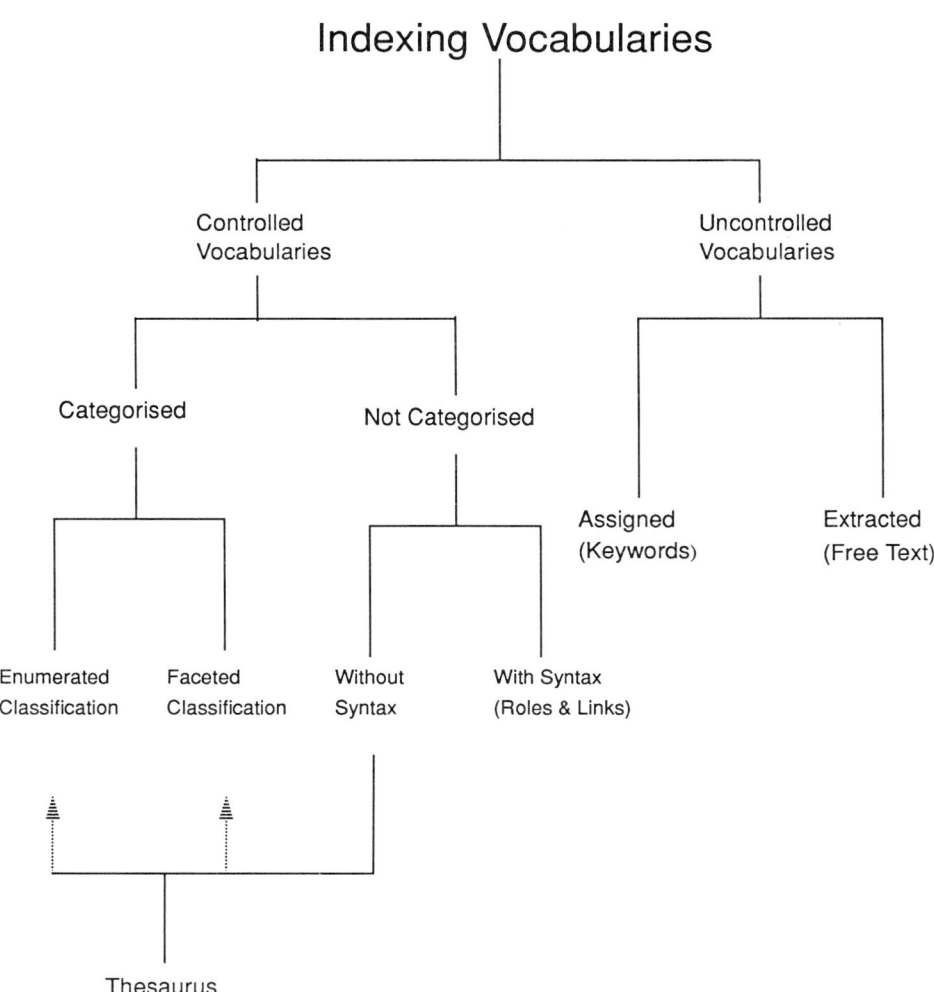

Fig. 6.2   Taxonomy of indexing vocabularies, adapted from Foskett (1982) and Frakes and Gandel (1990).

6.3.1   Uncontrolled Indexing Systems

These systems are either keyword-based or based on terms extracted from texts (free-text approach).

In a keyword-based indexing environment, the indexing terms that are assigned to documents are not controlled, i.e. the indexer has full freedom in choice of representations. This will often result in very inconsistent representations, especially for large collections of documents involving several indexers in keyword assignment.

In most Japanese software houses, reuse of software components is an integrated activity in software development. The components are assigned manually with keywords derived from the documentation or with application-oriented keywords. The tools applied for retrieval are very simple, usually tools for string searching in linear files (Matsumoto, 1987; Tajima & Matsubara, 1984).

In free-text systems, the indexing terms are derived automatically.

The free-text indexing method includes permuted indices like KWIC (KeyWord-In-Context) and KWOC (KeyWord-Out-of-Context) (Foskett, 1982).

It also covers indexing techniques where terms are derived from the full text of documents using an Information Storage and Retrieval System (IRS-system). (Salton & McGill, 1983). The printed and online version of the UNIX documentation (Kernighan & Pike, 1984) is an example of KWIC-indexing for software. This implies that all significant terms in titles of, for instance, UNIX utilities, can be used as search keys.

This facility is of course very helpful to experienced users of UNIX, but for an inexperienced user it does not give much help in finding a utility which the user needs, since it is necessary to know the specific term to search.

(a)   Free-text indexing of software

At AT&T Bell Labs, USA, a prototype of a software information system has been implemented in the IRS-system CATALOG (Frakes & Nehmeh, 1987). It comprises a small collection of program modules which form SUPER, a software system built at Bell Laboratories for interactive reliability analysis.

The textual descriptions required for each module are stored as individual records in the CATALOG system, and all single terms (minus stopwords) are sorted into inverted lists of indexing terms. The source code is not indexed, but stored as part of each individual record.

The retrieval interface features Boolean combinations of search terms, automatic truncation (wildcards) and partial matching techniques like phonetic matching.

There are two retrieval interfaces, a menu-driven interface for novice users, and a command-driven interface for expert users.

A major advantage of this approach is that it is economically feasible in the indexing phase, because of the automatic generation of index term lists, and the retrieval performance was evaluated as satisfactory by the users.

However, there are serious drawbacks to the approach. As in the UNIX help system, the user must know exactly the right terms to search. And even if the user enters a search term which matches the index of the system, valuable information may not be retrieved, because it is represented with other index terms in the module descriptions.

For instance, the search term 'Sorting' could match five descriptions of modules in the system, but miss descriptions of similar software modules containing related terms like 'Ranking'.

Further, the interface of such a system lacks guidance in restricting retrieval on very common terms, like for instance 'Files'. For optimum usage of an IRS-system, the user must be familiar with Boolean retrieval, where search terms can be combined with AND or NOT operators for restricting the search area and OR operators between synonyms for relaxing the search area.

Hence, this approach, though feasible in the indexing phase, is not very effective in the retrieval phase.

Further, the experimentation does not cover investigations on standard or generic representation methods for software, and it is therefore to be considered as an ad hoc approach to a Software Information System.

6.3.2 Controlled Indexing Systems

In Library and Information Science, the methods of controlled indexing for subject representation are regarded as indispensable for achieving both consistency in the terminology applied by the indexers of document collections, as well as often for shelf arrangement of books and other materials like musical recordings and videos.

Some methods are based on alphabetical lists or vocabularies of terms (single terms and compound terms) as candidate representations for documents.

Sometimes, the indexing methods are post-coordinate, meaning that the indexing terms are assigned as single units, which can be combined during retrieval using for instance Boolean operators in an IRS-system.

The post-coordinate indexing approach is flexible, but it does not capture contextual ambiguities. For instance, a query in the Inspec database expressed as

'FIND (Information Retrieval AND Software) /CT'

where the qualifier '/CT' limits the search to controlled indexing terms, retrieves references to documents on 'Information Retrieval for Software' as well as to documents on 'Software for Information Retrieval'. The approach is less critical in restricted subject domains.

In order to avoid such ambiguities in retrieval, some indexing systems feature roles and links to express syntactic relationships between indexing terms (Spang-Hanssen, 1976). A famous example is the PRECIS system (PREserved Context Indexing System), developed by Derek Austin for the British National Bibliography (Austin, 1974).

The controlled indexing terms can also be arranged in thesauri or classification systems.

A thesaurus is a list of indexing terms (verbal form) in which the semantic relationships between the terms are exposed, for instance synonyms, broader terms, narrower terms and related terms. A thesaurus can be diagrammed as a directed, acyclic graph (Sowa, 1984). It is not a tree structure, as a term can have several specializations (narrower terms) as well as several generalizations (broader terms) (ISO, 1985).

A classification system is a systematic list of terms in symbolic form, and consists of a schedule exposing the systematic arrangement, a notation for each node in the schedule and an alphabetical term entry index.

There are two main types of classification systems:

Enumerated classification systems feature tree-structured hierarchies of classes, where subdivisions of each class are done on uniform criteria, normally according to the individual scientific disciplines and their taxonomies, as in the CR Classification System (ACM, 1990) for Computer Science. The classes that constitute an array of classes must be logically separate (disjoint), but conceptually on the same level.

The enumerated classification systems are hard to maintain for very dynamic subject areas, as new developments in the field may require a revision of the entire classification scheme.

Faceted classification systems are more flexible. The theory of faceted classification was developed by S.R. Ranganathan (1967), based on the idea of universal knowledge structures, accordingly on a structuralistic viewpoint on knowledge organization.

One of his most famous theories is the universal facet formula of decreasing concreteness: PMEST (= Personality, Matter, Energy, Space and Time), which is a formal grammar of five facets or dimensions of knowledge.

In practice, faceted classification systems will feature enumerations within the individual facets. But still, the faceted systems are more open changes than the enumerated systems, as individual facets can be modified independently of other facets.

In spite of their lack of flexibility, enumerated classification systems are still the most common representation method for software, for instance in ACM's Computing Reviews Scheme (ACM, 1989), in the IBM Share System (Bolstad, 1975) and the taxonomy for Ada components created by G. Booch (1987). A faceted classification scheme for software has been conceived by R. Prieto-Diaz and has been implemented in prototype Software Information Systems at, for instance, GTE Laboratories and Contel, USA.

A prototype of a software information system featuring a thesaurus has been developed by the ESPRIT project Practitioner.

We will briefly look into the two latter approaches.

(a) Faceted classification of software

Prieto-Diaz's faceted classification scheme was designed according to Ranganathan's theories on faceted classification and comprises six facets (Prieto-Diaz, 1985).

The first three facets cover the technical aspects of a software component (Function, Objects, Medium) and the remainder cover system or application-oriented facets (System Type, Functional Area, Setting).

In the first prototype (Prieto-Diaz & Freeman, 1987), the facets were implemented as six tables in a relational database system, where the tables contained a number of test terms for each facet. The citation order, or synthesis, of the facets is fixed, constituting syntactic representations of the test components which resemble sentential structures, e.g.

> COMPRESS | FILES | DISC | FILEHANDLER | DB MANAGEMENT
> | CATALOG SALES

for representing a component, which compresses data files on a disc in a database management system in the application area of catalog sales.

The process of facet analysis was guided by interviewing potential users of the classification system, in casu software developers, who also supplied the test terms in the facets. The terms of each facet were arranged in conceptual graphs (term networks), exposing the semantic relationships between them in a thesaurus-like manner (the semantic distances were quantified with weights).

The faceted classification system may be considered as a conceptual representation of programmer knowledge of software, and is therefore an excellent basis for building an advanced User Interface or an 'Intelligent' Intermediary Mechanism for a Software Information System with facilities for, e.g., browsing in knowledge.

So far, the prototype implementations have not realized the full potentials of the classification system. For instance, the fixed citation order has not merely been applied for classification of components, but was also implemented in the retrieval interface, which implies that a search statement must begin with a term from the first facet. Further, the prototype systems have not implemented possibilities for assigning or selecting more than one term in each facet (Prieto-Diaz, 1990; Prieto-Diaz & Freeman, 1987).

(b)   Thesaurus design for software

PRACTITIONER is a five-year project under the European ESPRIT R&D programme, comprising teams in the software companies Asea Brown Boveri and PCS Computer Systeme, Germany, Brunel University, UK, and the system house CRI, Denmark.

PRACTITIONER is distinguished by focusing on reusable software concepts, that is software at all levels of abstraction, including documentation and ideas from the early phases of the software lifecycle (Boldyreff, 1989).

The ultimate goal for the project is to develop a Software Information System for pragmatic software reuse, which has been realized in the prototype system PRESS (Practitioner REuse Support System) (Olsen & Bisgaard, 1989).

PRESS features a thesaurus-based approach for representing knowledge of reusable concepts.

The thesaurus covers terminology compiled from domain analysis, for instance covering the technical domain and the application domain of a software concept.

The thesaurus is an important part of the User Interface or Intermediary Mechanism of the PRESS Software Information System.

For each domain, the terminology is structured in a semantic term network, comprising the standard ISO thesaurus relationships (ISO, 1985), e.g.:

Top Term   (TT)
Broader Term   (BT)
Narrower Term   (NT)
Related Term   (RT)
Synonyms   (SYN)

Because of the constant development in the terminology in most domains, particularly in the area of software, the PRESS thesaurus features relationships for new terms (NEW) and old terms (OLD).

The thesaurus provides capabilities for relaxing or restricting the search area for the user of PRESS.

A request for a software concept on parsing, expressed in a query with the search term 'Parser', can be expanded algorithmically to include search terms like 'Compiler' or 'Interpreter', which are Related Terms.

It is also possible to perform a command-driven retrieval using an extended version of the Common Command Language (CCL) (ISO, 1989), where the user activates the thesaurus by adding thesaurus qualifiers to his/her search terms. For instance 'parser + RT' for retrieving concepts on parsing, compiling and interpreting.

A great advantage of applying a thesaurus for representing software is that it is flexible, that is open to additions and modifications. Further, it is a natural language approach to representation, which means that it is more user-friendly for retrieval than a classification system using notations for subject representation.

A major drawback of the approach is the effort of thesaurus maintenance and particularly the effort of thesaurus construction. Part of the construction process can be automated, for instance collecting terminology from machine-readable sources like dictionaries, but the process of term network construction is mainly conceptual.

For successful construction of a thesaurus for a large domain like, for instance, the domain(s) of software, the thesaurus creator should be supported by thesaurus software, which e.g. automatically generates reciprocal relationships between terms and comprises tools for term clustering according to both linguistic and statistic information (automatic compounding, term co-occurrences).

6.4   KNOWLEDGE REPRESENTATION TECHNIQUES FOR SOFTWARE

Alternative approaches to building Software Information Systems are based on methods for Knowledge Representation and Language Understanding developed in the field of Artificial Intelligence (Winston, 1984).

These methods, when applied for IR-systems, rely on more complex representations of knowledge than normally found in classification systems and thesauri, often featuring rather sophisticated syntactic arrangements of the knowledge in order to support natural language queries.

According to Belkin & Croft (1987) and Winston (1984), there are two main types of knowledge representation formalisms:

1.   Rule-based techniques, where the subject information is expressed in formal logic.

2.   Graph-based techniques, where specific examples include semantic nets and frames.

6.4.1   Rule-based Representation

The rule-based representation method is the most popular formalism in knowledge engineering, that is in building expert systems. Rule-based representations are often built according to rules like:

>   IF   condition 1
>   condition 2
>
>   THEN   action 1
>   action 2

This formalism has been applied for advanced user interfaces to IR-systems, for instance in the RUBRIC system (McCune *et al.,* 1985).

An example of a rule-based Software Information System is the MES (Modeling Expert System) by Rosales and Mehrotra (1988), which guides the user in selection of reusable code modules in a very large software system at AT&T Bell Labs., namely a transmission system of 1 million PL/1 lines.

The critical problem with the rule-based approach is the effort of expressing the information in formal logic. Currently, this is done manually in all experimental systems (Belkin & Croft, 1987).

6.4.2 Graph-based Representation

Graph-based techniques like semantic nets and frames have also been applied in Software Information Systems (Frakes & Gandel, 1989).

Semantic nets are directed graphs with nodes of conceptual objects, for instance natural language terms, and arcs expressing semantic or syntactic links (slots) between the objects.

Frames are collections of semantic net nodes and slots that together describe a stereotyped object, act, or event, for instance a software component (Winston, 1984).

Frames are the most common data structures for building natural language interfaces to IR-systems (Belkin & Vickery, 1989). Specifically interesting in this context are the so-called case frames, where it is possible to produce uniform sentential representations of subject information in restricted domains (Winograd, 1983).

(a)   Case frame representations of software

A case frame is a data structure which is used for representing sentential structures of natural language terms, where each frame corresponds to a sentence with slots for each grammatical case.

For instance, a case frame grammar can be designed according to the idea of conceptual dependency (Schank, 1972).

Conceptual dependency was originally proposed as a method for producing uniform representations for natural language sentences and provide one depth representation for a number of natural language sentences. The structure of a depth representation has three categories of fundamental concepts or cases, namely nominals, actions and modifiers. The syntactic relationships between fundamental concepts or cases are called dependencies.

The British ECLIPSE project has performed an experiment in representing reusable software components using the idea of conceptual dependency (Wood & Sommerville, 1988), based on the following grammatical categories for software:

1.   Conceptual actions correspond to the fundamental functions that the component covers.

2.   Nominals correspond to the components, and to objects that are manipulated or produced, and to objects providing a context for an action.

3.   Modifiers are descriptors of actions or objects.

The case frame representation was realized in a prototype, comprising a minor test collection of UNIX software components.

The header of each case frame is labelled 'Component Descriptor Frame' and covers the conceptual action of a UNIX component with slots for all possible conceptual objects (nominals). Modifiers for actions and objects were not implemented, but specified as links. Consider the example descriptor frame (or network) for the UNIX component 'grep', which is a utility program performing a simple string search in linear data file in Fig. 6.3.

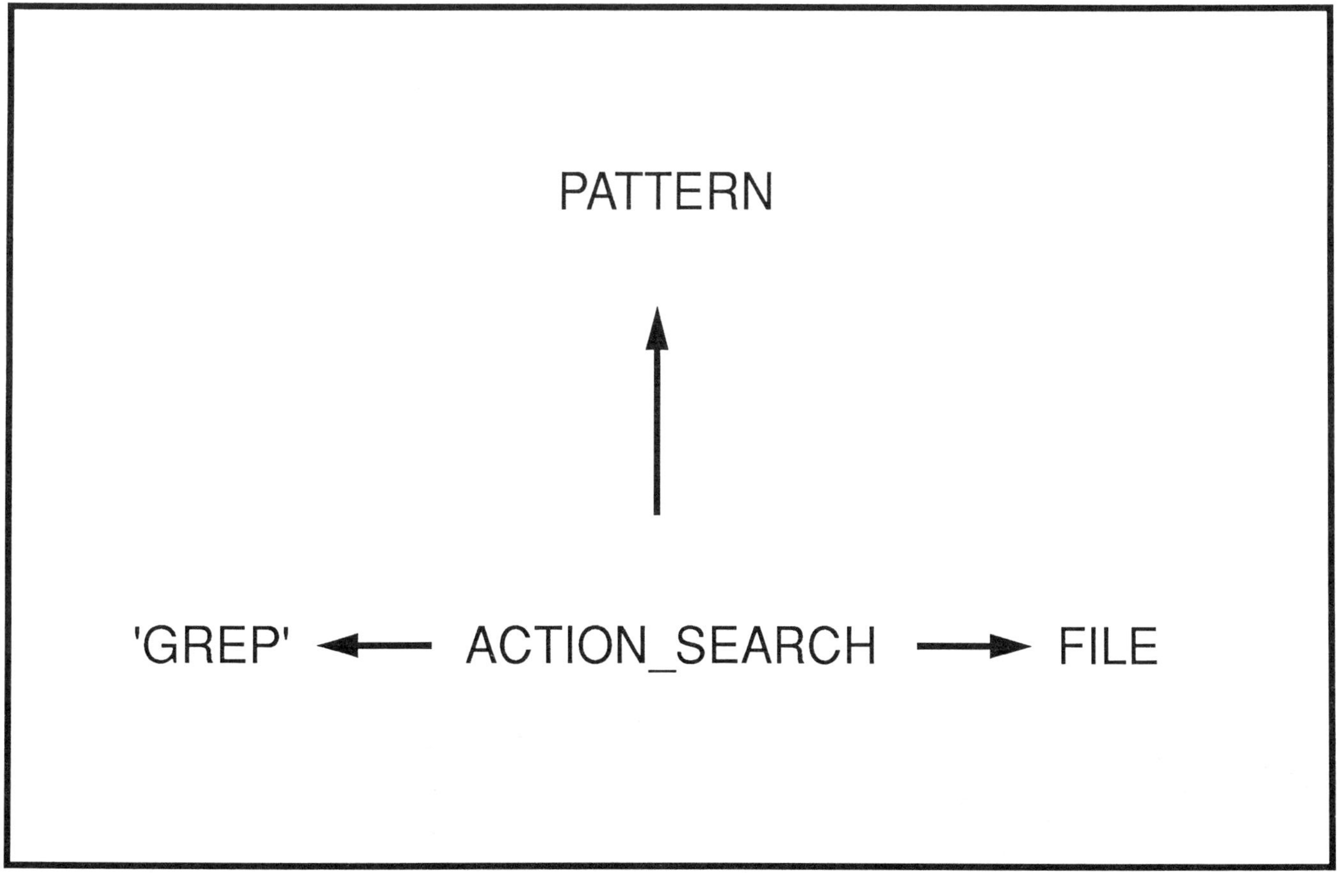

Fig. 6.3   Representational network for the UNIX utility 'grep'.

This frame ('action_search') has three slots, the component itself ('grep'), the object that is searched for ('pattern') and the object that is involved in the action of search ('file').

The prototype features a window-based retrieval interface with a form-based retrieval dialogue. In cases, where a search term entered by a user does not exactly match any representations of UNIX utilities, the search is expanded to an appropriate conceptual action or nominal (e.g. parser – compiler). This approach is a partial matching technique, corresponding to a searching thesaurus approach.

Further, the prototype features a browser for guidance through a semantic network structure of component descriptors.

In the ECLIPSE approach, the case frame grammar is only applied for representation, not for parsing natural language queries.

This has been partly realized in the NLH/E system, developed at the University of Karlsruhe (Tichy *et al.*, 1988). NLH/E is a prototype Software Information System, currently containing more than 130 case frame representations and descriptions of Common LISP modules.

The user can enter queries to the system in natural language. The parser does not support all possible features of natural language (tenses, moods), and the input is therefore restricted to imperative sentences or nominal phrases, e.g.

'concatenate two lists'
or
'set intersection in lisp'

For supporting partial matching of search terms applied in the queries, the parser features a genuine thesaurus of terms which are possible fillers in the case slots of NLH/E frames. The grammar constrains syntactic combinations of terms to meaningful sentences. For instance, a sentential representation like 'The programmer debugs the car' will be rejected by the grammar, because the nominal term 'car' does not fit the rules for possible objects of the action 'debug'.

The case frame approaches of ECLIPSE and NLH/E may be considered as natural language approaches to Information Retrieval Techniques for reusable software. They are clearly related to faceted classification approaches and syntactic indexing languages.

The advantages of the approaches are that they provide the basis for building user-friendly retrieval interfaces, where the user does not have to apply a formal query language like CCL (ISO, 1989) for inputting a request to the system.

However, the complexity of the representation, though clearly an advantage in the user interface, is at the same time a major disadvantage. It is very difficult to build the representational structure, and maintenance of the parser is time-consuming. Further, the grammar may be too restrictive for describing all possible items to be entered in the system.

6.5   SUMMARY OF APPROACHES AND FUTURE DEVELOPMENTS

In the beginning of this paper a model for IR of software was presented, showing a situation where a user, a software engineer, interacts with an intermediary mechanism for searching reusable software. This model represents an ideal retrieval situation and can hence be regarded as modelling the requirements to a Software Information System.

How do the approaches that have been made so far for building Software Information Systems live up to this ideal?

The uncontrolled indexing methods for reusable software, proposed in the Japanese software factory approach, and particularly in the AT&T approach, are very feasible in the indexing phase, that is processes belonging to the left side of the model. However, the user, represented by the right side of the model, is left in the dark, unless she is very familiar with both Boolean retrieval techniques and with the precise terminology of the covered subject areas.

One method for optimizing the representations of a free-text indexing approach is to restrict the number of indexing terms using linguistic or statistic methods for automatic indexing (Vickery & Vickery, 1989). Linguistic methods for automatic indexing are still in their infancy, but excellent examples include the prototype tool SIMPR, developed under the ESPRIT programme (Gibb & Smart, 1990), and the SPIRIT parser (Debili & Fuhr, 1989). Statistic methods are more common. They implement various models like the vector space model and the probabilistic model (Salton & McGill, 1983; Van Rijsbergen & Sparck Jones, 1973).

The controlled indexing methods and the case frame representations provide uniform representations for software.

Some of these representations, especially the faceted approach, the thesaurus approach and the case frame approaches, are very good foundations for building automated intermediary mechanisms, as the semantic and syntactic links between the individual search elements are helpful for guiding the user in query formulation.

Among the approaches featuring uniform software representations, it is only the PRESS tool which offers facilities for free-text searching in software documentation as a supplement to menu-driven retrieval. This flexibility in the user interface makes the tool attractive to users in all possible stages of IR-knowledge, including novice as well as expert users.

For the development of future Software Information Systems, it is worth considering approaches which combine a thesaurus or a knowledge-base with a free-text retrieval system (IRS-system).

Recently, there has been a great deal of R&D in developing advanced retrieval mechanisms for IR-systems.

Originally, the goals of these experiments were to automate human intermediaries (librarians) in bibliographic database searching. Hence, these systems are usually built as front-ends which give suggestions to the user for database selection, perform automatic dial-ups to chosen database hosts, provide standard retrieval interfaces with uniform syntax and search term vocabularies for query formulation. (Vickery & Brooks, 1987).

The experience gained in these experimentations, has provided profound insights into how users interact with information retrieval systems (Belkin & Vickery, 1985; Mark Pejtersen, 1988). Today, many of the results are being realized in a new (second) generation of the so-called OPACs (Online Public Access Catalogues), which are end-user interfaces to automated library systems. The new OPACs will be user-friendly interfaces, guiding the end-user (borrower) in performing complex retrieval tasks like subject searching.

Indeed, one of the most important points which has been brought into attention in the R&D activities in intelligent IR-systems is the information problems and tasks of the users. In the area of software reuse, investigations in the tasks and work context of the software developers and other possible users, is one of the future challenges for R&D in Software Information Systems (Belkin, 1989).

REFERENCES

1. ACM (1990). CR Classification System. ACM Computing Reviews 31 (1), pp. 3-20.

2. Albrechtsen, H. (1990). Software Concepts: Knowledge Organisation and the Human Interface. In: Fugmann, R. (ed.) Advances in Knowledge Organisation, vol.1, pp. 49-63.

3. Austin, D. (1974). The Development of PRECIS: a Theoretical and Technical History. In: Journal of Documentation 30 (1), pp. 47-102.

4. Belkin, N.J.; Vickery, A. (1985). Interaction in Information Systems: a Review of Research from Document Retrieval to Knowledge-Based Systems (British Library: Library and Information Science Reports, 35).

5. Belkin, N.J.; Croft, W.B. (1987). Retrieval Techniques. In: Annual Review of Information Science and Technology (ARIST) 22, pp. 108-145.

6. Belkin, N.J. (1989). User Modelling for Software Reuse. In: Proceedings of the ACM SIGIR Conference, Boston (Massachusetts), June, pp. 255-256.

7. Boldyreff, C. (1989). Reuse, Software Concepts, Descriptive Methods and the Practitioner Project. In: ACM SIGSOFT Software Engineering Notes 14 (2), pp. 25-31.

8. Bolstad, J. (1975). A Proposed Classification Scheme for Computer Program Libraries. In: SIGNUM Newsletter 10 (2-3), pp. 32-39.

9. Booch, G. (1987). Software Components with ADA. Menlo Park (California): Benjamin/Cummings Publishing.

10. Debili, F.; Fluhr, C. *et al.* (1989). About Reformulation in Full-Text IRS. in: Information Processing and Management 25 (6), pp. 647-657.

11. Foskett, A.C. (1982). The Subject Approach to Information/4th edition. London: Clive Bingley.

12. Frakes, W.B.; Gandel, P.B. (1990). Representing Reusable Software. In: Information and Software Technology (in press).

13. Frakes, W.B.; Nehmeh, B.A. (1987). Software Reuse through Information Retrieval. In: SIGIR FORUM 21 (1-2), pp. 30-36.

14. Fugmann, R. ed. (1990). Advances in Knowledge Organisation. Frankfurt/Main: Indeks Verlag (Proceedings of the International ISKO-Conference, 1, Darmstadt, 14-17 August 1990) .

15. Gibb, F.; Smart, G. (1990). Structured Information Management Brings New Techniques for Processing Text. In: Online Review 14 (3), pp. 160-171.

16. Ingwersen, P. (1987). Towards a New Research Paradigm in Information Retrieval. In: Wormell, I (ed.). Knowledge Engineering: Expert Systems and Information Retrieval. London: Taylor Graham, 1987, pp. 150-168.

17. ISO (1985). Documentation – Guidelines for the Establishment and Development of Monolingual Thesauri.

18. ISO (1989). Documentation – Commands for Interactive Text Searching (ISO 8777).

19. Kernighan, B.W.; Pike, R. (1984). The UNIX Programming Environment. Englewood Cliffs (New Jersey): Prentice-Hall.

20. Lancaster, F.W. (1986). Vocabulary Control for Information Retrieval/2nd edition. Arlington (Virginia): Information Resources Press.

21. McCune *et al.* (1985). RUBRIC: a System for Rule-Based Information Retrieval. In: IEEE Transactions on Software Engineering 11 (9), pp. 939-945.

22. Matsumoto, Y. (1987). A Software Factory: An Overall Approach to Software Production. In: Freeman, P. (ed).: Software Reusability. Washington: IEEE, pp. 155-177.

23. Olsen, L., Bisgaard, K. (1989). PRESS Design Description. Birkeroed: CRI (P1094-CRI-LO + KIB-WPE2.2-Report-0086/01).

24. Pejtersen, A.M.; Goodstein, L.P. (1988). Beyond the Desk Top Metaphor: Information Retrieval with an Icon Based Interface. In: Proceedings of the Interdisciplinary Workshop on Informatics and Psychology on Visualization in Human-Computer Interaction, 7, Sharding, Austria, 23-27 May 1988.

25. Prieto-Diaz, R.; Freeman, P. (1987). Classifying Software for Reusability. In: IEEE Software (1), pp. 6-16.

26. Prieto-Diaz, R. (1985). A Software Classification Scheme (Doctoral Dissertation). University of California: Department of Information and Computer Science.

27. Prieto-Diaz, R. (1990). Implementing Faceted Classification for Software Reuse. IEEE (in press).

28. Ranganathan, S.R. (1967). Prolegomena to Library Classification/3rd edition. Bombay: Asia Publishing House.

29. Rosales, S.; Mehrota, P. (1988). MES: an Expert System for Reusing Models of Transmission Equipment. In: Proceedings of the Conference on Artificial Intelligence Applications, 4. IEEE Computer Press, pp. 109-113.

30. Salton, G.; McGill, M. (1983). Introduction to Modern Information Retrieval. New York: McGraw-Hill.

31. Schank, R.C. (1972). Conceptual Dependency: a Theory of Natural Language Understanding. In: Cognitive Psychology 3, pp. 552-631.

32. Sowa, J.F. (1984). Conceptual Structures: Information Processing in Mind and Machine. Reading (Massachusetts): Addison-Wesley.

33. Spang-Hanssen, H. (1976). Roles and Links Compared with Grammatical Relations in Natural Languages. Copenhagen: The National Society for Scientific Literature (vol. 40).

34. Tajima, D.; Matsubara, T. (1984). Inside the Japanese Software Industry. In: IEEE Computer 17 (3), pp. 34-43.

35. Tichy *et al.* (1988). NLH/E: a Natural Language Help System. University of Karlsruhe: Department of Informatics (Interner Bericht no. 13).

36. Van Rijsbergen, C.J.; Sparck Jones, K. (1973). A Test for the Separation of Relevant and Non-Relevant Documents in Experimental Retrieval Collections. In: Journal of Documentation 29, pp. 251-257.

37. Vickery, A.; Brooks, H. (1987). Expert Systems and Their Applications in LIS. In: Online Review 11 (3), pp. 149-165.

38.   Vickery, B.; Vickery, A. (1989). Information Science in Theory and Practice. London: Bowker-Saur.

39.   Winograd, T. (1983). Language as a Cognitive Process. Reading (Massachusetts): Addison-Wesley (Vol. 1: Syntax).

40.   Winston, P.H. (1984). Artificial Intelligence/2nd edition. Reading (Massachusetts): Addison-Wesley.

41.   Wood, M.; Sommerville, I. (1988). An Information Retrieval System for Software Components. In: SIGIR FORUM 22 (3-4), pp. 11-25.

7 Analogy in software reuse

A.G. Sutcliffe

City University

7.1 INTRODUCTION

To deliver true productivity gains software reuse has to be effective at the specification stage of development. The major cause of errors in software development can be traced to requirements analysis and this phase is also acknowledged to be one of the most difficult parts of the software engineering. Software reuse can offer a solution to this problem. Specifications residing in CASE tool repositories encapsulate domain knowledge and solutions to many problems. However, to deliver reuse two problems have to be solved:

1.   The retrieval problem; an appropriate specification has to be retrieved for reuse in the new problem domain.

2.   The customization problem; previous specifications rarely meet the needs of a new application exactly, hence some tailoring of the old specification is necessary. An essential precursor to customization is understanding what the previous specification represents.

If these two problems can be solved then a CASE tool environment with automatic code generation facilities could support reusable development of software specifications.

7.2 AN APPROACH

We propose that analogy can be used to solve these problems. Analogical matching is the human cognitive process of reusing knowledge in problem solving. This can be applied to problem solving in software engineering applications. Analogy has further advantages in that it unlocks a wider variety of previous solutions for reuse than less powerful techniques, e.g. matching on similarity, classification. Similarity matching offers only software evolution, i.e. reuse within closely related domains. Analogy can support reuse across domains. The intuition that this may be the correct approach comes from two sources:

1.   Use of abstraction as a general principle in software engineering; the generalism inherent in the process of abstraction encourages inter-domain applicability of software constructs.

2.   The observation of contractor practice in industry, where approach to a problem and its solution often relies on previous memory of analogically matched solutions, e.g. 'it's that type of problem'.

Furthermore, cognitive studies of system development have shown that experienced practitioners rely on domain knowledge and rich memory schema of previous solutions when they start with new problems (Guidon and Curtis 1988, Vitalari and Dickson 1983). However, analogy is a complex mental process and human performance in analogical reasoning tasks is not always effective (Gick and Holyoak 1985). Use of analogy may therefore require considerable active tool support to deliver efficient and accurate software reuse.

7.3   INVESTIGATION OF ANALOGICAL REUSE

We have studied the process of specification reuse focusing, in particular, on the customization problem.

Initial studies used a paper-based scenario to test if reusability improved performance. Two experimental conditions were used; reuse of a specification with an analogically matched domain (the concrete specification), and secondly reuse of an analogically matched abstract specification. Both reuse conditions improved performance in terms of completeness of specification over a control group, although the error rate was similar in all conditions. Recognition of the abstract analogy was more effective, but reuse effectiveness overall was better for the concrete specification. Thus although fewer subjects recognized the match, those that did fared better with the concrete specification. From further analysis it appeared that the reason for this difference was a tendency to copy reusable specifications rather than understanding them. Concrete specifications appear to invoke more reasoning before reuse and this reduces errors (Sutcliffe and Maiden 1990b).

Follow-up studies with experts and novices have produced a model of the reuse process and provided further evidence that specification reuse improves performance (Sutcliffe and Maiden 1990a). Experts use analogically matched specifications to transfer knowledge to the new domains, as a prompt in developing understanding of the new domain and as scenarios against which to test specifications of the new application. Experts also spent more effort understanding the analogy in abstract terms. Expert analogical reuse therefore appears to contribute to several aspects on problem understanding and development of the solution. Novices showed similar behaviour but tended to spend less effort on understanding the analogy and copied more of the specification. Understanding the source specification, as is manifest in expert practice, appears to be an important determinant of success (Sutcliffe and Maiden 1990c).

7.4 CONCLUSIONS AND CURRENT WORK

Our studies have demonstrated that analogical matching of specifications can be an effective means of software reuse. However it is not without its problems. We believe that supporting understanding is going to be a crucial determinant of successful specification-level reuse. In light of this, a tutorial component is necessary within any reuse-supporting CASE tool.

Our current work is progressing in two directions. First, research is in progress to address the retrieval problem. Cognitive theories of analogical reasoning are being used to design an intelligent retrieval engine. Important attributes of specifications, search and matching heuristics are suggested by cognitive theory. These can be used to guide the dialogue with the software developer to acquire appropriate facts about the new domains, and to invoke efficient search procedures to retrieve candidate specifications from a repository. The key to a successful approach is to match specifications using a model-based approach rather than classification schemes. Inferential searching on the structural and semantic properties of conceptual models offers potentially more powerful retrieval than classification schemes which are limited by the wealth of the lexicon employed and the discipline of software developers in adhering to standard terms for classification and subsequent retrieval.

The second work area is in didactic support for comprehension of retrieved specifications. Here we are using techniques derived from learning theory and research in Intelligent Tutoring Systems. Our previous empirical work suggests that partial exposure and incremental development of reusable specifications should be advantageous. In addition, reusable specifications appear to have an important role in validating the development of the new application. Support for comprehension requires an explanation facility to help the software developer understand the relationship between the new domain and previous specifications. Indeed, explanation will also be necessary for selection of the appropriate specification(s) to reuse, because machine-based retrieval is unlikely to achieve a perfect match. We therefore conceive of a cooperative assistant system with initiative remaining with the system developer.

Design is in progress and implementation will commence shortly. This work will result in a 'proof of concept' demonstrator specification reuse support tool.

REFERENCES

Gick, M.L. and Holyoak, K.J. (1980), Analogical Problem Solving, Cognitive Psychology, vol. 12, pp. 306-355.

Guindon, R. and Curtis, B. (1988), Control of Cognitive Processes During Software Design: What Tools are Needed?, Proc. CHI '88 Human Factors in Computing Systems, Eds. Soloway, E. , Frye, D., and Shepard, S.B., pp. 263-269, ACM Press.

Sutcliffe, A.G. and Maiden, N. (1990a), Software reusability: Delivering productivity gains or short cuts. In proceedings of Interact-90, Eds Diaper, D., Gilmore, D., Cockton, G. and Shackel, B., pp. 895-902, North Holland.

Sutcliffe, A.G. and Maiden, N. (1990b), Specification reusability: Why tutorial support is necessary. In Proceeding SE 90, BCS Conference on Software Engineering. Ed. Hall, P.A.V., pp. 489-509, Cambridge University Press.

Sutcliffe, A.G. and Maiden, N. (1990c), Cognitive Studies in Software Engineering. In proceedings of 5th European Conference on Cognitive Ergonomics, Urbino, Italy. Ed. Van der Veer, G.

Vitalari, N.P and Dickson, G.W. (1983), Problem solving for effective systems analysis: An experimental exploration. CACM, vol. 26(11), pp. 948-956.

Part Three

Object-oriented Methods

8 How applicable is the object-oriented approach to the IS environment?

R. Jones

Software Development Monitor

8.1 INTRODUCTION

Everything, it seems, must today be object-oriented: languages; user interfaces; CASE tools. You name it, and you can bet that its vendor says that it is – or soon will be – object-oriented.

As ever, however, the academics and the hype merchants of the computing world are up and running off towards the horizon before the IS workers toiling away at the codeface are even crawling. In short, whilst seminars like this discuss the minutiae of object-orientation, most IS practitioners are in no position whatsoever to exploit object-oriented techniques and tools. More than that, I doubt whether many of those techniques and tools are yet applicable to the IS environment anyway.

This paper is meant to act as a sort of restrainer on the wilder fantasies of object-oriented evangelists, in as much as those fantasies relate to the IS environment.

But it isn't all doom and gloom. Whilst being sceptical of the degree to which IS staff can yet exploit object-orientation, I'm already in little doubt of the pivotal role of object-oriented techniques and technology in the future of IS software development. So this isn't, entirely, a negative paper.

8.2 SOME BASE POINTS

There are three 'base points' that this paper takes as read:

8.2.1 The Primary Problems Facing IS Staff are not Technical

Certainly, IS staff do face several immensely difficult technical problems: the need to embrace relational database technology; the need constantly to migrate existing applications to new technical environments; massive problems in maintaining existing software.

However, it is my contention that the major problem facing IS staff is primarily a cultural problem. Put succinctly, the IS world does not understand business, business certainly does not understand IS. Unless we find mechanisms for solving that cultural problem, all the technical innovations in the world – including the uptake of object-orientation – will not help IS staff build the applications their business peers so desperately need.

8.2.2 Information Engineering is a Good thing

By that, I mean generic information engineering that is software engineering plus – plus a whole range of facilities optimized to cope with the characteristics, such as shared data, of the particular genus of application built within the IS environment. Information engineering incorporates a number of techniques – such as 'user friendly' analysis diagrams and prototyping – that help explicitly in overcoming the cultural problems that I discussed earlier. In addition, information engineering captures, at a very high level of abstraction, most of the information required to build applications.

By working at such a high level of abstraction, developers can ensure that any design errors are captured very early in the development lifecycle.

8.2.3   Object-oriented is a Good Thing

By that, I mean that I accept totally the power – not to say the elegance – of object-orientation as a technical mechanism for cutting code. I fully expect it to become the dominant technical mechanism for cutting code in most sectors of the computer industry over the next five years.

8.3   BEST CURRENT IS PRACTICE

Is the IS profession getting any better at its job? To an extent, yes. I believe that, in a small number of IS shops, many of the major problems facing the IS profession are already being cracked. My newsletter, Software Development Monitor, regularly prints independently researched case studies that confirm the success of what I term the 'modern' approach to software development. That approach encompasses, broadly, the use of a methodology that falls within the generic information engineering camp, the use of prototyping to support the methodology, and the use of appropriate levels of automation within the software development process.

Already, there is a gradual uptake of CASE attitudes in the wider sense – encompassing, for example, the need to embrace repository technology as soon as it becomes mature enough – and some uptake of re- and reverse engineering. Above all, I detect a real commitment within these shops to cracking the basic cultural IS problem I outlined earlier.

That is to say, IS managers are increasingly assessing the techniques they use within the development process – especially analysis techniques – from a cultural perspective: does what I am about to do help build bridges with my users during development or not? Of course, technical issues remain, but they are secondary, subordinated to the wider cultural ones.

I had better add I suppose that the number of sites reacting in this way is still fairly small. However, the major hardware vendors are pushing their prime accounts in this direction. IBM's AD/Cycle, for example, reflects the world of information engineering. ICL's view of software development has always broadly mirrored this point of view.

8.4 OBJECT-ORIENTATION BASIC

According to a recent Ovum report, although the term 'object-oriented' is now widely used, no universal definition exists. 'It is generally agreed that it covers a set of properties each of which can exist in isolation from the others. However, the inclusion or exclusion of particular properties is still controversial. In reality, the power of modern object-oriented systems arises from a unique combination of ideas that build on and enhance each other'.

Ovum defines the term object-oriented in terms of four basic properties:

- Data and procedures are combined together in entities known as objects;

- Messages are used to communicate between these objects;

- Similar objects are grouped into classes;

- Data and procedures can be inherited within a hierarchy of classes.

Ovum says that any system (language, tool or methodology) is object-oriented 'if it supports all four of these concepts; if it supports only the first two concepts, the system is object-based; if it supports the first three, it is class-based.'

8.5 THE ATTRACTIONS OF OBJECT ORIENTATION

Although I'm sceptical to the degree to which object orientation can currently be of use to the average IS department, I'm in little doubt of the technical benefits that derive from using it to cut code. In particular, because process is directly attached to the data it deals with, any changes to program code should remain isolated. Indeed, it should be very difficult to produce the 'ripple bug' effect often associated with making amendments to existing procedural code.

Because data and process are tied so closely together, it becomes easier to 'grow' software with the object-oriented approach. Prototypes can consist simply of discreet units of completed code, with other elements of code either missing or acting as simple 'pass through' message switches.

The proponents to object orientation also say that its use leads to greater reuse of software components. Admirable though reuse is, I'm not so sure that it is a function of object orientation. Partly, it's a function of the fact that most systems currently being built with object orientation are 'green field'. That makes it easier to set up a control mechanism for identifying and cataloguing potentially reusable pieces of code.

In any case, the major problem associated with any reuse programme is not primarily technical. Rather it is clerical and organizational. How do you set up mechanisms for identifying reusable code? How to ensure that programmers check for reusability before they start to code? How do you implement 'minor variations' of an already identified reusable procedure? And so on.

Object orientation may make a marginal difference in implementing reuse, But any major reuse program is largely a matter of will, not of technicalities.

Every new technology spawns its own cliches. The biggest one so far in object orientation is 'object orientation mirrors the way the world works'. That may be true as far as writing what I called 'preidentifiable' software is concerned – for example, software to control the operation of an electrical component. But, for the average IS system, that phrase is really a nonsense.

I see no evidence yet that object orientation offers any better mechanisms for performing business systems analysis than the techniques offered by information engineering already do. What is more, I don't yet believe that many object-oriented practitioners have yet spent the necessary time studying business analysis problems to enable them to comment either way.

8.6 OBJECT-ORIENTED PROBLEMS FOR IS STAFF

And that, as far as I'm concerned, is the crux of the object-oriented problem for IS staff. Perhaps it takes someone who now works as a journalist to be churlish about the new, supposed, life-savers of the software industry, the object orientationists.

Well, here goes. From where I sit, I see object orientation being run by a bunch of techie evangelists who have little appreciation of the real problems associated with writing software to support business operations, and who consequently have no real concept of the cultural barriers that a techie approach to software development builds and perpetuates.

As I've noted already, I'm impressed by the object-oriented approach to code cutting. It seems possible, even likely, that that approach will become the norm in software engineering projects. But it's taken a long time for IS software developers to realize that methods that work within, for example, the realtime environment are simply inappropriate within the IS environment. That, if anything, should be the lesson learnt from the last five years of trying to implement information engineering.

The major problems facing IS departments still revolve around getting close enough to the business to enable IS staff to model business reality within the computer systems they are building to automate that reality. Information engineering works precisely because it concentrates on concepts, like shared data and the linking of IS plans to business plans, that force IS staff to deal with the minutiae of business.

The degree to which object-oriented techniques can be successful, or even useful, within the IS department depends almost totally, in my view, on their ability to mimic the 'business-related' aspects of information engineering. If object-oriented techniques simply move IS staff further away from – as opposed to closer to – business, they will, like many other well-loved software engineering methods, prove ineffectual in helping software developers build the innovative IS systems that most organizations are currently crying out for.

That's the crux of the object-oriented question as far as IS staff are concerned. Already, of course, the object-oriented bandwagon is up and running ominously fast. Sadly, most of the loudest proponents of object-oriented simply don't understand the difference between software and information engineering, and are thus, in their ignorance, more than happy to tout object-oriented as panacea for all software development ills, including the ones that currently afflict most IS departments.

So, the first thing that IS staff looking to assess object-oriented techniques should do is to discount almost entirely any vendors or pundits who claim that it is simply enough to transfer object-oriented (or, indeed, any) methods unaltered from software engineering environments to their information engineering counterparts. Anyone who still believes that the problems of most IS departments are primarily technical in nature should be promptly shown the door, no matter how impressive his/her object-oriented credentials.

Oh, and incidentally, even if I thought that the object-oriented approach would work in the IS environment, there is, as yet, little in the way of software development methods and technologies that looks likely to be of much use to the average IS software developer looking to exploit that approach in the immediate future.

8.7   OBJECT-ORIENTED METHODS FOR IS STAFF

The whole area of software development methodologies is one fraught with problems. But I use one basic litmus test to decide whether or not a method is likely to prove useful within the IS environment. It is this: does the method include business analysis techniques that are likely to help bridge the cultural divide between IS staff and their business peers?

If it does, I term the method a generic information engineering method. If it does not, I term it a software engineering method. Note, however, that all information engineering methods should also include all the elements traditionally found within a software engineering method. To repeat what I said earlier: information engineering is software engineering plus.

Sadly, most existing methods for implementing object orientation fall within the 'software engineering' camp. Whilst they're very useful for helping software developers build software to control a fighter plane, their use in helping the average business analyst to define the scope of, say, a customer sales and invoice system is fairly minimal.

It is thus very difficult to see how any IS staff who may have been using generic information engineering techniques can yet usefully attempt to start working with either object-oriented technologies or object-oriented techniques.

There are some object-oriented methods emerging that look hopeful, as far as IS staff are concerned. One such is ObjectOry from the Swedish company, Objective Systems. The interesting thing about ObjectOry is that it uses a variant of the key information engineering analysis technique, entity modelling. In fact, entity modelling is one of three high-level analysis techniques used by ObjectOry.

ObjectOry's entity modelling is very similar to the techniques used by most IS staff. The main difference is that ObjectOry 'understands' the relationships between entities.

A second technique, called Use-Case modelling is somewhat similar to dataflow diagramming, in that it identifies 'scenarios' in which business processes are instigated and controlled. And, like entity modelling and dataflow diagramming, ObjectOry iterates the use of entity and Use-Case modelling to build up a true picture of the business environment being automated.

But ObjectOry also encompasses a third technique that is specifically optimized for object-oriented computing. 'Services modelling' tries to identify atomic pieces of processing that can be attached directly to data objects.

ObjectOry uses all three techniques to build a high-level model of a proposed system. It then uses a variety of proprietary techniques to break those models down to real object-oriented programs. Objective Systems says that ObjectOry is being used by major organizations in Sweden.

For my own part, I'm not totally happy that ObjectOry can really satisfy all the needs of IS software developers. For example, it isn't apparent to me how one would link ObjectOry into the back-end of a traditional strategy planning exercise, something which is relatively easy to do with traditional information engineering.

Other interesting players in this area are Interactive Development Environments, with its OOE methodology, and Bachman Information Systems, who are already making early noises about the techniques needed to make a traditional relational database – DB2 – look like an object-oriented database to applications written for the IS environment.

In the UK, two organizations are carrying out particularly interesting work.

First, Information Systems Associates is building a methodology that works at the strategy planning/business analysis level. This attempts to identify which business problems might be best solved by using an object-oriented/knowledge-based approach, as compared to those that might best be served by using a traditional algorithmic approach.

Finally, DCE is the only methods organization I'm aware of that is trying to combine together the best technical features of object orientation with the best 'cultural' features of generic information engineering. In a recent article that appeared in Software Development Monitor, one of DCE's consultants claimed that object orientation offered a better approach to business analysis than information engineering. However, DCE is still a lone voice and I believe it has some work to do yet before it comes up with a combined object-oriented/information engineering methodology.

It's worth pointing out in detail at this stage the basic difference at the analysis level, between object orientation and generic information engineering.

8.8 TREATING DATA DIFFERENTLY

Within information engineering, the concept of shared data is pivotal. Most existing programs within the IS environment implement the concept that data belongs to a program or to an application. That concept was an historical necessity when those programs were being written. Now, however, we believe that data is a corporate resource that belongs to all applications, not just one or two.

Information engineering uses techniques that 'factor out' data from the processes that manipulate it. This is based on the concept that, whilst process changes frequently to reflect changing business practice, data remains relatively stable across time. Information engineering treats the separate data and process elements relatively separately all the way down the development lifecycle, up to the point where data is implemented as databases, and process is implemented as programs that manipulate those databases.

By contrast, the object-oriented view of the world sees data and process as closely interlinked. At the very highest levels, process is directly attached to the data it manipulates. When an object-oriented 'program' wants to manipulate another piece of data, it sends a message to that data, asking that a portion of the data's process carry out the necessary manipulation.

It's worth labouring this point because it outlines just how fundamental a shift of mindset is needed to move from the information engineering view of the world to an object-oriented one.

I'm not sure that many IS staff will ever make that shift of mindset. For example, the shift of mindset to move from, say, unstructured programming to structured programming – or from unstructured analysis to structured analysis – is fairly straightforward: there's no real change of paradigm, simply a refinement of an existing one. But I would estimate that each of those changeovers took at least ten years to complete within the IS industry.

The object-oriented paradigm is an order of magnitude more difficult to comprehend. It make take well over a decade to implement it within the average IS environment.

8.9 OBJECT-ORIENTED TECHNOLOGY FOR IS STAFF

Object-oriented technology for IS staff is still painfully thin on the ground.

Certainly, at the programming level, all the techie tools that are generally available are, of course, equally available to IS staff. But again, any IS manager who thinks he's going to solve his fundamental problems by teaching his staff to program in C + + is living in cloud-cuckoo land.

At the next stage up, there is a whole range of fairly interesting object-oriented-like technologies for building 'front-ends' to either existing, or new, IS-oriented applications. Actor is an interesting tool in this respect. In addition, of course, all the new GUIs appearing on the scene – Presentation Manager, Windows, the various flavours of workstation windows, windows '4GLs' like Easel – certainly have an object-oriented touch and feel.

Few object-oriented tools target the mainframe environment. A notable exception is Sapiens, an application generator targeted at the IBM environment. Originally developed in Israel, and now distributed worldwide, Sapiens implements large elements of the object-oriented approach to software development.

For example, in a Sapiens application, there are no programs. Developers define processing by means of rules which, in turn, are directly attached to the business data items to which they relate. Sapiens then 'parcels up' each item of business data with all its associated rules, thereby implementing the most fundamental facet of the object-oriented paradigm.

Of the traditional vendors of 'power tools', Ingres is making the earliest moves to embrace object-oriented technology. It already has extensions to its relational database that are arguably object-oriented, in that they attach elements of processing directly to data objects. In addition, it has launched a 4GL that includes many elements of the object-oriented paradigm.

CASE tool vendors have largely eschewed the object-oriented approach – in terms of the diagrams the tools support – at least as far as the IS environment is concerned. Leading exceptions in this respect are Objective Systems – which is committed to automating ObjectOry fully with CASE technology – and IDE.

The most recent release of the impressive Bachman CASE toolset for the IS environment includes a number of intriguing extensions that are of a broadly object-oriented nature. For example, the Bachman toolset now enables software developers to define 'methods' – lumps of processing – for attachment to individual entities within an entity relationship diagram. Indeed, of all the CASE tool vendors, I am happy that Bachman will probably be the first to include support for object-oriented methodologies within its IS CASE toolset.

Object-oriented database technology is still in its infancy, although vendors such as Ontologic are already into second-generation products. Interestingly though, many of those vendors seem already to accept that there will never be a large market for their technology in the IS environment. They expect to sell most of their technology into 'new' markets, such as imaging, multi-media, etc.

The attitude of traditional database vendors to object orientation isn't yet clear. It seems highly unlikely however that the Oracles and Sybases of this world will rush into adding object-oriented functionality to their products. In the medium term, I expect to see a healthy market for interface products that offer software developers an object-oriented view into existing database architectures.

8.10   CURRENT SOFTWARE DEVELOPMENT TECHNOLOGY AND OBJECT ORIENTATION

Intriguingly perhaps, although there may not be much use of object orientation by IS staff in the medium future, nearly all the tools that those staff use to build non-object-oriented systems are themselves becoming object-oriented.

For example, most CASE tool vendors already use object-oriented techniques to develop the CASE tools they market to IS departments. Index Technology – vendor of the Excelerator CASE product – has been working for over a year to build a second-generation CASE tool based around the Ontologic object-oriented database. Texas Instruments uses highly innovative object-oriented techniques to help it build code-generation technology that can target any number of different runtime environments from the same analysis-level design models.

And then there is the question of the technology that is to underpin what is already seen as the cornerstone of most IS software development architectures: the repository. Most existing repositories use relational database technology. Even IBM's Repository Manager – the linchpin of AD/Cycle – is based upon DB2 relational tables.

However, a number of vendors – notably Softlab with Maestro and LBMS with its recently acquired Meta Systems' PSL/PSA repository – claim that relational database technology can neither offer the modelling flexibility required within a repository, nor the performance needed to cope with the complexity of model required fully to scope a business application as it is being developed.

That conflict has yet to be resolved. Certainly, in the short to medium term, IBM will ensure that the relational repository rules the roost. But, in the long term, it seems highly likely that object-oriented will become the repository standard.

Another IS problem that is still to be resolved is the interaction between the current (IBM/360/Cobol) view of the development lifecycle – and the applications that

that lifecycle is used to produce – and what might be called the new 'GUI' view of the application world.

GUIs are obviously a good thing. They make possible the sort of intuitive application front-ends that increasingly computer literate users require. They make good use of workstation facilities, and help ease the introduction of client/server applications. As noted earlier, GUIs are inherently object-oriented. That's a real problem for most IS departments.

Not only must IS staff find a way of replacing 'dumb terminal' interfaces with new flavoured GUIs. They also have to find a way of insinuating the GUI/object-oriented view of the world into the back-end of 'dumb terminal' methodologies.

At the moment, we have the worst of all worlds. Typically, even a professional IS shop has to drop out of its structured methodology – and probably its CASE tool – as it designs its user interfaces, to start working in 'bits and bytes' mode with its new GUI whizz-bang technology. Again, it's difficult to see how that problem can be solved easily in the short term.

Most IS staff don't yet implicitly understand GUIs and object-oriented implementation. Most GUI vendors understand little of the mainframe lifecycle view of the world.

8.11 OBJECT ORIENTATION AND IS REVERSE ENGINEERING

I'm putting in this section simply as a marker, since there's not a great deal of work yet being done in this area.

Reverse engineering is primarily about trying to abstract logic from existing application code. In detail, it involves trying to disentangle process and data, so that the logic implicit in a program's data and process code can be stored separately in a CASE repository. On the data side certainly, the Bachman toolset already has highly impressive capabilities in this area.

Of course, with object orientation, trying artificially to create this separation between data and process is less important. For that reason, I expect the growing number of vendors working on reverse engineering to start exploring the use of the object-oriented paradigm as a possible 'target' for, at least, first cut reverse engineering.

One of the references for this paper – the Blenheim Conference – does also include an interesting case study at Brooklyn Gas in New York. Here, Andersen Consulting led a team that successfully reverse engineered a massive IMS application into a 'homegrown' object-oriented system, complete with self-made message passing and so on.

I'm not aware, however, that anyone else as yet has tried to mimic this approach.

8.12   OBJECT-ORIENTED PRESSURE GROUPS

There are already a number of interesting pressure groups in the object-oriented world.

The Object Management Group (OMG) is a sort of cross between a standards committee for object orientation and a vendors' cartel. OMG has already done an enormous amount of work in defining standards and procedures for building object-oriented databases, service interfaces to those databases, message-passing systems, and such like.

The Object Interest Group (OIG), by contrast, is a sort of IS users' cartel. Set up by a number of major user organizations in the UK, the OIG's mission is to find out 'what the hell all the fuss is about object orientation and whether it is of any use or interest to the average IS department'. Cleverly, OIG is manipulating vendors to give up their time freely in helping the OIG's members answer these and other questions. I commend the OIG to any user organization.

8.13   CAN THE AVERAGE IS DEPARTMENT USE OBJECT-ORIENTED TECHNOLOGY TODAY?

As a sort of summary, let me answer that question in three ways: no, yes, and maybe.

No

I can't yet see much use for object-oriented databases within the average IS department. In any case, the vendors of those products aren't really targeting the IS department yet.

More critically perhaps, there is still a real dearth of object-oriented methods capable of matching in any way the sophistication of information engineering during business analysis.

To repeat my caveat for the final time. The average IS developer just doesn't need the sort of technical silver bullet that object orientation purports to be. What he/she desperately needs is a good methodology that can help bridge the cultural divide between IS staff and their business peers, and that can then interface to the code-cutting technologies that are needed to convert the business models derived during analysis into operational systems.

I see no evidence yet that current object-oriented methods provide the necessary – prerequisite – business analysis support, although it's worth keeping an eye on the work being done at DCE.

Yes

There are of course a number of IS applications where the use of software engineering methods – as opposed to information engineering ones – may be highly appropriate. For example, if a financial services organization is building a complex ATM network, then the use of information engineering would probably represent overkill. In those circumstances, the technical problems probably outweigh the business problems, and the use of object-oriented techniques and methods would certainly be valid.

Inevitably as well, IS staff, especially those within the IBM environment, are going to have to start building applications soon that have a GUI front-end. In the short term, they will need all the help they can to circumvent problems associated with working at a fairly low level of detail with new GUI tools. Object-oriented methods and design may certainly be of help under those circumstances.

And, as noted earlier, most IS staff will soon be using tools – CASE, repositories, and such like – that were themselves built with object-oriented techniques and technology.

Maybe

IS staff should be selective in their use of products from vendors such as Ingres that offer object-oriented extensions to traditional databases and 4GLs. As object orientation moves ever more into the world of hype, so the chances of pseudo-object-oriented technology turning into a solution in search of a problem become greater.

Similarly, although Sapiens is probably an exception, IS staff should be wary of obtaining object-oriented 'power tools' – such as 4GLs – until they have identified the real business problems that they are trying to solve. This also applies to the use of CASE tools that claim to support the object-oriented view of the world.

8.14 BUT THE APPLICATIONS WORLD IS CHANGING

This paper has really concentrated upon the applicability of object orientation to the sorts of applications that IS departments have traditionally built. That's because, by and large, the average IS professional is still building – or, more likely – maintaining those applications. However, it would be foolish to ignore the fact that the nature of applications being demanded by end-users is changing.

Furthermore, as newer types of application delivery technology become available, IS staff should be looking to exploit that technology wherever possible. Exploiting that technology may prove to be far easier if IS staff embrace at least elements of the object-oriented approach. Already, some IS applications are storing and manipulating new types of data, for example, image, sound, BLOBs, etc.

In addition, the economic dynamics of downsizing are already leading to an increasing use of client/server networks. In this sort of environment, the traditional 'dumb terminal' approach to building systems is simply inapplicable. Developers should be looking to exploit GUIs within client/server environments. That requires the use of object-oriented techniques.

There is no longer a homogeneity of profile for IS applications. I've mentioned cooperative processing already. Other application types that are becoming more prevalent include: decision support systems, 'information intensive' systems, and knowledge-based systems.

Each of these potential advances in software development and/or delivery technology typically require changes in the way that software is developed. As those changes occur, so IS professionals must start to investigate newer techniques, one of which must obviously be object orientation.

8.15   OBJECT-ORIENTED PLAN OF ACTION FOR IS DEPARTMENTS

What should the IS professional do about object orientation today?

Well, the first thing he/she should do is to remind himself of the nature of most of the problems currently faced by his department. Few of those relate directly to technology, or to the need to embrace, willy-nilly, every new technology that comes along.

Key to the success of the IS department is understanding and matching the information needs of the remainder of the business. Any view of object orientation should be filtered rigorously through that lens.

You shouldn't care how good the technology is. Ask the question – does it help you build business solutions that better meet the requirements of your business peers? More than that, are the techniques that you will need to use to build those solutions with object-oriented technology amenable to the sort of user involvement that is critical to their successful implementation? If object orientation can't pass those tests, don't use it today.

The second thing that IS staff should do is to ignore the hype and ranting that currently emanates from all too many object-oriented techies and evangelists. Hardly any of them actually understand the way that the average IS department operates. Virtually none have any idea of the difference between the average software engineering environment and the average information engineering environment.

Again, the watchword is: does all this new technology stuff actually help me build better systems that are verifiable by end-users? If it doesn't (yet), wait until it does, because trying to implement yet another technical silver bullet is the last thing the average IS department currently needs.

Certainly, any IS department with even a half-hearted interested in object-oriented technology should investigate the Object Interest Group.

Finally – all my caveats and brickbats notwithstanding – object-oriented technology is too important to ignore. IS departments should delegate at least one person to maintain a watching brief on both object-oriented methods and object-oriented technology.

REFERENCES

Worthwhile references within the object-oriented literature to the realities of the IS environment are still pretty thin on the ground. For any serious student, the following will make a good starting point.

Proceedings of Object-oriented Techniques, 31st May/1st June 1990, available from Blenheim Online, 081 868 4466.

Object-oriented Systems: The Commercial Benefits, published by Ovum, telephone 071 255 2670.

Object-oriented Techniques for the IS Environment, Software Development Monitor, volume 1, number 11, available from Perfectsure Ltd, on 0954 780358.

Beyond Information Engineering Towards Object Management, Software Development Monitor, volume 2, number 8.

Waiting For 00-DB2, Software Development Monitor, volume 2, number 9.

9   The impact of software reuse on object-oriented methods

R. Hodgson

Interactive Development Environments Ltd

9.1   INTRODUCTION

Traditionally system development proceeds by a step-wise transformation from the problem domain (Schultz 1985). Analysis then design then implementation as illustrated in Fig. 9.1. Each phase depends philosophically on our appreciative system as illustrated in Fig. 9.2.

Analysis concerns itself with the understanding of domains and the elicitation of system requirements. Requirements are often thought of as 'out-there' in the real-world waiting to be discovered. An analysis method leads to their capture and, by transformation, a design, ideally with no distortions.

Irrespective of whether requirements are 'out-there', or evolved by experiencing ideas in action, the notion of transforming an analysis model into a design model is inappropriate for object-oriented systems built from reusable components.

A reuse approach raises considerations about 'bringing' existing models to the analysis and design process.

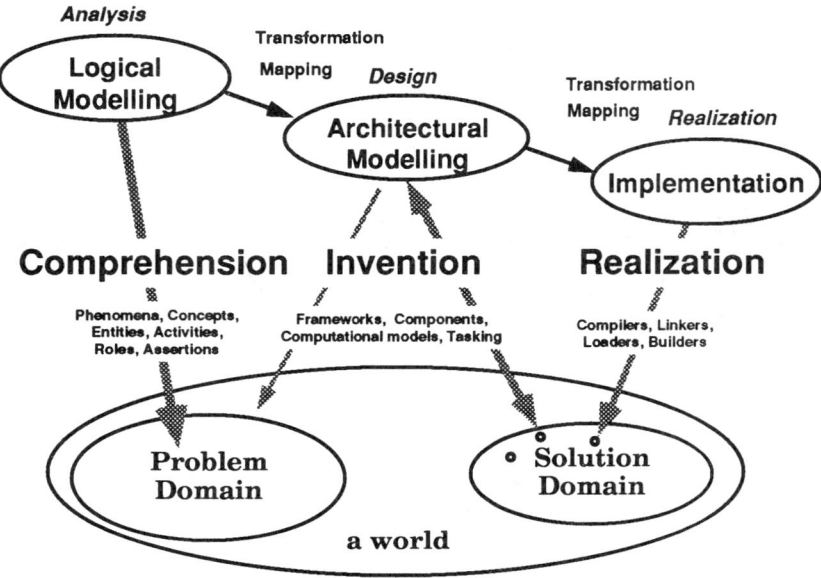

Fig. 9.1 Development phases.

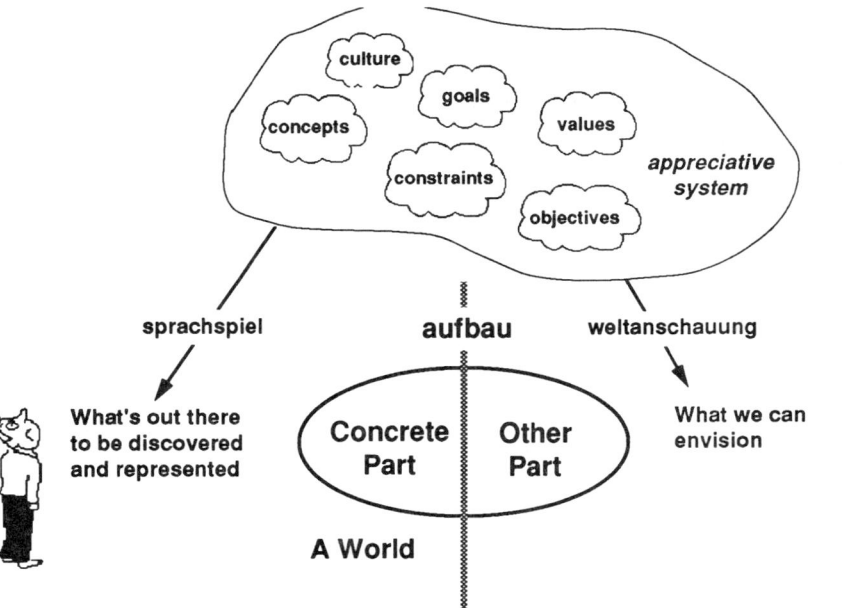

Fig. 9.2 The ontology of systems analysis.

Analogical reasoning (using metaphors) encourages analysis with design (with prototyping) then implementation (Barman 1989, Sutcliffe 1989, Vosniadou 1989).

Analysis is distinguished from design as the specification of what a system does as opposed to how it will do it. Objects present their behaviour externally through the set of actions for which they take responsibility. The specification of the object is what it does. 'I am what I do' is a sentiment from Morita psychotherapy (Reynolds 1984) that applies as much to objects as it does to people.

In all this, the term design presents a difficulty. Suggesting too much the activity or result of creating something, is design just the description of how the system is put together and the process by which it happened? Of greater appeal is 'architecture', evocative of structure and style.

In other words, we understand design reuse to be the reuse of architectural components and frameworks. And if we are to agree reusable architectures then some agreement on the applications to which they may be suited must also exist.

9.2   REUSE: THE STORY SO FAR

Re-inventing the wheel is so symptomatic in programming that our attitude is it's quicker to re-create a piece of software than to understand someone else's.

Hardware components are designed from the outset with reusability in mind. Digital and analog circuitry have interfaces and interconnections that are well understood. When faced with a new component we quickly familiarize ourselves with its functionality and external appearance by looking for where buses connect, and where input, output and control connections are located. Not so for software.

Many of today's systems were built using methods and languages offering poor support for change. Structured analysis and design without architectural partitioning and structured programming without modularity are obstacles to software reuse. At worst the reusable component is at the level of the data structure such as the array and structure, or language constructs such as sequence, iteration and alternation. Said by Brad Cox to be about equivalent to resistors, capacitors and pieces of wire (Cox 1986).

Poor partitioning can result from a strictly top-down approach to structured design resulting in highly pervasive global data. A piece of data is given to a procedure to be transformed in some way, either to change the state of itself or to give rise to new data. By necessity this data is stored outside of the functions that operate upon it. At worst all of the data becomes global frustrating any attempts to partition the system. At best, modules are still attached to disjoint pieces of global data, the module interfaces may be elegant but the module is not reusable without the global data. Transplanting the module into another application requires the global data to fit into new global data areas.

Global problems of this sort are reduced by information hiding (Parnas 1972). Modularity is achieved by encapsulating items of data with the functions to be performed on that data behind a well-defined interface. Interface procedures or, in the jargon of object-orientation, operations, manage access to the data.

But even if good disciplines of encapsulation are followed, other problems may persist preventing the integration of modules of software developed at different times and by different people. Conformance must exist for access to shared resources and intercomponent communication. The protocols required are dependent on the overall architecture, there must be compatibility to the supporting architecture and its mechanisms for messaging and concurrency control.

Even with these problems solved, we do not ensure malleability. Elegant packages and classes might result, but ultimately malleability depends on preserving architectural integrity of the system. Our components must behave consistently with other components of the system. Simply, the changing (or introduced) component must continue to do something useful in context.

Designing reusable components is not just a matter of deciding what data and functions should be encapsulated. Components only become usable in the context of architectures.

An architecture doesn't just arrive out of nowhere, but evolves from agreements on computational mechanisms, paradigms and other inventions that undergo evolution.

Architectures are agreed general structures that become assimilated into the industry's language giving rise to names like 'parser', 'graphics kernel system (GKS)', windowing system' and 'object management system'.

The architectural view focuses on frameworks of generalized designs and sees reuse as an issue of plugability. Compatibility with the architecture of the new application requires our components to behave consistently with other components. Simply, the component must do something useful in the new context.

A component becomes usable when it fits into an architecture. To be reusable it must possess the following qualities:

- it anticipates other contexts of use

- the component is 'findable'

- it is capable of being understood

● all of the services it requires can be provided.

Generalizing a component is not just a technical matter. Commitment and support will be needed from the organization. The dilemma of building for tomorrow's projects and finishing today's will have to be resolved.

Daniel Weinreb at OOPSLA 1988 posed the following question:

How is writing a reusable module different from writing an ordinary module? When you write an ordinary module, it's part of a particular program. You know exactly who the module's callers will be, and what they require of the module. But a reusable module must satisfy the needs of many callers, including anticipated callers that haven't even been written yet! How can you specify your module so that it will turn out useful and suitable for programs whose requirements are yet unknown? This is the fundamental challenge of reusable code.

Fortunately our choice of languages today includes object-based and object-oriented languages such as Ada, Modula-2, C++, Objective-C and Eiffel.

The promise of object-orientation originated as a programming paradigm embracing the concepts of encapsulation, messaging, classes and inheritance (Cox 1986, Goldberg 1983, Madsen 1988, Meyer 1988, Schmucker 1986).

Not only are these ideas powerful for creating interesting implementation architectures, but also for capturing the representation of a domain.

Object-orientation models a domain by identifying entities and their behaviour. This style of designing replaces functional decomposition, where a system is based on the functions it performs with general functions decomposed into specific ones.

With object-orientation, the structure of the software system is based on interactions between entities and not the mapping of system functions into processes. Functions and data are defined in context with the data they govern; they are grouped together according to the data abstractions they manage. We might liken objects to small computing machines, enacting the behaviour of their domain counterparts by requesting operations of each other. Objects mean components need not be restricted to stateless subroutine libraries or complete software subsystems such as a graphics library or an operating system.

9.3   APPLICATIONS AND ABSTRACTION

We choose to see an application as a hierarchy of related domains. By discovering common and disjunct domains we partition our problem space and isolate common behaviour.

For example, consider the list of applications below, where some attempt is made to group similar applications:

- **Supervisory Control And Data Acquisition** (SCADA): batch process control systems, alarm surveillance systems, trading-room systems, Automatic Teller Machine (ATM) networks;

- **Command and Control Systems:** air traffic control systems, mission-critical communications systems, telecommunication network management;

- **Direct Control Systems:** embedded process control instrumentation, vending machines, machine control systems;

- **Resource Management Systems:** warehouse systems, production planning, vehicle rostering systems, hospital bed allocation;

- **Scheduling Systems:** manufacturing systems, timetable scheduling systems;

- **Decision Support Systems:** medical diagnosis, computer fault diagnosis, strategic planning systems;

- **Information Systems:** library systems, software reuse repositories;

- **Interactive Design Tools and Environments:** CAD, CAE, CAM, CASE;

- **Non-interactive Tools:** compilers, interpreters and translators.

Characteristic domains might be found by thinking about:

- even and action-based behaviour;

- logic or rule-based inferencing behaviour;

- algorithmic functionality;

- information structure;

- resource management;

- user-interface management.

It is commonly believed that a domain might be characterized along three viewpoints: entity, behaviour and function. These three axes are illustrated with examples of popular notation in figures by requesting operations of each other. Objects mean components need not be restricted to stateless subroutine libraries or complete software subsystems such as a graphics library or an operating system.

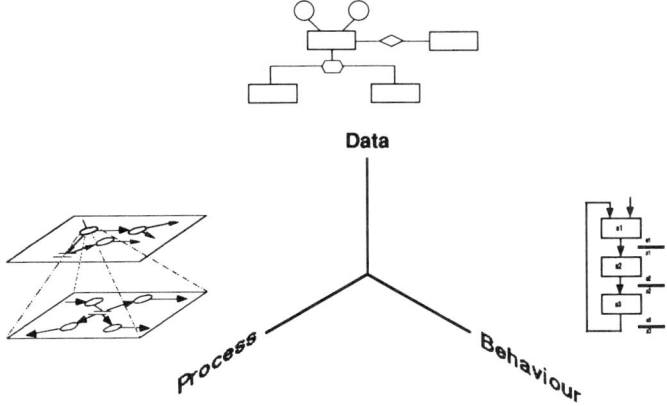

Fig. 9.3   Axes of abstraction.

Object modelling is an integration of different viewpoints. An object, with varying degrees, embodies aspects of all three dimensions, as depicted in Fig. 9.4. It interacts with other objects with standard protocols as illustrated in Fig. 9.5.

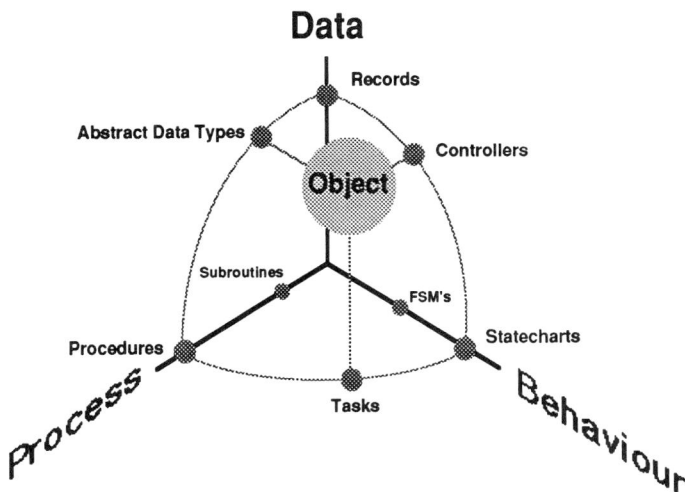

Fig. 9.4   Objects and abstraction.

Without state, objects are more reusable as exemplified by the numerous mathematics and statistical libraries that are reused.

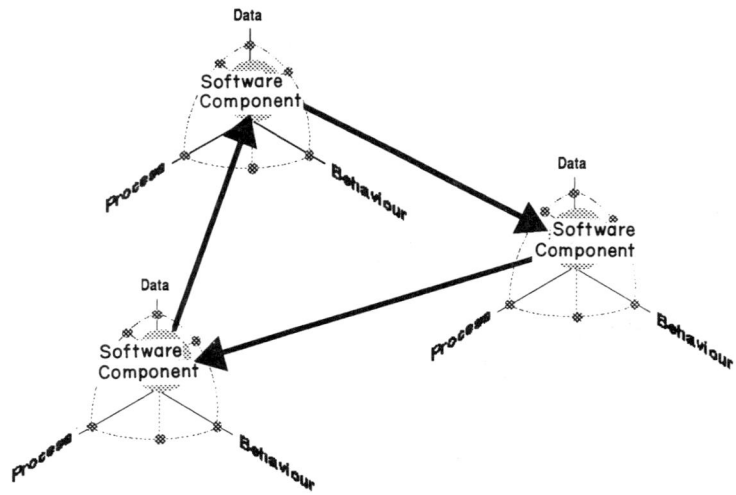

Fig. 9.5   Reuse depends on context.

Objects that are simple abstract data types such as complex numbers do not have any memory of their use and have no state.

With state, objects present a more complicated contract of use. Preemptions and concurrent threads of execution make it important that potential clients of a component have a thorough understanding of the interface.

Objects then are potentially mini-systems and we should expect the techniques for single system abstraction to be of help.

Entity modelling captures the properties and relationships of entities (Chen 1979). Properties are represented in attributes that record the changes in the values and states of the entity as it performs its operations. Often attributes are simple quantities that are characteristic of the entity, perhaps its colour, weight, or velocity. Other attributes may in themselves be entities, ranging from simple abstract data types such as cartesian coordinates to more complex entities that are parts or associated entities.

Many notations for information modelling exist. Irrespective of which modelling notation is used, entity analysis is governed by the abstraction processes of aggregation, association and generalization (Manfredi *et al.* 1989, Smith and Smith 1977).

Aggregation of objects related by properties allows us to build compositions of entities which may then be viewed without having to know their structure. But aggregation, or composition, should not be confused with specialization and generalization which allows common characteristics of classes to be grouped into more general classes. Classes are connected in inheritance or sub-type relationships with the general classes. Classification is powerful not only for sharing attributes but also for sharing behaviour, supporting system evolution through incremental modification. Association abstraction expresses other relationships between entities; how entities depend or make use of each other.

Often these dependencies express a causal relationship delineating action in a system. If we annotate these relationships with the events and actions that characterize the association, the resulting models, 'entity-action' diagrams, assist the allocation of operations to classes.

As an example, consider a flight reservation system which requires the modelling of aircraft, routes and flights. 'Aircraft' and 'route' are entity abstractions and 'flight' is an associated entity. The existence of the entity 'flight' depends upon an 'aircraft' and a 'route'. Rather than the 'aircraft' or the 'route', it is the 'flight' entity which is associated with other entities such as passengers, cargo and crew. Adding a passenger to a flight may clearly be seen to be an operation associated more with the 'flight' entity than with the 'aircraft' or the 'route' entities.

Most current object-oriented analysis methods make use of entity abstraction techniques (Loomis 1987, Shlaer 1989, Coad 1990). Their differences lie in the treatment of actions and services. Coad depicts actions simply as directed connections on the information model. Shlaer uses state transition diagrams to define the services provided by an object, a strong modelling correspondence to Jackson Entity Life Histories.

Strong event-oriented systems require methods that support behavioural modelling. An object may exhibit states or different conditions throughout its lifecycle and a method must assist allocation of actions to objects. Behaviour is expressed in terms of managed events and causal actions. Changes in state occur as a result of the event history of the object. In turn the ability of the object to respond to events may be constrained by its state.

Objects can execute their lifecycles in isolation but also in coordinated lifecycles with other objects. Such behaviour may be modelled as a Finite State Machine (FSM), an Entity Life History (ELH) or a Petri Net (PN) model. Concurrency complicates ELH models when multiple concurrent threads of behaviour are present. FSM and PN models are simpler – the composite state being the set of active states for FSMs and the graph marking for PNs.

A domain model begins as a collection of entities surrounding which there are conditions that describe situations that can develop in the domain. The instance of such a development is an event. Events cause activity in the domain and modelling proceeds by discerning the types of action that may occur.

A typical approach to finding objects using object-oriented domain analysis is as follows:

● develop an entity-relationship model to identify object boundaries and relationships giving a definition of what each object contains;

- annotate the entity-relationship model with the events and actions that occur between associated entities and producing an event-list for each object;

- consider the actions that are performed by each entity by expressing where events originate and which objects are responsible for actioning them;

- capture these decisions in an object communication diagram, which might be the same model as the entity-relationship model;

- develop the behavioural view of the object by modelling states and transitions based on the set of events for which the object is responsible. Express the actions that happen in the states of the state model (Moore model) as opposed to on the transitions (Mealy model). Indicate any generated events (signals) as outputs of the states;

- for objects that have a high degree of processing, optionally produce a process model that captures all of the actions as the processes contained within the object. Show how each process is involved with the objects data, how any generated events are sent outside of the object;

- repeat these steps for all objects and until the objects are fully refined.

For capturing functional requirements of an application, Yourdon/DeMarco data flow analysis is a well-proven approach. Techniques for finding application objects by grouping processes and stores have been proposed (Carter 1990, Ladden 1989, Seidewitz and Stark 1986, Seidewitz 1987, 1988). The resultant objects tend to be role encapsulations with names like 'manager' and 'handler'.

Radically different schools of thought exist on methods for object-oriented design. Many current approaches to object-oriented methods retain a traditional viewpoint on the notion of a problem domain and a solution domain, a contrived division between the so-called 'real-world' and the system to be built.

Across the method camps and the exploratory-programming camps, there exists a philosophical division of some sort. The empiricist tradition is that a problem is 'out-there' to be captured. The normative camp believes that systems are created from agreements on what can be envisioned. Not 'out-there' in the real-world, but 'brought-to' the problem-at-hand and created out of our intentions. The very notion of their being a 'real-world' is in question and imaginary-worlds are equally at play (Ehn 1988, Winograd 1986).

Representative of the new school in design is responsibility-driven design, also termed anthropomorphic design (Barry 1989, Rosson 1989, Wirfs-Brook 1989).

Responsibility-driven design realizes a solution as a set of communicating cooperative objects. Each object takes responsibility for managing what it knows about and has needs in order to carry out its responsibilities. An object has relations with information components and also with other objects which act as colleagues or collaborators, its acquaintances. The shift in view is away from a data-centred or function-centred perspective of a domain towards a behavioural view.

Object-oriented design is not viewed as an abstracted process of defining objects as:

$$Object = Data + Process + Behaviour$$

but as the concrete process of personalizing objects with responsibilities for performing roles as defined by their scripts and interactions with other actors:

$$Object = Responsibilities + Needs + Colleagues$$

We single out two important factors that are driving the debate on object-oriented design methods. First, object-orientation encourages new ways of looking at systems, raising considerations about reuse early in the design cycle. Second, frameworks that offer abstract designs raise the computing structures available in the solution domain making it difficult to fit a transformational approach to method with the pragmatics of iterative design based on the 'chosen' frameworks (Anderson 1990, Daniels 1990, Gossain 1990).

Object-orientation brings the new possibility of constructing a system based on generalized reusable design frameworks. To apply these frameworks we must separate out the characteristic domains of our system and apply the appropriate methods to modelling what is left and to constructing the connections between domain structures. Examples of governing domains include:

- networks (graph theory)

- routers (topology)

- schedulers (manufacturing)

- planners (operations research)

- controllers (control theory)

- manufacturing processes (process technologies).

The common theme of all these examples is that they model a well-formed theory from a domain of discourse (suggested in parentheses) in a generalized way.

9.4 OBJECT-ORIENTED DESIGNS

The plural 'designs' is intended. Rather than pursue the topic of object-oriented design method forwards in an abstracted way, it is interesting to look at how object-oriented systems are built, so as to find what techniques and methods might support the underlying design idioms.

Whatever our design method, the objects we build with are:

- surrogates for the real-world that act as external or context objects;

- domain objects that capture a theory of knowledge and provide the framework of a generalized algorithm or model of behaviour. Examples can be found in the theory of graphs, networks, scheduling etc.;

- application objects that express the specification of the use of a domain with control and service abstractions that capture the functions of the application;

- reusable computational objects that augment the resources of a computing platform. Examples are generic stacks, queues and collection classes.

Design methods have always being governed by the concepts supported by programming languages. For structured design, it is easy to see how traditional procedural languages fit with an overall design strategy – module calls involving parameter passing and shared data are ideas modelled directly.

In object-oriented programming languages we encounter a wide range of concepts: encapsulation, class, instantiation, composition, inheritance, delegation, polymorphism, genericity, objects as variables, messaging and self-recursion. And the list grows with the adoption of the object-oriented paradigm in other areas of software technology. For example, work on object-oriented databases is introducing ideas such as persistence, granularity and versioning of objects.

The richness of object-oriented concepts has raised the power of the computational environment far above what we have for structured design methods. It is unreasonable to relegate these concepts by speaking of them as the concerns of implementation level detail, object-oriented design methods should be judged on their ability to handle a full complement of object-oriented concepts. Herein lies the difficulty for design methods, finding abstractions leading to the design idioms that object-oriented concepts promote.

Recent work has suggested criteria for distinguishing among languages purported to be object-oriented (Blair, Gallagher *et al 1989*. Wegner and Zdonik 1988):

Object-based = encapsulation + unique identity

Class-oriented = Object-based + set-abstraction + inheritance

Object-oriented = Class-Oriented + polymorphism + self-recursion

To say we are doing an object-based design, methods must support encapsulation; the packaging of functions with data into objects with unique identity. For class-oriented design, there must be support for sharing specifications of collections of like-objects, either with classes or with prototypal objects and delegation. To say we are doing object-oriented design, we must aim for consistent message protocols between objects, strong polymorphism and good behaviour factoring with self-recursion in abstract classes.

Encapsulation, or information hiding is the simplest level a design method must support. Data is held with the operations that manage and control that data behind a well-specified interface, a well-known and agreed principle of good design, first described as information hiding (Parnas 1972).

Often we can partition an object's data into other objects. We must be clear on how to draw the object boundary when considering these compositions. Design decisions are taken on how much access to sub-objects should be provided at the parent's interface and the trade-off between partitioning and execution efficiency.

An object becomes usable to other objects through the provided operations (and exported types) it defines. This interface expresses the contract that a client (user) commits itself to when it makes a use of the object. Objects will use operations of other objects (requested operations). Just as an application requirement exists for the use of a domain entity, we can say that a specification exists for the use of an object. This specification is a set of operations belonging to a protocol, much like a communications protocol. Common operation semantics across objects standardizes interfaces and supports better architecture frameworks and component reusability.

Operations can be clarified from three viewpoints: system boundary, object interface and execution model interface. The system view is outside the system boundary and relates to the notion of a logical or context diagram. From this we discern efferent, transform and afferent operations at the highest level of abstraction. The object interface boundary is a service provider-user viewpoint where we distinguish the view from the requestor from the view from within the responder. The view from the responder's perspective is concerned with what behaviour is expected by the outside world. Whereas the requester's view is how other objects appear as service providers. The execution model interface deals with lower details of the underlying architecture such as memory management and tasking. Operations are categorized by Booch (Booch 1986) as:

- primitive operations for accessing the underlying representation of the object;

- enquiry operations that obtain data from an object;

- constructor operations that alter the values and states of the object's data: initialization, modification and finalization;

- iterator operations that permit parts of an object to be visited.

Much of the thinking to date on object-oriented design has dwelled on objects but it is the notion of a class for specifying and localizing the behaviour of a collection of similar instances that is central to the object-oriented paradigm. Additional method support for building reusable classes should address:

- class definition with support for class variables and class operations (if supported);

- separate consideration of the interface provided for clients (users of object instances) from the interface provided for potential specializations of the class (class to subclass interface);

- management of dependencies between classes;

- support for class client use: a class may use another class to define a component within itself either by reference or declarative inclusion. Classes therefore also contain use hierarchies;

- class splitting: the ability to split big classes into small classes;

- class melding: the ability to compose a larger class out of smaller ones;

- the provision of a class browser;

- support for object creation (instantiation), finalization and destruction.

To facilitate reuse, object and class interfaces should be designed with polymorphism. A variable may then reference objects of different classes at run-time using the same names for operations and arguments to carry-out requests. We should not have to resolve the differences between specific objects, we simply request an operation of the object:

> Compute the routing times for a network by visiting every node and using the 'processing-time' method appropriate to whatever object happens to be under selection.

Operations are bound at run-time to specific operations in a receiving object. What an operation does is therefore a matter for the receiving object as resolved by its immediate class or some inherited feature of a super-class. The invoker has an understanding of what is being done, but delegates the details and responsibility of how it is done completely to the responder.

Polymorphism is the means by which a standard set of operations can be defined, a common protocol across objects (classes). This simplifies architectural frameworks by removing the need to commit and resolve interactions to specific objects.

9.5   REUSE PARADIGMS

Depending on the object-oriented concepts supported by the implementation language or system, 'object-oriented reuse' means:

- component composition

- component configuration

- virtual machine abstraction

- generic component instantiation

- class specialization

- abstract superclasses

- generic frameworks.

9.5.1 Component Composition

A component is constructed of other components either statically through a strict encapsulation mechanism, or by references to external objects. Strongly typed languages tend to follow the strict encapsulation method, whereas languages that support object references might adopt a dynamic construction technique and require methods to build a composite object.

Communication between components may be by static linkage between caller and callee or by dynamic messages bound at run-time to the receiving object. Dynamic binding results in more malleable designs by removing the need to commit a client to interactions with specific objects. Provided new components conform to the protocols dictated by the client, no change of the client code will be needed.

9.5.2 Component Configuration

Components distributed across different address spaces require inter-communications. A common approach is based on the concept of Remote Procedure Calls but this has the disadvantage of requiring explicit naming to be held at each communicating site.

To build components for reuse in configurations than cannot be anticipated location transparency is required. Architectures are based either on virtual nodes, or message ports. Local components route their messages to a configuration-dependent destination. Reuse requires that all configuration management be delegated to other objects that support the interconnection paradigm.

9.5.3   Reuse using Generic Components

Component specifications may also become reusable by instantiating a generalized model in a new problem domain. Mechanisms bind problem-specific names and types to generic parameters.

Genericity is the idea of parameterizing a software component so that it can serve as a specification for making new components that will work on other data types.

Generic components will often require more than a data type. For algorithmic features of the component to function properly on new data types they will require new functions for generic functions. An example is Booch's passive iterators for building generic reusable components using generic function parameters in Ada (Booch 1987).

Genericity is a good way of providing tested reusable components and a design method should support the definition of generics separately from their use.

Genericity is not an alternative for inheritance and the contortions that result from attempting this equivalence should be avoided (Meyer 1986, 1988).

9.5.4   Inheritance-based Reuse

In data modelling 'data normalization', one-fact-in-one-place, is important for structuring information. Through inheritance we have the ability to organize classes into hierarchies giving rise to the possibility of 'behaviour normalization', that is the idea of one-behaviour-in-one-place (Drake 1989).

Inheritance is fundamental to object-orientation and has given rise to many design idioms (Anderson and Gossain 1990, Johnson and Foote 1988, Wegner and Zdonik 1988):

- type conformance

- class specialization

- abstract classes

- generic frameworks.

Type conformance, or substitutability, is a strict (disciplined) use of inheritance where an instance of a subclass is acceptable wherever an instance of its superclass might be used. For example Escort and Toyota are subclasses of car and we should expect either to be usable wherever we use a car. Strict inheritance is concerned with maintaining conceptual integrity in a class hierarchy. Classes are related semantically in an 'is-a' relationship with subclassing done in strict accord with the type signatures of the class hierarchy.

Inheritance is often used in a style of programming known variously as 'programming by difference', 'differential programming' and 'programming by exception'. New classes are defined by finding their closest relatives. Inheritance reuses as much code from the collections of like-objects, either with classes or with prototypal objects and delegation. To say we are doing object-oriented design, we must aim for consistent message protocols between objects, strong polymorphism and good behaviour factoring with self-recursion in abstract classes. Encapsulation, or information hiding, is the simplest level a design method must support. Data is held with the operations that manage and control that data behind a well-specified interface, a superclass is possible but some operations are overridden by operations in the new class. Specializing an existing class often involves introducing new instance variables and operations to support unique features of the new subclass. Differential programming is a common approach to code reuse but it does have problems. Some insecurities are:

- The concrete superclass manages data abstractions and state which might not be meaningful to the new subclass.

- Liberally connecting to superclasses to borrow parts of their data and behaviour brings the danger of unanticipated behaviour from an operation in a superclass.

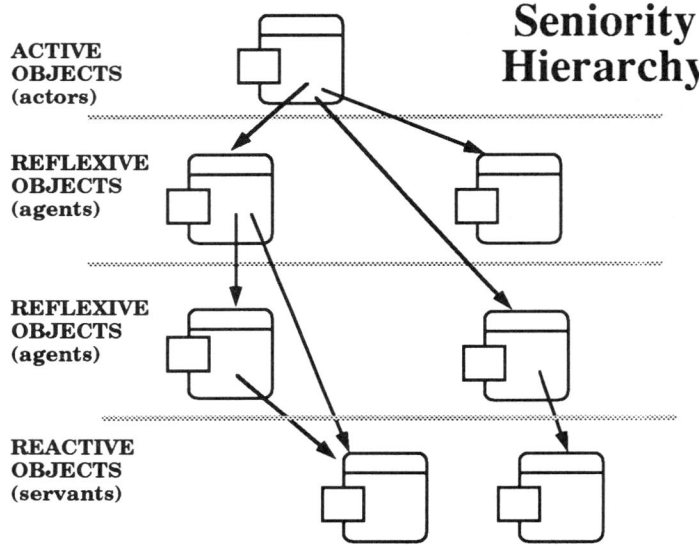

ACTIVE OBJECTS (actors)

REFLEXIVE OBJECTS (agents)

REFLEXIVE OBJECTS (agents)

REACTIVE OBJECTS (servants)

Seniority Hierarchy

Fig. 9.6   Actor-agent-server architecture.

A situation to watch out for is partial inheritance of concrete superclasses, that is, superclasses which have instances. It is invariably better to split the concrete class so that the shared part can be isolated into an abstract superclass.

Abstract classes are those that never have instances. Their purpose is to 'factor-out' common behaviours so that subclasses might safely inherit behaviours without inappropriate instance structure. Migrating methods to new abstract superclasses benefits greatly from multiple inheritance.

Insecure inheritance from a concrete superclass can nearly always be transformed into an abstract superclass hierarchy. In this way the behaviour of an existing software component is reused but at the expense of having to modify the definition of the original concrete classes. Experiences of this iterative re-design of existing classes have been recently reported (Gossain 1990).

Abstract superclasses can be used to define general behaviour which invokes specific behaviour from subclasses where necessary. Subclass code is required on the basis that most things are done well enough by the superclass, but some things should be done specifically in the subclass. In other words an operation in the superclass defines the overall strategy and at some point in its execution it invokes an operation of the subclass to deal with the specifics of the particular object. This technique requires the notion of 'self' so that a superclass can request an operation of the specific object on whose behaviour the superclass operation is invoked.

Behaviour sharing among class hierarchies is the basis of the powerful architectural idea of frameworks prescribing what is expected of subclasses. The superclasses provide standard, that is, generalized operations, or protocols.

An important tenet in software architecture is the definition of an interface between components. Hiding the implementation of an object and providing a specification for its use, the interface forms the contract between a client and the object. But to date, object-oriented design methods have only addressed interfaces between objects: so-called seniority hierarchy. With inheritance relationships between classes and instance objects within classes, in total there are three interfaces to consider (Fig. 9.7):

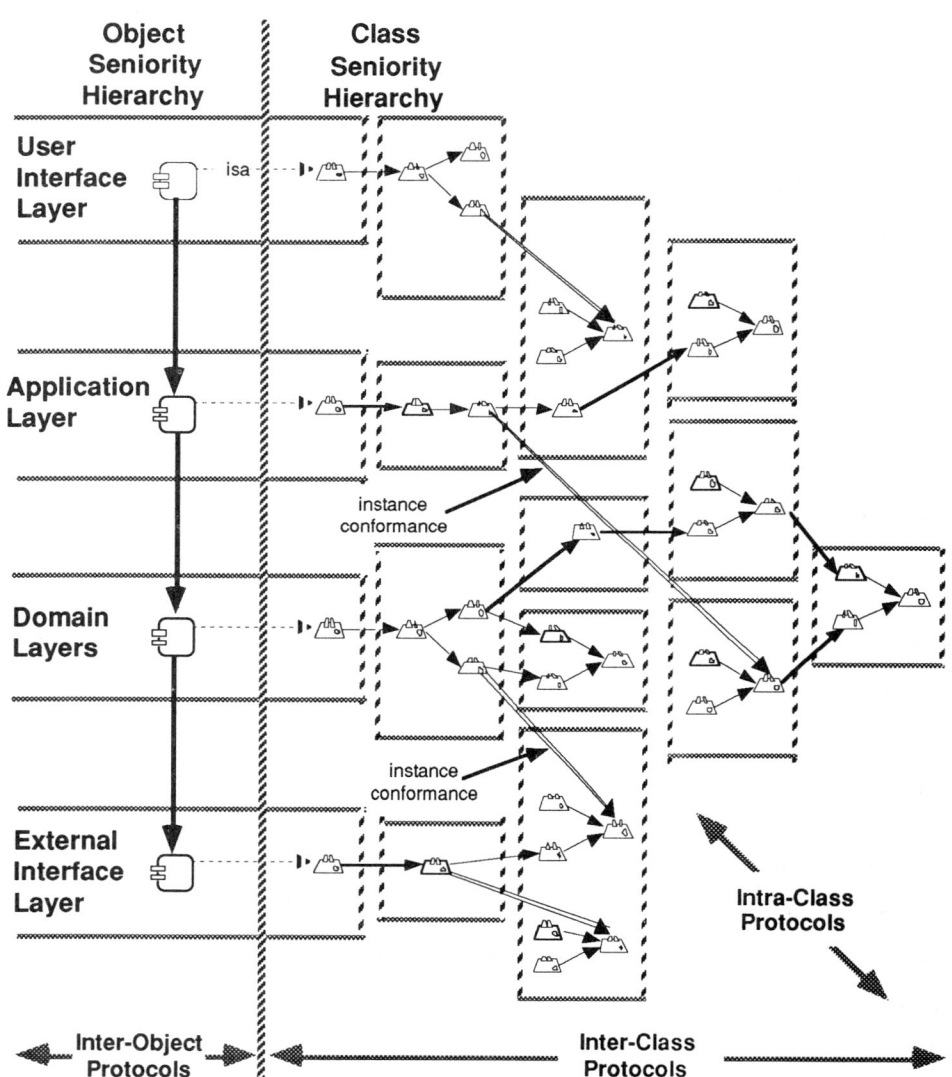

Fig. 9.7   Extensible integrated domain model architecture.

- an interobject interface between object instances often referred to as the 'object seniority hierarchy';

- an interclass interface between a class and its inherited ancestors governed by the operations expected of the class invoked by self-recursion in the inheritance hierarchy;

- an intraclass interface between the methods of a class and the classes with which it is associated (so-called acquaintance classes). This interface is the delegated requested protocol against which objects must show type conformance.

Contracts expressed by interclass and intraclass protocols are neglected by existing object-oriented design methods.

9.5.5   Reuse from Generic Frameworks

Reusable frameworks represent a shift in perspective away from the idea of a component plugging into a new application towards the idea of an application plugging into an existing structure.

Generic frameworks provide an architecture with a 'general' way of doing things. The framework amounts to a 'blank' application with the overall structure present but requiring specific functionality from application-based subclasses.

Patterns of interaction are prescribed in the protocols between the abstract classes. The framework is an abstract design. Specific operations required at different places and times in the generalized behaviour of the superclasses are provided by the application subclasses.

Classes of the application are in effect servers to the framework classes. The design approach is an inverted architecture, where the application is driven by the framework. Such frameworks are 'open' and design proceeds by finding out how the application might be 'plugged' into the framework. Not top-down design, nor bottom-up but design-by-analogy – how the application behaviour is analogous, by specialization, to existing more generalized models.

Examples of frameworks are:

- Smalltalk foundation classes (Goldberg 1983);

- ICpak201 Objective-C MVC classes (Knolle 1989, Stepstone 1989);

- NIH (OOPS) Smalltalk look-alike library (Gorlen 1987);

- MacApp from Apple Computer Inc. (Schmucker 1986);

- ET + +, a C + + user interface framework (Gamma 1989, Weinand 1988);

- Model-View-Controller (MVC) architecture for user interface management (Krasner 1988).

Applications that have reused these frameworks include:

- Intermedia at Brown University, USA using MacApp (Meyrowitz 1986);

- WEBS (Woven Electronic Book System), Univ. of Fribourg using MacApp (Pasquier-Boltuck 1986);

- Virtual Instruments using Smalltalk, Fluke Mfg. Co., Inc. (Bhaskar 1986);

- INSIST uses Smalltalk, Philips Research Labs., Sunnyvale, USA (Van der Meulen 1987);

- Fabrik for visual programming using Smalltalk, Apple Computer (Ingalls 1988).

Inheritance-based component libraries are 'black-box' frameworks which serve as subsystems to an application. Black because they do not involve specialized behaviour from any client application subclasses. Examples of 'black-box' component libraries are:

- Public domain C++ class libraries: GNU G++ library, Symbol tables, 3D graphics, matrices, image libraries, FFT classes, 2D user interface classes, fast shared memory allocation, bit manipulation classes, linked lists, Hash functions (Coggins89);

- Common View User interface classes (Glockenspiel);

- Booch's Ada Software Components (Booch 1987);

- Booch's C++ Software Components (Booch 1990).

At lower (deeper) architectural levels, solution domain objects provide reusable components such as sets, containers, queues and stacks. Such objects might be thought of as building-blocks offering higher abstractions to raise the power of the underlying computing environment.

9.6 REUSABLE ARCHITECTURES

A number of architectures are emerging from the experiences of using object-oriented design:

- Client-Server architectures;

- Layered Virtual Machine architecture;

- Actor-Agent-Server architecture;

- Responsibility-Driven Actor (or Anthropomorphic Actor) architectures;

- Extensible Integrated Domain Model (EIDM);

- User interface architectures: Model-View-Controller (Krasner 1988) and Presentation-Abstraction-Control (Coutaz 1989).

9.6.1 Client-Server Architecture

The client-server model is the basis of many architectures and notably 'Layered Virtual Machines'. A distinction is made between a client invoking services from a server. Models differ in the semantics of the contract between the client and the server and in the symmetry of the relationship with regard to the need to name correspondents. Other behavioural differences arise in support of concurrency and atomicity.

Recently a use of a client-server-service model has been reported for a C + + industrial automation project (Menga 1989).

9.6.2 Layered Virtual Machine Architecture

A Layered Virtual Machine (LVM) architecture is constructed as a hierarchy of layers where each provides services to its higher layer. At each layer, sets of services are provided by the instruction sets of abstract machines. In this manner the functions of the application are refined into orders for abstract state machines, themselves issuing orders to lower abstract state machines. At the lowest level of the architecture we can introduce entity abstractions that act as surrogates of their real-world counterparts (Nielsen 1988).

9.6.3   Actor-Agent-Server Architecture

The Actor-Agent-Server model forms the basis of Booch OOD (Booch 1986), Nasa's GOOD method (Seidwitch 1986) and the European Space Agency's HOOD method for Ada (Heitz 1987).

An actor is defined as an object which only requests operations of other objects and provides no operations itself. An agent provides and requests operations and a server only provides operations. Figure 9.6 illustrates the seniority hierarchy that results.

9.6.4   Responsibility-Driven Actors (RDA)

This architecture is based on the Actor model of programming which is also known as anthropomorphic programming (Barry 1989, Wirfs-Brook 1989, Rosson 1989).

In keeping with the concepts of Hewitt and Lieberman, Actors are responsible for performing roles and conduct their activities by sending messages to each other (Hewitt 1977, Lieberman 1986).

A system is modelled by thinking about the responsibilities, needs and collaborators (fellow cast members) of each object as explained earlier in the paper.

Typically architectures employ objects that are personifications of roles. Analogies of organizational models result in objects such as managers, workers, secretaries and couriers.

Architectural reuse is facilitated by the adoption of metaphors. Analogical reasoning helps us choose design approaches by testing for behavioural similarities in the target application (Vosniadou 1989).

9.6.5   Extensible Integrated Domain Model Architecture

A strategy for reusable designs is to separate the concerns of a system into domain models and application models, or 'use-of-domain' models (Ganti 1990).

A domain model is built by modelling the concepts and phenomena present in the domain, without considering how it will be used. What is important are the key abstractions and behaviour. The application can then be evolved independently (Fig. 9.7).

Domains can be:

- entity domains of 'real-world' objects that capture the characteristic properties of those objects;

- algorithmic domains that capture a well-formed theory such as planning, routing, control theory and scheduling;

- application domains that express the functional abstractions of specific application uses of the entity domains;

- entity domains of a computational nature that provide computing abstractions such as sets, stacks, queues, lists and trees;

- architectural frameworks that provide the structure of the computing solution such as multi-tasking operating systems, messaging mechanisms and distributed computing paradigms.

A domain model is built by modelling the concepts and phenomena present in the domain, without considering how the domain will be used. It often turns out that the real-world is not very interesting with respect to objects and has shallow hierarchies. On the other hand, algorithms can be rich in objects and have deep hierarchies.

Domain layers are reusable across different applications and can have subdomains that help to decompose the structure of our problem into cooperating class hierarchies. By understanding the anatomy of an application we can reuse general designs that model a well-formed theory. For example from the theory of graphs we can produce a domain model that is reusable for applications as diverse as network management, flexible manufacturing and PCB layout. From operations research, we can capture ideas in abstract classes for planning systems.

An extensible layered domain architecture captures the entities and properties of the domain. Provided the protocols of the model are observed, extensibility allows the domain model to evolve in a different lifecycle to the application and multiple applications to share the same domain models. Figure 9.7 illustrates how the application layer drives the domain model layers. The figure shows a view of the interactions between objects and classes and how an inheritance-based architecture has more than one plane of use hierarchy. Self-recursion among classes causes other control threads.

Reusing domains requires creative thought in fitting known models to new problems. It requires us to separate the functionality of differing applications from the domains which govern them. Domains are separated from their use and we regard an application as a 'use-of-domain' layer.

Consider the design of a commodity trading system. The domain model would capture concepts such as commodity, standard contract, spot price, futures price and exchange rate. Another domain model would capture the notions of a bid and a bidding strategy. The application would interface with these models and make use of their protocols.

Another example from industrial automation industry is a flexible manufacturing system (FMS). An FMS has domain models for equipment, materials, and batches. A further domain model might capture the notion of a route as a network of work-cells. Generic algorithms for traversing a network could be used to calculate route times by messaging more specific subclasses for processing times at each point on the route. The applications are separated from the models but comply with the domain protocols.

Traditionally the domain model is pervasive throughout an application. Changes to accommodate new objects in the domain are difficult to make. Moreover the domain model cannot be shared by another application.

An extensible domain model captures the entities and properties of the domain. As long as the protocols of the model are observed, extensibility allows the domain model to evolve in a different lifecycle to the application and multiple applications to share the same domain models.

9.7 REUSABLE SOFTWARE ENGINEERING

The component-oriented viewpoint of software development recognizes that there are different concurrent lifecycles to components, applications and abstract designs.

Black-box components evolve by adaptation without suffering changes to their interfaces. Their specifications determine their usefulness and reusefulness. Adaptation preserves the interface and only concerns itself with how well the component performs. 'Fitness for purpose' is the only consideration.

Applications evolve to meet new system requirements in response to how the experience of using a system raises new considerations. Such evolution might place new demands on existing components, possibly requiring their replacement.

Evolution of an application might also result in new distinctions about the structure and behaviour of their governing subdomains. In an inheritance-based design, reorganization of the class hierarchies is typical. Reported experiences indicate that a class hierarchy undergoes considerable re-melding and refinement as a system and the understanding of its underlying domains evolves (Anderson 1990, Gossain 1990).

Evolution of class hierarchies casts doubt on the viability of a software libraries industry. Except in well-understood domains, particularly those governed by standards such as networking, user interfaces and graphics, it is hard to envisage a components industry that will not be required to provide source code.

9.8 CASE SUPPORT FOR OBJECT-ORIENTED REUSABILITY

How will object-oriented software engineering be adopted? There will be no revolution and adoption in each industry segment will be different. The information systems community will look for ways of mapping the identification of entities and relationships into classes; see for example Coad/Yourdon Object-Oriented Analysis (Coad 1990). The real-time structured analysis (SA/RT) community may wish to transform data flow diagrams and control specifications into objects and methods (Carter 1990).

Not one method for 'going object-oriented' but across all industries, different methods for structuring domain models to those used for capturing the functional requirements of the application level. While traditional methods might be adaptable, new methods will be called for to support the evolution of domain models, to support the evolution of class hierarchies and to guide the re-engineering of existing systems using layered domain models.

For many people will be the idea of eventually doing object-oriented development. A transition from existing designs by re-engineering and hybrid object-oriented systems. These considerations have led Interactive Development Environments (IDE) to take the initiative of publishing a standard notation for expressing object-oriented designs, Object-Oriented Structured Design (OOSD), (Wasserman 1990).

OOSD supports the re-engineering of both sequential and concurrent systems by recognizing the importance of passive and active objects. The goals of OOSD are summarized as:

- support for a wide variety of systems;

- support for object-oriented concepts;

- support for re-engineering through hybrid system construction;

- design reusability;

- support for code generation;

- analysis method independence.

OOSD is a notation for expressing the architecture of a software system. Figure 9.8 illustrates a subset of the OOSD notation.

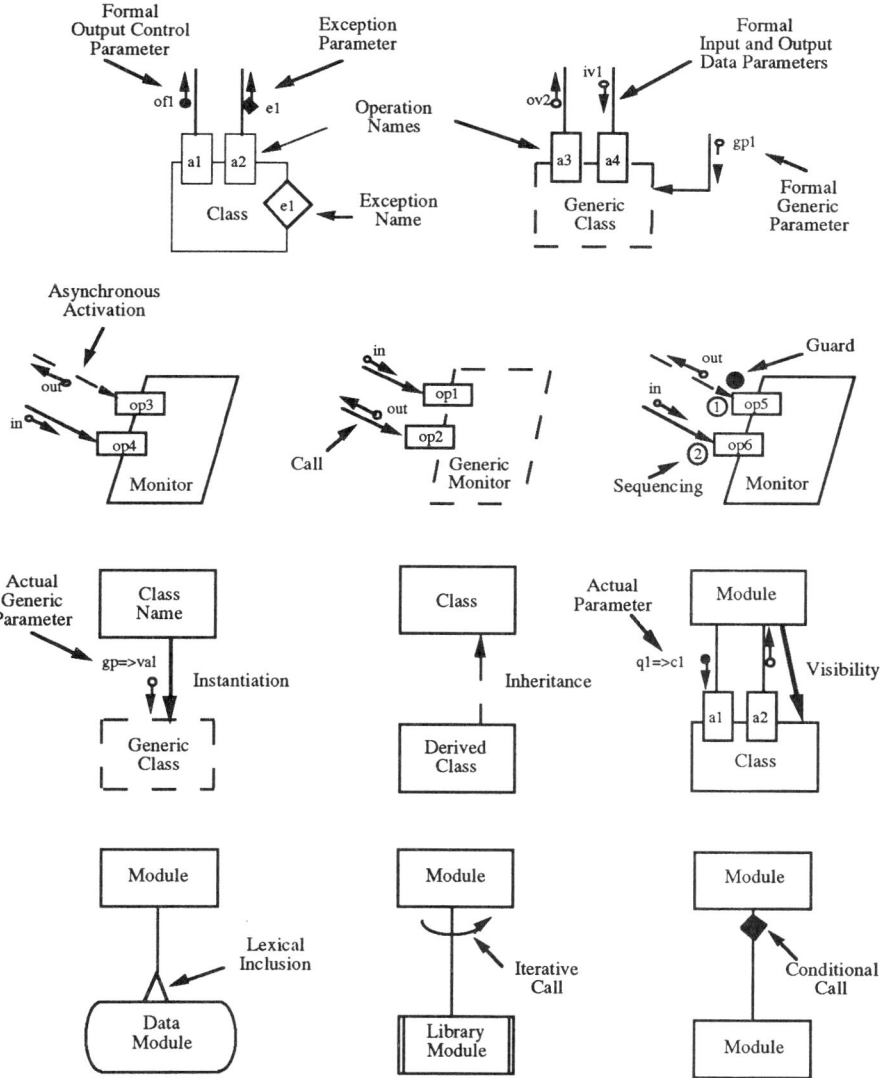

Fig. 9.8   Basic OOSD notation.

Central to the OOSD approach is the retention of useful ideas from structured design such as interface definitions, modularity and hierarchical composition, in conjunction with a full set of object-oriented concepts ranging over objects, classes, genericity and inheritance. The basic ideas of OOSD come from four foundation sources:

- structure charts in Structured Design;

- Booch's notation for Ada packages and tasks, generalized to be language-independent;

- class hierarchy and inheritance principles from object-oriented programming;

- Hoare's monitors for concurrent programming.

Building software using reusable components and architectures can benefit considerably from CASE support. A minimum set of facilities that a Reuse CASE environment might offer are:

- a reuse catalogue powerful search and retrieval mechanisms;

- an extensible set of constraints that govern how components can be combined by aggregation or through associations;

- mechanisms for interconnecting components;

- architectural idioms that are configurations of components for generic application and computational models;

- guidance for using existing components and configurations;

- guidance and methods for assimilating new components and configurations into reuse repositories.

Automated support for reusability is provided in OOSD through a reuse library. The reuse library is a controlled library that can contain validated designs.

Automated support for reuse provides not only the reuse library, but also a browser whereby designers can search the library for useful components and a mechanism for using selected components. Users select library units from a reuse catalogue along with desired interface features. OOSD/ADE then draws the specific use of the object automatically.

The reuse facility must support both a reference to a component in the reuse library, and the ability to copy and modify that component external to the reuse library, with the resulting modified component as a candidate for addition to the library. Users refer to the definition of an object while navigating through a design by zooming into that object in the reuse library.

The reuse catalogue of OOSD must also support the object-oriented paradigm in the full, reusing components through the various design idioms of inheritance and instantiation.

9.9   REUSE NEEDS COMMITMENT

Methods are ultimately governed by the norms and values of an organization. Reuse may well be technically feasible but ultimately it needs commitment from the organization.

A generalized component will take longer to develop and it has been reported that the benefits from reuse may not be felt until after the second or third reuse of the component.

We continue to be faced with more challenging software projects and the requirement for software engineers continues to grow at up to 25% per annum. Reuse will become more and more crucial to ensuring successful software developments.

Procuring software components and subsystems will increasingly be important to a company's competitive strength. For this reusability to be effective, new design methods, agreed architectures and CASE support will be increasingly important.

9.10   CONCLUSION

The paper has dealt with a broad perspective of object-orientation choosing to look at the question of reuse from the perspective of architecture.

Objects by their very nature encourage a different way of looking at the world, which must be accommodated within the traditions of systems analysis.

Potentially every object is a system in its own right. Techniques used for single-system abstraction are the right ones for objects. What is new for objects is dealing with what happens in the time and space between objects.

Work continues on:

- how to classify so that separate underlying domains are discerned to give reusable abstract designs;

- how to provide method support for behavioural factoring in class hierarchies;

- how to provide an environment that supports the different lifecycles within an object-oriented approach to software reusability.

ACKNOWLEDGEMENTS

The author is grateful in various ways to Steve Cook, John Daniels, Bruce Anderson, John Deacon, Anthony Wasserman and other colleagues at Interactive Development Environments.

REFERENCES

Anderson, B. and Gossain, S. Software Reusability using Object-oriented Programming. (UK IT 1990, University of Southampton, 22nd March), 1990.

Barman, M.A. Shifting Paradigms for Software Development. In Proceedings of the Third International Workshop on Computer-Aided Software Engineering (CASE'89, Imperial College, London, UK, July 17-21), p. 100, 1989.

Barry, B.M. Prototyping a Real-Time Embedded System in Smalltalk. SIGPLAN Notices 24, 10, pp. 255-265, October 1989.

Bhaskar, J.S. Peckol, J.K. and Beug, J.L. Virtual Instruments: Object-Oriented Program Synthesis, ACM Sigplan Notices 21, 11, pp. 303-314, November 1986.

Blair, G.S., Gallagher, J.J. and Malik, J. Genericity vs Inheritance vs Delegation vs Conformance vs, Journal of Object-Oriented Programming, 2, 3, pp. 11-17, September/October 1989.

Booch, G.S. Object-Oriented Development, IEEE Trans. on Software Engineering 12, pp. 211-221, February 1986.

Booch, G.S. Software Components with Ada, Structures, Tools, and Subsystems, ISBN 0-8053-0610-2, Benjamin/Cummings Publishing Company, Inc., 1987.

Booch, G.S. and Vilot, M. The Design of the C++ Booch Components, In ACM SIgplan Notices, Vol. 25, No. 10, October 1990 (OOPSLA ECOOP'90, Ottawa, Canada, 21-25 October 1990), pp. 1-11, ACM, 1990.

Carter, C. Object-Oriented Design: a common sense fusion of methods (Stp UK User Group Conference, Spiders Web Hotel, Watford, England, May 1990), 1990.

Chen, C. The Entity-Relationship Model: Toward a Unified View of Data. ACM TODS 1, 1979.

Coad, P. and Yourdon, E. Object-Oriented Analysis, ISBN 013-629122-8, Prentice Hall, 1990.

Coggins, J.M. The Best of comp.lang.C++. C++ Report 1, 6, pp. 9-10, June 1989.

Cox, B. Object-Oriented Programming: An Evolutionary Approach, Addison-Wesley, 1986.

Daniels, J. Object-Oriented Design: Refinement or Transformation? (OOPS-30, Strand Palace, London, 9th March 1990), pp. 62-63, 1990.

Drake, R. A conversation at an OOPS meetings, 1989. Personal communication.

Ehn, P. Work-Oriented Design of Computer Artifacts, ISBN 91-86158-45-7, Arbetslivscentrum, Sweden, Stockholm, 1988.

Gamma, E., Weinand, A. and Marty, R. Integration of a Programming Environment into ET++, A Case Study. In Proceedings of the Third European Conference on Object-Oriented Programming (ECOOP1989, Nottingham University, England, July), pp. 283-297, ISBN 0 521 38232 7, Cambridge University Press, 1989.

Ganti, M., Goyal, P. and Podar, S. An Object-Oriented Software Application Architecture. In 12th International Conference on Software Engineering, Nice, France, pp. 212-220, IEEE Conputer Society Press, 1990.

Goldberg, A. and Robson, D. Smalltalk-80: The Language and its implementation, Addison-Wesley, Reading, Mass., 1983.

Gorlen, K.E. An object-oriented class library for C + + programs. SP&E 17, 12, pp. 899-922, December 1987.

Gossain, S. and Anderson, B. An Iterative-Design Model for Reusable Object-Oriented Software. In ACM SIgplan Notices, Vol. 25, No. 10, October 1990 (OOPSLA ECOOP'90, Ottawa, Canada, 21-25 October 1990), pp. 12-27, ACM, 1990.

Heitz, M. HOOD: Hierarchical Object-oriented Design for development of large technical & realtime software, CISI Ingeniere, 1987.

Hewitt, C. Viewing Control Structures as Patterns of Passing Messages. AI 8, pp. 323-364, 1977.

Hodgson, R. On the question of Object-Oriented Method (OOPS-30, Strand Palace, London, 9th March 1990), pp. 50-51, 1990.

Hucklesby, P. Two controversial opinions from the Eiffel camp (OOPS-30, Strand Palace, London, 9th March 1990), pp. 36-37, 1990.

Ingalls, D., Wallace, S., Chow, Y.Y., Ludolph, F. and Doyle, K. Fabrik: A Visual Programming Environment, SIGPLAN Notices 23, 11, pp. 176-190, November 1988.

Johnson, R.E. and Foote, B. Designing Reusable Classes, OOP 1, 2, pp. 22-35, June/July 1988.

Kennedy, A. and Carter, C. Structured Analysis and Structured Design with Ada: A pragmatic Object-Oriented Approach, Ada UK 1989 10, 3, 1989.

Knolle, N.T. Variations of Model-View-Controller, JOOP 2, 3, pp. 42-46, September/October 1989.

Krasner, G.E. and Pope, S.T. A Cookbook for Using the Model-View Controller User Interface Paradigm in Smalltalk-80, OOP 1, 3, pp. 26-49, August/September 1988.

Ladden, R.M. A Survey of Issues to be considered in the development of an object-oriented development methodology for Ada, ACM Ada Letters IX, 2, pp. 78-88, March/April 1989.

Lieberman, L. Using Prototypical Objects to Implement Shared Behaviour in Object-Oriented Systems, ACM Sigplan Notices 21, 11, pp. 214-223, November 1986.

Loomis, M.E.S., Shah, A.V. and Rumbaugh, J.E. An Object-Modeling Technique for Conceptual Design, Proceedings of ECOOP'87, Paris, special issue of BIGRE 54, pp. 325-335, 1987.

Madsen, O.L. and Miller-Pedersen, B. What object-oriented programming may be – and what it does not have to be. In Proceedings of the European conference on Object-Oriented Programming, ECOOP'88 (ECOOP'88, Oslo, Norway, August), pp. 1-20, ISBN 3-540-50053-7, Springer-Verlag, 1988.

Manfredi, F., Orlando, G. and Tortorici, P. An Object-Oriented Approach to the Systems Analysis. In Proceedings of the 2nd European Software Engineering Conference (ESEC'89, Warwick, England, September), pp. 395-410, Springer- Verlag, 1989.

Menga, G., Morisio, M. and Russo, G.L. A Framework for Object-Oriented Design & Prototyping of Manufacturing Systems. In Proceedings of the Second International Workshop on Software Engineering and its Applications (Toulouse, France, December 4-8), pp. 587-603, ISBN 2-906 899-30-5, 1989.

v. d. Meulen, P.S. INSIST: Interactive Simulation in Smalltalk, ACM Sigplan Notices 22, 12, pp. 366-376, December 1987.

Meyer, B. Genericity versus Inheritance, ACM Sigplan Notices 21, 11, pp. 391-405, November 1986.

Meyer, B. Object-oriented Software Construction, ISBN 0-13-629049-3, Prentice-Hall, 1988.

Meyrowitz, N. Intermedia: The Architecture and Construction of an Object-Oriented Hypermedia System and Applications Framework, ACM Sigplan Notices 21, 11, pp. 186-201, November 1986.

Nielsen, K. and Shumate, K. Designing Large Real-Time Systems with Ada, ISBN 0-07-046536-3, 1989.

Pasquier-Boltuck, J., Grossman, E. and Collaud, G. Prototyping an Interactive Electronic Book System Using an Object-Oriented Approach. In Proceedings of the European conference on Object-Oriented Programming, ECOOP'88 (ECOOP'88, Oslo, Norway, August), pp. 177-190, ISBN 3-540-50053-7, Springer-Verlag, 1988.

Parnas, D.L. On the Criteria to be Used in Decomposing Systems into Modules. Communication of ACM 15, 12, pp. 1053-1058, December 1972.

Rosson, M.B. and Gold, E. Problem-Solution Mapping in Object-Oriented Design, SIGPN Notices 24, 10, pp. 7-10, October 1989.

Reynolds, D. Playing Ball on Running Water, ISBN 0-85969-483-6, Sheldon Press, London, 1984.

Rumbaugh, R. Relations as Semantic Constructs in an Object-Oriented Language, ACM Sigplan Notices 22, 12, pp. 466-481, December 1987.

Schmucker, K.J. Object-Oriented Programming for the Macintosh, ISBN: 0-8104-6565-5, Hayden Book Company, 1986.

Seidewitz, E. and Stark, M. General Object-Oriented Software Development, SEL-86-002, 1986.

Seidewitz, E. Object-Oriented Programming in Smalltalk and Ada, OOPSLA'87 Proceedings pp. 202-213, 1987.

Seidewitz, E. and Stark, M. Towards a General Object-Oriented Software Development Methodology, Ada Letters 7, pp. 54-67, July 1987.

Seidewitz, E. General Object-Oriented Software Development: Background and Experience, 21st Hawaii International Conference on System Sciences, 1988.

Shlaer, S. and Mellor, S.J. An Object-Oriented Approach to Domain Analysis, ACM SIGSOFT SEN 14, 5, pp. 66-77, 1989.

Smith, J.M. and Smith, D.C.P. Database Abstraction: Aggregation and Generalization. ACM TODS 2, 2, 1977.

Smith, M.K. and Tockey, S.R. An Integrated Approach to Software Requirements Definition Using Objects, IDE User Group Proceedings March 1989, 1989.

Stepstone: Objective-C Product Information, The Stepstone Corporation, 7 Glen Road, Sandy Hook, CT 06482, 1989.

Sutcliffe, D.A.G. and Maiden, N.A. Analogy in the Reuse of Structured Specifications in a CASE Environment. In Proceedings of the Third International Workshop on Computer- Aided Software Engineering (CASE'89, Imperial College, London, UK, July 17-21), pp. 148-150, 1989.

Vosniadou, S. and Ortony, A. Similarity and Analogical Reasoning. ISBN 0-521-38935-6, Cambridge University Press, 1989.

Ward, P. How to Integrate Object-Orientation with Structured Analysis and Design, IEEE Software 6, March 1989.

Wasserman, A.I., Pircher, P.A. and Muller, R.J. The Object-Oriented Structured Design Notation for Software Design Representation, IEEE Computer 23, 3, pp. 50-63, March 1990.

Wegner, P. and Zdonik, S.B. Inheritance as an Incremental Modification Mechanism or What Like Is and Isn't Like (ECOOP'88, August 1988), pp. 55-77, ISBN 3-540-50053- 7, Springer-Verlag, 1988.

Weinand, A., Gamma, E. and Marty, R. ET+ + – An Object-oriented Application Framework in C +. SIGPLAN Notices 23, 11, pp. 168-182, November 1988.

Winograd, T. and Flores, F. Understanding Computers and Cognition: A New Foundation for Design, ISBN 0-89391-050-3, Ablex Publishing Corporation, New Jersey, 1986.

Wirfs-Brock, R. and Wilkerson, B. Object-Oriented Design: A Responsibility-driven Approach, SIGPLAN Notices 24, 10, pp. 71-75, October 1989.

Part Four

Reverse Engineering and Re-engineering

10 Reverse engineering – hype, hope or here?

A. Frazer

The Institute of Software Engineering

10.1 INTRODUCTION

Five years ago, any discussion on reverse engineering within the computing industry would have centred around the analysis and duplication of a hardware system. In fact, the generally accepted definition of reverse engineering was 'the process of developing a set of specifications for a complex hardware system by an orderly examination of specimens of that system'.

Raise the subject of reverse engineering today, especially amongst software engineering practitioners or CASE vendors, and hardware component analysis or chip design will not even be considered. Reverse engineering of software systems is in vogue. Interest has been growing rapidly over the last eighteen months and concrete evidence of the viability of software reverse engineering has started to appear. Of 480 research papers and computing articles relating to or mentioning reverse engineering published during 1990, over 300 have been concerned with software reverse engineering.

Major seminars or conferences have been taking place at the rate of one every eight weeks in the UK alone, and users are starting to come forward and testify to actual benefits obtained.

Of course, healthy argument still persists, with protagonists and antagonists arguing over even what is theoretically possible or impossible. What is undeniable is that many users see themselves entangled in an ever increasing maintenance workload and are desperately seeking assistance from a new breed of CASE tool. Equally undeniable is the fact that the number of products claiming reverse engineering capabilities is increasing rapidly.

The reverse engineering bandwagon has been gathering speed for some time and now has sufficient momentum to ensure its relevance for years to come. It seems likely that, in the long term, many of the concepts now emerging from reverse engineering tool vendors will prove as important to software developers as current information engineering ideas.

Although we seem to be past the stage of excessive marketing hype (it passed more quickly this time than with many other new ideas or products, perhaps since the target market was that of the experienced software development professional), a legacy of confusion remains.

What is reverse engineering? Why is there so much interest in it? What can it achieve now and what is the best way to approach it?

These are amongst the questions which this paper seeks to answer.

Note: The technology under consideration in this paper lies entirely within the domain of software reverse engineering. Reverse engineering of hardware is not discussed. In addition, although reversal from object code to source code is possible, the main thrust both of this paper, and of the CASE tool vendors, is directed at reversal from human readable inputs (e.g. source code, database schemas, etc.) to higher levels of abstraction.

10.2 WHAT IS REVERSE ENGINEERING?

10.2.1 Software Development Lifecycle and Deliverables

Before considering the 'Re' terms it is important to establish a background frame of reference against which we can position or compare our 'new' definitions. The obvious candidate for this will be our present understanding of the software development lifecycle model, be it the traditional waterfall, the Boehm spiral or some other less well-known form. While we expect there to be iteration within the stages of the lifecycle and perhaps recursion, the general directed graph nature of all these representations will let us define forward (downward) and backward (upward) activities.

For our purposes and in the interests of representational simplicity, we shall choose the waterfall lifecycle model shown in Fig. 10.1.

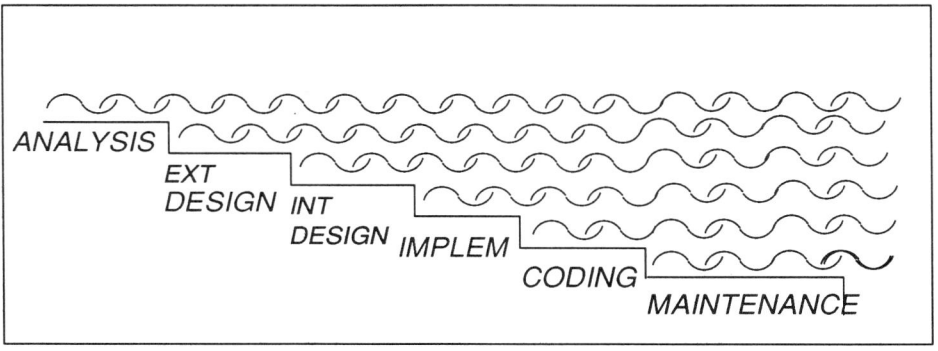

Fig. 10.1 The waterfall model of software development.

It is also important at this point for us to be able to identify the deliverables produced at each succeeding stage. The availability of these deliverables will serve to identify the stage under consideration at any one time. A sample list of deliverables, by no means exhaustive but sufficient for our purposes, is given in Fig. 10.2.

10.2.2 Terminology

Although reverse engineering is emerging as a major link in the software lifecycle, its growth has, in common with most new technologies, been hampered by confusion over terminology.

However, whilst a variety of process descriptions and definitions, or meanings, is to be expected at this stage, a consensus appears to have been reached on some of the central terms.

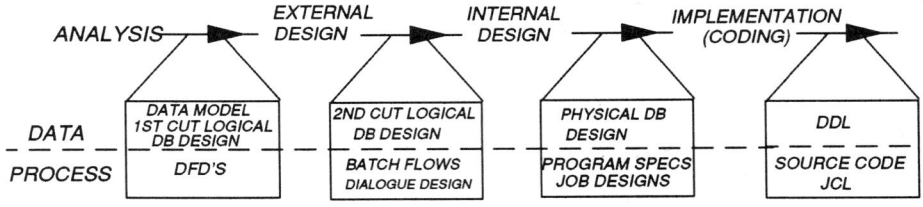

Fig. 10.2 Sample lifecycle stage deliverables.

Forward Engineering: is the traditional process of moving from a high level of the development model to a lower level with the production of the associated deliverables. Until recently the simple phrase 'software development' was sufficient to cover most needs, however it has become necessary to introduce forward engineering to distinguish the forward or downward activities from those performed during reverse engineering. Until the advent of reverse engineering, the lifecycle model was in theory only ever traversed in one direction.

It should be noted that in the process of moving from a higher to a lower level, whilst there is an increase in the amount of detail obtained, there is of necessity, always some loss of 'meaning' (Fig. 10.3).

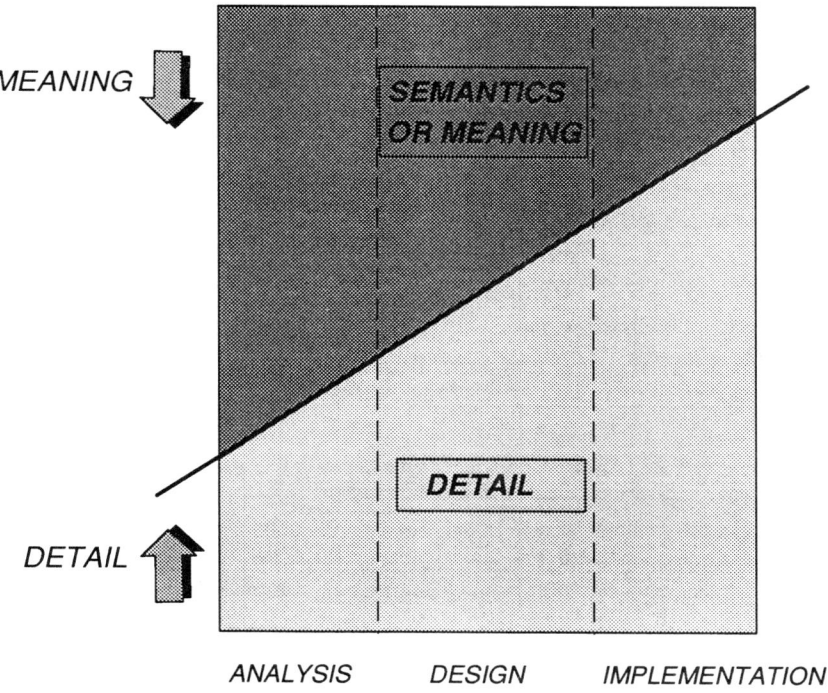

Fig. 10.3 Loss of meaning across lifecycle stages.

Reverse Engineering: can be defined as the process of analysing a subject system to:

- identify the system's components and their interrelationships;

- create representations of the system at a higher level of abstraction.

[Chikofsky/Cross 1990]

Alternatively: 'Reverse Engineering is a process to support the analysis and understanding of data and processing in existing computerized systems' [LBMS]. 'It aims to extract the contents, structure, and flow of data and processes contained within existing software systems in a form amenable to enquiry, analysis and documentation' [Jones 1988].

Reverse engineering involves the extraction of design elements from an existing system. It does not involve modifying the target system or generating new systems.

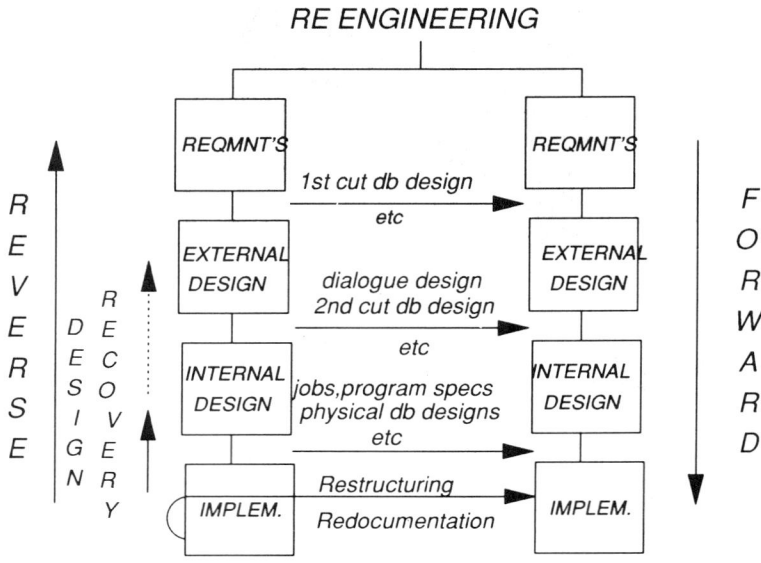

Fig. 10.4   Reverse engineering and related processes.

Redocumentation: is the production of a semantically equivalent representation (often paper-based) of the target system at whatever level of abstraction is being addressed. Typically documentation tools are used on existing source code to produce dataflow diagrams, data models, structure charts or text-based process definitions. Interestingly enough, many documentation tools perform tasks of a similar nature to reverse engineering tools, although they fall short of storing the results in a form amenable to further analysis, reporting or manipulation.

Design Recovery: is the process whereby an approximation of the design of a target system is achieved. It recreates design abstractions from a combination of all known current system information. (i.e. source code, documentation, analyst 'head knowledge', etc.). It attempts to produce the design elements which could reasonably be expected to have been produced as deliverables during the forward engineering process.

Restructuring: is often performed as a precursor to reverse engineering, although it can also be beneficial in its own right. It is the transformation from one representation of a system into another without altering the system meaning or functionality. Most commonly it is applied to source code in order to make it conform better to structured programming principles. This often involves physically moving blocks of code round in the program in an effort to remove 'goto' statements.

Re-engineering: is the process of reverse engineering a subject system to a chosen level of abstraction and then reconstituting the system by means of forward engineering. Very often it also involves introducing modifications to the system functionality prior to forward engineering.

Re-systemization: is the term used by at least one vendor to describe the process of reverse engineering a system, removing the environment specific design and implementation restrictions and then forward engineering it under a new environment without altering the functionality.

10.2.3   Objectives of Reverse Engineering

Reverse engineering is not, of course, an end in itself. Its primary purposes are to provide an aid for comprehension and a basis for maintenance or future redevelopment. Incorporated in these are the following goals or objectives (Fig. 10.5).

- To Facilitate Reuse.

- To Provide Missing or Alternative Documentation.

- To Recover Lost Information.

- To Assist with Maintenance.

- To Migrate from one Hardware or Software Platform to Another.

- To Bring the System under the Control of a CASE Environment.

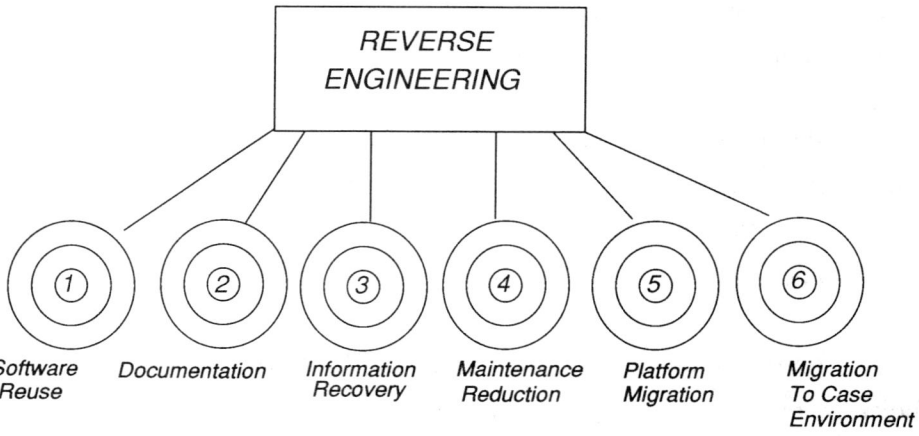

Fig. 10.5 Reverse engineering objectives.

Typically, systems seen as suitable candidates for reverse engineering exhibit one or more of the following characteristics:

- Design specifications are missing or incomplete;

- The code is poorly structured;

- The system requires excessive corrective maintenance;

- The documentation is out of date;

- Some modules have become overly complex;

- Migration to a new generation of hardware is required;

- Migration to a new software platform is required;

- Hard coded parameters are subject to change.

10.2.4 Benefits

The most obvious benefits sought are in terms of maintenance cost savings. However, although less tangible and harder to justify, gains can be achieved in other areas. A reverse engineering project would be expected to deliver benefits in one or more of the following areas:

- Maintenance cost savings;

- Quality improvement;

- Competitive advantage;

- Staff morale.

10.3   WHY IS THERE SO MUCH INTEREST IN REVERSE ENGINEERING?

The rapid growth in importance of reverse engineering has been fuelled by a number of factors, some of which are related to opportunity while others are related to necessity.   Of primary importance is the ever-increasing maintenance overhead experienced by many users, but also of significance is the general growth of the CASE market, current and projected staff shortages and the opportunities presented by re-engineering or re-systemization.

10.3.1   The maintenance crisis

Maintenance has traditionally been seen as the poor relation to the 'more creative' activity of software development.   Management has tended to view it as a mundane task and a 'necessary evil' and often the most junior programmers have been assigned maintenance as their first task.   However, with the spotlight now on the maintenance activity, attitudes are beginning to change.   There has been recognition that maintenance is not just 'bug fixing', but rather a complex amalgamation of activities often having much in common with development.   A number of different maintenance types have been recognised as follows (Fig. 10.6).

1.   Corrective maintenance is concerned with correcting errors discovered in the live system.

2.   Adaptive maintenance is concerned with making the software to adapt it to environmental changes such as new hardware or system software.

3.   Perfective maintenance involves improving the software by responding to user-defined changes and enhancing it by increasing its functionality.

4.   Preventative maintenance involves the updating of software to forestall future problems and accounts on average for 5% of the maintenance activity.

Each of the above involves interrogating existing code and documentation to ascertain process logic and structure.

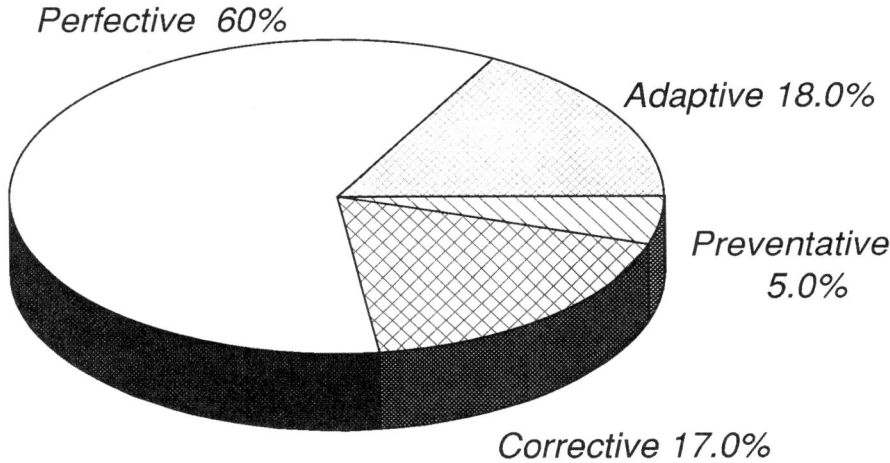

Fig. 10.6   Types of maintenance.
(Source: Centre for Software Maintenance, Durham.)

(a)   What activities does a maintenance task involve?

A programmer embarking on a maintenance activity will typically carry out a number of discrete tasks. First the change will be planned. Then time will be spent trying to understand what is already there. Having gained a clear understanding of the existing code, the change will be made, documented and finally tested. The IBM GUIDE Study on Maintenance gives the following breakdown of the time spent on each activity (Fig. 10.7).

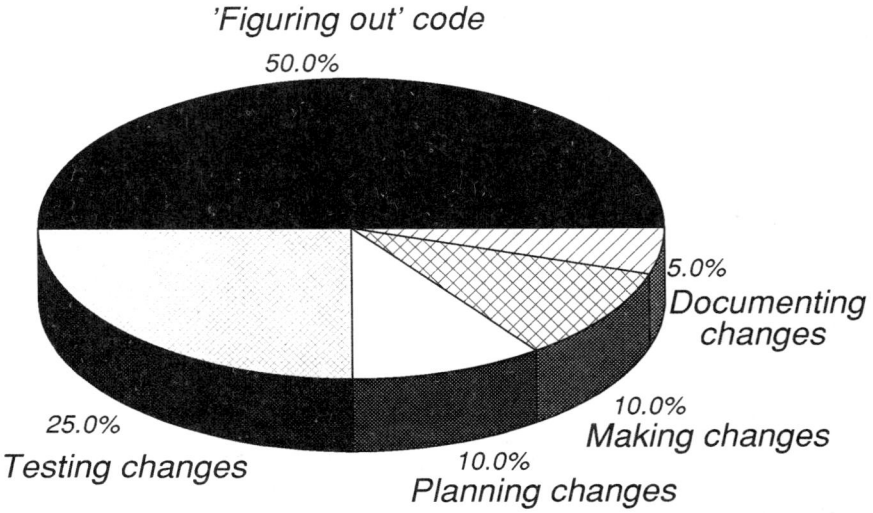

Fig. 10.7 Percentage time spent on each maintenance activity.
(Source: IBM: Guide Study on Maintenance.)

(b)   Magnitude of the maintenance overhead

Most conventional software development lifecycle models, such as the waterfall model, represent maintenance as a final stage appearing after testing almost as an afterthought and give no indication to its importance in terms of effort required. However, figures quoted by the Grindley Report from the Institute of Data Processing Management in 1986, indicate that rather than an insignificant activity, maintenance is the dominant activity of the lifecycle (Fig. 10.8).

These figures are, not surprisingly, reflected in the many surveys and reports recording maintenance as an overall percentage of the IS activity and in the attention-grabbing statistics and quotations appearing in many computing publications. Durham University's Centre for Software Maintenance reports that the UK spends £1 billion per year on software maintenance, while in the States, the Federal Government alone is estimated to spend $3.75 billion on maintenance annually: 23% of its total IT budget (Ref: Quality Assurance Institute).

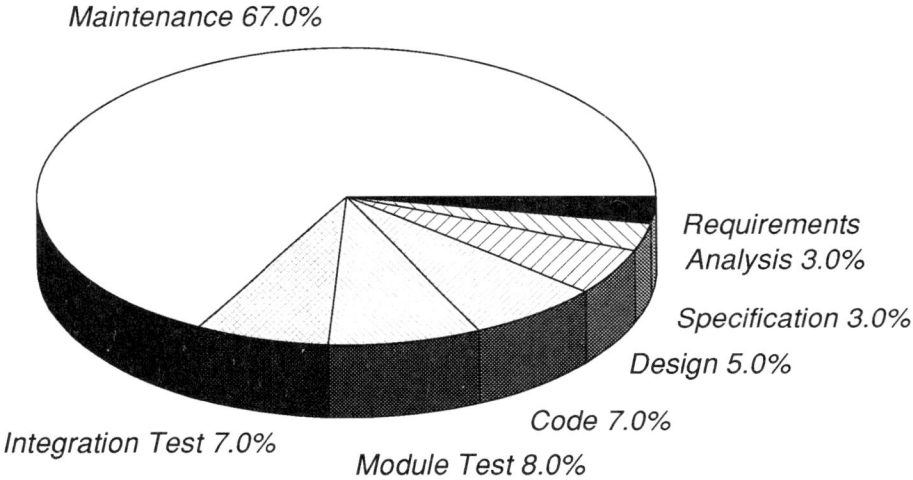

Maintenance 67.0%

Requirements Analysis 3.0%

Specification 3.0%

Design 5.0%

Code 7.0%

Module Test 8.0%

Integration Test 7.0%

Fig. 10.8 Lifecycle cost distribution.
(Source: The Grindley Report, The Institute of Data Processing Management, 1986.)

A report produced by the Gartner Group in 1987 projected that maintenance as a percentage of IS budget would rise from 80% in 1987 to a staggering 95% in 1995 (Fig. 10.9), and although the current figures in the UK are much lower (an average UK figure of 32%-44% is indicated by a recent survey conducted by Ovum), a similar maintenance growth rate is anticipated. Obviously anything that can retard this growth rate or promote greater productivity in the maintenance task will be welcomed with open arms by hard pressed IS managers. The potential of reverse engineering to assist in these areas is reflected by the intense interest currently shown by the maintenance community.

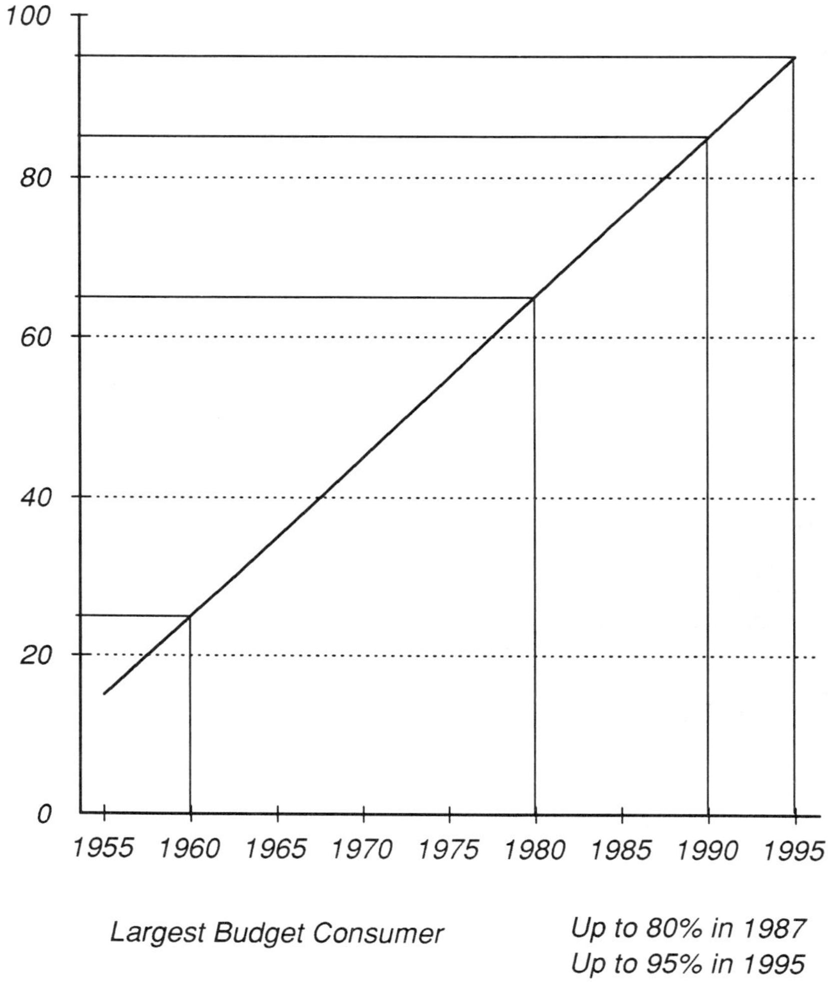
100
80
60
40
20
0
1955 1960 1965 1970 1975 1980 1985 1990 1995
Largest Budget Consumer
Up to 80% in 1987
Up to 95% in 1995

Fig. 10.9 Maintenance as a percentage of IS budget.
(Source: Gartner Group Report, 1987.)

10.3.2 The Skills Shortage

Accompanying the increase in demand for maintenance staff is the growing skill shortage. The current situation is illustrated by the results of a Computer Weekly/ NCC survey published in December 1989 indicating skill shortages in all areas. Shortages are expected to become more acute in the future with a study by Data Logic concluding that there will be a shortfall in software maintenance staffing levels over the next ten years due to the falling European birth rate and a corresponding reduction in numbers of school leavers. The study anticipated a resulting 'dramatic deterioration' in service levels.

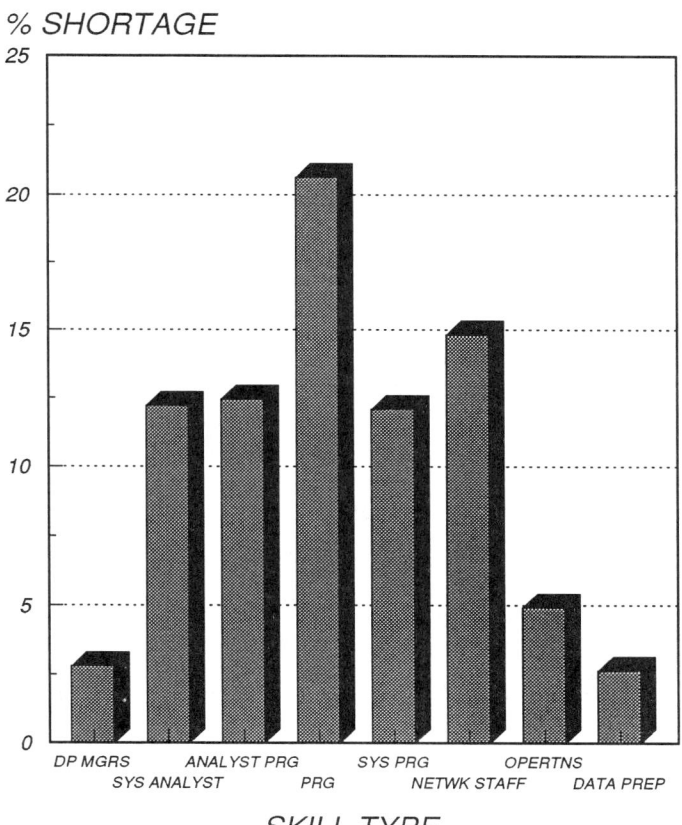

Fig. 10.10   Current shortage of staff by skill area.
(Source: Computer Weekly/NCC Salary Survey, December 1989.)

10.3.3   Opportunities for Users, Software Houses and Consultants

Given the well-documented maintenance crisis, skill shortage and ever-changing hardware and software environment, it is obvious that the software industry is facing greater challenges today than ever before. Reverse engineering is emerging as one of the most significant developments in the short history of software engineering and the opportunities are immense for those able to provide genuine solutions for very real problems. Dividing the software engineering community into end users and consultants or software houses, the following opportunities can be identified:

(a) End users

1.   Productivity Increase – one of the central objectives of reverse engineering is to reduce the maintenance overhead on existing systems. Given that maintenance – in all its forms – is a necessary and important part of a product's lifecycle, the aim must be not to minimize it (with the exception of corrective maintenance), but to make maintenance staff more efficient, thereby increasing maintenance productivity and releasing additional resources for new development.

2.   Product Life Extension – very often the decision to scrap a system and redevelop it will be taken because it is no longer viable to maintain it. Possibly the system has been amended so often that the initial task of understanding the design from the code is just too difficult. Reverse engineering the system will prolong its life by providing design documentation to aid comprehension, by bringing it under better control and by highlighting selective areas for redevelopment.

3.   Quality Improvements – although quality is difficult to define, reverse engineering or re-engineering a system will ensure that its construction adheres to structured techniques and exactly reflects the design documentation. The system will be brought under methodology control and quality should be more easily maintained. Corrective maintenance tasks should be fewer and more easily performed and, overall, a better quality product should result.

4. Platform Migration – business considerations will often dictate the need for a system to be transferred to a new hardware or software platform. Reverse engineering followed by forward engineering will facilitate this transfer, while also permitting design enhancements to take advantage of any new hardware or software features introduced.

5. Staff Morale/Turnover – with the shortage of skilled staff, morale can be an important consideration within a large IS department. The introduction of reverse engineering with its associated tools and techniques and in association with the embracing of a full lifecycle methodology, will help transform maintenance from a 'black art' into an engineering discipline. Although there may be initial resistance, ultimately the maintainer's professional status will be enhanced along with job satisfaction and thus morale.

(b) Software houses/consultants

1. Third Party Maintenance – a number of software houses already offer third-party maintenance services and with the trend towards facilities management, the demand for this type of service will increase. Obviously, a software house which can avail itself of reverse engineering tools and techniques to provide a more efficient service will be well placed in a competitive market. There should also be economies of scale here with the possibility of using selected tools on more than one project, although licensing arrangements will need to be carefully checked with the tool vendor.

2. Reverse Engineering Services – reverse engineering is a long way from being completely automated, and the success or failure of a project still depends to a large extent on human skills. Many users embarking on their first reverse engineering project will look to experienced consultants for advice and guidance in areas such as project management and training, or even for the provision of a complete turnkey solution.

3.   Package Enhancement/Conversion – software houses dependent for much of their income on sales of packaged software find there is a constant need to enhance their product to meet the latest competition. Package life can be divided into four stages: the development stage, with high costs and little or no income; the introductory stage, where costs can still outweigh income; the mature stage which is the real revenue generating stage and the old age stage where few sales are made because the product can no longer be enhanced due to original design limitations. Reverse engineering will offer the opportunity to extend the length of the mature stage by permitting enhancements to remain cost effective for longer than would otherwise be possible.

4.   Reverse Engineering Product Development – reverse engineering is a new technology with many products still in their infancy and offering limited functionality. Product trends or market leadership have not yet been established, but what is apparent is that the possibilities for automation far outstrip what is currently available, especially with respect to object orientation, expert systems and tool integration. Opportunities must exist for larger software houses and consultancies to develop and market their own reverse engineering toolsets.

5.   Application Blueprints – a recent development in the provision of software packages has been the trend towards application blueprints. With these, the vendor supplies the product in the form of design specifications which can be tailored by the user prior to forward engineering by means of an application generator. It should eventually be possible for a package vendor to produce a blueprint of an existing package by means of reverse engineering.

10.4 WHAT CAN BE ACHIEVED NOW?

10.4.1 Current Strengths and Weaknesses

As with any new technology, reverse engineering benefits from a number of strengths but also suffers from a number of weaknesses. It is likely that as the concepts of reverse engineering mature, so the capabilities of the associated products will increase and the weaknesses, apparent at present, will reduce or disappear. Nevertheless, the user considering embarking on a reverse engineering project should be aware of the present situation. The list given below is by no means exhaustive and is of necessity general in nature.

(a) Strengths

Apart from the pressing need for a solution to the maintenance crisis and skills shortage and the fact that many major consultants, CASE vendors and system suppliers have identified the area as worthy of substantial investment, the introduction of reverse engineering should have a positive impact on the following areas.

(b) Maintenance productivity

Significant benefits have already been experienced by a number of companies, mostly in the States, but more recently also in Europe.

(c) Repository

The use of reverse engineering in the maintenance of an 'old' system will force the adoption of a repository. This will become the IS department's own database, structured and organized in a logical way and accepting as input the deliverables from the reverse engineering or development processes. The availability of this repository for enquiry and update during future development and maintenance activity can only prove to be a strength.

(d)   Staff morale

Traditionally maintenance has been seen as a fairly dull activity with little creativity involved and has often been the responsibility of junior programmers. Often the maintenance team is the last to be given access to CASE tools or training in modern methods. However with the introduction of reverse engineering, maintenance staff will have greater exposure to CASE tools and should become more proficient in modern design techniques.

(e)   Market acceptance

Already many large users have shown considerable interest in existing products with pilot projects recently completed or currently underway in IS departments where the maintenance problem is felt most acutely. Amongst those most noticeably interested are banks, finance houses and insurance companies, but other notable projects have been run by such companies as Dupont, McDonnell Douglas and NASA. Even IBM have embarked on a collaborative research project using formal methods to reverse engineer CICS.

A recent survey by Ovum found that, of over one hundred respondents, one in eight already used some form of reverse engineering. Regarding market penetration, Ovum estimated, from information supplied by vendors, current sales of reverse engineering tools to be approximately $60m in the USA and $81m in Europe of which the UK accounted for only $6m. Ovum forecast a growth rate of 50% per annum fuelled both by a rapidly increasing supply of tools and an increasing user preoccupation with the maintenance issue.

10.4.2 Weaknesses

(a) Transient technology

When embarking on a reverse engineering project, decisions must be made as to which tools to include in the toolset. Some of these will be purely transition products which will have no further value to a company once they have performed their initial task. One example would be a code restructuring tool. However this would not always be the case as it is likely that reverse engineering toolsets would include repository management tools which would retain their value. In theory, having reverse engineered an application once to bring it into a more structured environment and under the future control of more structured development techniques, it should not be necessary to perform the exercise again. In the longer term, 10 to 15 years, some observers feel that the need for reverse engineering will have disappeared due to advances in forward engineering automation.

(b) Lack of integration

A major inhibiting factor in the rate of growth of the number of users embracing reverse engineering is the lack of integration of current tools and techniques. This is seen in a number of ways:

1. Current best practice when embarking on a reverse engineering project is to compile a portfolio of tools best suited to the specific requirements of the target system environment. Frequently the source code will require analysis and restructuring before being suitable for input to the tool performing reversal and populating the repository. It is often the case that the most suitable analysis tool will come from a different vendor to the chosen restructuring tool and that the reversal tool will come from yet another vendor.

2.   Weaknesses are also to be found in the level of integration of reverse engineering tools with existing CASE tools and the user could easily find that integration between his current strategic CASE products and his selected reverse engineering toolset is poor or non-existent.

3.   Few current development methodologies make allowances for the inclusion of design information obtained from the reverse engineering 'bottom-up' approach.   Most are based on the familiar top-down school of software engineering.   However, experience teaches that 'top-down' development can seldom be used exclusively and that very often existing systems must be taken into consideration.

Fortunately there is a school of thought emerging which promotes new and more complete methodologies which will encompass maintenance and hence reverse engineering in a new software engineering lifecycle. Eventually we should see users adopting full lifecycle methodologies with either integrated CASE toolsets or CASE tools with a much higher level of inter-operability.

In addition to the above, it should be remembered that a badly designed system cannot be re-engineered into a well designed one without significant analyst and designer input. In fact there will be instances where a system requires so much design alteration that to rewrite will be a better solution than to re-engineer. This is not necessarily a weakness or a strength, merely an observation.

10.5   WHAT TOOL SUPPORT IS AVAILABLE NOW?

10.5.1   Types of Tool

It is possible to break down existing and probably most future tools used in reverse engineering projects into four broad categories:

- Software Resource Analysers;

- Code Converters;

- Code Improvement Tools;

- Reverse Engineering Tools.

A sensible approach for anyone wishing to commit wholeheartedly to reverse engineering concepts – hoping ultimately to adopt a full lifecycle development methodology including reverse engineering for all projects – would be to start with the most basic forms of reverse engineering and successively embrace the techniques and tools leading to higher levels of abstraction.

It seems unlikely, for example, that it will ever be possible to abstract 'business logic' essence directly from spaghetti code. So, a prerequisite for reverse engineering – of process logic at least – is probably some form of code restructuring. By the same token, it would seem foolhardy to embark on a possibly expensive restructuring exercise without first using analysis tools to gain an insight into the quality or otherwise of an existing software resource.

At the moment many organizations embarking on a reverse engineering project will require to compile toolsets from a variety of vendors. Ultimately, however, it seems likely that all maintenance/reverse engineering functions may become available within integrated product sets.

(a) Software resource analysis tools

Documentation Tools – one of the major problems associated with the maintenance of existing software systems is the lack of documentation. Documentation tools aim to assist with the maintenance task by producing paper-based representations of the design of a program, job or file and often use reverse engineering techniques to do so. However, as the results are not stored in a repository for further manipulation, their use in a reverse engineering/re-engineering project is limited.

Static and Dynamic Analysis Tools – These tools are marketed on the basis that, before a programmer can actually alter program code, he or she must spend much time working out which code to alter.

Although the tools that fall into this category are technologically the simplest in reverse engineering terms, they are probably the most attractive to IS staff in the short term.

As the names suggest, static analysers assess code independently of input data or code execution while dynamic analysers perform their assessment by exercising the code.

(b) Code converters

These tools convert from one language to another, e.g. from Cobol to C, and can often be quite sophisticated, even emulating source support environments on the target platform. Their use in a reverse engineering context is to make more tools available. For example, there are few, if any, tools available to reverse engineer DEC Dibol, and so one approach would be to convert the Dibol system to Cobol and then reverse engineer it. However, code conversion, even with the best converters, is not a trivial exercise and in many cases a better approach will be to adapt a selected reverse engineering tool by commissioning a new 'front end' parser.

(c) Code improvement tools

Restructurers – the theory underlying the use of code restructuring tools is fairly straightforward: structured code is good; unstructured code is bad. Given estimates that 60% of Europe's programs are unstructured monoliths, there ought to be a large market for restructuring tools.

The claimed benefits of restructuring are illustrated in an example provided by Language Technology, and illustrated below (Fig. 10.11). It compares the cost of adding 3000 lines of new code to an unstructured system of 50,000 lines with that of adding the same number of lines to the same size structured system.

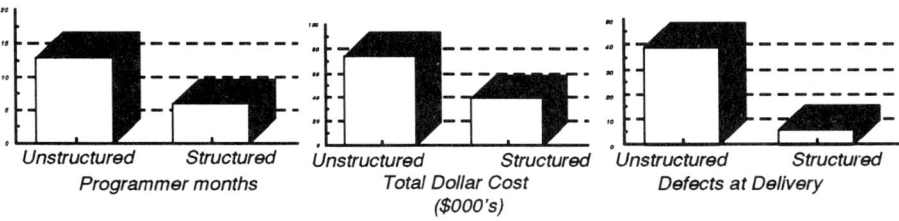

Fig. 10.11 Effect of the availability of structured code during a major enhancement project.
(Source: Language Technology.)

Reformatters – do not strictly improve the code, however they do improve the code layout, primarily by using indentation to ease reading and hence facilitate comprehension. If reverse engineering tools are available for a particular environment, a reformatter will provide no additional benefit.

Debuggers – allow the internal behaviour of a program to be investigated, typically by offering trace facilities and permitting insertion of break points for interactive evaluation and improvement of the code. Some debuggers will also provide guidance on how the code should be improved.

Data Standardisers – provide the capability of searching data definitions in source code to ensure that in-house naming conventions are adhered to. Once again these tools will provide no additional benefit if reverse engineering tools are to be used, since standardization will be simpler at design level using a populated repository than at code level.

(d) True reverse engineering tools

These tools reverse code and/or data by one or more levels of abstraction, populating a repository with the resulting design artefacts and their relationships. Available tools vary in what they attempt to abstract, their level of automation (and hence the anticipated level of user intervention) and the richness of the repository which they use. There are currently more than forty tools operating over a wide range of hardware and software platforms which fall into this category.

10.5.2 Hardware and Software Platforms Covered

As mentioned above, there are at present more than forty products on the market performing a reverse engineering function, and a great many more which aid the process by restructuring, re-documenting or analysing source code.

The hardware platform best covered is the IBM mainframe range for obvious reasons, with DEC and Hewlett-Packard also well provided for. Other hardware platforms covered include Bull, CDC, DG, ICL, Tandem and Unisys.

The language targeted by the greatest number of products is Cobol, again for obvious reasons, with products also available for Fortran, Pascal, C, Ada, Basic and a host of minor languages.

A summary of the most common environments supported is given in Fig. 10.12. It should be noted that this table is not exhaustive and also that coverage is being steadily increased, with suppliers often enhancing the collection capabilities of their tools to meet a user's specific environmental requirements. One area worthy of special note is support for reversal of 4GLs such as Ingres and Oracle. Presently this is only provided by DEFT from Deft Inc. in Canada, but it is an area in which additional activity can be expected in the future.

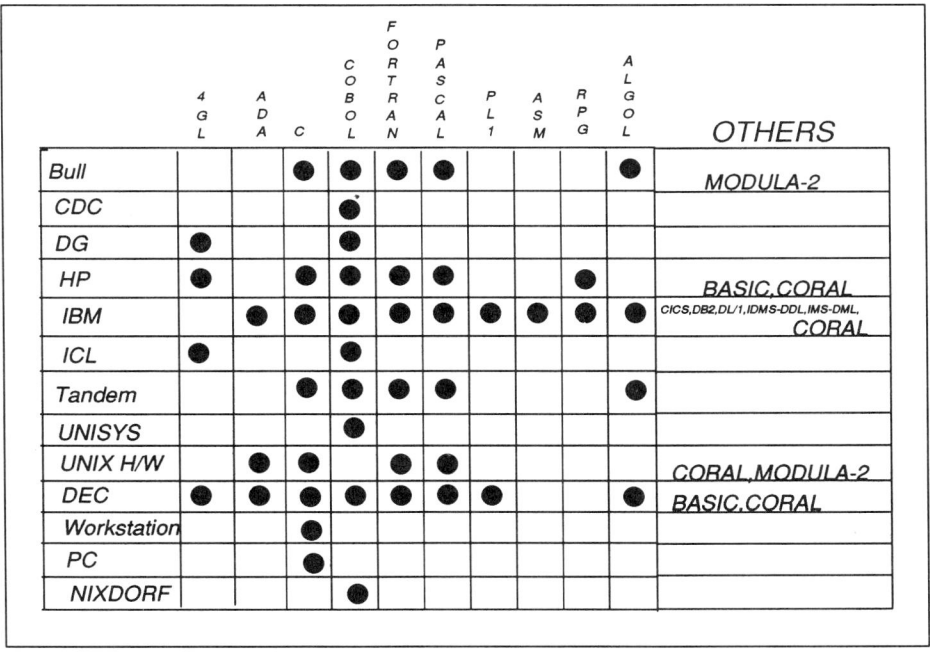

	4GL	ADA	C	COBOL	FORTRAN	PASCAL	PL1	ASM	RPG	ALGOL	OTHERS
Bull				●	●	●				●	MODULA-2
CDC				●							
DG	●			●							
HP	●		●	●	●	●			●		BASIC,CORAL
IBM		●	●	●	●	●	●	●	●	●	CICS,DB2,DL/1,IDMS-DDL,IMS-DML, CORAL
ICL	●			●							
Tandem			●	●	●	●				●	
UNISYS				●							
UNIX H/W		●	●		●	●					CORAL,MODULA-2
DEC	●	●	●	●	●	●	●			●	BASIC,CORAL
Workstation			●								
PC			●								
NIXDORF				●							

Fig. 10.12   Environments supported by reverse engineering tools.

10.6 MAKING A START

10.6.1 Selecting a Suitable System for Reverse Engineering

Before embarking on a reverse engineering project, the candidate system environment and the availability of automated support should be carefully considered. Reverse engineering techniques can be applied to all systems, but in some cases they will not be cost effective or, indeed, even the best approach. Listed below are some questions worthy of consideration.

1.   **Are reverse engineering tools available for the environment?** Manual reverse engineering is possible and has been part of the maintenance activity (without populating a repository) for as long as maintenance has been performed. However, without the aid of automated tools the effort required to reverse engineer an existing system is likely to be similar to that required for developing a new one. If no tools are available but reverse or re-engineering is mandatory then conversion of the system into a supported environment could be undertaken. However, conversion in itself is a major exercise and introduces an additional level of complexity. A better approach might be to commission the tailoring of an existing tool to the required environment.

2.   **Is the code well structured?** For reverse engineering tools to abstract any useful design from the code they will expect that there has been a design in the first place, that the design is implicit in the code and that it has been implemented in a structured manner. It will be very difficult to obtain any useful design documentation from spaghetti code. If the code is poorly structured it will be necessary to use a restructuring tool on it. Often code analysis tools will also have to be used to identify 'good' and 'bad' code. Analysis and restructuring will of course involve additional expense for the project.

3. **Are structured techniques and CASE tools already in use for development projects and do staff clearly understand forward engineering techniques?** For the maximum benefit to be gained from a reverse engineering project, the target system must be brought under the control of a development methodology and subject to strict configuration management techniques. If this is not done the system will very quickly revert to its original state and design documentation will once again become outdated.

4. **Is the underlying business logic very dynamic?** The best candidate systems for reverse engineering are those in which the core requirements are stable, for these will have a high degree of reuse. Systems in which the underlying business logic changes frequently may well be at the limits imposed by their original design, in which case to redesign will be a better option than to reverse engineer.

5. **Is the system critical to the enterprise's operation?** If so and reverse engineering is required (for example to alleviate the maintenance burden), a sensible approach would be to identify the programs which would benefit most from reverse engineering (and then forward engineering) and to target these. The 80/20 rule, where 80% of the benefit is likely to accrue from reverse engineering 20% of the system, will often apply.

6. **Are the original analysts/designers/programmers still in the organization?** Given the current state of the art in reverse engineering tools, a considerable amount of staff input will be required, whichever tools are chosen. Thus the more staff expertise available for the project, the greater will be the degree of success. The staff members will eventually move on, so it will be better to 'capture' their design expertise now, than try to recreate it later.

7.   **How many languages does the system encompass?** Frequently a system will be comprised of three or more different languages. Perhaps the system will have been written in Cobol, with assembler subroutines and large numbers of JCL statements. Some tools will cope with this scenario but obviously the fewer languages involved, the simpler will be the exercise.

8.   **To what extent does the system interface with other systems?** If reverse engineering is a precursor to forward engineering, considerable care will have to be exercised to maintain the integrity of these interfaces. Even if no change to the code is anticipated, it will be difficult to abstract interface design information from one side of the interface and considerable manual intervention will be required.

9.   **To what extent are 'in-house' subroutines used?** If standard subroutines are used across a range of systems then it is likely that they will contain data and/or processes surplus to the requirements of any one system and manual intervention will be required to identify redundant code. The more numerous and complex the in-house subroutines, the greater will be the requirement for manual intervention.

10.   **How will the introduction of reverse engineering impact on working practices?** Introduction of new tools and techniques will involve widespread changes in the way maintenance staff work. The roles of developer and maintainer will merge to a certain extent, as will the roles of analyst/designer and programmer. Will staff readily accept new working practices or will there be resistance?

10.6.2 Selecting the Right Tools

Before setting out to identify which tool, or tools, to use for a particular project, it is important, as with any project, to identify the overall and intermediate objectives. Obviously the requirements will be different if a complete re-engineering exercise is planned than if selective program reverse engineering to assist with maintenance is planned. A reverse engineering methodology should be established and final and intermediate deliverables identified. It can be stated categorically that the wrong way to embark on a reverse engineering project is to see an impressive tool, buy it and then look for a way to use it.

For the purposes of this section we will assume that a re-engineering project is planned and that we wish to analyse an existing system, improve it where necessary, reverse engineer it, enhance the design, and finally forward engineer it into a new implementation.

Given this scenario, it would be necessary to compile a portfolio of tools for the project.

The following questions concentrate on what to ask a reverse engineering tool vendor, but most will be equally valid when considering other tools in the toolset.

1. Language Coverage – will the tool support the required languages and language variants? A tool that will support ICL Cobol will not necessarily provide support for Tandem Cobol.

2. Techniques Supported – will the tool support those design techniques currently used by the existing development methodology? Which types of design deliverables are supported.

3. Repository Support – what type of repository does the tool use and how rich is its meta data layer? A repository that is a simple data dictionary will not offer the versatility of a more sophisticated one such as the 'Object-Property-Role-Relationship' type and so the processes which can be performed on it will be more limited. Also important is whether or not the repository will be available to existing CASE tools.

4.   Environment – what environment will the tool run on?   Many reverse engineering tools (and CASE tools in general) now run on PCs or workstations, but others still require a mini or mainframe environment. Additional hardware costs, if any, will have to be assessed.

5.   Vendor Support – what level of support, training and consultancy services are available, how much is recommended and how much does it cost?   As with most first-time projects good solid experience is worth paying for.

6.   Tailoring – can the tool be tailored either by the user or by the vendor? Many sites will have developed their own idiosyncrasies over the years and it is not uncommon over a period of time for programmers to use shortcuts in their code, perhaps not adhering strictly to a language's syntax but realizing that certain variations will be allowed by a compiler. It is sometimes the case that the parsing section of a tool will require amendment to cope with these aberrations.

7.   Reference Sites – can visits to suitable reference sites be arranged?

8.   Type and Level of Abstraction – what level of support is provided for reversing each lifecycle stage?   Most tools provide automated support only for reversal from code to internal design, and in many cases this will be sufficient. Others provide assistance with higher levels of abstraction.

9.   Integration – how well does the tool integrate with other products, either from the same vendor or from other vendors? If a re-engineering project is being considered, are there forward engineering CASE tools to operate on the objects stored in the repository by the reverse engineering tool, and is automated code generation from these forward engineering tools a possibility?

10. Industry Standards – what is the vendor's position with respect to de jure and de facto standards – repository, networking, user interface etc.? Although somewhat of a minefield, standards will become increasingly significant and it is important that the vendor should reflect or complement your own strategy.

10.6.3 Points to Remember

(a) Garbage in, garbage out

If the quality of input is poor then automated reverse engineering will not improve it. If the input system substantially fails to meet user requirements then to re-design and rewrite will be a better option than to re-engineer.

(b) Total automation is not possible

It is impossible for a tool to capture all the information required for completely automated reversal. Information loss cannot be avoided during development and so will have to be restored manually. Lower stages of the development lifecycle provide greater detail but lose 'why' information.

(c) Beware of reverse engineering into a 'black hole' or cul-de-sac

It is important to have a clear development/maintenance strategy before reverse engineering. Beware of a 'I wonder if this report would be useful' approach.

(d) Staff training and motivation is essential

A new way of working is being introduced and there may be initial resistance from the old timers before the benefits become apparent. Try to win over the 'technical opinion leader' among the staff and the rest should follow.

(e) Large systems include, on average, three different languages (e.g. Cobol, Assembler, JCL), and many installations have non-standard language variants

How will selected tools handle this?

(f) Data conversion may be required

If re-engineering is required then user application data may need to be transformed from the old file structures to the new ones and significant effort may be involved. Care should be taken where the integrity of the file structures have been improved as existing good data may be rendered invalid.

10.7 CONCLUSIONS

Reverse engineering is not a new process, as any maintenance programmer will confirm. What is new is the attempt to automate it. With the maintenance crisis, reverse engineering addresses a problem which must be solved if the industry is to develop further, and as such is worthy of the considerable attention focused on it.

Considering the possible benefits, it seems to me in addressing the question posed by the title of this paper, that there is a singular lack of hype surrounding reverse engineering in comparison to many other technologies, that the hope expressed by many of its advocates is well founded and that the tools to make a positive impact are available here and now.

REFERENCES

Chikofsky, E.J., and Cross, J.H., Reverse Engineering and Design Recovery: A Taxonomy, IEEE Software, Jan. 1990.

Jones, R., Business Software Review, Jan./Feb. 1988.

FURTHER READING

Bush, E., Reverse Engineering. Proc. of Fourth Software Maintenance Workshop, Sept. 1990, Centre for Software Maintenance Ltd., University of Durham.

Calow, H., Adding a Reverse Engineering Flavour to Today's Methodologies. Proc. of From Software Maintenance Towards Reverse Engineering and Beyond, June 1990, Blenheim Online Ltd.

Munro, M., The Software Maintenance Context. Proc. of From Software Maintenance Towards Reverse Engineering and Beyond, June 1990, Blenheim Online Ltd.

Rock-Evans, R. and Hales, K. (1990), Reverse Engineering: Markets, Methods and Tools, Ovum Ltd., London.

Samuelson, P., Reverse Engineering Someone Else's Software: Is It Legal?, IEEE Software, Jan. 1990.

Sneed, H., Software Renewal – A Case Study, IEEE Software, July 1984.

Sneed, H., The Economics of Re-engineering. Proc. of Fourth Software Maintenance Workshop, Sept. 1990, Centre for Software Maintenance Ltd., University of Durham.

Walston/Felix, A Method of Programming, Measurement and Estimation, IBM Systems Journal, Vol. 17, No. 1, 1977.

11 Reverse engineering – not yet?

R. McGill

ADPAC Software Limited

'Reverse Engineering – Not Yet?' seems an odd title for a presentation at a reverse engineering seminar, however I believe that it is vital to consider this question before jumping into new techniques. Too often in the past has the data processing industry jumped on the bandwagon of an attractive-sounding concept before it was ready to implement it. The resulting failures are well known. Before we consider when to implement reverse engineering we must be sure of what it means and whether it is a good idea at all.

In essence reverse engineering is the process of extracting the fundamental design and structure of a system out of the already written code. This information must be available in a form which allows the redevelopment of the system thus utilizing the new technologies and advancements. Should we consider reverse engineering or should we start again from scratch?

Increasingly organisations are realizing the sense of this approach to development. Over the years companies have made terrific investments in systems development and in some cases one could say that the business *is* the computer systems. It makes no sense to throw this investment away especially when one realizes that the underlying data requirements of the organization remain static over long periods. While changes do and must occur the vast majority of the base data is already adequately described. Furthermore any new development areas have to interface to the existing systems so unless we know and can use the information about how our systems are put together, how will we be able to efficiently build interfaces to ensure the smooth integration of our computer systems?

Having decided to look at our existing code as a corporate data resource itself what are the difficulties associated with reverse engineering today?

(a)   Volume of Code. Computer systems have been developed over many years and there is a huge code base needing analysis by some method.

(b)   Lack of Expertise/Knowledge. Staff may have moved on and there are often few people with in-depth knowledge of how the systems are put together. Indeed in some cases the code appears to have been written to avoid understanding!

(c)   Inconsistent Standards. Over the last 10 to 15 years many different bandwagons have appeared: modular programming; flowcharting; e.g. structured programming; information engineering etc. Few sites are in the lucky position where all their systems correspond to one set of standards.

(d)   Little or no Documentation. Normally caused by the pressures on data processing departments to produce immediate results, system documentation is at best out of date – in many cases non-existent.

(e)   Systems not Streamlined. As systems have developed over the years, new areas have been bolted on, but due to the lack of understanding of the existing code, these add-ons have often introduced redundancy into the structures.

In summary, then the existing systems can often be described as poor quality. They may work correctly but the burden of maintenance is high.

There are three alternative approaches we can take towards reverse engineering. We can manually extract the information from our systems or utilize reverse engineering facilities today or improve the quality of our systems and then reverse engineer.

Manual analysis is clearly impractical. The mammoth task involved would rule this out alone even without the attendant dangers of incompleteness. Furthermore as we cannot stop the world we run the risk of never finishing the job at all.

If we attempt to use some black-boxed reverse engineering tool now we run into several problems. There are few tools available which address more than a small portion of the existing code and the poor quality of the existing systems means that the effort in redesigning these systems in order to avoid duplicating yesterday's problems becomes more than can be justified.

The only practical approach to moving forward is to firstly improve the quality of our existing systems. Once we have accomplished this task then the actual reverse engineering problem will reduce itself to a tiny proportion of today's problem regardless of the method chosen. In addition there are many other benefits today in improving our systems quality: maintenance will reduce due to smaller research phases; less experienced staff will become more productive; there will be more time to implement new techniques and the systems will be more flexible.

I am going to describe three practical cases where organizations have started to put in place quality procedures using PM/SS. It will be apparent that not only is the quality of their data processing improving but that their use of the product to understand the code allows them to contemplate genuine reverse engineering in their different environments.

11.1   IMPLEMENTING A DATA DICTIONARY

Norwich Union have made a strategic commitment to implement a Data Dictionary fully throughout their organization. This is fine in theory but, in practice, is extremely difficult to achieve. There are few, if any, companies who genuinely have a complete dictionary which is widely used.

The problems which arose are typical of most organizations. The effort necessary to manually load a dictionary with all the existing code far outweighs the resource allocated to the task. The burden is further compounded by the lack of consistent standards in naming and defining data over the years.

Typically, the actual development staff get little benefit from the dictionary until it is fully loaded and, further, see it as a burden upon themselves to provide the information.

Given the above difficulties it was clear to Norwich Union that they could not effectively implement their Dictionary without some automated assistance and consequently they bought in our product PM/SS. The product is used to take away all the manual research work and provide the information to the Dictionary staff which is necessary to rationalize the existing data structures. Once this exercise is carried out PM/SS is used to generate input to the Dictionary for the whole system. At the same time the rationalised names are re-applied to the source ensuring consistency with the Dictionary and upgrading the quality of the systems.

Even in new developments the same process is carried out so that any new system will go into production with standard datanames regardless of how they were initially coded. Use of automated tools like PM/SS thus allows the development teams to get the benefits of having an implemented data dictionary without putting an additional burden on their resources. In the worst case, Norwich Union have achieved a 10-to-1 improvement in loading all the information about a system to the Dictionary and in one particular case where the data was already rationalized managed to carry out an 11 man-year loading task within 1 man-month.

In the future, Norwich Union can look to having all their computer systems held on the Dictionary (regardless of whether they are IMS, DB2, FOCUS etc.) with consistent data and process naming conventions. Not only can they ensure complete coverage but they can enforce the standards they have laid down on datanames. This will put them in a position to utilize data-driven methods of system development in a truly practical way. Of course with consistency of naming across systems, their systems will become more easily understood thus reducing their general maintenance burden.

11.2 DOCUMENTING THE SYSTEMS

Barclays Bank are currently redeveloping their major Branch Accounting system and have realized the importance of defining a standard approach to documentation of their systems. Having defined their documentation needs they found, as most organizations do, that the development had been proceeding fast and that the newly developing system was not documented according to their standards. Given the size and complexity of the system they found that it was vital to be able to document this code in order to make enhancements manageable and to minimize the dependence on a handful of individuals with deeply specialized knowledge of the system.

Once again automation is seen as the key to achievement of the task. PM/SS was brought in to perform key documentation of the system and standard procedures have been developed to do this. The important features of the exercise have been in identifying all the component parts of a system (procedures, programs, called modules etc.) and then documenting groups of programs at a time. As well as documentation on the programs they also document file and database usage across the systems and prepare input to their data dictionary.

Obviously an automated toolset cannot supply all the documentation necessary for a system but current estimates say that 60% of the documentation can be produced automatically by PM/SS. Furthermore, the actual savings are greater than this, with the documentation being produced by clerical staff thus freeing up development resource.

The future benefits are clear to Barclays. The system-produced documentation can be automatically updated keeping it consistent with enhancements. Impact analysis will be quicker and more complete leading to faster and more accurate enhancements. Consequently the maintenance overheads will be reduced and staff will be more mobile between projects.

10.2   QUALITY MAINTENANCE

British Telecom International have a large development and support staff involved in their data processing operation and invest a high proportion of their budget in maintenance and enhancement activities. In keeping with most organisations, they are seeking ways to reduce the amount of resource tied up in these activities in order to provide a firm basis for developments utilizing the new technologies.

The problems to be addressed are fairly typical. There is a large volume of source code for which the documentation is poor or not up to date. Additionally they defined the need to enforce their standards and control the quality of code being written. PM/SS was considered as offering an integrated set of procedures that could be used to address all these issues.

The product is used to identify the impact of a change to a system and to assist in problem-solving tasks which normally have a high research content. By automatically documenting their systems, not only does the maintenance become easier but also the quality of the code improves as the benefits of adherence to standards are more visible. PM/SS is also used to monitor the quality of code being written, for example the programmer is provided with a skeleton program defining the structure to be developed, and at each walkthrough PM/SS is used to compare the structure of the code to the original design.

British Telecom estimates that they can save around 3 man-days per enhancement by automating the research phase and they will also achieve a more complete analysis. In the future they intend to have automatic quality assurance procedures providing more control in both the development and maintenance environments which will ensure a higher quality of system with less program crashes.

The examples given above, while showing different approaches to the problem of applying quality to existing code, allow us to draw some general principles.

A quality system should be one which does what it ought to, does only what it ought to, is understandable and is easy to change. Two key areas in achieving these principles are automatic creation of documentation and enforced standard data names.

Without quality procedures built in to our systems and methods, it is clear that it will be impossible to effectively utilize and integrate the major new areas of technology such as CASE, Application Generators, Methodologies. These will continue to be implemented on a piecemeal basis, not providing a true return on investment until a consistent set of procedures and methods are implemented throughout the organization.

Reverse engineering is a key part of tomorrow's developments. Only by utilizing the knowledge we already have about our business may we move fast enough to meet the challenges of tomorrow's business. Implementing reverse engineering requires quality systems. Quality systems in turn require an automated and enforced set of standards and methods. If we make the conscious effort today to build this environment then tomorrow we will be in a position to gain true competitive advantages from our computer systems.

12 From recursion extraction to automated commenting

A transformational approach towards reverse engineering of software to support reusability

C. Boldyreff and J. Zhang

Brunel University

12.1 INTRODUCTION

Searching for a satisfactory solution sometimes without any reassurance that a solution is possible presents a challenge in engineering a new system. Especially at the start of development, lacking a conceptual unity to the new system's form and content, we may take various wrong turnings. Throughout the development process, we continue to prune away possible solution paths until we reach the end-point of our development. We can contrast this with the process of examining an existing software system; and retrofitting what has been developed into more understandable forms. This process is called Software Reverse Engineering. In reverse engineering a software system, we do not attempt to recreate the history of the system's development, rather by examining the existing system, we attempt to establish its underlying theory and concepts. The principal artifact we have to examine is the system's source code; thus, a major task in Software Reverse Engineering is to develop or extract higher level description of a software system from its lower level source code description [RIC 88, SNE 89]. The higher level description of source code may be a collection of well-documented comments of source code units such as procedures and functions in Pascal [WIR 68, JEN 75], a collection of recursively defined procedures or first-order predicates in some very high level languages such as Lisp [McC 65, WIN 81] and Prolog [CLO 84, KOW 85] or a partition into high level modules of the source code [PAR 72]. Other very high level descriptions take the form of dataflow diagrams (DFDs), entity grid charts and structure charts (LDS), entity life history matrixes (ELH), logical dialogue outlines (LDO) for dialogue design, relational data analysis documents (RDA), composite logical data design documents (CLDD), and documents of process outlines, first cut data design, first cut program design and physical design control [for details, see MAR 85 and PRE 87].

Two main problems exist in extracting higher level descriptions from software systems' source code. Firstly, the higher the level of description you extract, the harder your work will be. For those very high levels of description listed above, it is even harder to envisage any automated solution to their extraction in the near future. Secondly, even if some higher level description extraction is possible, for example abstracting an algebra specification from source code, the naming of extracted components is problematic. Arbitrary naming will render any higher level specification useless simply because it will be unreadable. With these observations, we started our research at levels of description relatively close to the source code, and from the start, we have tackled the naming problem. For an independent discussion on the important role that names play in understanding source code, see Biggerstaff [BIG 89].

Although there has been substantial research in the areas of code restructuring [ARN 86], code analysis [HEN 83, CHE 86, AMB 88], design recovery [ARA 85, BIG 89], specification abstraction [PAR 86, RIC 88, WAR 88], etc., towards reverse engineering, less work has been done to enable automated documentation of source code [JAN 81, ANT 87, FOS 87].

12.2   AN OVERVIEW OF THE APPROACH

This paper describes a transformational approach to reverse engineering of software. Source code is first transformed into an equivalent recursive form that generalizes code segments into recursive procedures yielding a functional decomposition of the program. The user is responsible for naming and commenting each transformed procedure interactively. Each named code pattern is stored with its comments in a knowledge base to provide assistance with the naming and commenting process in future via intelligent pattern matching. Partial evaluation of user-provided comments can be further carried out to produce specific comments for each procedure call, thereby resulting in a final fully documented program. A semi-natural language specification of the program can be easily obtained by simply gathering together all comments associated with a particular code module. In general, the resulting program will be at a higher level of abstraction with much more modularized code segments, and will be more understandable for maintenance and reuse. No penalty for recursion need be paid at execution as the recursive form of the code is transformable back to a nonrecursive form.

Thus transformed and decomposed, the documented modules with their associated semi-natural language specifications are in a suitable form to be employed in the Practitioner project's canonical form of software concept descriptions – the Questionnaire [BOL 89].

12.3   PATTERNS OF TRANSFORMATIONS

In this section, we give several primary transformation schemes to bring Pascal loops into tail-recursive procedures. Compound statements begin ... end and multi-branch conditional statements if E then S1 then S2 are also transformed into new procedures.

In general, each transformation scheme has its particular application conditions; however, these are omitted here for simplicity. The output patterns of transformation schemes are not written strictly in standard Pascal, and are only for the illustration purposes; for example, all details regarding Pascal types have been omitted.

Pattern 12.3.1

From:

      while E do S;

To:

      unknown (X1,X2,...,Xm);

where

      procedure unknown (X1,X2,...,Xm);

      var Y1,Y2,...,Yl;

      begin

            if E then

            begin

                  S;

                  unknown (X1,X2,...,Xm);

            end;

      end;

and X1,X2,...,Xm are external variables, while Y1,Y2,...,Yl are the internals.

Pattern 12.3.2

From:

      repeat S1; S2;...; Sn until E;

To:

      unknown (X1,X2,...,Xm);

where

        procedure unknown (X1,X2,...,Xm);

        var Y1,Y2,...,Yl;

        begin

                S1; S2;...; Sn;

                if not E then unknown (X1,X2,...,Xm);

        end;

and X1,X2,...,Xm are external variables, while Y1,Y2,...,Yl are the internals.

Pattern 12.3.3

From:

        for I : = E1 to E2 do S;

where I is any enumerable scalar type.

To: unknown (X1,X2,...Xm,E1,E2);

where

        procedure unknown (X1,X2,...Xm,I,N);

        var Y1,Y2,...,Yl;

        begin

                if I then

                begin

                        S;

                        unknown (X1,X2,...,Xm,succ(I),N);

                end;

        end;

and X1,X2,...,Xm are external variables, while Y1,Y2,...Yl are the internals.

    We also have a similar pattern for I : = E1 down to E2 do S.

The following are patterns of transforming compound statements begin ... end and multi-branch conditional statements if E then S1 then S2 into non-recursive procedures. Other statements remain unchanged in the resulting program.

Pattern 12.3.4

From:

    begin

        S1; S2;...; Sn

    end;

To:

    unknown (X1,X2,...,Xm);

where

    procedure unknown (X1,X2,...,Xm);

    var Y1, Y2,...,Yl;

    begin

        S1; S2; ...; Sn;

    end;

and X1,X2,...,Xm are external variables, while Y1,Y2,...,Yl are the internals.

Pattern 12.3.5

From:

    if E1 then S1 else

    if E2 then S2 else

        ......   if En then Sn else Sn + 1;

To:

    unknown (X1,X2,...,Xm);

where

    procedure unknown (X1,X2,...,Xm);

    var Y1,Y2,...,Yl;

```
begin
        if E1 then S1 else
        if E2 then S2 else

                ......

        if En then Sn else Sn + 1;
end;
```

and X1,X2,...,Xm are external variables, while Y1,Y2,...,Yl are the internals.

12.4 EXAMPLES

The following give a few examples of applying the transformational schemes to Pascal code. Besides those primary transformation schemes described in the last section, other transformation rules, which are omitted here for brevity, are used to assist the transformation.

Example 12.4.1

From:

```
i : = 1;
while i < do
begin
        a[i] : = 0;
        i : = i + 1;
end;
```

To:

```
set_zero(a,1,n);
```

where

```
procedure set_zero (a,i,n);
begin
        if i < = n then
```

```
            begin
                    a[i] : = 0;
                    set_zero (a,i + 1,n);
            end;
      end;
```

Example 12.4.2

From:

```
      for i : = 1 to n do a[i] : = 0;
```

To:

```
      set_zero(a,1,n);
```

where

```
      procedure set_zero(a,i,n);
      begin
            if i then
            begin
                    a[i] : = 0;
                    set_zero(a,i + 1,n);
            end;
      end;
```

Notice that both Examples 4.1 and 4.2 result in the same resulting procedure. And in Example 4.1, some other transformation rules have been used to remove the i : = i +1 statement from the body of the procedure.

Example 12.4.3

From:

```
      for i: = n  downto 2 do
      begin
            large: = x[1];
```

```
        index: = 1;
        for j: = 2 to i do
        if x[j] > large then
        begin
                large: = x[j];
                index: = j;
        end;
        x[index]: = x[i];
        x[i]: = large;
    end;
```

To:

```
    select_sort(x,n,2);
```

where

```
    procedure select_sort(x,i,n);
    var large,index;   begin
            if i > = n then
            begin
                    assign_large_index(x,large,index,1);
                    select_large_index(x,large,index,2,i);
                    x[index]: = x[i];
                    x[i]: = large;
                    select_sort(x,i -1,n);
            end;
    end;
    procedure select_large_index(x,large,index,j,i);
    begin
            if j > = i then
            begin
                    if x[j]large then
```

```
                    assign_large_index(x,large,index,j);
                    select_large_index(x,large,index,j + 1,i);
        end;
end;
procedure assign_large_index(x,large,index,j);
begin
        large: = x[j];
        index: = j;
end;
```

The above program shows a transformation from a selection sort code written with loops into three recursive procedures. Procedure assign_large_index is called respectively by procedures select_large_index and select_sort. The names are assumed to have been given by the user who has governed the transformation process interactively. The resulting procedures decompose the code of the selection sort algorithm into sub-modules, and also generalize the functionality which has enabled assign_large_index to be called by select_sort.

12.5 AUTOMATED COMMENTING

Comments provided by the user for each transformed procedure in Example 4.3 are shown below:

```
select_sort(x,i,n):
－       {Sort X[I], X[I - 1], ..., X[N].}


select_large_index(x,large,index,j,i):
－       {Select the largest element LARGE of address INDEX among
                X[INDEX] and X[J],X[J + 1],...,X[I]}
```

assign_large_index(x,large,index,j):-
{Update LARGE and INDEX to X[J] and J respectively.}

Below are examples of commented procedures automatically generated from the user-provided comments by treating the comments as parameterized expressions and symbolically evaluating them substituting actual parameters for formal parameters:

```
procedure select_sort(x,i,n);
{Sort x[i], x[i - 1], ..., x[n].}
var large,index;
begin
        if i > = n then
        begin
                {Assign large and index to x[1] and 1 respectively.}
                assign_large_index(x,large,index,1);

                {Select the largest element large of address index
                among x[index] and x[2],x[3],...,x[i]}
                select_large_index(x,large,index,2,i);

                x[index]: = x[i];
                x[i]: = large;

                {Sort x[i - 1], x[i - 2], ..., x[n].}
                select_sort(x,i - 1,n);
        end;
end;
```

```
procedure select_large_index(x,large,index,j,i);
        {Select the largest element large of address index among
        x[index] and x[j],x[j + 1],..,x[i].}
        begin
                if j > = i then
                begin
                        if x[j] large then
                        {Assign large and index to x[j] and j
                        respectively.}
                        assign_large_index(x,large,index,j);
                        {Select the largest element large of address
                        index among x[index] and x[j + 1],...,x[i].}
                        select_large_index(x,large,index,j + 1,i);
                end;
        end;

procedure assign_large_index(x,large,index,j);
{Assign large and index to x[j] and j respectively.}
begin
        large: = x[j];
        index: = j;
end;
```

Semi-natural language definitions of the above procedures are generated automatically:

```
{Sort x[i], x[i - 1],...,x[n].}
begin
        if i > = n then
        begin
```

{Assign large and index to x[1] and 1 respectively.}

{Select the largest element large of address index among x[index] and x[2],x[3],...,x[i].}

x[index]: = x[i];

x[i]: = large;

{Sort x[i - 1], x[i - 2], ..., x[n].}

      end;

end;

{Select the largest element large of address index among x[index] and x[j],x[j + 1],...,x[i].}

begin

      if j > = i then

      begin

            if x[j] > large then

            {Assign large and index to x[j] and j respectively.}

            {Select the largest element large of address index among x[index] and x[j + 1],...,x[i].}

              x[j + 1],x[j + 2],...,x[i].}

      end;

end;

{Assign large and index to x[j] and j respectively.}

begin

      large: = x[j];

      index: = j;

end;

12.6 FROM TAIL RECURSION BACK TO ITERATION

The transformed recursive version of the program with automated comments serves as a good description for both software maintenance and software reuse. However, recursive programs are usually much more inefficient when executed than non-recursive programs. Since only tail-recursive procedures have been introduced, we can always transform the resulting code back into one of its equivalent iterative forms. In the following, we give two examples of such transformations:

Example 12.6.1

From:

```
select_sort(x,n,2);
```

To:

```
for i: = n downto 2 do
begin
        large: = x[1];
        index: = 1;
        for j: = 2 to i do
        if x[j] > large then
        begin
                large: = x[j];
                index: = j;
        end;
        x[index]: = x[i];
        x[i]: = large;
end;
```

Example 12.6.2

From:

set_zero(a,1,n);

To:

for i: = 1 to n do a[i]: = 0;

Notice that set_zero(a,1,n) can also be transformed into

i: = 1;

while i < = n do

begin

a[i]: = 0;

i: = i + 1;

end;

12.7 FUTURE DEVELOPMENTS AND CONCLUSIONS

The work described above is supported by an experimental transformation system implemented in Prolog. In the current system, there is no knowledge-based assistance provided although future plans include its provision. Within Practitioner, our goal is the reuse of software concepts realized in existing software. We hope to use the system described here to assist in population of a reusable software library. From existing source code, we have shown how semi-natural language documentation can be generated by a process of transformation and evaluation of user comments; whether such documentation forms an appropriate level software description suitable for conceptual reuse remains to be proven in practice.

REFERENCES

1. [AMB 88] James P. Ambras, Lucy M. Berlin, Mark L. Chiarelli, Alan L. Foster, Vicki O'Day and Randolph N. Splitter, MicroScope: An Integrated Program Analysis Tool, Hewlett-Packard Journal, August 1988.

2. [ANT 87] P. Antonini *et al.*, Maintenance and Reverse Engineering: Low-level Design Documents Production and Improvement, Conference on Software Maintenance, Austin, Texas, 21-24 September, 1987, pp. 91-100, 1987.

3. [ARA 85] G. Arango *et al.*, Maintenance and Porting of Software by Design Recovery, Proceedings Conference on Software Maintenance, CS Press, Los Alamitos, California, pp. 42-49, 1985.

4. [ARN 86] Robert S. Arnold, Tutorial on Software Restructuring, IEEE Computer Society, 1986.

5. [BIG 89] Ted J. Biggerstaff, Design Recovery for Maintenance and Reuse, IEEE COMPUTER, Vol. 22, No. 7, pp. 36-49, July 1989.

6. [BOL 89] Cornelia Boldyreff, Pat Hall and Jian Zhang, Reusability: The Practitioner Approach, Position paper printed in: Workshop 'Reuse' RESEARCH IN PROGRESS, Delft University of Technology, November 1989.

7. [CHA 84] F. B. Chambers, D.A. Duce and G. P. Jones (editors), Distributed Computing, Academic Press, 1984.

8. [CHE 86] Yih-Farn Chen and C. V. Ramamoorthy, The C Information Abstractor, IEEE, 1986.

9. [CLO 84] W. F. Clocksin, Logic Programming and Prolog, in [CHA 84].

10. [FOS 87] John R. Foster and Malcolm Munro, A Documentation Method Based on Cross-referencing, Proceedings Conference on Software Maintenance – 1987, pp. 181-185, 1987.

11. [HOA 85] C. A. R. Hoare and J. C. Shepherdson (editors), Logic and Programming Languages, Prentice-Hall, 1985.

12. [JAN 81] G. Jandrasics, SOFTDOC – A System for Automated Software Analysis and Documentation, Proceedings of ACM Workshop on Software Quality Assurance, April 1981.

13. [JEN 75] Kathleen Jensen and Niklaus Wirth, PASCAL User Manual and Report, Springer-Verlag, Second Edition, 1975.

14. [KOW 85] R. Kowalski, The relation between logic programming and logic specification, in [HOA 85].

15. [MAR 85] J. Martin and C. McClure, Diagramming Techniques for Analysts and Programmers, Prentice-Hall, 1985.

16. [McC 65] John McCarthy *et al.*, LISP 1.5 Programmer's Manual, The Computation Center and Research Laboratory of Electronics, Massachusetts Institute of Technology, The MIT Press, Second Edition, 1965.

17. [PAR 72] D.L. Parnas, On Criteria to be Used in Decomposing Systems into Modules, Communications of the ACM, Vol. 15, No. 12, pp. 1053-1058, December 1972.

18. [PAR 86] David Lodge Parnas and Paul C. Clements, A Rational Design Process: How and Why to Fake It, IEEE Transactions on Software Engineering, Vol. SE-12, No. 2, pp. 251-257, February 1986.

19. [PRE 87] Roger S. Pressman, SOFTWARE ENGINEERING, McGraw-Hill, Computer Science Series, Second Edition, 1987.

20. [RIC 88] Charles Rich and Richard C. Waters, Programmer's Apprentice: A Research Overview, IEEE COMPUTER, pp. 10-25, November 1988.

21. [SNE 89] Harry M. Sneed and Gabor Jandrasics, Inverse Transformation from Code to Specification, Proceedings Software Tools '89, Blenheim Online, London, 1989.

22. [WAR 88] Martin Ward, Transforming a Program into a Specification, Computer Science Technical Report 88/1, School of Engineering and Applied Science, University of Durham, January 1988.

13 Re-engineering business systems to use the next generation of software

S. Holloway

DCE Information Management Consultancy

13.1 INTRODUCTION

Although we now have a variety of tried and proven tools and techniques for business systems development, it can be said that we, as information systems developers, have failed. Baldock (1) summarizes the problem as follows: 'The rate at which software can be produced (which is a factor of the number of people available to do the work and their work output) had not kept pace...., contributing to an increase in the "application backlog" '.

Many large organizations have a 2 - 5 year backlog of applications. This backlog is not a large number of equal projects or tasks; it is a very diverse three-dimensional workload. The first dimension of the application backlog is different types of application. They range all the way from large scale new systems through ad-hoc requests to maintenance and enhancements.

It is important also to understand how this is divided. The Quality Assurance Institute (2) has shown that the maintenance proportion of IT's Budget has risen from 30% in 1963 to 80% in 1985. The US Federal Government spends 23% of its total IT Budget on maintenance. Durham University's Centre for Software Maintenance have estimated that in the UK, spending £1 billion per year on application will reveal that it requires a combination of program types in order to work. This is the second dimension to the application backlog. An application is no longer 100% batch or 100% online, it is a combination of these, and will involve both simple and complex processing. The third dimension of the backlog is the Application Lifecycle.

13.2 INFORMATION AS A RESOURCE

Naisbitt (3) talks about the fact that two hundred years ago we were basically an agricultural society involved in the growing of food to feed ourselves. About the turn of the nineteenth century we evolved into an industrial society where the measure of success of an organization was how many goods and products could be produced by an assembly line or in a factory. We were involved in the industrial society until the late 1950s when the introduction of the computer happened. With this, people realized that they could utilize information produced by the computer to achieve corporate success and growth. We then evolved into what is known today as the information society. Information is necessary for us to succeed in the 1980s and 1990s. This is substantiated by Edelman (4) who states that 'Information is the prime asset, second only to people.' I believe that everyone will agree that we are an organization's most important asset. Well just think how much more of an asset or how much more of a contribution these people could provide to the success of our organization, if we can supply them with meaningful, timely and accurate information with which to do their jobs. What is needed is effective information management to help us achieve corporate goals.

13.3   THE DEVELOPMENT LIFECYCLE

The development of corporate databases and information systems requires IT to build applications in a methodical manner. To achieve this and to meet the increasing user demand for information, a number of methodologies have been developed by consultancies.   Each of these off-the-shelf methodologies purports to cover the development lifecycle. Figure 13.1 shows a picture of a generic development lifecycle.

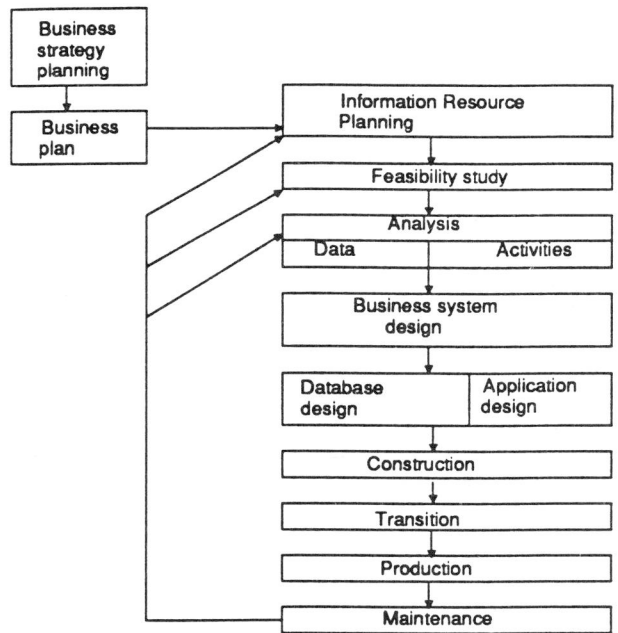

Fig. 13.1 Generic development lifecycle.

If one looks at how the software industry has responded to the needs of IT to automate the techniques used within particular stages, one will find that the maintenance phase is the least well supported.

CASE and 4GL technology has enabled IT development to produce better quality systems in a more maintainable format, but it only really caters for the development of brand new systems. A process that can be described in information engineering terms as 'Forward Engineering'. What is needed by the IT?

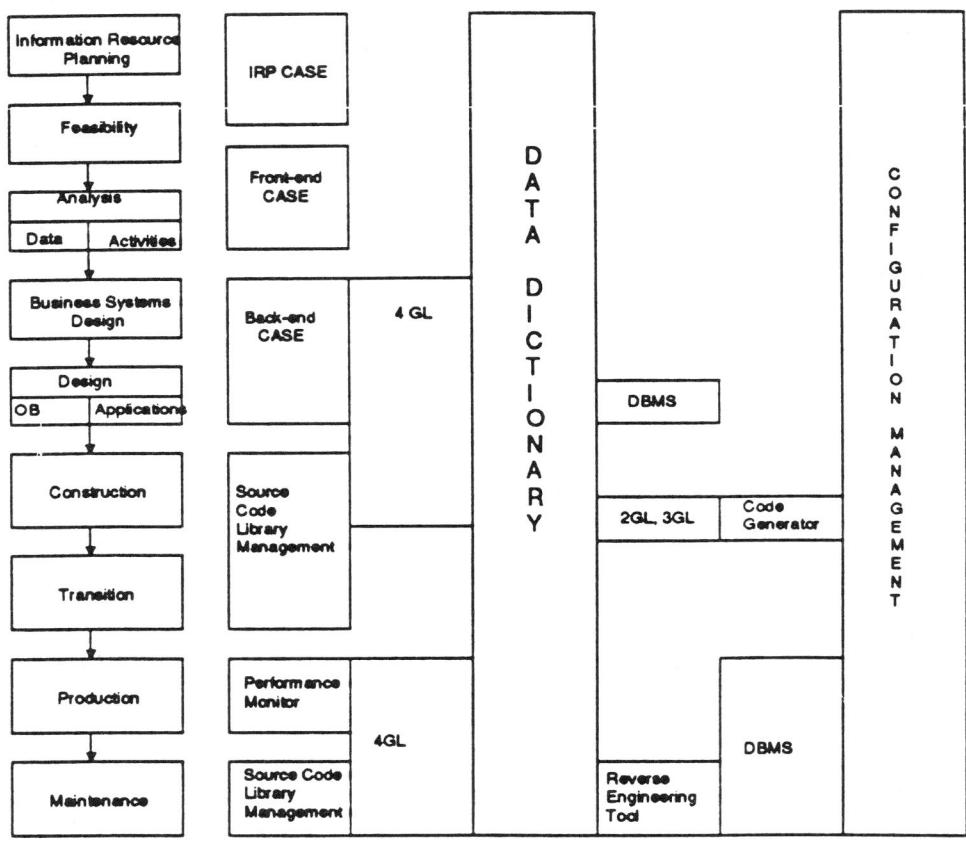

Fig. 13.2   Software assistance.

All IT sites now have major investment in the applications that they have currently in production both in terms of code and data structures. An organization's existing information systems are an irreplaceable corporate asset. New functionality has to be added routinely to these systems if they are going to continue to support business activities in an ever more competitive world. The problem is that the technological condition of most information systems makes the updating of these modifications difficult or impossible. In addition, to achieve performance or easier access, there is need to change the underlying technology base. This also suffers from the problems of modification. What they need is a means of enhancing and/or covering these applications. The answer lies in 'Reverse Engineering.'

13.4   REVERSE ENGINEERING

Reverse Engineering is the process of extracting the specification of a system from its functional objects and storing it and all relationships in an active repository. In other words, it is the process of taking the embedded knowledge that is stored in the code and data structures, and producing a conceptual model in the selected methodology style of the organization. Reverse Engineering on its own is no use, unless you can then move the result forward through enhancing or regenerating.

Re-engineering involves the process of Reverse Engineering of a particular system followed by a regeneration (and a forward engineering process) to create the system on a new technology platform.

The Reverse Engineering process can be viewed in terms of moving through four distinct stages. This is depicted in Fig. 13.3.

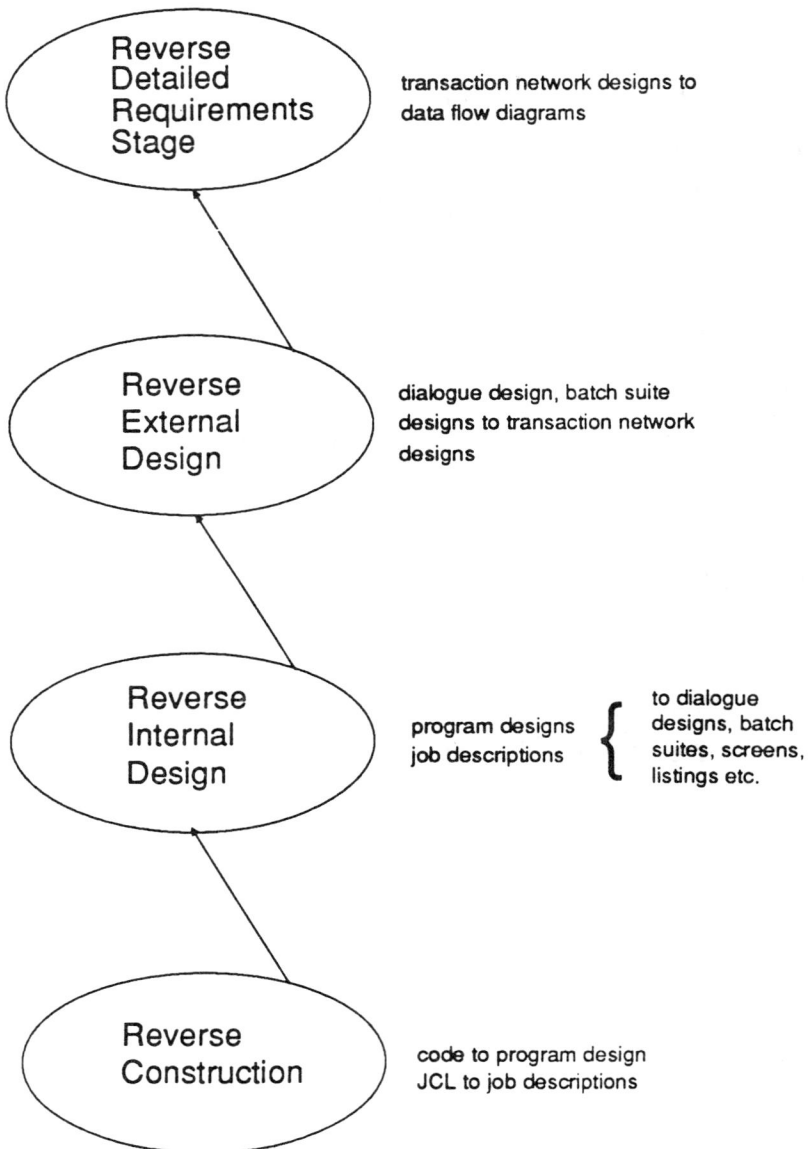

Fig. 13.3   The reverse engineering process.

The first stage – Reverse Construction – involves turning code to program design, JCL to jot description and database schemes to physical database design structures.

The second stage – Reverse Internal Design – involves the translation of the program design and job description into dialogue design, batch suites screen and screen and report designs.

The third stage – Reverse External Design – involves the translation of dialogue design, batch suite design and transaction network design.

The final stage - Reverse Detailed Requirements - involves the translation of physical database design into a conceptual data model, and of the transaction network designs to a functional model.

The process of re-engineering can never in my view be fully automated; there is and will always be a need for human interaction and human decision-making.

13.5 REVERSE ENGINEERING TOOLS

Reverse engineering tools cover a number of approaches to the analysis of existing systems and to the restructuring of existing code to improve both form and execution efficiency.

Russell Jones (5) in June 1989, proposed that Reverse Engineering Tools could be categorized into three distinct types:

- **Software Resources Analysis Tools.** These tools are marketed on the basis that, before a programmer can actually alter program code, he or she must spend much time working out which code to alter. Software analysis tools offer a way of building comprehensive module/program/job step/job cross-references. More advanced capabilities include the assessment of the complexity of programs – in terms of the processing they are trying to achieve and of the degree to which individual programs can be considered to be well structured. Examples of products in this category are PM/SS and PATHVU.

- **Code Restructuring Tools.** The restructuring process is based upon a number of key, well accepted, software engineering principles: the fundamental constructs of structured programs – that is, sequence, selection and iteration; the structure theorem and the mathematics behind structured programming. The method of converting unstructured programs to structured ones. Leading restructuring tool, notably IBM's Restructuring Facility, Language Technology (LTI)'s Recoder and Catalyst's Retrofit, analyse the basic structure of a program, reorganize it into well recognized constructs without altering the logical consistency of the program, and regenerate code, includung as many of the original program's landmarks as possible.

- **True Reserve Engineering Tools.** Here, we're moving into futures, because, with the well publicized exception of the Bachman tool for reverse engineering definitions from IMS and IDMS into DB2, no real reverse engineering tools yet exist. The hope there is that tools will emerge that are capable of abstracting the 'business logic' essence of a program direct from its code. The abstracted logic will be placed in a central CASE repository, where developers can mould it with design information gleaned during a normal 'forward engineering' process of analysis and design. The whole will then be used as the basis of new applications. At present there are three products which could be said to be early starters in this area, namely Bachman, Keith London/Metier Systems PLA/PSA and Delta Software's AEMILIO.

To be use to the average organization, Reverse Engineering Tools will need to have a number of essential characteristics.

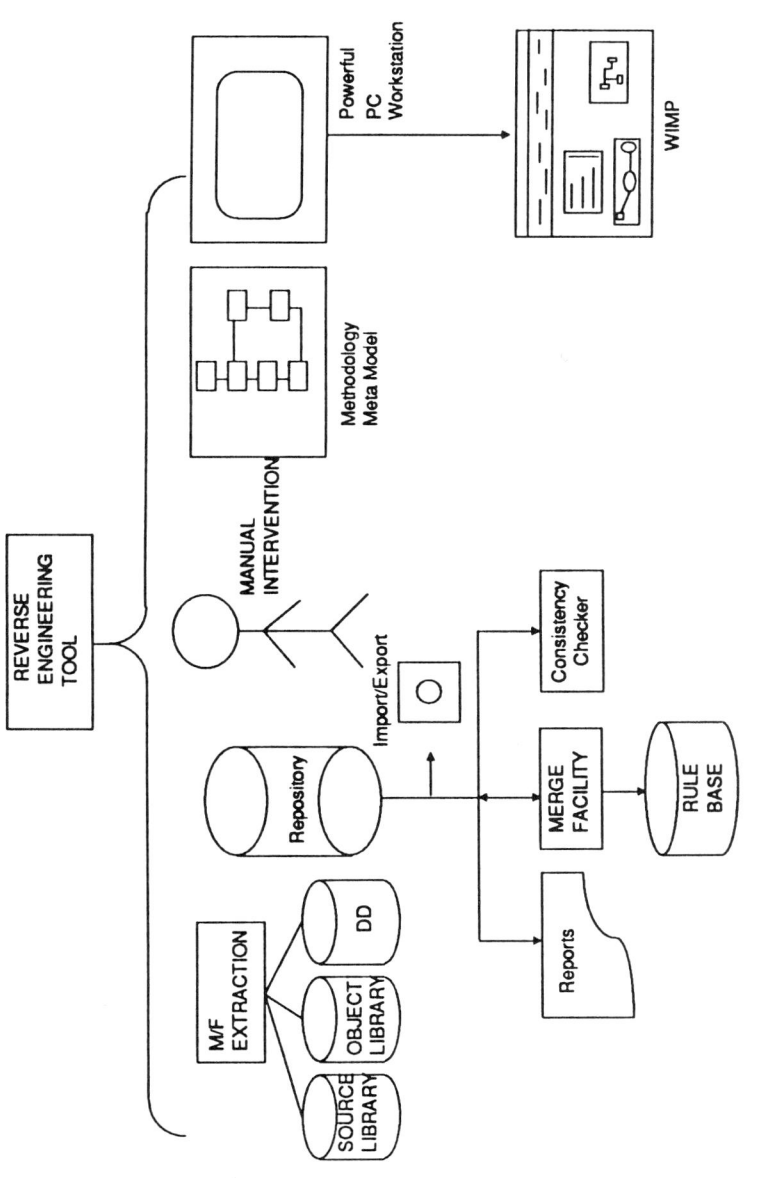

Fig. 13.4 Essential characteristics of a reverse engineering tool.

A Reverse Engineering Tool is a type of CASE tool and it has been recognized that a CASE tool consists of the following characteristics:

- A powerful workstation with a sophisticated WIMP user interface capable of supporting both naive and expert users that supports diagrams and text at a speed that is faster than pencil and paper;

- A repository or dictionary in which the information is collected, stored and indexed so that the information can be easily verified and reported on;

- A methodology meta model that describes the catgories of information that can be collected and describes the relationships and rules concerning the information objects.

A Reverse Engineering Tool needs two additional components and an extension. These are:

- Merge facility as an extension to the respository facilities set, which allows rules to be input to control the way in which information is gathered;

- Mainframe Extraction facility that enables the embedded knowledge to be extracted from the existing system sinks such as data dictionaries, source code libraries and object code libraries;

- Manual Intervention facilities that allow the user to adjust, manipulate and input information.

It is only with these characteristics that IT users will be able to move their organization to take advantage of new technology and techniques.

13.6 CONCLUSIONS

The current generation of CASE and 4GL software has only really tackled the forward engineering process – that of developing new systems or of complete redesign. What is needed by IT is a means of levering existing application into the new technology age, without having to go through the expensive cycle of redesign. Reverse Engineering in theory appears to be the way to achieve this. However, the current tools are in their infancy.

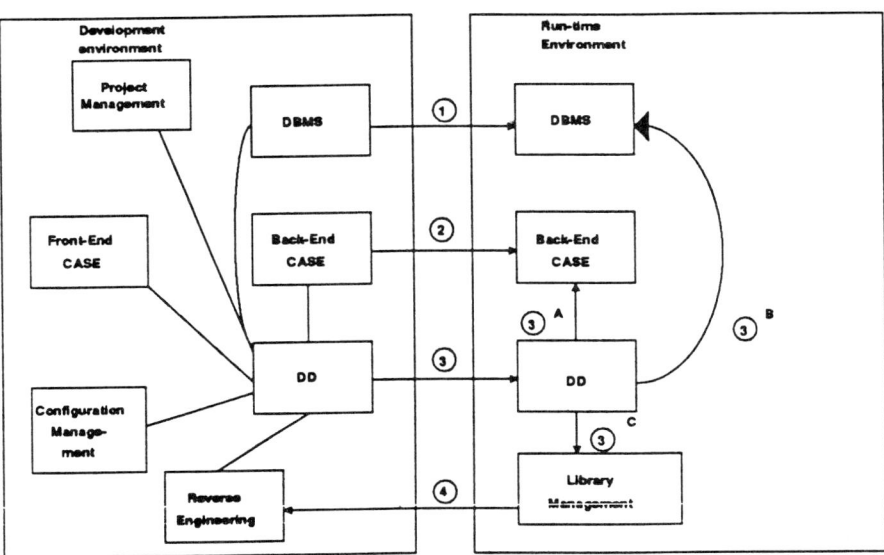

Fig. 13.5 The future IT development environment.

What IT needs is a development environment that allows and caters for the building of new systems and the enhancement and maintenance of existing applications to occur in a shared environment using similar tool and techniques. The keypin to the achievement of this goal is a requirement for a standard but non-proprietary repository.

REFERENCES

1. Information Systems Analysis and Design: Ways of accelerating the cycle and building better systems, R. Baldock. State of the Art Report 12:3, edited by E.E. Tozer, Pergamon Infotech Ltd, 1984.

2. The Quality Assurance Institute.

3. Megatrends: Ten new directions transforming our lives, J. Naesbitt, Macdonald & Co., 1982.

4. Resources: A challenge for American Business, F. Edelman, MIS Quality.

5. A Review of Current CASE Technology, Russell Jones, The Distributed Development Environment, The Art of Using CASE, edited by S.R. Holloway, Chapman and Hall, 1990.

14 Re-engineering – a practical methodology with commercial applications

R. Warden

K3 Group Limited

14.1 INTRODUCTION

This paper is based on a mixture of commercial experience and research. It describes some of the requirements of a methdology, the practical implementation of one, and the findings and results from case history projects.

For re-engineering to be commercially viable, then our methodology must cover all aspects of such a project. In this respect there is far more to a re-engineering project than the acquisition and use of a toolset.

14.2 WHAT WE MEAN BY RE-ENGINEERING

14.2.1 Introduction

The first problem we face in discussing re-engineering is to place it into context with many of the other terms often quoted. These terms include reverse engineering, inverse engineering, restructuring, recycling and forward engineering.

In particular the terms re-engineering and reverse engineering are used often, and generally very loosely. At times they seem to be interchangeable. We will start with a discussion of terms so that we can put them into some form of structure. This will enable us to consider methods and tools in a clearer perspective.

14.2.2 The Re-engineering Family

We consider that re-engineering is the generic term for a group of activities. In order to define them we must understand what re-engineering in general sets out to achieve in commercial terms.

We propose that the basic motive behind re-engineering is to improve a system in some way, without changing its functions. We find a variety of different motives in commercial environments. They include:

- a need to extend the useful economic life of a system

- a need to significantly improve the general maintainability of a system which is rapidly becoming unmaintainable

- a need to remove specific design or complexity problems to allow for some specific system expansion or integration

- a need to improve maintenance productivity either to allow future changes to be made more quickly, or to allow transfer of resources to development work

By comparison mechanically extracting a description of an application and implementing it in another language is not re-engineering. This is code translation, where the new system will faithfully reflect the code complexity, design errors and architecture errors contained in the original.

In commercial terms re-engineering implies some significant change to give improvement. This is fundamental.

We consider that re-engineering can be broken into two main phases. The first is reverse engineering and the second is forward engineering. Each of these phases in turn can be broken down into a family of activities.

This definition is different to some common notions which suggest that re-engineering concerns some form of 'restructuring' work at the program level, and that reverse engineering is the process of abstracting back to some high level specification. We find these notions lack structure and do not easily match the needs of the overall task. For example, even to 're-engineer' a single program it is necessary to reverse engineer it to a higher level of abstraction than the code level. Then it is necessary to forward engineer it in some new implementation.

An immediate consequence of our definitions is that for commercial work there is no point in reverse engineering from code to a higher level of abstraction if there is no forward path available to make improvements.

We can now discuss the two main phases in a little more detail.

14.2.3 Reverse Engineering

At the 1989 Workshop on Software Maintenance at Durham University, the concensus of opinion was that reverse engineering is the process of 'going backwards through the development cycle'. As we break down the development cycle into many phases, we should expect reverse engineering to contain many phases as well.

In the absence of a fully developed reverse engineering model we will consider that reverse engineering can be broken into a family of tasks at three major levels:

– at the implementation level

– at the design level

– at the business level

Implementation level reverse engineering is concerned with documenting code characteristics such as program structure, control flow complexity, internal data complexity and standards violations.

Design-level reverse engineering is concerned with documenting design characteristics such as modularity, coupling, cohesion, depth, factoring, and data and file design complexity. These characteristics may be documented at a partial or global design level.

Business-level reverse engineering is concerned with documenting in a non-procedural way the business functions which a system performs. Therefore the descriptions obtained are design independent.

A key aspect of reverse engineering is that with a code-only system, the process is bottom-up. Reverse engineering strategies have been proposed in commercial environments which require the topdown population of levels of documentation. Such strategies require very careful examination as they raise the question of information validation. For example, how can higher level data flow diagrams be validated if the lower levels of information are not available.

In summary, we consider that reverse engineering is essentially a documentation exercise, with the computer source code and JCL as the only reliable starting points.

14.2.4 Forward Engineering

Parallel with our family of three reverse engineering levels there are the forward engineering levels:

- code re-implementation

- application re-design (which may be global or partial)

- revision of the business specifications and develop of a new application architecture

There are many types of problem which may need to be solved in the forward engineering phase. Some typical ones we have found in commercial environments include:

complex procedure control flows

complex internal data usage

poor program structure

poor design decomposition

poor data or file design across one or more programs and databases

hard coded boundaries

standards violations

problems peculiar to an individual system

In the systems that we have looked at, we are rarely talking about problems inherited from the original development. In most cases these problems have arisen from two sources. The first source is from unstructured, defensive programming methods used to modify a system over a period of years. The second source is that the original design and implementation are no longer valid because the business requirements have changed.

For forward engineering to be successful it must be able to remove clearly defined types of problems.

14.2.5   The Re-engineering Driver

From this line of reasoning we obtain a very important conclusion. The problem types which forward engineering has to solve dictates the requirements of the reverse engineering process. That is, reverse engineering must be capable of extracting the necessary information to support the required re-engineering analysis work. As problems vary from system to system, so the reverse engineering requirements will vary too.

Even at the implementation level of re-designing a single program, reverse engineering is not trivial, neither is it achievable by some of the toolsets available.

As a simple example, the approach by several toolsets is to use a code restructurizer to remove GOTO-based logic in COBOL programs. Our experience is that these algorithms can be inadequate and generate less maintainable code. These algorithms do not appear to contain much knowledge about structured design principles, even when applied to single large program units. Therefore in rigidly applying structured programming constructs, they may all to easily violate design rules. We have noted other problems which this approach can generate, but we cannot discuss them all here.

For the complex GOTO type of problem we have to use a Knot Analysis to help understand the nature of the GOTO complexity before deciding on how it should be re-engineered.

14.2.6 Method versus Automation

Having defined that the needs of forward engineering dictate the requirements of the reverse engineering process, we also determine that we must identify the methods first and consider the tools second. This is fundamental to the design of a re-engineering methodology.

What becomes apparent at this point is that there is a significant human skills-based task in forward engineering, even when working at the program level. This should not be a surprise to us. Just as human skill is still needed to determine a system's original architecture, design and decomposition, so such skills are needed to re-engineer into a better state.

However we consider tools support is essential for non-trivial re-engineering work. Our primary area of concern is that reverse engineering tools extract the appropriate information for the forward engineering process.

14.3 REQUIREMENTS FOR A RE-ENGINEERING METHOD-ODOLOGY

14.3.1 Introduction

In this section we will consider aspects of constructing a re-engineering methodology for use in commercial environments. We will also consider what forms of automation are required and give some insights about the tools needed.

The first step in determining the requirements for a re-engineering methodology is to identify the general methods and principles required.

14.3.2   The Principles

- The principles which K3 uses as the basis for a re-engineering methodology are:

- re-engineering is only performed if there is an acceptable cost/benefit argument

- re-engineering implies improvement through re-design

- re-engineering removes poor design but recognizes and keeps good, simple design, even if it is unstructured

- re-engineering is reverse engineering followed by forward engineering

- forward engineering is the removal of specified problem types

- reverse engineering is driven by the problem types which need to be identified

- problems are identified and expressed as violations of structured design and programming rules, or in ways that a client may define

- tools do not drive the processes but must be tailored to a project environment

14.3.3 The Methods

There are a number of methods which can be used to support these principles. Those which K3 adopted for its methodology include:

worst/first analysis

a COCOMO-based method for re-engineering estimation,

static code and data analysis which includes using metrics and analysis techniques such as:

knot analysis/control flow analysis

McCabe complexity

factorization of logic

program depth

fan-in and fan-out

file or dataset usage

internal storage duplication

redundancy checking

standards violations

re-engineering analysis and specification

cosmetic re-engineering

structural re-engineering

parallel and regression testing

documentation

14.3.4 Automation of Methods

There are some major conceptual difficulties with reverse engineering backwards through the lifecycle, and they place constraints upon the degree of automation that can be applied.

During the original system specification and design a significant amount of non-procedural business knowledge will have been used to make decisions about a system's architecture, data design and procedural processing. These decisions are often not documented during development, let alone updated and made available during maintenance. Therefore any automated reverse engineering tool is not going to be able to re-generate this knowledge from procedural code alone.

An aspect of this issue relates to arbitrary structures in both data and procedural logic design and implementation. The question is how can an automated approach recognize and deal with such structures?

Another problem is the choice of language in which to express information about a system which is extracted using tools. Current systems development is still done largely using natural English, or quasi-languages derived from English. These methods of expression are not rigorous, and can be misinterpreted. Furthermore they can be difficult to check for validity and consistency.

Any automated reverse engineering tools will need to express aspects of a system, whether procedural processing or data design, in a formal and rigorous way. If they cannot then it will be difficult to validate the functions of a reverse engineered system against the system it replaces. For example, even with the relatively simple concept of code restructurizing, the current tools do not mathematically validate the restructured code in a demonstrable form.

Above all, until re-engineering methods are fully described it will be very difficult to provide acceptable automated solutions. We should not be dismayed at this notion, for it applied to the development and acceptance of CASE tools for software development.

One can look at this problem another way. The IT industry has made a significant investment in CASE tools, and they are now becoming quite widely accepted. By comparison there has been very little automation applied to the processes of software maintenance. We cannot expect to automate a conceptually demanding task such as re-engineering from such a lack of experience of the use of tools and methods in maintenance.

Currently we have defined a number of generic requirements for tools to support re-engineering. They are:

ability to tailor to the problems types of an individual project

ability to handle mixed language systems

ability to analyse partially rebuilt code

ability to offer interactive graphical displays of large volumes of information

We have found the last requirement to be very important. Voluminous reports and metrics from, say, static analysis can be difficult to interpret by a re-engineering analyst. However, a graphical display of structures combined with the abilities to query and edit them can help identify major problems very quickly.

14.4 IMPLEMENTATION OF A METHODOLOGY

14.4.1 Introduction

This section describes some of K3's work in implementing a methodology to perform commercial software re-engineering. This is based partly upon the successful completion of re-engineering work and also on discussions with large IT users about their own re-engineering requirements.

There are three major phases in our approach which are:

re-engineering review

pilot project

main project

14.4.2 Re-engineering Review

With any large system there are some key questions which must be answered before any re-engineering work starts. They are:

what are the motives for performing re-engineering?

which parts of the system require re-engineering?

what additional work will be needed to support a re-engineering project?

is there an initial cost/benefit justification for performing re-engineering?

We have developed a number of techniques aimed at answering these questions. They are applied in a Re-engineering Review, which is a short study of a system. During this time the review performs a number of tasks which include:

assess the current ability of the system to respond to business change

identify areas/problems which business and technical staff consider important

determine current system sizings using several metrics

determine volume and distribution of the annual change traffic determine likely re-engineering areas through a worst/first analysis

determine likely re-engineering areas through a software reliability analysis

determine likely re-engineering areas through a backlog analysis

determine the state of any documentation that may be essential to the re-engineering process

From all of these items we produce a Re-engineering Assessment Report of a system. We note that it is possible for this review to conclude that re-engineering is not justified on business grounds, or that a system's problems are so severe that they can only be solved through complete redevelopment.

14.4.3 Pilot Project

Following the Re-engineering Review we perform a pilot project. This project has to address a number of key technical re-engineering issues. They include:

determine the re-engineering criteria by which the work can be judged to have been done correctly

determine the tools required

determine the methods for system revalidation

calibrate the estimation method so that more accurate estimates of the work can be made

set a schedule and priorities

We will expand on two issues, re-engineering criteria and tools support.

Some typical re-engineering criteria include:

> standardize data names and remove redundancy/aliasing

> redesign poorly factored logic

> reduce excessive depth

> remove excessive fan-in/fan-out

> remove control flow knots

> remove working storage duplicate record definitions

> improve functional cohesion

> remove standards violations

> remove unnecessary files or datasets

To support this type of work we have to ensure that the correct tools are available. The minimum requirement is an accurate data dictionary and a procedure code analyser. Most large systems have a data dictionary facility. The common problem, particularly with mixed-language systems, is the lack of an appropriate procedure code analyser.

We have developed our own analysers specifically for re-engineering work. These tools differ significantly from any commercial tools in the following respects:

> they can be tailored to check for each project

> they can analyse incomplete code

they can check for recursion in non-recursive languages

they can display structural design information in a true graphical display

the re-engineering programmer can interactively examine/modify structure displays in order to understand design problems

We have analysed code from different mainframes by downloading the source to a PC, on which the tools run. This approach has handled code sets of 100,000 lines NCSS with no difficulty. For very large systems there is no reason why parsing routines cannot be written to run on the host machine, with the extracted logical data downloaded to the PC for input to the structure processor and other analysis tools.

The pilot project is conducted in the following way:

from the review at least two programs are selected

tools are modified/used to demonstrate the required analysis capability

re-engineering criteria are set

the programs are re-engineered

the results are validated

an interim report is generated commenting on what can be achieved and defining the scope of the main project

The last task of the pilot project is to arrive at firm estimates and to derive a project schedule for the main project.

In summary, the purpose of the pilot project is to exercise the methods and tools for reverse and forward engineering so that they can be refined for the main project.

14.4.4 Main Project

The main project involves performing the same processes on each of the program units selected. However, we loosely describe, the most pertinent one as 'the programs are re-engineered'. We will describe this in more detail. There are several steps involved in reverse then forward engineering which include:

updating the specifications

analysis and production of detailed re-engineering specifications

cosmetic re-engineering

structural re-engineering

testing and acceptance

final documentation

To discuss all of these tasks in detail is beyond the scope of this paper. Therefore we will discuss three major tasks of cosmetic re-engineering, structural re-engineering and documentation.

Cosmetic re-engineering is the task of improving the readability of programs/modules by:

standardizing data names

removing redundant names/structures

standardizing layouts

inserting additional comments about program functions

This task may sound trivial, but in fact it has been found to make a significant difference to the speed at which a system can be understood. This not only benefits the forward engineering work, but also provides lasting value. Therefore we perform cosmetic re-engineering before implementing other items from a re-engineering specification.

Structural re-engineering is the skilled task of implementing the major requirements of the re-engineering specifications. As we stated earlier, problems are defined and treated, wherever possible, in structured programming or design terms.

At any point during this work the re-engineering programmer may wish to re-analyse the current programs/modules to check on their correctness. A tool's ability to analyse incomplete code in a partial state of reconstruction is vital. We do not consider it acceptable for a tool set to be able to analyse complete code, i.e. only at the very beginning and end of the re-engineering process.

Another very important task is that of re-documentation. To perform acceptance testing it is essential to have accurate functional descriptions. This type of documentation cannot be generated automatically as it is business function orientated. We have to use specialist technical authors to assist re-engineering analysts. The technical authors also make use of the outputs from the code analysis.

14.5 RE-ENGINEERING FINDINGS AND RESULTS

14.5.1 Introduction

The findings and results that we can report are based on re-engineering at the program and partial design levels. We can report data from re-engineering work completed nearly a year ago, so that we have the very important views of maintenance staff on their experiences with the re-engineered code.

First we will discuss some of the findings; that is, some of the problems we have had to solve. Secondly we will discuss the results, which will be expressed in a number of ways. Finally we will make some summary comments.

14.5.2 Findings

The findings are essentially the results of the reverse engineering and the re-engineering analysis processes. The first point of interest is that even within a given application system there can be a diverse range of problems. An individual program will show its own problem set, which may be different from any other being examined. The following examples of problems are taken from the re-engineering analysis of about 50 COBOL programs totalling 150,000 lines NCSS.

One program of 3500 lines procedure division had a McCabe complexity of over 500 and contained conditional recursion between two complex sections. Apart from the fact that recursion is not permitted in COBOL, the current conditions excluded a recursive path. However, the complexity of the sections of code represented a great danger that through further modification a recursive path could be enabled. The high McCabe number represented a formidable testing problem.

Another program of about 4000 lines procedure code had a fan-out ratio between a controlling section and other PERFORMed sections of 1:28. The controlling section was not a transaction centre, and there was no justifiable design reason for this excessive fan-out.

In some programs we found that there were multiple internal storage definitions of record structures. In some cases there were as many as six definitions of a particular structure. From the program's history we deduced that as new functions were added, programmers were reluctant to use existing data structures and defined new versions of them. This had led to a high degree of internal data complexity which made the procedural code very difficult to follow.

Many programs used non-standard datanames, particularly in internal working storage data structures. This problem is allied to the previous one. The overall maintenance problem generated by these two problem types acting together was considered to be as great, if not greater, than that of 'spaghetti code'.

In a program of 2900 procedure division lines we found a section of code, quite well down the logical structure of the program which contained a major part of the control logic. This was a problem of poor factorization, where there were not clear divisions between the higher level controlling procedures and the lower level processing logic.

A number of programs exhibited excessive depth, which in COBOL terms is the number of PERFORM levels in a program. (For non-COBOL readers the PERFORM statement can be simplistically compared with a procedure CALL in other languages.) The maximum depth we recorded was 16, indicating that a programmer may need to track code through 16 different levels of processing in order to understand what is happening. This was a function of poor program design.

The programs varied enormously in style. Some were designed using PERFORMed sections in order to give a reasonable structure. Others contained many

GOTO commands within sections, but these were control flow jumps down the code. We consider some of these examples as benign uses of GOTOs, particularly when they represent simulated CASE statements. There were some which displayed the classic 'spaghetti code' control flow complexity. Techniques such as knot analyses combined with graphical displays identify these problems very quickly. However, we do not consider 'spaghetti code' to be the most frequent or the most important problem type to solve.

In other programs we found poor handling of I/O functions. In particular we found that an I/O function could be called from many different places. This type of problem was shown rapidly from graphical displays of code structures, where it was possible to examine all of the routes into sections of code performing I/O.

In a few large programs we found that their structures contained natural divisions. That is that at a low level of the program structure all processing would be routed through one section. This gave the clue that further modular decomposition was needed to simplify the processing.

Finally, in this list of examples, we found a number of large programs which contained individual COBOL sections (or procedures if you wish) which contained more than 30% of the entire program code. These sections performed a number of processing functions, and often contained 'spaghetti code' as well. These were examples of poor functional cohesion.

These findings are only meant to give an example of the problems which our commercial re-engineering must solve.

Some findings of a different nature that are also important is how the work breaks down in a re-engineering project. A typical breakdown is:

33% reverse engineering/re-engineering analysis

20% forward engineering

15% updating specifications and other documentation

20% revalidation

12% other

Without the correct tools support for the reverse engineering phase we estimate that this task would at least have doubled, and the accuracy of the work would have reduced significantly.

14.5.3 Results

The results of re-engineering work can be expressed in two basic ways. First, they can be measured in terms of the technical re-engineering criteria determined in the pilot project. Secondly, they can be assessed by a longer term view of the staff who have to support the systems, and the cost/benefit arguments in favour of re-engineering. Following is a list of examples.

Code size was reduced by as much as 30% in some programs. This is a significant improvement, particularly for readers who consider that code size is a good measure of complexity. This included the removal of both redundant procedure code and data.

The McCabe complexity was reduced by up to 28% in some code. However, in some work we recorded a slight increase in the McCabe number. Some programs displayed logic splitting, and the re-engineering introduced new conditions. (We also found a very high correlation between McCabe number and program length.)

Performance was improved by as much as 15%. This was an unexpected and useful gain. Our re-engineering criteria normally require that performance should, at minimum, be the same for the new code.

'Spaghetti code' was removed, and this was measured explicitly using knot analyses.

Standards violations were removed.

Multiple internal data stores were reduced to single definitions.

Fan-out was reduced to normal design level ranges, e.g. 5 to 9.

Large procedures were split to improve functional cohesion.

Excessive depth was removed by redesigning control and processing logic.

Links between processing logic sections and file I/O sections were reduced by as much as 45%, thereby giving better control over I/O functions.

Datanames were standardized within programs, and with this the data dictionaries were also improved. Whilst we classify this sort of work under our term of 'cosmetic re-engineering' it does have a significant impact on the understandability of the code.

14.5.4 Summary

Trying to describe the success of re-engineering work is difficult. Improvements are often measured using various software metrics, and there is often disagreement about the measures used. For example, we find McCabe complexity useful. However, we have to use many complexity metrics as McCabe alone is totally inadequate.

The most important metric we have so far comes from the staff who have had to work with re-engineered code. They indicate that the time taken to make changes to re-engineered code is half that they would expect with the original code. This represents a doubling in maintenance productivity.

14.6 CONCLUSION

We consider software re-engineering to be a very large subject. We also believe that the IT industry is literally in its 'first day at school' in terms of re-engineering large commercial systems. The findings and results described are from early re-engineering work. Currently we are being posed much more significant re-engineering problems, e.g. the entire decomposition of 1,000,000 + lines of code and its subsequent reconstruction into a better design. In addition the re-engineering of databases is becoming topical, particularly for migration to new technologies like DB2.

Our initial experiences show that it is possible for re-engineering to be commercially viable. However, great caution is needed to determine all of the methods and techniques to be used before embarking upon automation. This is necessary partly because of the lack of general re-engineering experience and partly because of the wide diversity of problems that may be encountered.

Above all, we must not become hypnotized by specific toolsets or technologies, something which has happened in the IT industry before. For example, ten years ago 4GLs were seen as a technical solution to a more general productivity problem. Apart from the very mixed results from using 4GLs, most 4GL users now find that they will have great difficulty re-engineering 4GL systems because there are not the reverse engineering tools available to support these languages. It used to be claimed by some 4GL vendors that maintenance work would cut by up to 90%. The inability to reverse engineer a 4GL system means that the IT user may face the ultimate maintenance crisis which a 4GL was presumably meant to avoid – having to throw away a system and most of the knowledge it contains and redevelop a replacement from scratch.

15 Step-by-step transition from dusty-deck FORTRAN to object-oriented programming

M. Bardiaux and P. Delhaise

Plant Genetic Systems, U.C.M.B Laboratories

15.1 INTRODUCING BRUGEL

BRUGEL (for Biochemistry Research Utilities, Graphics, Energy and Language) is an integrated software for computer-assisted design of biological macromolecules. Like any such package, it contains four major application-level components:

- Model building tools: the ability to construct (models of) new molecules from previously known ones.

- Simulation tools: computing physico-chemical properties of modelled molecules.

- Analysis tools: to exploit the enormous amount of data generated by simulations, compute geometric and other properties, etc.

- 3-D interactive graphics.

It is important to note that, while electrical and mechanical CAD softwares were built by capitalizing on centuries of experience with drawing boards, chemical CAD is a very recent discipline, where no consensus exists regarding which questions are to be asked, to say nothing of how to compute them. Hence, the application contents of **BRUGEL** must evolve at least as fast as its implementation techniques.

In the context of this paper, the most interesting aspect of **BRUGEL** as an application is that the user interface is based on an object-oriented command language (without methods). Most commands perform one simple action, storing results in named objects that will be used as input for subsequent commands. However, objects at the command level do not currently enjoy uniform semantics, and moreover are not truly related to the object-management system that is used for implementing **BRUGEL**. Of course, this will be fixed in some future release.

15.2 WHY FORTRAN ?

The development of **BRUGEL** began 10 years ago using standard FORTRAN 77, and will be continued in FORTRAN, not only because of the cost of conversion, but also because FORTRAN remains the dominant language both in biology-oriented public-domain software and on the supercomputers that are absolutely required for the very compute-intensive simulations.

Two major problems encountered while developing any large application in FORTRAN are:

- Lack of expressive power: card format, 6-character identifiers, very few compile-time checks, no encapsulation mechanism at all. Although most compilers provide language extensions, their use compromises portability – a serious concern if one wants to benefit from a competitive market.

- Waste of the address space: all arrays must be given the largest size that one expects to need someday. Although most state-of-the-art computer systems feature both virtual memory and large physical memories, disks and boards are by no means cheap, and the needs for memory always seem to grow faster than prices decrease.

After being exposed for the first time to the UNIX cpp, we decided to write our own pre-processor, with similar specifications but tuned to FORTRAN, written in strictly standard FORTRAN and able to produce strictly standard FORTRAN. The macro facilities of bpp were then used to implement a dynamic memory management system. An unexpected result was that the system quickly started (and continues) to evolve towards a true object-oriented programming language.

15.3 THE BPP PRE-PROCESSOR

Bpp supports the cpp-like directives #define (useful replacement for the parameter statement), #if (useful for system-dependent unavoidable code, such as system calls and open options), #include (vital for modular development). Bpp macros have the same syntax and semantics as with cpp; their primary use is to hide the details of heap management behind a (more or less) standard-looking syntax.

Bpp also provides some non-universally available FORTRAN extensions that improve the quality of code, such as implicit none, unlimited line length, in-statement comments, unlabelled do/enddo loops, do while(), and unlimited identifier length (by maintaining a dictionary of re-mappings to 6-character identifiers).

Drawbacks: pre-processing takes time, can confuse symbolic debuggers, knows very little of FORTRAN syntax and nothing at all of semantics.

15.4 MEMORY MANAGER

15.4.1 Physical Level

Pointers in are similar to PASCAL or ADA pointers, i.e. they designate an object in a global area called the heap. Moreover, they are implemented in a portable way: not as addresses but as FORTRAN integers which are indexes in several large equivalenced common FORTRAN arrays (one for each primitive FORTRAN type).

Memory blocks in the heap are obtained by calling a pointer-valued function, which uses the most classical algorithm: non-roving first-fit with boundary tags and an avail list (see). When needed, and possibly under the operating system, the heap can be extended with extra virtual space (e.g. with malloc(3)).

15.4.2 Objects Level

Very early in the design of the memory manager, we decided that to be able to manipulate large and complex data structures, we could not rely on manual memory reclamation but had to use some automatic system. But any garbage collection algorithm requires run-time knowledge of the contents of reclaimed blocks, to be able to identify and follow pointers inside heap objects. (Note: unfortunately, we use a non-usual meaning for the word dereference, the normal meaning of which is what we call follow or designate.)

For this purpose, all heap objects are endowed with a header containing:

- Physical size (total space used in heap seen as array of integers).

- Type (pointer to a heap object known as type descriptor, which contains such things as name of the type, size of a scalar of the given primitive type reported to size of an integer).

- Some debugging information.

- Logical size (usable space in heap seen as array of the corresponding primitive type, exclusive of header).

- Reference count (see below).

Since we needed structured objects as type descriptors, that important facility was made generally available. Record types, however, are not described at compile-time but at run-time, by calling subprograms. This means that the first thing an application using bpp has to do is to call elaboration routines (ADA terminology) to initialize the heap manager and then create its own types, initialize static pointers to the special value NULL, etc.

15.4.3 User Level

Fresh objects are created by the function new (type,size) where type is a pointer to a type descriptor (these are manifested as common variables in #include files) and size is either the desired length for heap arrays, or a variant tag for records. Pointer variables are assigned a value, not with an assignment statement, but by using the _setq macro, which handles the details of reference counting (see below). Non-pointer elements of heap objects are accessed using normal FORTRAN semantics, except that macros are used instead of variables: predefined macros, or new ones added for improved readability. Example:

```
_setq(vec, new(typ_r8,10))

#define _vec(i) _r8(vec,i)

_vec(3) = 1.2
```

It is worth mentioning that the last statement will be pre-processed into

$$r8((vec + 4)/2 + 3) = 1.2$$

More complex bpp statements will result in very long FORTRAN statements, taxing the capabilities of some compilers.

15.5   AUTOMATIC MEMORY RECLAMATION

When we had to choose a garbage collection algorithm, it was soon clear that mark-and-sweep was out of the question since it requires all references to be reachable from a small number of root pointers, while in a FORTRAN implementation we would have many pointers in common, local and argument blocks. These could have been moved to special global areas, but it would have required another level of indirection and either non-dynamic resources or another memory manager.

Hence, we decided to reuse a reference-counting algorithm that had been developed by one of us (M. Bardiaux) and B. Marchal, while implementing a PROLOG interpreter (based, of all things, on parts of a LISP interpreter, itself written in ADA – influences still very much apparent in **BRUGEL**).

The basic rules are:

- Each heap object has a non-negative integer-valued property called reference count.

- When a pointer variable receives the 'index' of a heap object (i.e. references it), increment the reference count of the object.

- When a pointer stops designating an object (i.e. dereferences), decrement reference count.

- When the reference count goes down to zero, return the object to the free memory pool.

Drawback: as is well known, reference-counting is unable to reclaim structures containing circular references. We are now adding debugging tools to detect such cases.

15.5.1 Functions and Anonymous Pointers

A tricky situation occurs when a pointer returned by a function is used as argument of another subprogram, since the reference is in the call packet and thus anonymous. This has been solved by adding the following rules:

- reference all pointer arguments at entry and dereference them at exit.

- All pointer-valued functions return their result with a reference count of zero. Hence, an extra check is needed at each dereference against the possibility that the object is actually a function result to be returned.

Drawback: out and inout (in ADA terminology) pointers must be avoided (anyway it is much better to write functions returning a pointer to a list of pointers).

Drawback: user subprograms must be festooned with housekeeping code at entry and exit. We are currently extending the bpp pre-processor to generate that code automatically.

15.6 ERROR HANDLING

The conceptual model of errors in bpp is based on the ADA exception, i.e. the program can be in one of three states: no exception; an exception was raised; an exception was raised but is being handled. Exceptions are implemented as pointers to strings (the name of the exception), manifested as common variables in #include files.

However, FORTRAN does not offer a portable mechanism to transfer control from the point where an exception was raised to the point where it will be handled. Even non-portable mechanisms (such as setjmp/longjmp under UNIX) would not allow us to dereference heap objects while pointers are popped off the stack. That goal is achieved by adopting a fixed style of control flow: all subprograms should exit immediately after a called subprogram returns with exception raised; all subprograms should exit immediately after entry if an exception was raised. In this context, entry means after reference-ing all pointer arguments, and exit-ing includes dereference-ing pointer arguments and local pointer variables (reference and dereference act even when an exception was raised).

Hence, although several subprograms might be called before the exception is handled, they should have no effect. Pointer-valued functions allow us to reinforce this security by designating the resulting object through a local pointer and committing it to the returned pointer at the last time before exiting.

15.6.1 Interruptions

Many operating systems allow users to interrupt a running program. In **BRUGEL**, when such an event arises, we would of course like to abort the current command rather than terminate the whole program. However, the FORTRAN runtime library is usually not interruptible. This problem was relatively easily solved by limiting the system-dependent part of event handling to the raising of an exception.

15.7 DEBUGGING FACILITIES

A first set of tools contains subprograms to check or dump heap objects, using information from their type descriptor. These are callable from FORTRAN, from the parser, and, under UNIX, from the symbolic debugger.

A second set consists of redefinitions for the interface macros between user code and the heap, allowing tracing and type and index range checking at each access to heap objects in a source file.

Of course, the heap manager also maintains and prints statistics about current and peak memory usage.

Drawbacks: as usual when using a pre-processor, symbolic debuggers have no knowledge of macros.

15.8 TOOLS LIBRARY

15.8.1 Conversion

Subprograms are provided to convert between heap arrays and 'classical' FORTRAN arrays (i.e. declared via dimension), such as:

        _pointer function copy_i4(vector, nelem)
        subroutine export_i4(ptr, ito, maxelem)
        _pointer function others_bit(logicval, number)

15.8.2 Arrays and Records

While conversion subprograms must exist for each basic type, the following ones can be programmed to be universal since all pointer arguments carry with them the full description of the designated heap objects:

        _pointer function conc(p_to_ar_1, p_to_ar_2)
        subroutine copy_slice(into,li,ri,from,lf,rf)
        _pointer function slice(p_to_ar,l,r)
        logical function equal(pl,pr) ! non-recursive

A need is currently felt for the possibility of handling totally arbitrary data structures, so we will add functions such as equivalent (recursive), duplicate (recursive copy) and decircularize.

15.8.3 Coded Output

The style of coded output mimics the ADA text_io package, because we felt it provided maximum security by avoiding mismatches between the lengths of formats and I/O lists. A typical output statement would be

```
call fprint_tokr4(bru_out, var, '(e10.3)')
```

The first argument is actually a pointer to a Logical-unit Description Block. The ldb level (sitting on top of the FORTRAN runtime) provides line buffering and margin and page control, but also more original features such as inactivation and mirroring. We are currently adding the possibility of directing output to line-structured memory files rather than FORTRAN files.

15.8.4 Coded Input

BRUGEL has no full-fledged coded input system, because most user input is done via the command interpreter. Limited facilities exist for question-and-answer-style input during execution of a command, and for reading card-format data files of known structures, such as energy parameters libraries and Brookhaven Protein Data Bank files.

15.8.5 Machine-independent Binary I/O

Our current installation is a network of UNIX machines and relies on the NFS protocol. It was considered necessary that binary files of known structure could be read by BRUGEL running on any machine in the network, regardless of the host that had produced them. To achieve this goal, binary files contain a label block, and data blocks contain size and type tags. The bpp binary I/O system currently supports only read and write of 'classical' FORTRAN arrays, because full, efficient binary I/O of arbitrary heap structures will be possible only through memory-mapped files.

Moreover, FORTRAN runtime libraries usually endow binary files with a record structure that we do not need, resulting in poor performance. When possible under a given operating system, **BRUGEL** uses raw file access (e.g. by direct calls to read(2) under UNIX).

15.9 WHAT ABOUT METHODS ?

In the context of object-oriented programming, the term method conventionally refers to subprograms designated in the type description of an object to perform specific operations. We are only now considering their use in bpp, for several reasons:

1. The accessibility of type descriptors at runtime already allows a fair amount of genericity, although limited to primitive types and operations.

2. The implementation of the use of methods implies the writing and maintenance of a few subprograms, in assembly code and dependent on the compiler architecture. We have only recently decided that the added expressive power was worth the extra development costs.

3. The coding style in **BRUGEL** has been strongly influenced by ideas from functional programming, and thus is not always compatible with object-oriented programming style as found in textbooks.

15.10 EFFICIENCY

One may (and we had to) wonder whether the potentially very complicated statements generated by the pre-processor will not result in an unacceptably sluggish software. We have observed that performance measurements give very different results depending on the hardware used as well as on the task required of **BRUGEL**, and must also be assessed using different criteria.

15.10.1   Compute-bound Tasks

On superminis, supermicros and workstations, the complexity of post-bpp code does not seem to be a problem for optimizing compilers. Anyway, the bottleneck is usually floating-point computations, and the indirection overhead is mostly hidden.

On minisupercomputers, however, vectorizing compilers do not fare as well: the fact that all data is in a single array seems to make them overcautious; many loop-constant expressions are not factored out but rather vectorized. Although 'full vectorization' can be achieved, many unnecessary vector operations are generated. Since floating-point vector operations are executed quickly, the indexing overhead is strongly apparent. For the most compute-bound subprograms, the only effective solution has been to make the heap invisible by transmitting heap data to subroutines as 'standard' FORTRAN arrays.

15.10.2   Computer-assisted Design

In this case, the true measure of efficiency is not raw speed (although **BRUGEL** is somewhat sluggish on low-end 68020-based systems), but efficient memory management, and the number of application-level features that could be added using the object-oriented approach.

15.11   HISTORICAL VIEW AND CONCLUSIONS

At this point, although some original features have been mentioned, one might well wonder whether this is not another case of 'reinventing the wheel'. The interesting aspect is that development started at a time when object-oriented techniques were far from being recognized software production tools. **BRUGEL** has evolved by selecting from various programming languages which features were promising enough in this particular context to warrant implementation. As mentioned in the introduction, each such feature had to compete, not only with others, but with the necessary priority to development of new application-level functionalities. This demonstrates, in a sense, that object-oriented programming is a natural approach to software development. But the order in which features were introduced is also indicative of their priority in practical cases: an object-oriented command language came first, but dynamic memory allocation with automatic reclamation was the next step, while it is at best a secondary design goals in languages such as C + + and Objective-C.

Finally, do our initial reasons (re-evaluated in 1985) for sticking with FORTRAN and adding our own ingredients still apply? Unfortunately, yes. VAX/VMS FORTRAN 77 is becoming a lingua franca but cannot be called a standard, even de facto. As far as we know, FORTRAN 88 is not to feature a pointer type. The only rich and strictly standardized language, i.e. ADA, is still generally expensive. And C-based object-oriented languages are still young.

As in the old Chinese curse, we do live in interesting times!

REFERENCES

1. Delhaise, Ph. *et al.*, Analysis of data from computer simulations of macromolecules using the CERAM package, Journal of Molecular Graphics, Vol. 3, No. 3, September 1985.

2. Jensen, K. and Wirth, N., PASCAL User Manual and Report, Springer-Verlag, 1975.

3. Knuth, D., The Art of Computer Programming, Vol. 1: Fundamental Algorithms, Second Edition, Addison-Wesley, 1982.

4.   Ichbiah, J. *et al.*, Reference Manual for the ADA Programming Language, ANSI/MIL-STD-1815A-1983, Castle House Publications, 1983.

5.   Allen, J., Anatomy of LISP, McGraw-Hill, 1978.

6.   Cox, B.J., Object-oriented Programming: An Evolutionary Approach, Addison-Wesley, 1986.

7.   Angell, I.O. and Griffith, G., High-resolution Computer Graphics Using FORTRAN 77, Macmillan, 1987.

16 A graph method for technical documentation and re-engineering of DP-applications

J. Grumann and P.J. Welch

Grunmann Daten-Kommunikation

16.1 INTRODUCTION

This paper explains what we, Grumann Daten-Kommunikation, mean by the term technical documentation and restructuring and why we consider them to be of importance in all DP environments but particularly in the commercial sphere. A set of methods and tools is described designed to extract and present this information.

Within this document we have not made explicit reference to much of the extensive literature on the subject. This is partly because this is not a review paper, equally however because the literature is so vast that this would have been impracticable. Many of the ideas presented here are well known, many are at least to our knowledge new. We know of no literature source where the present connection of these concepts is available.

Technical documentation is the precursor to a multitude of commercial activity based on technical information about DP applications. This information can be required for verification, auditing, metrication, validation, porting, maintenance, extension and last but not least restructuring purposes. The term static analysis which could be considered synonymous is considered here a subset of technical documentation since it is usually applied within the framework of only one of the above situations and often with a fixed aim in mind.

Our approach to technical documentation is to capture the entire and complete Application as an Application Graph consisting of a series of connected Functional Directed Graphs which allow the abstraction of information about the application in various Spaces, the most well known of which are the Control Space and the Data Space.

While it is not possible to extract the Functional Specification from the application code, it is possible to Document the Functionality in such a manner that meaningful decisions can be made about whether, how and at what cost the application can be overhauled, including possible restructuring, or smaller maintenance tasks carried out.

Logical inconsistencies of the program such as unused code, bad control structure, bad readability, unused data etc. can be marked for attention. Actual structure and flow paths of control and data can be extracted and checked for internal consistency and for consistency with either a functional specification if this is available or with the users of the application. Once this information has been extracted in the desired form, meaningful decisions can be made about what re-engineering strategy should be adopted for the application. The graph form described, combined with the information extracted from it, allow for the transformation of the application in various ways for various reasons. Restructuring is one of these transformations, others are mentioned at the end of this article.

16.2   TECHNICAL DOCUMENTATION

What is a DP-Application?   In data processing, the term application is quite well defined as being all the functionalities used for a particular, identifiable and discrete purpose. This means that where a part of a total application can be completely separated from another, communication only occurring through permanent storage media, that this can be treated for most purposes as a sub-application[1].

The starting point for technical documentation is the sources for the application. For the complete technical documentation obviously the complete sources must be available. This includes not only the program sources but system control program sources, data dictionaries, etc. Further information is required on such things as exact versions of the system control program and transaction monitors.

What is Technical Documentation?   By technical documentation, in the whole, we mean all information which can be extracted from the sources listed above. This definition includes all metrication results, all possible static analysis techniques, all listings, cross-reference tables, data usage logs etc.

Technical documentation starts with the premise that the application runs, and runs correctly. It can easily point to inconsistency within the application, unused paths, data etc. and badly styled code; it cannot from itself say that any structure or unusal occurrence is incorrect.

---

1   A sub-application only exists when referred to the whole of which it is part.

What is Not Technical Documentation? Technical documentation does not reveal any reason that a program does anything, nor reveal the reason for it doing it in a particular manner.

Neither a formal, nor functional, nor technical specification of an application can be extracted from the code. In general it is impossible to say what the designers and programmers wished to do only what they did do.

Thus all specifications, designs, application user manuals, error logs, operator experience, etc. are not part of technical documentation and form what we refer to as the total documentation. In the use of the technical documentation this information is important but it is not involved in its extraction.

Input is only required from the DP personnel using or maintaining the application when sources are missing, overcomplete[2], incorrect, out of date or in some other way incomplete. It is a prerequisite for successful technical documentation that all source information is available and it has been shown that a fully functional application can be generated on-site with exactly and only these sources.

Uses for Technical Documentation?   The aim of technical documentation then, is to capture the complete functionality of the application and to make this available in different views, levels of compaction or detail, as lists or graphics, online or batch.

---

2   Duplicates, unnecessary modules etc.

Obviously for different purposes different views[3] and levels of detail are not only desirable but essential. The metric presented in the documentation must be that requested by the user of the information and not that which it is convenient to produce. Most DP departments and software houses have different standards for their in-house technical documenation, different work patterns etc.

The Key to Successful Technical Documentation is thus:

- The information base used in the generation of the various views of the application should be 100% complete.

- The information base used in the generation of the various views of the application must be generated immediately prior to or during the maintenance action and on the exact sources which are to be maintained.

- The tools producing the different views from this information base must work directly against the information base rather than using intermediate abstractions.

- The tools must be generic in nature and thus be capable of producing slightly differing views with a minimum of re-programming effort.

Our current approach is aimed primarily, but not exclusively, at the commercial and business sector. Here one often encounters large and unwieldy applications, written a long time ago in unstructurable languages such as COBOL-74. Even where such applications have substantial documentation, this is often out of date after repeated and unstructured maintenance. Even if no tool is available to help in

---

3   Here the term **view** refers both to listings and graphical output.

extracting technical documentation, or even to automatize it, at least a minimal technical documentation must inevitably be carried out at some stage in the maintenance process.

Even in new applications and even where a formalized, structured, development method has been used, the documentation rarely corresponds completely to the current state. In all cases the use of automatizable tools to update the documentation before and after maintenance is to be recommended.

16.3 RESTRUCTURING

The term *Restructuring of a DP-Application* without any further explanation is undefined. The term *DP-Application* is not the problem, but what does Restructuring mean? Obviously to change the structure of the application, but the structure of which part and in what manner. There are several possibilities :

- change the style and comfort of input and output, i.e. the design of the user interface

- change the environment where the application runs to port to another computer or layered product

- change the time-consuming functions or algorithms, here improvement of performance would mean restructuring in the sense of optimizing

- change the coding style into a special form of programming language, here restructuring would mean translation or adaptation

- change the program functions into an equivalent but totally different form of processing and handling such as parallel processing

The list of possible and in a liberal sense useful changes could be expanded even more and every interpretation of the item restructuring would make sense. Irrespective of the reason for restructuring there are, however, several common aspects.

1.   In order to be able to restructure one must have an exact knowledge and representation of the structure as it is at present.

2.   The restructuring represents a transformation of this structure to a more highly desired structure.

3.   In order to carry out the restructuring this transformation should be algorithmically expressible in terms of the structure representation.

4.   After restructuring the application must be expressed in terms of program code which can be compiled and executed, a back transformation is required.

5.   The original and restructured application must be input/output identical byte for byte. Here input and output are defined as the data or actions which are processed by the application. Any change must be explicitly defined and flagged as an enhancement.

6.   The restructured application may still have to interact with external influences such as databases, standard subroutines.

7.   The customer requirements must be satisfied. A restructured application where all the statements are automatically rearranged to produce pretty flow diagrams, the input and output design is styled for optimal ergonomics and a complete redesign of the database is carried out is certainly academically ambitious and rewarding but nobody will want to pay for it in practice.

As with technical documentation the key to restructuring is flexibility. The restructuring transformation should be expressible in some generic way so that small or large changes to the transformation algorithms can be made without having to change the programs which carry out the transformation.

16.4   THE APPLICATION GRAPH

The aim of the application graph is to achieve a mathematical representation of the application which is algorithmically accessible and contains all of the information about the application. Because of the definition of the application as all sources including JCL, CICS[4] etc., this must be in a language-independent form to be compatible. Obviously at most 100% of the information in the sources can be extracted, i.e. if the sources are incomplete or false then incomplete or false information is produced.

There is, under some circumstances, a problem with interpreter-type languages such as Basic. In languages such as C Assembler or Fortran, alternative paths are usually chosen according to the value of some variable, this presents no problem because the set of possible paths is apparent from the code, even if the actual choice at run time is governed by a terminal input. In Basic it is not uncommon[5] to specify a jump address from a terminal input. Thus the set of possible paths is any line in the program. Although in principle it is possible to model this in the graph, the graph would become meaningless simply because the program is meaningless without information about the range of meaningful terminal inputs.

---

4   Here the trademarks for IBM products are used, other vendors have similar products with different names.

5   This is **possible** in most languages, but much less common and in all cases really dirty programming.

The choice of modelling method and representation should also be such that there is a minimal restriction on the set of possible abstractions of the information contained. That is the method must not be restrictive to a particular form of technical documentation. The problem with most available static analysis tools is that they can only produce a very limited range of abstractions, designed for a particular purpose or standard.

It should be mentioned here that many items, such as files, data dictionaries etc. to which one usually assigns a very static character are, in the application-graph analysis, also graphs which have a well defined directional component. For example, an indexed file which is read and/or written is in its data flow practically indistinguishable from a subroutine.

16.4.1 Functional Directed Graphs

The application, as defined by the sources, contains three types of information. At a particular place in the application there is information which is always the same however this point was reached - static information. At a particular place there is also a definition of direction, i.e. the next part of the application to be accessed -directional information. Finally at many places in the application there is functional information, firstly about what and how data should be processed, secondly about under what circumstances a particular direction should be taken.

In order to provide a mechanism for the capture of all these types of information an approach was adopted based on the use of functional directed graphs as described by Boehm and Weise[6] and illustrated in Fig. 16.1. This is not the place for full mathematical details but some points should be mentioned here.

1. Both nodes and edges are subdivided into Input - (x^-) and (y^-), Operator – KO_{xi} and BO_{yk}, and Output – (x^+) and (y^+).

2. The actual connection of nodes and edges is achieved through separate Connection Operators – KAO_{xj} and BAO_{yk}.

3. Thus the only difference between the nodes and the edges is that edges can only connect nodes with other nodes, and nodes can only connect edges with edges. Nodes can have multiple input edges and/or multiple output edges, edges connect exactly two nodes. Both nodes and edges are otherwise structurally identical.

16.4.2   Transformation Of Program Code

(a)   Resolution level of code

Once the mathematical model is identified, it is necessary to perform the transformation from the code into the chosen graph form. This is roughly equivalent to the compilation step in normal DP practice but is considerably more extensive because the aim is not to produce executable code for a particular machine but a graph form which is both 100% self-contained and independent of the machine and source language. This involves the storage within the graph structure of all the information which is usually kept in system tables etc. The system interaction, commonly referred

---

6   F. Boehm, G. Weise, Graphen in Datenverarbeitung, Verlag Harri Deutsch, Frankfurt, 1981.

to as the environment, must be modelled in the same, language-independent, way as the normal program code.

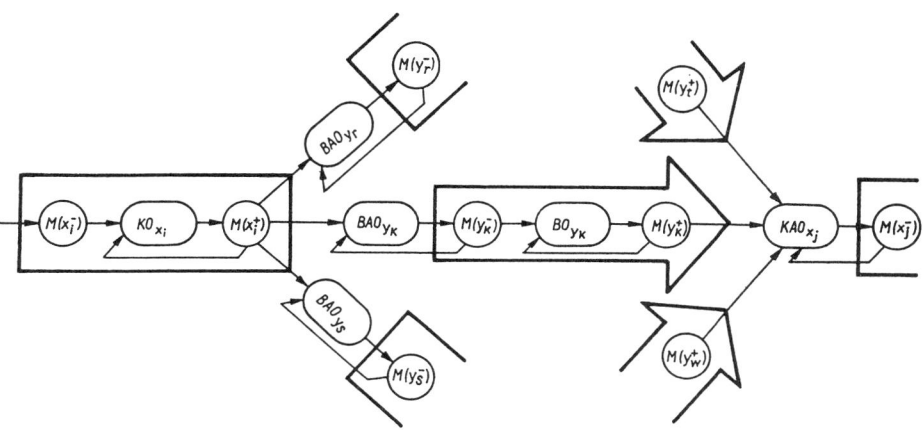

Fig. 16.1 Principles of the functional directed graph.

KO_{xi} – Node Operator

KAO_{xj} – Node Connection Operator

$M_{(xi}{}^-)$ – Node Input Marker

$M_{(xi}{}^+)$ – Node Output Marker

BO_{yk} – Edge Operator

BAO_{yk} – Edge Connection Operator

$M_{(yi}{}^-)$ – Edge Input Marker

$M_{(yi}{}^+)$ – Edge Output Marker

The technique could be compared to the production of a common assembler code for all the application modules. Thus a common component set for all the languages must be identified so that all higher abstractions can be broken down into terms of a few common components.

Anyone familiar with a number of different computer languages will realize that this level of resolution is necessarily well below both the normal statement level and also the normal variable level and in some cases below many more recent assembler languages.

The major additional difficulties in comparison to the assembling of programs are the requirements for documentation and back transformations.

- For documentation purposes we need to know inside the graph exactly from where and how a component was generated in the code so that it can be documented.

- For the back transformation we need to be able to reconstruct the code in its original form starting with the graph. Without any reference to the original sources this is impossible but the reference to the source has to be very tight, carried out at a byte level, and thus needs to be generated and tagged into the graph units very carefully.

Luckily these two requirements can be fulfilled concurrently with a single mechanism.

(b)   Inter-procedural connection

An application is modularized in as much as it is built up of separate pieces of code. After compilation the modularization of the run-time application follows this structure quite closely. It is possible, using rules for structured programming, to treat the application as a single 'giant' program and investigate whether the high-level modularization is structured and thus likely to be maintainable on a system level, see Section 5.

However, once the application is broken down to the aforementioned low level, it is possible to rebuild the application in different ways, suppressing the previous interfaces between modules. Such logical flow diagrams can provide details of the logical structure of the application which may be completely hidden in the code.

The situation for the data flow is even more marked. The controlling factor for the application 'direction' is of course the order in which the statements are written down. One can, however, define a mapping of the application whereby the direction is given by something one can refer to as the data flow. This is significantly different to the control flow and in this mapping the modularization of the program can become something else again.

Thus it is highly desirable to be able to generate a graph – or set of sub-graphs – which encompasses the entire application so as to be able to generate such information about different logical structures in the application.

16.5 MAPPING INTO CONTROL SPACE

The most well known space for the documentation of an application is the control space. This is the space usually presented in more or less detail in program flow charts. Here the direction of the edges is given by a transformation of the order of the statements in the source code.

In general, consecutive statements are executed consecutively, but when high-level statements are broken down into the assembler primitives their order can be somewhat different. This is, however, usually noticeable only in the fine details.

16.5.1 Constructional Elements

The following constructional elements or common component set are found to be sufficient to model the control flow of an application in the required detail, see Fig. 16.2.

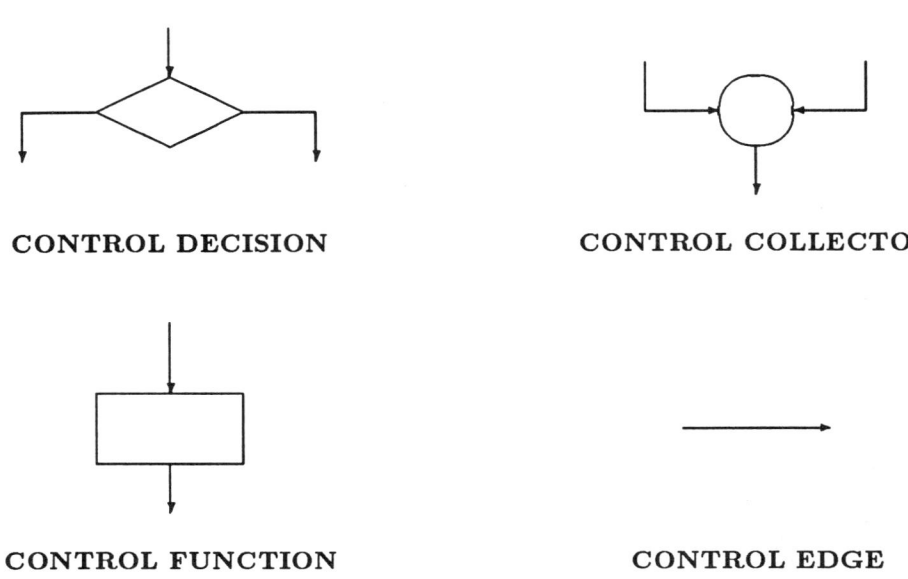

CONTROL DECISION

CONTROL COLLECTOR

CONTROL FUNCTION

CONTROL EDGE

Fig. 16.2   Constructional elements of the control graph.

Graph Control Function   This has exactly one input edge and exactly one output edge.

Actions in the program mapped according to the control flow which do not lead to alternative paths, or do not combine them, lead to a control function in the control flow graph.

Control Decision   This has exactly one input edge and two output edges.

This should not only be identified with an IF statement. An IF statement leads to at least one control function which calculates the value of an internal boolean value followed by a decision node which is equivalent to the resulting branch instruction in assembler. Loops also result in at least one control function and one decision node.

Control Collector   This has two input edges and one output edge.

Again, the FI construction does not always represent a collector in the control flow graph. For example, if a GO TO is present in an IF construction then the collector is usually the label referred to in the GO TO instruction. There are always exactly as many decision nodes as collectors.

Control Edge   This has one input node and one output node.

The control edge connects the nodes in the control flow graph and is responsible for the transport of the data which is processed in the nodes.

16.5.2   Elementary Constructs

All programs which run on von Neumann Machines, can be modelled in terms of the above primitives. We have further defined a restricted set of combinations of these building blocks for the purpose of defining a structure criterion which is described in the following and in Figure 16.3.

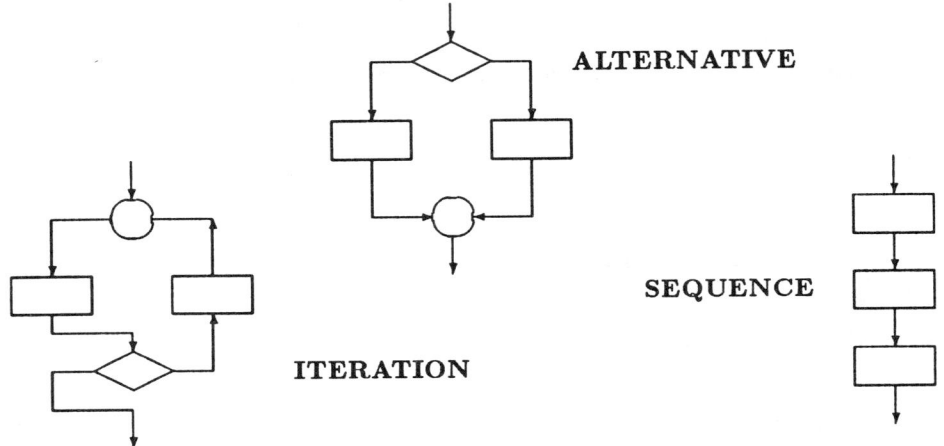

Fig. 16.3   Elementary constructs of a structured control graph.

Sequence A series of one or more control functions.

Alternative A decision node, two alternative control functions and a collector.

> This is similar to an IF-THEN-ELSE-FI in most program description languages.

Iteration A collector, control function, decision and a further control function.

> This is similar to a DO-WHILE-DO-ELIHW, our generalization of the loops found in most program description languages.

All of these elementary constructs have exactly one input edge and exactly one output edge. Thus all of these elementary constructs can be globalized to the form of a control function at a higher hierachical level. If a program is composed only of these elementary constructs this procedure can be carried out until the entire module is representable as a single control function.

This structure condition is considerably more restricted than most conventional structure conditions. It has, however, the major advantage that the readability of the control flow is maximized and that a whole range of well-defined and relatively simple algorithmic transformations are possible on the resulting structured graphs.

In the case of technical documentation of unstructured programs, similar globalising rules can be used, by representing any sub-graph which has exactly one input and exactly one output as a pseudo control function, irrespective of the structure of the contents.

It is often assumed that the presence of GO TOs, and other internal jumps such as BREAK, in a program necessarily means that the program is unstructured. This is not the case; such jumps mean that the structure of the code in terms of the order of statements does not correspond well with the actual structure of the executable modules. Very little is said about the structure of the resulting module in terms of any structure criterion.[7]

16.5.3   Pictorial Presentations

For the purposes of technical documentation pictorial presentations must be flexible in content, in structure and in depth of detail. In the practical use of such tools in the maintenance phase it is necessary that restricted questions can be answered. For

---

7   See the example in Section 16.5.3 (c).

instance that only details of system calls are presented without further details which are irrelevant for this purpose.

It is vital for the acceptance of such tools, that the documentation is generated at the time that the maintenance action is carried out and that it is generated directly from the sources which are being maintained. Most software engineers have bitter experience of documentation which is in principle up-to-date but is in fact some months or years old, or even simply wrong.

(a) Standards

It must be possible to produce flow diagrams corresponding to all the various standards DIN, IEEE, etc. from the same graph, as well as being able to accommodate local variations in these standards corresponding to various in-house practices. On the other hand it must not only be possible to produce these. The method for the analysis of the graph must not restrict the set of possible presentations.

(b) Zooming

In particular, the presentation of only structures at a particular fixed level of resolution is not tenable. It should be possible to present the application as a global system flow diagram and selectively zoom in on a particular module. Inside this module it must further be possible to select a small part of the module to be presented in detail but still be able to see its connection to the rest of the module.

In the case of a graph which satisfies the structure condition mentioned above this is particularly easy since sub-units of the graph have at all 'magnifications' a single entry and exit edge.

(c) Connection to code

It must be possible to make a direct connection, in a physical as well as a logical sense, between the graphic objects in the pictogram and the original source code.

This becomes less easy when presenting the logical structures resulting from the analysis of the language-independent graph structure. The documentation of the logical structure of the application represents the actual processing structure of the data. The code-language structure is a way of realizing a particular functionality and the transformation from programming language to control structure is not always simple.

For instance the programming of loops in COBOL-74 using the GO TO instruction in the construction – LABEL-CODE-IF-THEN-DO-GO LABEL-FI – was practically inescapable because of the inefficiency of the PERFORM statement. Although conventionally the 'readability' of these constructions at a COBOL code level is often considered poor, the structure of the resulting code is completely equivalent to a while XXXX do XXXX statement in C and equally well structured. The equivalent COBOL-74 PERFORM statement is not very readable since the paragraph which will be performed is some distance away in the code.

It is necessary for a usable technical documentation that such structures can be presented both in terms of the language structure and in terms of the actual control structure. Additionally, as mentioned above, we have the code structure which is the order of the texts describing the statements in the program file. These three levels of resolution are distinct and should be presentable separately or in combination.

16.5.4 Documentary Presentations

The same requirements on flexibility apply to the documentary presentations. Here a fixed set of system call, subroutine call, cross-reference etc. tables is insufficient since

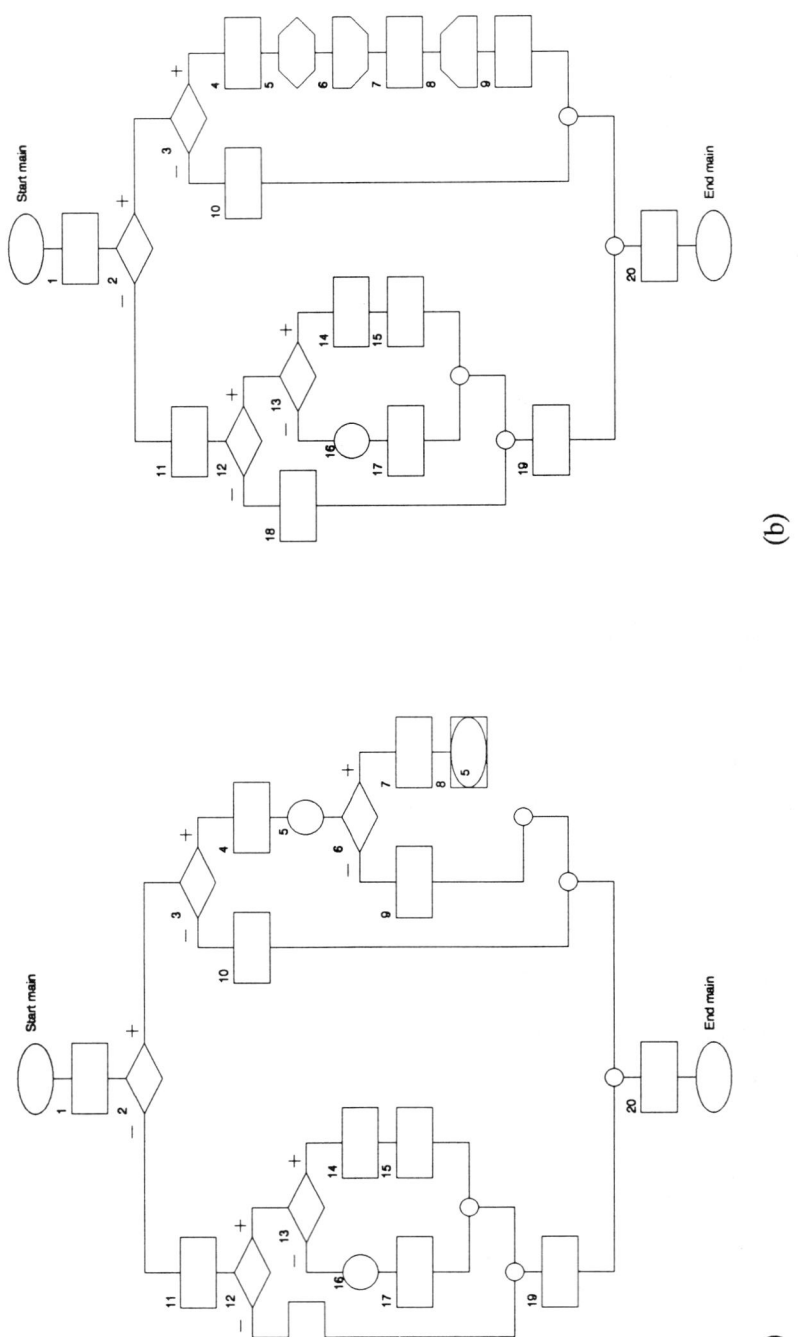

Fig. 16.4   Examples of pictorial presentations of data space showing different representations of the same program module.

the structure of such tables is equally a transformation of the application space as are the pictograms. The use of report generator tools is particularly useful in this respect.

16.6   MAPPING INTO DATA SPACE

As mentioned above, it is possible to define a data space where the direction in the application is given not directly by the control flow but by the logical connection of the data.

The title *Data Processing Application* reveals that the primary aim of such applications is to process data, not to write pretty control flow graphs. While the data aspects have received much attention in data-bank design and other directions, in normal DP applications the considerations of data structure and usage within and between program modules have often been given little attention.

Part of the problem is that there are a lot of tools and methods for structured programming in terms of control structures but very little concerned with structured data. Further, any data structure criteria would have to be programmed in terms of control functions and the transformation from structured data – to control-flow – to code is largely unknown.

The following Constructional Elements, are sufficient to model the data flow of an application in the required detail, see Fig. 16.5.

Data Function A data function can have many inputs and many outputs. Each time an assignment is made to a variable, a data-function node results, input edges transport the functions with which the input data should be processed. The no-operator function NOP is also required.

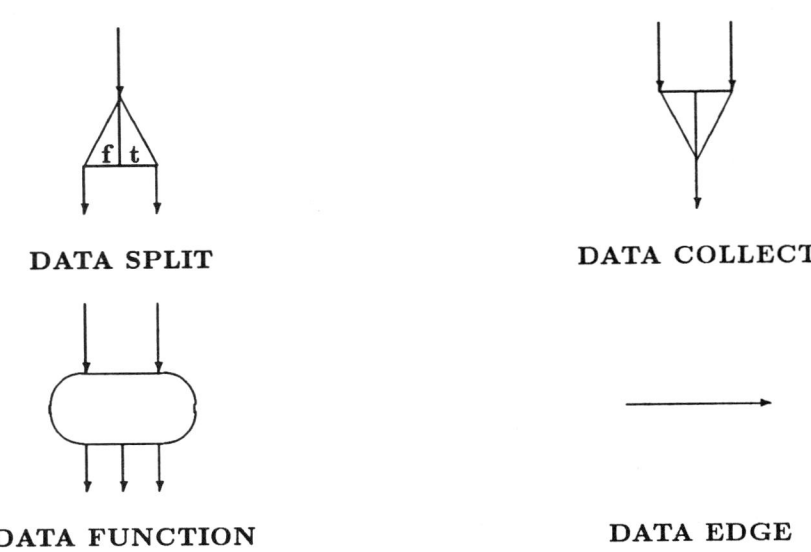

Fig. 16.5 *Constructional elements of the data graph.*

Data Edge The data edge connects data nodes and provides the functions required for the data assignments. Here the UNITY function and the NULL function are also required to fully describe the functionality of the data edges.

The data definition within a single graph is an edge without a previous node, as are parameter transfers from and to other modules.

Data Split   This has one input which is the node corresponding to the value of the internal boolean variable resulting from a decision control node. It has two outputs corresponding to the two possible values P, and P*, for the predicate truth value of this boolean variable. The two outputs are connected to two nodes corresponding to the two alternative assignments[8] resulting from the alternative paths of the control flow decision. For each variable assigned within an alternative or iteration a data split results.

Data Collect   This has exactly two inputs and one output and is the corollary to the data split, 'collecting' the two alternative assignment values for a single variable immediately after the end of the scope of the alternative and combining them to a single assignment value. All three impinging nodes thus represent the same variable.

The functionality of the data split, data collect and two of the three assignment nodes formally belongs inside the data edges themselves and can be included there both in the theoretical framework and in the graph structure.

There are, however, practical problems involved in the handling and interpretation of the resulting graphs when the edge functions are included in a real storage structure. In the present data design for the storage of the graphs it has been possible to reduce the functionality of the edges to that of direction only thus allowing the storage of the nodes alone, the edges being formed simply by joins between nodes in the relational design. It is not yet fully clarified whether the modelling of additional edge functions will be necessary. In this case the edges would have to be specifically included as data elements in the database. It is probable that this problem will be finally

---

8   Including NOP assignment if necessary.

decided in the course of the amalgamation of control and data graphs to a unified application graph.

16.6.1   Elemental Constructs

There are elemental constructs in data space which have their equivalents in control space. In the data space, however, a single alternative or iteration applies to only a single variable. An alternative in control space is expanded in the data space into a number of 'data-parallel' alternatives, these have a single data function node corresponding to the setting of the internal boolean variable. From this, radiate as many edges as there are assignments to distinguishable variables inside the alternative. Each of these variables has its own data split which marks the two initial assignments and its own data collector which collects the final[9] assignment values for this variable at the end of the alternative.

Above we have recognized that the resolution of the control flow is possible at at least three levels – the code, the language structure and the elemental structure similar levels seem to exist in the data flow based on the programmed data structures rather than the programmed control structures.

From the point of view of the data flow, there is a local component of direction to the graph which is necessarily the same as that for the control flow. An event in the control graph which precedes another data-dependent event cannot succeed it in the data graph. However, processing events which are not data-dependent on each other appear in the data graph in parallel, irrespective of the order in which they are actually programmed in the code. Between any two given connected points in the data graph

---

9   The initial and final assignments can, of course, be a single assignment.

there must be an equivalent path in the control flow, but the length of the equivalent path can be very different. Non-data-related events in the control flow graph need have no equivalent paths in the data flow.

The parallelism of data flow inside alternative constructions is mirrored by parallelism between modules. The transfer of parameters is forced by the control flow to take place over physical data interfaces which are defined by the code. It is probable that logical data interfaces will result from an analysis of applications which have no direct parallel in the control flow. The aim of the present work is to make such logical data usage patterns visible as well as documenting the physical usage patterns forced by the program itself for comparison. A portion of the data flow graph containing as many exactly matching data-collects as data-splits can be considered as a data-function with the observed number of input edges and output edges. In general any number of data function nodes can be gathered together to form a more complex data function node. This forms a corresponding concept to that of globalization of the control flow graph. Little is known about data-structure criteria at this level. In particular it is not clear what happens to the control flow when one undertakes such globalizations in data space and vice versa.

16.6.2   Pictorial Presentations

Very little experience is available of the best ways of presenting data flow diagrams, particularly where these diagrams are extracted from existing applications. The pictures produced are difficult to interpret, mainly we think because they are unfamiliar. Our experience shows a similar learning curve to that for control flow diagrams. The pictorial representation of the data flow is made more difficult because of the logical parallelism of independent data events which quickly leads to a rather confusing web of lines. It is probable that such representations, as also for reports, will need to be restricted to a single variable to be clear. There is thus a requirement for interactive, dialogue controlled tools in the technical documentation of data flow.

An alternative style of pictorial representation of the data flow shown in Fig. 16.7[10] leads to less confusion between the various variables and possibly shows the data usage structure more clearly. The connections to the code and the control graph are, however, far less evident.

16.6.3 Documentary Presentations

The documentation of the data flow should include the functional representation of a given assignment value in terms of its input variables – the data function. In principle it is possible to document the data function of a final result of an application in terms of all related input variables.

As a first step, flexible dependency tables in both directions would be of enormous help in maintenance tasks. These would show data which are affected by a change in the value of a particular input or data which contribute to a particular output.

Meaningful methods and presentations are being investigated in case studies in the commercial sector as well as in-house.

---

10   Recommended Diagramming Standards for Analysts and Programmers,
       J. Martin, Prentice-Hall, 1987.

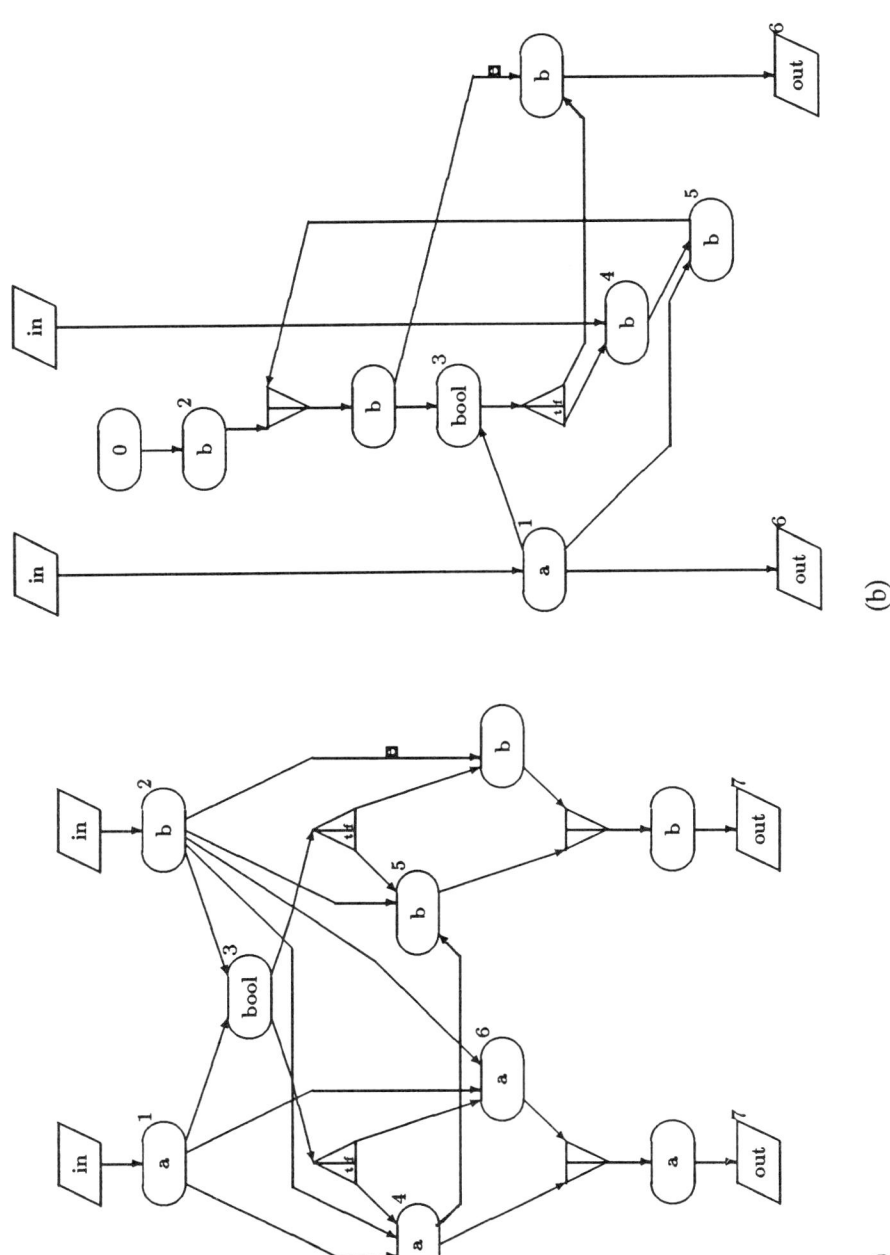

Fig. 16.6 Examples of pictorial presentations of data space.

16.7   APPLICATION SPACE

Both the control space and data space are mappings which have a common basis – the application. In both cases the one-to-one connection to the other space has been made a primary requirement on the realization of the transformation. In this way it is hoped that we can establish a generalized application graph of which control flow and the data flow are both mappings. This would make it possible to browse between both spaces at will and investigate for example the data around a control structure and vice-versa.

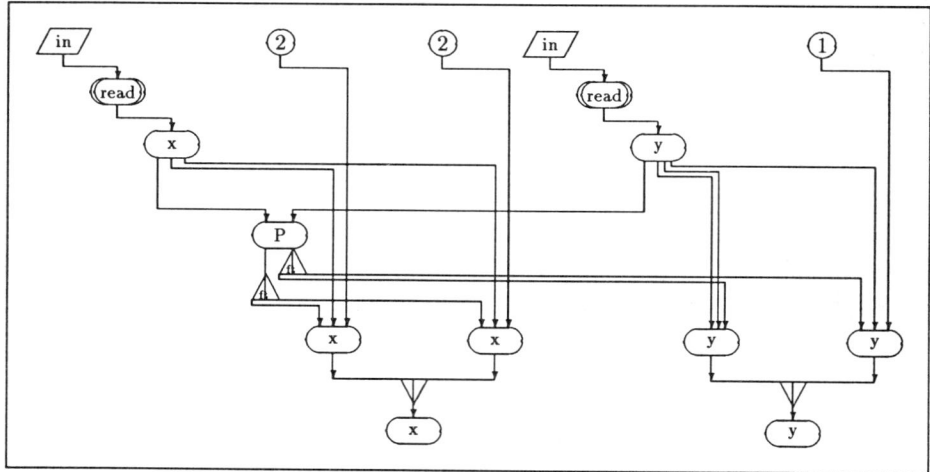

Fig. 16.7   Data flow graph in alternative presentation, adapted from J. Martin.

One approach is based on the commonality of the data between control and data flow. A datum can be considered in the control flow to be an edge. In the data flow it is clearly a node. If it is possible to generate a graphical unit for the datum which is structurally and functionally identical in both of the spaces, this could form a common element. Thus the application graph could consist of only two information structures: control nodes ≡ data edges and control edges ≡ data nodes.

The alternative approach is to generate both the control flow graph and the data flow graph and include in each a bi-directional mechanism which connects the two. This would have the advantage that the two current mappings discussed above are directly extractable.

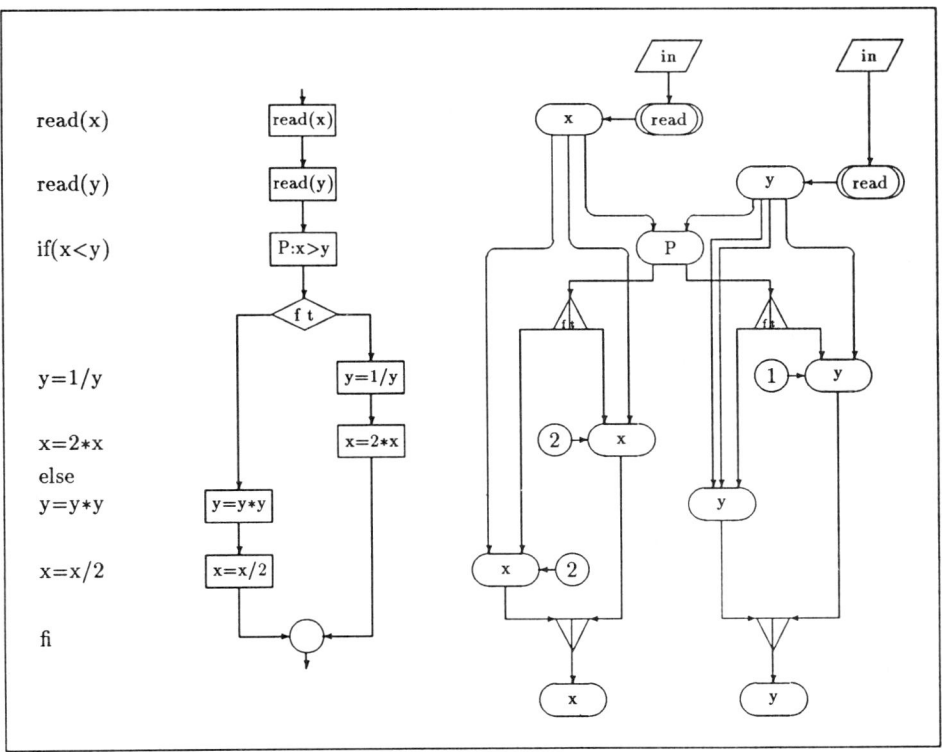

Figure 16.8 Example of combined view: code, control flow and data flow.

It seems unlikely that the structure criteria for the control flow and possible structure criteria for data flow could be mutually exclusive. How far it will be possible to establish a unified structure criterion for control and data simultaneously is understandably unclear.

Figure 16.8 shows a pictorial representation of the code, the control flow graph and the data flow graph for a simple program example. The potential advantages of simultaneous, mixed or alternate viewing of the three representations of the application should be clear.

16.8   TOOL SET

16.8.1   Graph-SDDB

The structure of the Graph Units corresponding to the various elements in the mathematical model is established in the data dictionary of a common relational database. ASCII files and C structures for all programs are derived automatically from this structure, generating C include files, so that changes can only take place globally and consistency is assured.

The relational database is used only for the storage and retrieval of the complete graphs this requires that functions such as add, delete etc. are available to manipulate the intermediate ASCII files directly.

16.8.2   Transformers

(a)   Source to graph-SDDB

Transformers have been developed for COBOL and C based on the UNIX compiler generating tools Lex and Yacc. The tight reference to the source is established on a byte level – each graph unit containing such a connection to the code producing it.

Because of the peculiar structure of the COBOL language, it was found to be necessary to split the transformer into a number of distinguishable Lex and Yacc steps which run either in series or in parallel within a common main program.

(b) Graph-SDDB to source

For technical documentation purposes alone it is not strictly necessary to be able to carry out the back-transformation from graph to code. The concurrent establishment and testing of the back-transformation is, however, the only way to ensure consistency and accurately test that the graph structure completely represents the source. Furthermore, for the extension of the graph method to restructuring and other purposes, the back-transformation is an absolute must and is being developed and tested strictly in parallel to the forwards transformation.

16.8.3 Report and Dialogue Generators

The production of fixed styles of graphics or list reports is not consistent with the marketplace, where each software house has its own standards and wishes. Further, as mentioned above, a small desired change in a report should lead to a changed report program which still operates directly against the information base SDDB. Such changes should not be patched on to information which has already been extracted and thus transformed.

It is therefore desirable, and necessary for commercial success, to be as flexible as possible in the generation of reports. This requires the use of code generators which operate against some sort of 4GL. Report and dialogue programs have been and will be produced using our in-house code generators, CGLR (C-Graphik-Listen-Rahmen) and CDR (C-Dialog-Rahmen,) which are programmed in an SQL type 4GL producing portable C code which interfaces with X-Windows OSF- Motif and the C interface of common relational database products. The generators themselves are not part of the technical documentation toolkit but will be used to produce updates etc. as required.

16.8.4 Restructuring Tools

These have been dealt with in general terms above. The basic principle used in the development of these tools, as in all the other tools is flexibility. Restructuring is in general a transformation of the structure of the program. The tools for this transformation must be as independent as possible of the details of the particular transformation as possible. This is simplified by the adoption of the SQL interface between the database and all programs. Many SDDB graph-unit structures are directly expressible in terms of a single SQL-type select statement.

The pragmatic approach adopted is to restructure the data and the control successively until both structure criteria are satisfied. Although little experience has up to now been gathered with this technique applied to data flow, the possibilities are extremely promising for such considerations as parallel processing, database design, identification of logical modules etc. In these cases the control flow is clearly subsidiary to the data flow, our aim is to be able to produce at least 99 executable codes from the restructured data flow.

16.8.5 Remodularization Tools

(a) Identifying reusable modules

If the outlines of the functional domain of a module in the graph space can be defined it can be marked within the graph database including all attached data and extracted.

The extracted module will contain the functionality required but also a lot of irrelevant code. The irrelevant code must be removed, still leaving the required code in a connected state for both data and control.

(b) Configuration of interfaces

The module, freed of unnecessary code, is normally no longer executable. In particular the interface to the outside world can suffer because of the internal rearrangement. It will be possible semi-automatically, with online support, to rearrange data definitions and input and output before further configuration including possible restructuring with a particular aim in mind – the target use and environment.

16.8.6 Metrication Tools

(a) Generation of product metrics

The graph approach described above enables the extraction of almost all details of the structure of the application, including of course those several different styles of metrics conventionally referred to as software product metrics.

(b) Reliability metrics

Another function of the metrics tools is to highlight features of the program which are implicit in the structure but are not directly visible and which may not be what the programmer really desired. A concrete decision must then be made by the programmer about whether the construction is intended.

(c) Test case generation

For a given test strategy, defined in terms of the functional specification of the application, the tools can be used to help define the test procedures for the application. If an output variable K should be tested, from the data graph it is possible to specify which input variables are relevant. If all control paths are to be tested at least once, these can be fixed in terms of the data input and output to these paths.

Part Five

Reuse and Re-engineering for Parallel or Distributed Hardware

17 Re-engineering software for distributed execution

S.J. Goldsack

Imperial College of Science, Technology and Medicine

17.1 INTRODUCTION

The availability of cheap microcomputers has encouraged the development of system based on networks of such machines, cooperating to provide the overall functionality required by the application. Such systems have several advantages over conventional uniprocessor systems:

- Performance: Concurrent execution of the code in the different machines provide greater overall throughput with low cost.

- Reduced communication needs: The programs required to conduct control of an extended plant can be geographically distributed, placing processing power close to the devices and plant-objects involved in the system. Processing of high urgency can therefore be done without transferring large amounts of data to and from a central site. Long distance communication is reduced to general coordination of the system. Compared with transferring raw data to a single central site, this requires a smaller bandwidth, reducing both cost and sensitivity to noisy environments.

• Adaptability: Hardware and software may be adapted and reconfigured to adapt to changing needs of the environment and the availability of new devices and processors.

• Fault tolerance: Failure of hardware in a distributed system may not cause total failure. Reconfiguration of software can permit degraded execution with reduced hardware, or replacement hardware may be on standby to assume the functions of the damaged processors.

To set against these advantages, it must be recognized that communication between processors over a network involves delays which may be difficult to predict, but which will often exceed by orders of magnitude the delays in accessing data or processes in the same processor.

17.2 DEVELOPMENT OF DISTRIBUTED PROCESSING SYSTEMS

Distributed software may be written in a number of different ways. Two extreme approaches are:

(a)   A separate program is written for each machine in the network, and inter-machine communication is handled by the operating system and its associated communication primitives. The programmer introduces explicit calls on these primitives to handle the passing of messages between the otherwise independent programs.

(b)   The programs for the application are written by the application program without regard to the way in which the program will eventually be executed in the network. Communication between machines is transparently handled by the compiled system, so that the programmer need not distinguish, for example, between a call to procedure in a remote node of the network and a call to one which is locally resident. The compilation system will handle the first by a normal subprogram call and return mechanism in the same machine, while compiling the second into appropriate sequences of send-and-receive primitives to use the message-passing facilities of the networking system.

17.2.1   The Separate Program Approach

It is evident that the first solution provides a straightforward and universally available technique, but is unsatisfactory for programming systems for our purpose. Since the network communication is explicitly coded into the application software, it will never be possible to run the programs in a network structure different from that for which the system is built, and there is no possibility of change to reconfigure the system, following failure, for example. Software written this way is non-portable and non-reusable. There is no possibility of extending the network and adding new capabilities without amending large parts of the existing system. We therefore reject the approach as a solution to coding modern distributed systems.

17.2.2   The Single Program Approach

The second approach is more promising. In principle, a programmer could compose a single logical program, defining the functionality of the system, while ignoring completely the possibility of its eventual distributed execution, leaving to the compiler the task of subdividing the work of the program between the processors in the network introducing remote communication where necessary to achieve the overall effect as specified by the source program. A program initially written without consideration for possible distributed execution could be recompiled to run in different hardware architectures. The intelligent compiler would be supplied with some definition of the structure of the network of processors to be used as a target, and the appropriate collection of program units for the different machines would be automatically produced with their communication built in.

In practice, however, this is unrealistic. Apart from the fact that a compiler with the appropriate degree of intelligence is difficult to write, the resulting code would be subject to potentially unacceptable delays. Even a simple assignment statement might be between items residing in different machines, and involve handshaking messages across the network; moreover it would be difficult to predict performance with any accuracy, since the user would never know whether or not an operation would involve networking delays. Although some attempts have been made to develop systems of this kind, we shall not consider this approach further here.

17.2.3   An Intermediate Approach

In the first of these techniques the programmer must have (and build into the code) knowledge not only all about the decomposition of the problem into separable parts but also all about the network architecture and the operating system communication mechanisms; in the second he need concern himself with neither. The most satisfactory approach, however, lies between these limits.

It is the proper role of a programmer to take account of the composition of the problem domain, identifying how the application is structured; it is his role to design software components responsible for managing the parts of the total system. The programs should define the communication between these components in a machine-independent way, independently both of the hardware and of the operating system. It is the role of the compiler to arrange these machine-dependent details. With this separation of responsibility, all details of the network architecture and operating system are invisible to the programmer, and the software may be reconfigured to run in a different network with minimal change.

Thus, in this approach, the programmer is aware in writing the program that distribution is intended. The components are written in such a way that communication between them is defined (typically as procedure and function calls) independently of whether they will ultimately be executed in the same node of the network or not. Thus flexibility is maintained, and it is the system designer and programmer who are responsible for recognizing which are the time-critical activities which cannot reasonably be subjected to the long and unpredictable networking delays, so must be handled within a single component. The components represent a kind of granularity of the code, providing the system with units of allocation. Construction of systems in such a way largely separates the concerns of functionality from those of configuration.

In practice most work on distributed programming has concentrated, in one way or another, on this second approach.

17.3 DISTRIBUTABLE PROGRAMS

From the above discussion it is clear that designing distributed programs involves the recognition of components to serve as units of distribution, allocation and reconfiguration and, potentially also, of reuse. In connection with Ada programming the term virtual node was coined to describe these units of distributed execution (Tedd et al. 1984), (Hutcheon and Wellings 1988), (Goldsack et al. 1987), (Atkinson et al. 1988), and in the remainder of this paper that name will be used for such structures in Ada and, where appropriate, extended also to corresponding units in other languages.

17.3.1 The Concept of a Virtual Node

Virtual nodes are a convenient name for the components composed by a programmer to form units of distribution and allocation (and possible reconfiguration) in a network. However, it would be wrong to consider that they have been introduced solely for the purpose of distribution. It has been remarked that the composition of the program components must take account of those aspects of the system which require close cooperation and high communication speed. It is natural, therefore, that they map closely onto the application structures; control of a well-defined subsystem in the external world will be managed, or modelled, by a program component which can be expected to run in a single machine. Thus, the concerns of network decomposition are closely related to those of system modelling. A well-designed program for an application will naturally be structured in terms of components having many of the features required by virtual nodes. A virtual node must be viewed as an abstraction from the application domain, as well as a convenient unit of distribution. This mapping becomes more apparent when the considerations of reconfiguration for fault tolerance are included; any replacement of code will usually be for some well-defined subsystem of the application.

The following list gives some of the main properties of virtual nodes:

- They model well-defined abstractions of the application.

- They encapsulate their state, communicating with others only by message passing (usually represented as procedure calls). They must never share direct access to data of other nodes.

- To model active entities in the system, they should be able to have independent 'threads of control', so that they can execute concurrently with others.

- In the terminology of Structured Analysis and Design (see for example Page Jones 1983) they represent modules with high cohesion and low coupling.

- For interaction with other virtual nodes they should use the same communication protocols for local (intra-processor) communication and for remote (extra-processor) communication. This property has been referred to as communication transparency.

- Ideally, to provide a degree of flexibility, maximizing the separation of the functionality and the configuration of the system they should be separately compilable, and constitute 'types' in the language, so that a system may contain many copies of a virtual node structure, and they may themselves be organised into structures such as arrays and records.

- Again ideally, they should use an indirect naming scheme, so permitting communication with other virtual nodes to be redirected dynamically during reconfiguration.

It can be noted that textbooks of software engineering would list many of these properties as appropriate for modules of design in any software system.

17.3.2   Communication between Virtual Nodes

Since virtual nodes are expected to communicate over a network, it is evident that, in the implementation of internode communication, information flow between the parts of the program will be by message passing. The natural way to represent message transfer between program units in conventional language terms is by defining suitable subprograms. Outgoing messages are represented by 'in' parameters while returned messages can be handled as 'out' parameters or as results from function evaluations. This does not rule out the access by one unit to data stored in another if the programmer considers that appropriate; a suitable procedure or function to access the data and return its value as a message on request from a remote node can be provided. However, direct visibility of data, permitting direct assignments to and from it, are impossible.

The use of procedures for describing interactions between virtual nodes provides the property of communication transparency, required by the above list of properties. If communicating virtual nodes are to be loaded into the same processor, then normal implementation of the procedure call is adequate; if they are to communicate over the network, then the call must be implemented as a remote procedure call. Details of this implementation would ideally be hidden from the programmer, in an environment where it is supported by the language implementation; however, relatively simple transformations of code can be used to replace the remote procedure calls by suitable sequences of calls on the communications primitives of the runtime system. The compiler can then compile separate load modules for the separate machines   Details may be found in the book describing the DIADEM approach (Atkinson et al. 1988). Such transformations can be implemented manually or by software tools. Of course it could be argued that this technique represents a return to the use of separate programs, which was dismissed in the first section. However, this is not really the case; type checking can be maintained in the communication between the program components in the different machines, and the programmer does not necessarily need to know about the transformation techniques. Moreover, the program can be restructured without affecting the application, by redoing the transformation.

The essence of this development approach lies in the separation of concerns of the programmer for issues of modularization, structure and functionality of the parts on the one hand and of allocation and configuration on the other. A change in the configuration does not impact on the decisions about the functions of the components.

7.4 PROGRAM STRUCTURES FOR VIRTUAL NODES

We shall consider here two alternative ways of constructing programs structured in the way described above. In the first, a special language is used to enable the programmer to give appropriate instructions to a compiler about the distribution. In the second the programs are written in a conventional language, possibly enhanced by the addition of compiler directives.

7.4.1 Using a Special Language

The use of a purpose-designed language, providing structures with appropriate properties, clearly has much in its favour. If a programmer can encapsulate program components in syntactic structures, these can be recognized as 'virtual nodes' by the compilation system. With suitable choice of the semantics of the components they can be given all the properties required of such objects. Typically, a second stage of programming defines the population and communication patterns of these virtual nodes, often using a different language. The rest of the configuring of the actual program on the network can then be done automatically. A typical and well-designed language with the appropriate properties is CONIC (Dulay *et al.* 1987). In this the designer composes programs in terms of task modules, which correspond to the virtual nodes, and group modules which cluster one or more task modules into larger structures intended to execute on a machine. Work on the CONIC system has included consideration of techniques for dynamic reconfiguration (Kramer and Magee 1985).

Other languages and environments developed explicitly for the development of distributed programs are Communication Port (Mao and Yeh 1980), Argos (Liskov 1982), Galaxy (Kung and Kung 1985).

17.4.2 Using a Conventional Language

Use of a special language is not always convenient. It does not, for example, satisfy the requirement for the use of the Ada language in the development of defence systems;

nor does it provide an immediate solution to the reuse of existing programs written for some standard hardware, re-engineered for execution on a network. (Though recoding of an existing design into such a language could be considered.) Moreover, many programmers are understandably reluctant to adopt different languages for programming distributed and uniprocessor systems. A uniprocessor system is, after all, only the limiting case of a distributed system for a network of one machine. For these reasons we must consider the use of languages which were not originally designed for use in creating network software. These could include any of the 'classical' languages such as FORTRAN, Pascal or Ada.

It is evident that the convenience of a language depends on the extent to which it provides structures whose properties correspond to those of virtual nodes listed above. The main properties of virtual nodes are in fact provided by a number of languages which support modularity of the kind represented by classes in Simula, packages in Ada and modules in Modula. These share the feature that they export (i.e. make visible to other components through a defined interface) sets of procedure and function specifications, and encapsulate their implementations with the state variables in a definition body which hides it from any direct access by other components. In this category fall abstract data types, where structures and their appropriate operations are packaged in this way. All access to such data is through subprograms placed in the interface by the system designer.

The Simula class was the original source of the idea, exploited in languages commonly referred to as 'Object Oriented', in which the modules are derived from class definitions. Classes are 'types' or templates for constructing objects which are also called class instances. References to objects are through class instance variables, which are pointers to instances of the class. This provides indirect naming, so that communication of a component can be defined in terms of some partner whose actual identity need not be determined until a later time. This is crucial in giving fully the separation of concerns mentioned earlier. Although Ada packages provide the encapsulation required, separating the specification of the interface from the body of an object, they do not possess the features of (dynamic) replicability and indirect naming, which is one of the causes of difficulty in the use of Ada for distribution and (especially) reconfiguration.

Without some suitable language features providing such a unit of encapsulation, programmers are unprotected from errors, but may still be able to structure their programs in the appropriate way, ensuring, by the application of an appropriate discipline to their work, that data structures are associated with the operations which act on them, and that no external use is made of the structures without calling the procedures implementing the appropriate operations. Surprisingly, perhaps, FORTRAN 77 subroutines can be defined with multiple entries, and it is not difficult to organize these as a collection of access procedures for the internally defined data.

Because, as remarked above, multiprocessor systems execute components in parallel, the equivalence of the behaviour of a program in distributed form and that in a single processor is most apparent if the language used supports concurrency, so only languages with that feature are really convenient for use as languages for distributed execution. In fact, much effort in this area has concentrated on the Ada language, and it will be convenient to review some of that work in this paper.

We shall see shortly, however, that the flexibility required for creating virtual nodes which are also adaptable for reuse in different systems, and for reconfiguration following fault detection, suggests that the object-oriented approach should be adopted, and that objects can be the appropriate units to serve as virtual nodes.

17.5 DISTRIBUTING ADA PROGRAMS

The development of techniques for distribution of Ada programs has received a great deal of attention for several reasons.

1.   Ada was designed in the first place for use in the programming of 'embedded computer systems'. These include the kind of distributed control systems discussed above.

2.   Ada supports concurrent execution of components called tasks.

3   It has support of the US Department of Defense and, in principle, its use is required for the development of software for defence systems both in Europe and the USA. Its successful use in this field can have important benefits.

4.   It has signally failed to deliver its expected benefits in the distributed field.

As we saw above, the Ada package does not possess the properties of a type, so cannot be used as a template for creating multiple instances. Moreover, it cannot be indirectly referenced, so there is no potential for flexible naming schemes. On the other hand, the task does possess these features, but can only be used inside some other structure. Thus a network of tasks cannot be used to compose a distributed program either.

Because of its importance, there have been a number of projects to study how best to overcome these shortcomings of Ada and use it effectively in this domain. Although attempts have been made to compile single Ada programs for distributed targets, notably by researchers at Honeywell (Cornhill 1983) and at Michigan University (Volz et al. 1985) most work has concentrated on attempts at using Ada's own structures to support the definition of units suitable for distribution.

17.5.1 Virtual Nodes in DIADEM, Aspect and DRAGON

Several Ada-oriented projects have proposed structural units for virtual nodes.These include DIADEM (Atkinson et al. 1988), Aspect (Hutcheon and Wellings 1988), and DRAGON (Di Maio et al. 1989). A further example is (Fantechi et al. 1986). Diadem chose to structure each virtual node as closely as possible to a complete Ada program, with a main program which is a procedure. Each VN defines an interface in the form of a package exporting a task specification. Apart from calls from one node to task entries in another, each unit is an independent program. Aspect, on the other hand, chose to use a package as the main program unit for a virtual node. The differences are relatively small and based on technicalities of the way in which Ada programs are elaborated. In neither case is the dynamic creation of virtual nodes fully supported, though DIADEM does offer some capability of defining a restricted form of virtual node type.

In the DRAGOON project discussed in some detail below a much more radical approach has been taken. An Ada-related language called DRAGOON has been developed which is truly object-oriented and in which classes can be developed incrementally through the use of compile time (static) inheritance; the power of the object-oriented approach for reuse is fully exploited. However, unlike most OONs, objects in DRAGOON can be 'active' and execute concurrently with others. They can also, therefore, be appropriate units of allocation, the virtual nodes.

17.5.2   The DRAGOON Approach

The DRAGOON project (Esprit No. 1550) aims not only to support the distribution of Ada software, but also its reuse and to support fault tolerance through its dynamic reconfiguration. Several possible strategies were considered as a means of unifying these diverse goals, but it became clear that the techniques of object-oriented programming would offer the best framework.

As well as promoting good programming practices, such as modular design and separation of concerns, object-oriented languages possess a number of features serving to encourage software reuse. Although Ada is sometimes claimed to be object-oriented (because the package provides the encapsulation and interface which are part of the characteristics of an object, so that it is possible to represent the basic notion of objects in Ada), the language does not directly support the mechanisms of inheritance or the dynamic binding which are mainly responsible for the power of object-oriented programming from the point of view of reuse. Furthermore, as we saw above, its packages lack also the flexible naming which is provided by indirect referencing.

Few object-oriented languages address the question of distribution, or even the prerequisite notion of concurrency. The few that do, such as Emerald (Black *et al.* 1987), do not support inheritance and so do not provide the reuse advantages of object-oriented programming. In Ada, concurrency is a built-in feature of the language. However, as we remarked above, Ada's tasks prove unsuitable for direct use in structuring objects.

Realising the project goals within an object-oriented framework, therefore, not only involved devising a technique for implementing the principal mechanisms of object-oriented programming in Ada, but also extending the object-oriented paradigm to handle concurrency, distribution and reconfiguration. The project team therefore developed a language called DRAGOON (Distributable, Reusable Ada Generated from an Object-Oriented Notation), which supports all the importance of object-oriented languages, but also extends the conventional inheritance model to handle aspects of concurrency and distribution. Tools for converting DRAGOON programs into Ada have been designed, so one way of viewing DRAGOON is as a design language for Ada.

Although the object-oriented features of DRAGOON have been designed in the spirit of Ada, and follow the language's syntactic conventions so far as possible, DRAGOON, unlike DIADEM, does not stay faithful to the Ada standard.

17.5.3   Overview of DRAGOON

The fundamental concept in an object-oriented language is obviously the 'object'. This is a program entity which presents an external interface in the form of a set of operations or methods, and which possesses a state that 'remembers' the effect of these operations. It therefore has the main properties required of virtual nodes. An object is accessed from other objects by means of a reference (or pointer) variable, usually termed an instance variable. The instance variables of an object referencing other objects are hidden from the rest of the system by being encapsulated in a manner similar to the local variables of an Ada task or package. However, it is important to realize that the objects which they reference are not necessarily logically parts of the object, and may not be so encapsulated.

The reference stored in an instance variable may be changed dynamically by direct assignment or be used as a parameter of a method call. This enables a program to change the values of instance variables during execution so that calls are directed to the methods of a different instance of the appropriate class. This provides flexible naming, so that dynamic reconfiguration is possible.

Closely related to the notion of an object is that of a class, which is a template, or 'object type', from which any number of structurally identical objects may be created. Classes act both as types in the language, and as separately compilable units of modularity. As such they naturally form units of reuse, but as in other object-oriented languages the possibilities for reuse in DRAGOON are further enhanced by the mechanisms of multiple (static) inheritance, polymorphism and dynamic binding.

DRAGOON is not, however, a 'pure' object-oriented language in the sense of Smalltalk (Goldberg and Robson 1983) and Emerald in which all data items must be represented as objects. This is because there are many entities that need to be represented within computer programs which do not correspond naturally to objects; these are typically 'qualities' such as 'greenness', or 'pure' abstractions such as numbers and boolean values. Although the 'pure' object-oriented model can be weakened to handle these concepts, as demonstrated by Smalltalk, most object-oriented languages for commercial software development, such as Eiffel (Meyer 1988), C++ (Stroustrup, 1986) and Objective C (Cox, 1986) include primitive data types (e.g. REAL, INTEGER, CHARACTER, BOOLEAN) supporting traditional 'value-oriented' programming.

DRAGOON goes much further than these languages in that it incorporates the full typing scheme of Ada (except task types). It is, therefore, a fully 'mixed', or 'hybrid', language completely supporting 'value-oriented' as well object-oriented programming. Whether a particular abstraction should be modelled as a 'class type' or 'data type' is the choice of the programmer, although the DRAGOON design method provides assistance in this judgement. In order to allow conventional (Ada-style) type declaration to be shared by a number of classes, DRAGOON permits the use of stateless packages called template packages. These serve as convenient repositories for defining conventional data types, subprograms and exceptions. All variables in DRAGOON must be defined in class bodies. DRAGOON classes differ from those found in most other languages in that they possess separate specifications and body parts which, in the style of Ada packages, are separately compilable library units.

Since DRAGOON is intended for use in the same application domains as Ada, it adopts a similar policy of strong typing in order to improve program correctness. Moreover, to minimize run-time overheads, DRAGOON also adopts the Ada philosophy of performing as much checking as possible at compile time (i.e. statically) by ensuring that all assignments are compatible with their declared type. In an object-oriented context this transposes into the goal of ensuring that no assignment (whether direct, or by the matching of actual and formal method parameters) could result in a method call being directed to an object which is not able to service it.

Since an heir class generally inherits all the methods and variables of its ancestor(s) it can be used in any context where one of its ancestors is expected. Therefore, like other object-oriented languages (e.g. Eiffel, Smalltalk) DRAGOON uses the inheritance hierarchy as the basis for determining the type compatibility of classes. A class is assignment-compatible with another – that is, a subtype (or subclass) of it – if, and only if, it is its descendant. The reverse assertion is not true in DRAGOON, however, because it is possible to remove inherited methods from the interface of an heir class.

Like languages such as Eiffel (Meyer 1988) and POOL (America 1987), DRAGOON also includes the notion of generic classes which can be parameterized with respect to both data or class types.

17.5.4 Concurrency

The section above has introduced the main 'sequential' features of the language, which are fairly typical of object-oriented languages. As remarked above, any language wishing to support the development of distributed embedded applications, however, must also provide some means of describing concurrency. Although a number of concurrent object-oriented languages have been developed, this is an immature field, and no previous language has successfully combined concurrency features with the inheritance mechanism. DRAGOON introduces a number of new concepts which aim to rectify this situation.

There are three main issues which must be addressed by languages intending to facilitate the design of concurrent systems:

- the generation of concurrent execution threads (or processes),

- inter-process communication,

● inter-process synchronization.

DRAGOON has abandoned the Ada model of tasks and handles concurrency for active objects in the same way as most of the other object-oriented languages which support concurrency (e.g. POOL (America, 1987), Emerald (Black *et al.* 1987)). An object in DRAGOON may optionally be provided with a thread which executes concurrently with the threads of other objects and with invocations of its own methods by calls from other objects. Essentially this approach unifies the notion of an object from the object-oriented world and a process from the operating systems and parallel processing worlds. Objects can model active agents in the world, coexisting with and conducting their affairs concurrently with others. In DRAGOON the thread of an object is activated by invocation of the special START method which is automatically part of the interface of an object possessing a thread.

Having identified the object as the unit of concurrency in DRAGOON, it is natural to use the method call as the mechanism for communication between them. This approach is also taken by the other languages cited above. However, DRAGOON differs from these in that the method call is always synchronous – that is, the caller is blocked until the method call completes. If asynchronous communication is required this can be constructed by the application programmer using some form of buffer object.

When it comes to the strategy for achieving synchronization DRAGOON differs more significantly from other approaches. Although it shares the basic philosophy of regarding an object as a form of 'monitor' which shields its internal state from erroneous concurrent access, it adopts a completely different approach for specifying the access protocol. In virtually all imperative concurrent languages adopting a monitor-like approach to the protection of data, the designer of the 'monitor' is responsible for explicitly encoding the access protocol, whether it be by means of semaphores, condition variables or, in the case of Ada, select statements and guards. This protocol, therefore, is embodied in the code of the component, despite the fact that it is completely independent of the 'sequential' operations for accessing the data.

To make it possible to reuse the 'sequential' parts of an object with different access protocols, DRAGOON allows the required synchronization conditions to be superimposed on a purely 'sequential' class by a form of inheritance known as behavioural inheritance . Behavioural classes use a simple form of deontic logic (Genolini *et al.* 1989) to specify a generic behaviour in terms of formally named sets of methods. As such they are not normal classes, and cannot be directly instantiated. The formal names are matched to the actual names of the methods of the sequential class when the behaviour is inherited.

17.5.5 Distribution in DRAGOON

At first sight, classes/objects from the object-oriented programming world would seem ideal constructs for acting as virtual nodes in the partitioning of software for distribution (Atkinson and Goldsack 1989). They possess many of the properties laid out above as important for supporting configuration flexibility:

- classes are separately compilable 'types' from which multiple instances (i.e. objects) can be instantiated,

- objects communicate through well-defined interfaces by a message-based protocol,

- they name each other indirectly using reference semantics,

- they may possess an independent thread making them into autonomous processes.

There is, however, one fundamental aspect of objects which impairs their suitability to act as virtual nodes. They do not safely encapsulate their internal states.

This might seem a surprising statement to make, given the frequency with which the modularity and encapsulation properties of objects are emphasized. However, object-oriented languages employ reference semantics for identifying objects and cannot guarantee protection of their state. Although communication between them is expressed in terms of method calls, the use of indirect references breaks down the encapsulation barriers and means that objects can be passed references enabling them to access and manipulate the 'internal' state of others.

This problem exists wherever indirect references are used to identify data structures. In Ada, for example, using access types to refer to tasks makes it possible for tasks instantiated within a package body to be accessed from any other part of the program to which the access value is communicated, regardless of the scoping rules that otherwise apply. The problem is particularly troublesome in 'pure' object-oriented languages which only provide indirectly identified objects as the means of representing state, because it is not possible for an object to communicate any information about its state to another object without also conceding permanent visibility. Furthermore, objects in different machines use different address spaces, and references in one machine have no relevance in providing access to data in another.

If virtual node objects designed for possible dispersal over a network cannot communicate by transferring object references, how can they communicate? One approach might be for the objects themselves to be copied over the network, rather than references to them. However, difficult questions are raised about the efficiency and semantics of such copying especially for active objects with threads. The solution adopted in DRAGOON is to restrict virtual nodes to communicating by forming messages composed of values of conventional data types, for which purpose the programmer has the full power of Ada at his disposal. While this means that the power of the object-oriented paradigm is slightly weakened for the purposes of modelling distributable applications, it gives rise to a much simpler and more natural model of remote communication, and reinforces the motivation for the mixed programming paradigm.

It is not desirable, however, to restrict all communication between objects to being by means of data values, since this would rule out the use of many of the most powerful features of object-oriented programming. Reference semantics is invaluable for exploiting the properties of polymorphism and dynamic binding which are so important for reuse, and essential for permitting the sharing of objects. It is essential to permit all these powerful features to be used in building distributable objects, since these may be large modules composed of many other objects. All that is required to support the virtual node approach to distribution is to prohibit the exchange of state references between objects intended to be potentially distributable – that is, virtual node objects.

17.5.6   Executable Objects

As with other object-oriented languages, programming in DRAGOON involves the construction of new classes using instances of those already defined. Normal application classes built in this way can be submitted to the compilation system for use as components in the further definition of new classes, but cannot actually be 'executed' because they simply represent textual definitions of the class functionalities. In other words, they define 'lightweight' processes (objects) which can only execute in the run-time system of another surrounding object.

In any language for distribution a mechanism is required for describing executable objects which correspond to fully-linked, binary, load modules – that is, 'programs'. This is achieved in DRAGOON by extending the use of multiple inheritance to distinguish between the 'heavyweight' and 'lightweight' forms of a class.

To create an executable version of a particular virtual node class, the programmer must define a subclass which inherits from the application class concerned and also from a special execution support class.

By inheriting from an execution support class, the interface of the application class is enriched by the operations that can be performed on processes in the environment in which they are to be executed, and will include the command to start execution. In practice, therefore, it acts as a directive to the compilation system that the necessary steps should be performed to generate a relocatable binary image for execution. The formation of such an executable object will, in general, depend on the nature of the hardware and operating system of the host machine, and on the particular language run-time system. There are, therefore, many different kinds of execution support class modelling the properties of executing programs in different environments.

Like the behavioural classes introduced above, execution support classes are not classes in the normal sense, since they cannot be instantiated independently. Their only function is to serve as parents of virtual node classes endowing them with the quality of executability. Another property they share with behavioural classes is that they do not have bodies. They cannot, in fact, be defined by applications programmers, but are supplied with a DRAGOON development environment as an interface to its compilation facilities.

17.5.7   Physical Node Classes

Allied with the multiple inheritance mechanism, execution support classes provide a means of defining executable 'heavyweight' versions of application objects. In order to build a complete, functioning distributed system, however, it is necessary also to have a way of representing the hardware architecture of the system and the different types of machines it contains. DRAGOON, therefore, also uses the concept of physical node classes as abstractions of the individual processing elements in the network. As well as providing an abstract model of the network nodes to which instances of executable classes may be allocated and executed, physical nodes are used to specify the interface to the services offered by the hardware. Thus, hardware operations which may be activated by the software (or as operator commands) are represented as methods in the interface of the physical node class.

Physical node classes are the natural complement of execution support classes. Each physical node class represents a particular type of processor/ environment that may be used to execute DRAGOON software, and will only accept executable objects that have inherited from an appropriate execution support class – that is, have been compiled by a suitably targeted compiler. Similarly, executable classes that are descendants of a particular kind of execution support class can only be executed on the appropriate type of physical node. Together with execution support classes, therefore, physical node classes facilitate the description of all the different types of components that need to manipulated in the configuration of fully heterogeneous networks.

17.6 CONFIGURING DISTRIBUTED APPLICATIONS

Following the definition of the executable objects, the building of a distributed application involves three different steps:

- describing the hardware configuration (i.e. the number and connection pattern of physical nodes),

- describing the software configuration (i.e. the populations and connection pattern of executable modules),

- and describing how they are matched (i.e. which modules execute on which machines).

In special languages for distributed systems, there is usually an independent configuration language to describe these steps, and even in DIADEM this stage was not handled in Ada. In DRAGOON a uniform approach is used, and all the different entities that need to be manipulated to perform these tasks are modelled as instances of different kinds of classes. The configuring of distributed systems is therefore performed in the normal object-oriented style by the creation of objects, assignment of object references to instance variables, and the passing of parameters in method calls.

There are two basic ways in which these operations can be invoked. By viewing the terminal as an active object in the system, the required operations can be performed interactively from the command line by the human operator. Alternatively, the required actions can be described in a class just like other ordinary operations. Such a class is treated like any other class, and must inherit the appropriate execution support class in order for its instances to be executed. Unlike ordinary classes, however, this class is able to bring about the creation of other 'heavyweight' objects in the system.

There is no reason why the operations of instantiating 'heavyweight' executable objects, and passing their references to others in method calls, should be contained in only special 'configuring' classes. Because DRAGOON provides an explicit distinction between 'heavyweight' and 'lightweight' objects, any object may safely manipulate any other kind of object, including physical node and executable objects. The task of configuring a system can therefore be distributed throughout the executable objects in the system, and once the class responsible for starting the elaboration process is activated from the command line, the process will continue automatically.

Given a set of class definitions which model the application, their execution in a different network configuration, or in networks of different, possibly heterogeneous, machines can be engineered by rearranging the ways in which the classes are combined into executable objects, and loaded into machines.

Reconfiguration and extension of the network to contain additional machines may be handled dynamically by suitable manipulation of the reference variables.

17.7   DISTRIBUTION OF EXISTING PROGRAMS

In a discussion of re-engineering, it would be unreasonable to omit some discussion of the re-engineering of programs already in use on a monoprocessor to run on a network. Enough has been said in the preceding sections to show that the feasibility of doing so will depend on several factors. First, and most important, is the question of how well the original code was designed and written, and also how well it was documented. As a model of some application world, it must reflect the structure of that world, and if good software engineering practice was followed, then it should not be difficult to extract the parts which constitute the potential 'virtual nodes' of a distributed implementation. If the language has good modular structure, these may be reused in constructing executable components to serve as load modules in a networking implementation.

If direct sharing of access to data by different components has been used, then some restructuring is needed. The true owner of the data must be identified, and the data lodged in the appropriate node. Subprograms are then provided in the interface to give the necessary access to others. If there is a large amount of such data, and it seems better to make it a virtual node on its own, then all the programs may access it from the new interface. How difficult these sorts of changes will be depends crucially on how disciplined was the original data access.

Care will be needed to ensure that the components may execute concurrently without destroying the behaviour. Synchronization will be necessary to ensure the integrity of shared resources, but if synchronization is so strong that effectively only one node can execute at a time (mirroring the monoprocessor system for which the code was created), most of the potential benefits of distribution will have been lost.

Most likely, however, it is only the design that can reasonably be reused, with the existing programs guiding the coding in a more suitable language.

17.8 CONCLUSION

This paper has presented the importance, in the development of distributed software, of separating the stage of definition of the functionality of components intended to serve as units of distribution, from the stages defining the configuration and allocation to hardware nodes in a network, and has shown how software components should be structured to enable them to be managed flexibly in a network of (possibly non-homogeneous) processors.

The most novel feature of the treatment has been to show how the consistent view of program development in the object-oriented style can be used to support all the stages of the process of constructing a distributed system, distinguishing between objects which will be used to form parts of executable modules and others which are executable units. Restructuring, both within and between load modules, for purposes of reconfiguration to satisfy new requirements in the system's evolution or following part failure of a system, or for some other reason, such as a mode change in an executing system, is conveniently supported.

A few words discussing the extent to which the structuring techniques described might be applied to the distribution of programs written in other languages, not directly intended for distribution, suggest that the prospect for the reuse of code are limited, but that a good design should transfer well to a distributed style.

ACKNOWLEDGEMENTS

I am pleased to acknowledge the help, in preparing this paper, of Colin Atkinson, who has been an associate both in the DIADEM project and subsequently in DRAGOON. He has made several important contributions to the presentation given here. Insofar as the ideas described in this paper rest on the results of the DRAGOON project, it is a pleasure also to acknowledge the contributions of all the partners in that project, but especially Andrea Di Maio of TXT(Milano), the lead partners in DRAGOON, and Rami Bayan of GSI/TECSI, Paris.

REFERENCES

1.   America (1987). POOL-T: A Parallel Object Oriented Language, in Object Oriented Concurrent Programming MIT Press, pp. 199-220.

2.   Atkinson, C., Moreton, T. and Natali, A. (1988). Ada for Distributed Systems, The Ada Companion Series, Cambridge University Press.

3.   Black, A., Hutchinson, N., Jul, E., Levy, H., and Carter, L. (1987). Distribution and Abstract Types in Emerald, IEEE Transactions on Software Engineering, vol. SE13, no. 1, January 1987.

4.   Cornhill, D. (1983). A Survivable Distributed Computing System for Embedded Applications Programs Written in Ada, Ada Letters pp. 79-87.

5.   Cox, B.J. (1986). Object Oriented Programming – An Evolutionary Approach, Addison-Wesley Publishing Company.

6.   Di Maio, A., Cardigno, C., Bayan, R., Destombes, C., Atkinson, C. (1989). DRAGOON: An Ada-based Object Oriented Language for Concurrent, Real-time, Distributed Systems, Systems Design with Ada, Proc. Ada-Europe International Conference, Madrid, June 1989.

7.   Dulay, N., Kramer, J., Magee, J., Sloman, S. and Twidle, K. (1987). Distributed System Construction: Experience with the CONIC Toolkit, Experiences with Distributed Systems: Proc. International Workshop, Kaiserslautern, FRG, 1987.

8.   Fantechi, A., Inverardi, P. and Lijtmaer, N. (1986). Using High Level Languages for Local Network Communication: A Case Study in Ada, Software-Practice and Experience, 16(8), pp. 701-717.

9.   Genolini, S., Di Maio, A., Cardigno, C., Goldsack, S. and Atkinson, C. (1989). Specifying Synchronization Constraints in a Concurrent Object-Oriented Language, Proc. First Int. Conf. on Technology of Object Oriented Languages and Systems (TOOL'89), Paris – La Defense, November 1989.

10.   Goldberg, A. and Robson, D. (1983). Smalltalk-80: The Language and its Implementation, Addison-Wesley.

11.   Goldsack, S.J. and Atkinson, C. (1989). An Object Oriented Approach to Virtual Nodes: Are Package Types an Answer?, Proc. 3rd Int. Workshop on Real-Time Ada Issues, Nemacolin Woodlands, Farmington, PA, June 1989.

12.   Goldsack, S.J., Atkinson, C., Natali, A., Di Maio, A., Maderna, F. and Moreton, T. (1987). Ada for Distributed Systems – A Library of Virtual Nodes, Ada Components: Libraries and Tools, Proc. Ada-Europe International Conference, Stockholm, The Ada Companion Series, Cambridge University Press.

13.   Hutcheon, A.D. and Wellings, A.J. (1988). Supporting Ada in a Distributed Environment, Proceedings of the 2nd International Workshop on Real-Time Ada Issues, Ada Letters.

14.   Hutcheon, A.D. and Wellings, A.J. (1988). The Virtual Node Approach to Designing Distributed Ada Programs, Ada User 9 (Supplementary), December 1988.

15.   Kramer, J. and Magee, J. (1985). Dynamic Configuration for Distributed Systems, IEEE Transactions on Software Engineering. 11(4).

16.   Kung, A. and Kung R. (1985) Galaxy: A Distributed Real-time Operating System Supporting High Availability. Proc. Real-time Systems Symposium, San Diego.

17.   Liskov, B. (1982). On Linguistic Support for Distributed Programs IEEE Transactions on Software Engineering, 8(3).

18.   Mao, T.W. and Yeh, R.T. (1980). Communication Port: A Language Concept for Concurrent Programming. IEEE Transactions on Software Engineering, 6(2), pp. 194-204.

19.   Meyer, B. (1988). Object Oriented Software Construction, Prentice Hall.

20.   Page-Jones, M. (1983). The Practical Guide to Structured Systems Design. Yourdon Press.

21.   Stroustrup, B. (1986). The C + + Programming Language, Addison-Wesley.

22.   Tedd, M., Crespi-Reghizzi, S. and Natali, A. (1984). Ada for Multi-microprocessors. Cambridge University Press, Ada Companion Series.

23. Volz, R.A., Mudge, T.N., Naylor, A.W. and Mayer, J.H. (1985). Some Problems in Distributing Real-time Ada Programs across Machines, Ada in Use, Proceedings of the Ada International Conference. The Ada Companion Series, Cambridge University Press.

18 Converting sequential applications software for parallel execution with Strand88 harnesses

D. Catton

AI Limited

18.1 INTRODUCTION TO STRAND

Strand is a general purpose concurrent programming language with a clear, simple parallel execution model. It allows programmers to develop efficient portable software which can then run on a wide range of multi-processor machines of different types and configurations. Strand programs can easily be written to dynamically determine and exploit the underlying hardware configuration and multi-processor architecture. Strand is designed to be extensible in that existing sequential code written in conventional programming languages can be linked into and executed from Strand programs.

The Strand Project recently won the 1989 British Computer Society's award for Technical Achievement.

STRAND88 is the first commercial implementation of the Strand language. It is available on a wide variety of shared and distributed memory multi-processor machines and also runs on single processor machines. It is currently available on Sun3/4 series Workstations, Sun SparcStation, Sequent Symmetry.Intel iPSC/2, Encore Multimax, MIPS RISComputer and the Transputer under Helios and Express. Versions are also under development for the NCUBE, Meiko and BBN Butterfly.

18.2   INTRODUCTION TO STRAND HARNESSING

A Strand harness provides a convenient migration path from sequential to parallel processing whilst maximizing the investment in existing valuable sequential code.

Conceptually a harnessed application can be thought of as 'chunks' of sequential foreign code with a potential to execute concurrently, managed by a Strand program which provides the necessary synchronization and communication.

Strand's Foreign Language Interface provides the capability to extend and enhance the Strand language by incorporating foreign code and as such provides the basis for the development of a Strand harness. An outline of the use of the Foreign Language Interface is included as part of the following case study and further information on the Foreign Language Interface can be found in the Strand User Manual.

The primary reason for harnessing an application is the enormous potential it provides for exploiting the latent parallelism within an application. Harnessing can result in substantial improvements in performance. A harness written in Strand also provides two additional benefits, portability and scalability:

Strand's portability immediately allows a harnessed application to execute on a wide variety of hardware platforms (see above);

Strand's ability to dynamically determine and utilize multi-processor resources enables a harnessed application to fully exploit additional processors without modification to the software. Distribution algorithms can be employed which are sensitive both to the available machine resources and the complexity or irregularity of the problem to hand, dynamically mapping processes to processors so as to maximize processor utilization.

To successfully implement a Strand harness requires the existing software to conform to the following important criteria:

- the application would benefit from an improvement in performance/portability;

- the software must be *w* in a language which is supported by the Foreign Language Interface,currently this includes C and Fortran;

- the software should be sufficiently modular and well designed to enable the sequential code to be decomposed into appropriately sized 'chunks' which have the potential to execute concurrently.

Once an appropriate application has been identified and the feasibility of a harness established, the existing sequential code is decomposed into appropriate 'chunks' of code.

The size of each 'chunk' will relate to a function or procedure in the foreign language but otherwise is application-specific. The only guide is that each 'chunk' should be sufficiently large and independent so as to reduce possible communication bottleneck and remove the possibility of a process deadlock occurring, i.e. where two or more processes require information from each other in order to continue. For this reason harnessing is said to provide relatively coarse-grained parallelism. The process of decomposition is achieved using either:

- functional decomposition, where a problem is decomposed into independent subproblems each of which provides part of the solution;

   and/or

- data decomposition, where several similar processes are created for each operation on independent data to solve the problem.

   Once the appropriate foreign language routines have been identified and suitable Strand procedures defined using the Foreign Language Interface, the final stage is to write a Strand program which implements an appropriate parallel algorithm.

   The following case study should further serve to illustrate the harnessing technique.

18.3   A CASE STUDY

A Strand harness has been designed and built to parallelize existing Fortran wave modelling software developed as part of the Joint North Sea Wave Project (JONSWAP) by Newcastle University and Imperial College. The wave modelling software forms part of a larger application for McDermott Engineering who manufacture oil rigs, and will be concerned with calculating average and maximum stresses on their oil rigs for fatigue calculations.

   The Fortran software models the velocity and acceleration of seawater, moving according to some roughly periodic wave motion, across waves calculated at a series of points over a specified time period. The problem is ideally suited to parallelization since the calculations for a given point at a given time are entirely independent of each other. A previous version of the software was actually written using a Parallel Fortran running on Transputers. The alogorithm will be explained with reference to the Fortran implementation which will then be contrasted with Strand harnessed Fortran implementation.

The original Fortran software consisted of three files: a configuration file, which provided a static allocation of software tasks to physical processors; a master file, which included initialization code, code to calculate the required results for a portion of the points and finally code to write the results to file; and a slave file, which included explicit message passing code and replicated the code to calculate the results for a given set of points. Figure 18.1 illustrates how the original parallel Fortran software implemented the parallel algorithm.

The transputers in the Parallel Fortran version of the code are arranged in a pipeline with the front end transputer reading and writing input and output data from disk. The transputers divide the points between them, calculating velocity and acceleration components at each point for each timestep from the start time up to some maximum time. The calculation is parameterized by a variety of data including some common array data, generated on the front end transputer during the initialization phase. These data and the calculation points are passed forward down the pipeline using message-passing primitives provided in the Fortran. At each timestep the transputers post the velocity and acceleration components calculated during that timeslice back up the pipeline, forwarding their own values and those received from processors further down the pipeline. Thus, adjacent transputers must synchronize after each set of values is calculated before continuing on to calculate results for the next timeslice. Results are written to file by the front end transputer as they arrive.

The existence of a parallel version of the algorithm simplified the task of decomposition and resulted in the definition of three new Strand procedures:

- seaparams, which read some boundary parameters from a file prior to initialization;

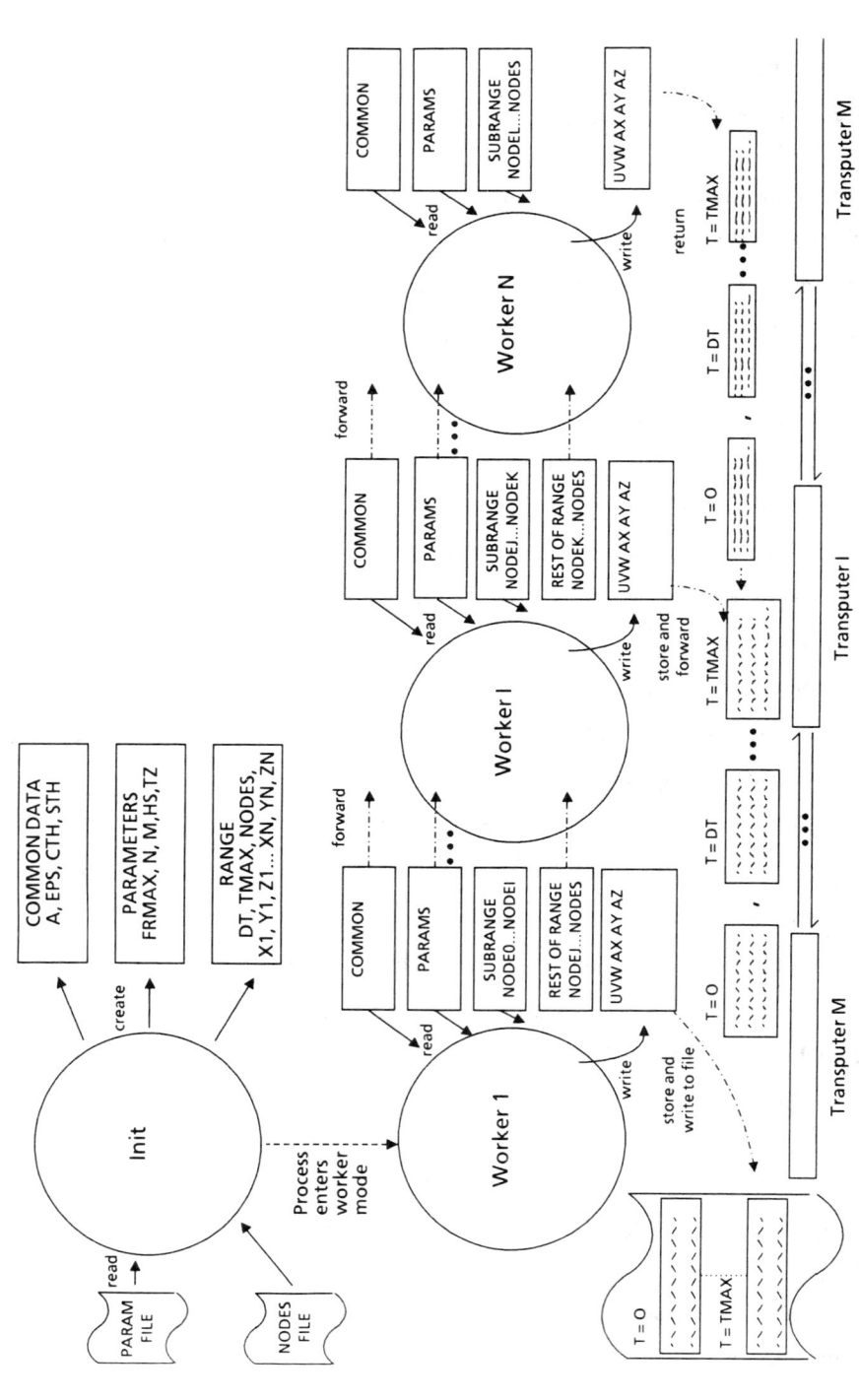

- seainit, which calls the Fortran initialization code; this creates some common data using Fortran arrays which are then passed by Strand to each calculation;

- seaslv, which calls the Fortran code calculating the velocity and acceleration of the seawater at a given x,y,z point at a given time.

The input-output code was rewritten as a C procedure for simplicity. The body of the other two procedures is substantially unchanged from the original with the exception that the message passing and file-handling code is deleted and the local data originally initialized by the message-passing routines is instead supplied as arguments to the subroutines.

Finally, the actual Strand program which distributes the work over the available processors was provided by the simple adaptation of some standard 'manager/worker' software. Figure 18.2 (see Appendix) illustrates the Strand implementation of the parallel algorithm.

The number of workers in the configuration is a parameter of the Strand program. The manager and store process run on one processor and the workers are distributed one per spare processor in the multi-processor configuration. The double width lines represent streams of data passing between Strand processes. The single lines represent dataflow from a writer process to a reader process. Transfer of data from one processor to another happens automatically. The processes involved merely read or write Strand variables to achieve this distribution of data.

Note that the store process and the manager process share the same stream of point vectors. The manager allocates each point to a free worker. The workers generate the associated component values by calling the seaslv routine, then post another request to the manager. The store process writes the position and time values and the velocity and acceleration components to file. If the component values have

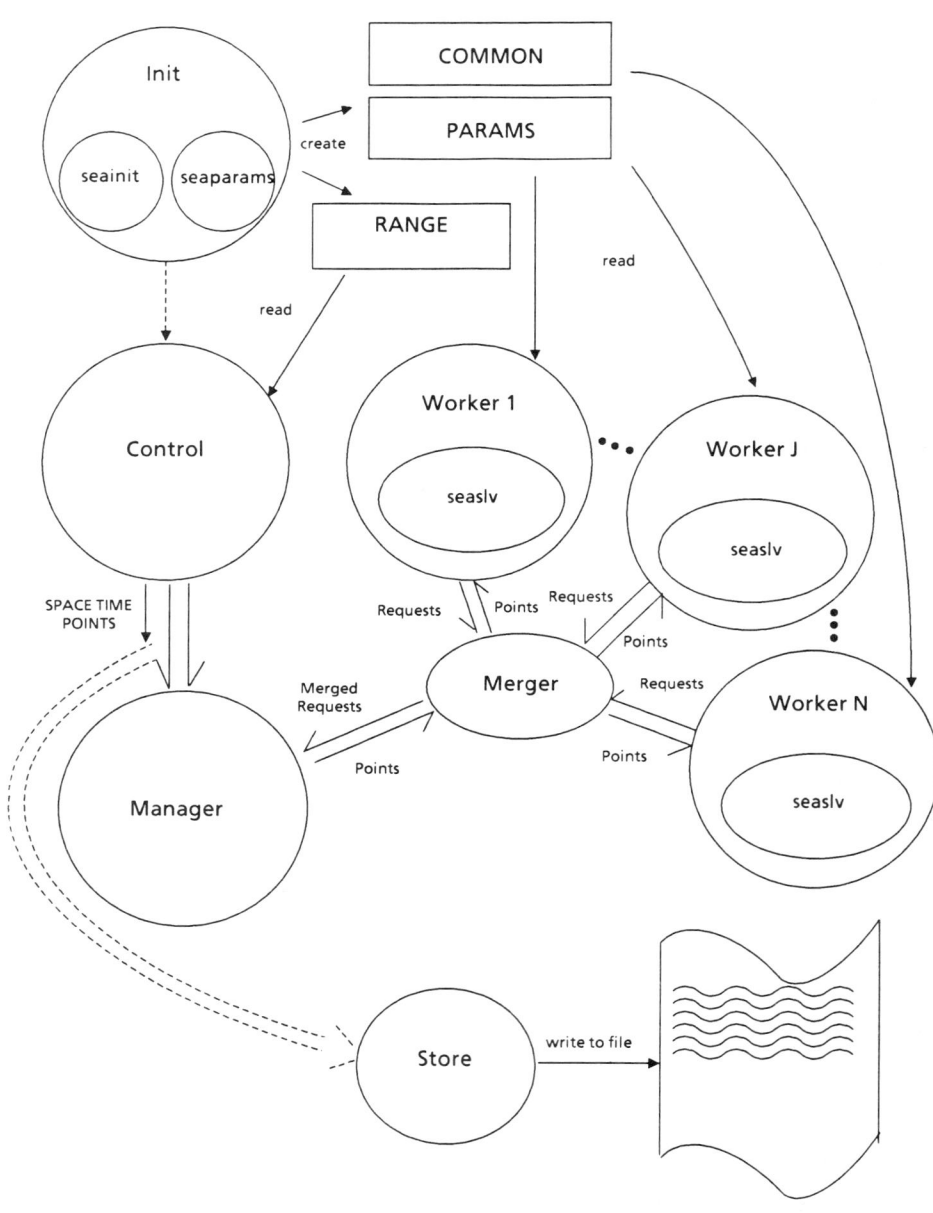

Fig. 18.2 Strand process and data distribution.

not yet been written into a point vector the store process will automatically suspend, waiting for a worker to generate them.

A comparison of the Parallel Fortran implementation and the Strand implementation highlights several important features of Strand:

- The Parallel Fortran version is not immediately portable or scalable since it requires specific configuration code to statically allocate the processes to available processors;

- Strand's portability and scalability removes the restrictions on hardware and immediately allows a harnessed application to take full advantage of any available processors;

- The Parallel Fortran version includes explicit message-passing code to transfer data between processors;

Strand requires no such explicit code:

- The Parallel Fortran version requires replication of the code which calculates the results for a set of points at the specified time interval;

- The Strand version requires no such replication of code and implements a more flexible and machine-independent algorithm.

The case study also illustrated the two mechanisms which are provided for passing data between Strand and foreign languages:

- STRAND88's Foreign Language Interface provides a facility for the declaration of user datatypes. These are used by Strand programs to distribute foreign language data structures for use by foreign code which are opaque to Strand. This latter technique is used in the harness example to distribute the common Fortran arrays created by the Fortran initialization code.

18.4 RESULTS

The following timings were obtained running the wave harness on a 16-node Intel hypercube (iPSC2) using a simple worker-manager distribution algorithm. Tasks were allocated as a single timepoint (X,Y,Z,T quadruple) at which to calculate the velocity and acceleration component values. The manager process was run on one node and between 1 and 15 worker processes run on the other nodes. The time quoted is real time in seconds, i.e. the elapsed time from startup of the harness program to its completion of the harness algorithm. The parameters used for the run were as follows:

mean pk-pk wave height (HS):	10.0
meters mean wave period (TZ):	10.0 seconds
#frequencies in spectrum (N):	50
#angles in 2-d summation (M):	20
max freq/avge freq (MAXFR):	5
random generator seed (JRAN):	100
maximum time value (TMAX):	100.0
seconds sample time (DT):	2.0 seconds
#points calculated (NODES):	10
#timepoints (NODES*TMAX/DT):	500

The timings obtained using a simple manager worker distribution were:

#nodes/workers	elapsed time (seconds)	processing rate (#timepoints/second)
2/1	164.5	3.04
3/2	83.6	5.98
4/3	57.7	8.67
5/4	61.4	8.14
6/5	56.4	8.86
7/6	59.6	8.39
8/7	56.1	8.91
9/8	55.2	9.06
10/9	51.5	9.71
11/10	52.3	9.56
12/11	53.2	9.40
13/12	53.7	9.31
14/13	51.2	9.77
15/14	50.6	9.88
16/15	52.6	9.51
Control timing:	110.5	

(single processor manager/worker)

The elapsed time was measured by hand. Repeated readings established the error to be approximately ± 0.25 seconds.

Timings were also obtained for two optimized distribution schemes using a 4-node iPSC2. In the original 16-node case workers returned results by assigning each of 6 return arguments to the appropriate component value. In the first optimized scheme the values were returned by assigning one return argument to a 6-tuple containing the component values. This allows the STRAND88 implementation to return all 6 values to the manager at once, in theory providing for up to 6 times less communications overheads in returning results. The timings are as follows:

#nodes/workers	elapsed time (seconds)	processing rate (#timepoints/second)
2/1	127.0	3.94
3/2	64.7	7.73
4/3	43.4	11.55

In the second optimized scheme tasks are allocated by passing a point with the timestep and end time. The workers calculate component values for the point at each timestep up to the maximum time, returning the component values in a list. This cuts down on much of the manager/worker communications and also allows return data to be combined by transferring one or more sets of component values in each return message. The timings are as follows:

#nodes/workers	elapsed time (seconds)	processing rate (#timepoints/second)
2/1	114.2	4.38
3/2	56.0	8.93
4/3	44.6	11.21

18.5 ANALYSIS OF RESULTS

The results obtained from the 16-node iPSC2 tests show a linear speed up in performance with 2-4 nodes/1-3 workers in the configuration. Comparing the timings for one worker against the control figure for a sequential program running on one node, there is an initial overhead of about 50% in distributing the control. This overhead is more than recovered when running with two workers and the gain continues with the addition of a third worker. However, thereafter there is little gain (and at some points even a loss) in performance with the addition of further nodes. The chaotic behaviour after four nodes displays fluctuations up and down in processing rate which appear to repeat in the same pattern across runs. The results reflect the fact that use of a dynamic distribution scheme requires significant numbers of data transfers to allocate work. The chunks of work allocated are obviously large enough to justify the extra work involved in dispatching them because a speed-up is obtained with a small number of processors. However, the rate at which processors return for more work leads to contention very quickly with increase in nodes.

This contention effect is commonly observed in programs which employ a centralized control agent such as a manager/worker configuration. The application would benefit from a higher computation/communication ratio. This can be obtained either by minimizing the amount of communications involved or performing more work in response to each communication. The control timing obtained for a sequential implementation gives some idea of the overheads involved in communications performed for this original naive implementation. Even with 1-3 workers (i.e. little or no contention) it could be seen that each worker was only spending about 65% of its time actually running the Fortran code.

The first attempt to optimize the code works by batching up the data being transferred. Instead of assigning six component values, the workers assign one variable with a six-element tuple. This allows the STRAND88 implementation to return all six values in one message. The decrease in communications time is dramatic. Comparison of the single worker timings with the control timing reveals a drop from 55 seconds communications/110 seconds computation time down to 17 seconds communications/110 seconds computation time, i.e. from 50% to 12%! This decrease in communications overheads would allow further workers to be added to the configuration without reaching the contention limit without changing. N.B. work is in progress to perform some of this message batching automatically without the programmer having to consider the data transfer issues arising from a particular distribution scheme.

The second attempt to optimize the code works by performing more per communication performed. Each worker calculates the whole set of component values at a point across the time interval and returns a list containing all the resulting component values. This approach can be seen to decrease further the communication overheads. However, there is a wrinkle which surfaces when three workers are used. The timing for three workers does not increase linearly. This is because there are only ten points used in the calculation. With three workers this means that two workers calculate component values for three points decreases the number of tasks and beyond a certain point this can lead to workers going idle. In reality the computation would be performed at more than ten points, however the example is useful for didactic purposes.

It is worth emphasizing that both optimizations were obtained from the original Strand program by changing only a few lines of the program. All three versions were implemented by about ten Strand procedures consisting of around fifty lines of code. The Fortran code employed in the Strand version is almost identical to the original program code once the parallel Fortran constructs are removed.

18.6   CONCLUSION

The evidence provided by this case-study indicates that the technique of producing parallel harnesses for existing applications written in sequential programming languages offers significant potential for:

- 'Future-proofing' – many organizations are now so dependent on their data processing capabilities that they could not continue to function without them. STRAND88 harnesses offer, for the right applications, an effective means of making the transition from today's sequential hardware to the increasingly prevalent parallel hardware without major investment in replacing applications software which functions perfectly adequately in many cases.

- Improved performance – Parallel processor architectures offer the promise of greatly improved performance at lower cost, provided that existing applications can run on them. STRAND88 harnesses offer a means of extracting the latent parallelism in existing applications and allowing them to take advantage of the improved hardware performance provided by manufacturers.

- Portability – STRAND88 has been designed from the outset as a portable language and is already available on a wide variety of hardware platforms, with many more to follow. Once an application has been harnessed, the same code can be run on many platforms, with further economies for users. As new hardware becomes available, it is a minimal task to deliver harnessed applications to users compared to the re-work which is all too often required today.

APPENDIX

```
----------------------------------------
                seainit.f
----------------------------------------

        SUBROUTINE SEAINIT(SYNC,A,EPS,CTH,STH,HS,TZ,N,M,
    >              MAXFR,JRAN,TMAX,DT,FRMAX)


        REAL*8 CTH(M),STH(M)
    1   ,PI,HS,TZ,G,S,GAM,FM,ALP,DW,FR,SIG,B,SP,A(N,M)
    2   ,EPS(N,M),TMAX,TH,DTH
    3   ,FRMAX,DT


        INTEGER SYNC,N,M,I,J,L,JRAN,MAXFR


C USE CLOCK TO SET JRAN SEED IF (DEFAULT) JRAN LE. 0


        IF (JRAN.LE.0) CALL ICLOCK(JRAN)
C       WRITE(*,*)'JRAN = ',JRAN
        JRAN=MOD(JRAN,259200)
        G=9.819239
        PI=3.1415927
        S=2.0*PI*HS/(G*TZ**2)


        IF (S.GE.0.037) THEN
           GAM=10.54-1.34/SQRT(S)-EXP(3.775/SQRT(S)-19.0)
        ELSE
           GAM=0.9+EXP(18.86-3.67/SQRT(S))
        END IF


        FM=(0.6063+0.1164*SQRT(GAM)-0.01224*GAM)/TZ
        ALP=(2.964+0.4788*SQRT(GAM)-0.3430*GAM+0.04225*GAM**1.5)*S**2
        sum=0.0


        DO 1010 L=1,M
           TH=(L-0.5)*PI/M-PI/2.0
           CTH(L)=COS(TH)
           STH(L)=SIN(TH)
1010    CONTINUE
```

```
        DTH=PI/M
        FRMAX=MAXFR*FM
        DW=FRMAX*2.0*PI/N


        DO 1020 J=1,N


           FR=(J-0.5)*MAXFR/N
           SIG=0.07
           IF (FR.GT.1.0) SIG=0.09
           B=EXP(-0.5*((FR-1.0)/SIG)**2)
           SP=ALP*G*G/(2.0*PI)**4/(FR*FM)**5*EXP(-1.25/FR**4)*GAM**B


           DO 1030 L=1,M

C GENERATE RANDOM PHASE USING UNIFORM DEVIATE METHOD


              JRAN=MOD(JRAN*421+54773,259200)
              EPS(J,L)=FLOAT(JRAN)*2.0*PI/259200.0
              SUM=SUM+SP*0.5*PI*CTH(L)**2*DTH*DW
              A(J,L)=G*CTH(L)*SQRT(PI*SP*DW*DTH)


1030       CONTINUE


1020  CONTINUE


        SUM=SUM/HS**2
        SYNC = 0


        RETURN
        END
```

```
----------------------------------------

         seaslv.f

----------------------------------------

   SUBROUTINE SEASLV(SYNC,X,Y,Z,T,FRMAX,
   >              N,M,A,EPS,CTH,STH,U,V,W,AX,AY,AZ)


    REAL*8 X,Y,Z,T,FRMAX,A(N,M),EPS(N,M),CTH(M),STH(M)
   1 ,U,V,W,AX,AY,AZ
   2 ,FRAD,RK,EKZ,Q,CS,SN,PI,G


    INTEGER N,M,L,J


    PI=3.1415927
    G=9.819239



     U=0.0
     V=0.0
     W=0.0
     AX=0.0
     AY=0.0
     AZ=0.0


    DO 1020 J=1,N


       FRAD=(J-0.5)*FRMAX*2.0*PI/N
       RK=FRAD**2/G
       EKZ=EXP(RK*Z)


       DO 1030 L=1,M


          Q=FRAD*T-RK*(CTH(L)*X+STH(L)*Y)+EPS(J,L)
          CS=EKZ*COS(Q)*RK*A(J,L)
          SN=EKZ*SIN(Q)*RK*A(J,L)
          U=U-CTH(L)*CS/FRAD
          V=V-STH(L)*CS/FRAD
          W=W+SN/FRAD
          AX=AX+CTH(L)*SN
```

```
                  AY=AY+STH(L)*SN

                  AZ=AZ+CS


1030      CONTINUE


1020   CONTINUE


       SYNC = 0


       RETURN

       END
```

```
-----------------------------------------
             mwboot.std
-----------------------------------------
-compile(resolvent).

-exports([boot/3,merge/2]).


boot(N,Control,Data):-
    make_tuple(N,RTuple), % tuple of streams written by workers
    merge(R,Requests), % merged into one stream
    manager:manager(Control,Requests),    % manager gets Control
    boot_workers(0,N,R,Data).     % workers gets Data


boot_workers(N,N,R,_):- R:=[].% all worker processes added


boot_workers(I,N,R,Data):-
    I < N |
    I1 is I + 1,
    R :=[merge(Requests)|R1],
    worker:worker(Requests,Data)@I,   % add worker on node I
    boot_workers(I1,N,R1,Data).   % add rest of workers
```

```
-----------------------------------------
          manager.std
-----------------------------------------
-compile(resolvent).
-exports([manager/2]).


manager([Task|Tasks],[task(Request)|Requests]):-
    Request := Task,        %got  task and request,
    manager(Tasks,Requests).  % assign to worker and recur


manager([],[task(Request)|Requests]):-
    Request:=done,      % no more tasks
    manager([],Requests). % tell worker to finish


manager([],[]).    % all workers finished
```

```
----------------------------------------
            worker.std
----------------------------------------
-compile(resolvent).
-exports([worker/2]).


worker(Requests,{FrMax,N,M,A,Eps,Cth,Sth}):-
    Requests:=[task(Task)|More],  %ask for task and enter loop
    worker(go,Task,FrMax,N,M,A,Eps,Cth,Sth,More).


worker(_,done,_,_,_,_,_,_,_,Requests):-
    Requests:=[].      % no more tasks, so no more requests


worker(Go,{X,Y,Z,T,U,V,W,AX,AY,AZ},FrMax,N,M,A,Eps,Cth,Sth,Requests):-
    data(Go) |    % previous task finished - run this one
    seaslv(Sync,X,Y,Z,T,FrMax,N,M,A,Eps,Cth,Sth,U,V,W,AX,AY,AZ),
    Requests:=[task(Task)|More],      % ask for another
    worker(Sync,Task,FrMax,N,M,A,Eps,Cth,Sth,More).  % loop
```

```
-----------------------------------------

            seapar.std

-----------------------------------------

-compile(free).

-exports([test/2,wave_forces/2,store/2]).


wave_forces(File,Ms):-

    string(File), Ms > 0 |

    test(Vecs,Ms),      % get data

    store(Vecs,File). % write to file


test(Vecs,Ms):-% call seaparams to get parameters from file

    seaparams(Sync1,Ps,Ns,HS,TZ,N,M,MaxFr,JRan,TMax,Dt),

    L is M * N,% create common block datatypes

    userblank(100,L,8,A),

    userblank(100,L,8,Eps),

    userblank(100,M,8,Cth),

    userblank(100,M,8,Sth),    % initialise common data then run

    seainit(Sync,A,Eps,Cth,Sth,HS,TZ,N,M,MaxFr,JRan,TMax,Dt,FrMax),

    init_seaslv(Sync,Ms,Ps,Dt,TMax,FrMax,N,M,A,Eps,Cth,Sth,Vecs).


init_seaslv(Sync,Ms,Ps,Dt,TMax,FrMax,N,M,A,Eps,Cth,Sth,Vecs):-

    data(Sync)|    % wait for initialisation then boot manager

    mwboot:boot(Ms,Vecs,{FrMax,N,M,A,Eps,Cth,Sth}),

    times(0.0,Dt,TMax,Times), % generate all timepoints

    do_points(Ps,Times,Vecs).


do_points([],_,Vecs):-

    Vecs :=[].


do_points([P|Ps],Times,Vecs):-

    do_times(P,Times,Vecs,MoreVecs),

    do_points(Ps,Times,MoreVecs).


do_times(_,[],Vecs,MoreVecs):-

    Vecs:=MoreVecs.


do_times({X,Y,Z},[Time|Times],Vecs,MoreVecs):-
```

```
    Vecs:=[{X,Y,Z,Time,U,V,W,AX,AY,AZ}|Vecs1],
    do_times({X,Y,Z},Times,Vecs1,MoreVecs).


times(T,Delta,TMax,Times):-
    T < TMax |
    Times := [T | More],
    T1 is T + Delta,
    times(T1,Delta,TMax,More).


times(_,_,_,Times):-
    otherwise |
    Times := [].


store(Vecs,File):-
    list_to_string([10],NL),   % write header and then loop over data
    write_file(File,'Wave Forces Output Data',_),
    append_file(File,NL,_),
    append_file(File,NL,_),
    append_file(File,'X     Y     Z    T',_),
    append_file(File,NL,_),
    append_file(File,'  U     V     W    AX      AY       AZ',_),
    append_file(File,NL,_),
    append_file(File,NL,_),
    store1(Vecs,File).


store1([],_).       % all done


store1([{X,Y,Z,T,U,V,W,AX,AY,AZ}|Vecs],File):-
    data(U),data(V),        % ensure results are on this node
    data(W),data(AX),
    data(AY),data(AZ) |
    real_to_list(X,LX,)      % generate string for line, write and loop
    real_to_list(Y,LY),
    real_to_list(Z,LZ),
    real_to_list(T,LT),
    real_to_list(U,LU),
    real_to_list(V,LV),
    real_to_list(W,LW),
```

```
real_to_list(AX,LAX),
real_to_list(AY,LAY),
real_to_list(AZ,LAZ),
list_to_string(LX,SX),
list_to_string(LY,SY),
list_to_string(LZ,SZ),
list_to_string(LT,ST),
list_to_string(LU,SU),
list_to_string(LV,SV),
list_to_string(LW,SW),
list_to_string(LAX,SAX),
list_to_string(LAY,SAY),
list_to_string(LAZ,SAZ),
string_to_list(SX,L,[9|TX]),
string_to_list(SY,TX,[9|TY]),
string_to_list(SZ,TY,[9|TZ]),
string_to_list(ST,TZ,[10|TT]),
string_to_list(SU,TT,[9|TU]),
string_to_list(SV,TU,[9|TV]),
string_to_list(SW,TV,[9|TW]),
string_to_list(SAX,TW,[9|TAX]),
string_to_list(SAY,TAX,[9|TAY]),
string_to_list(SAZ,TAY,[10]),
list_to_string(L,S),
append_file(File,S,_),
store1(Vecs,File).
```

```
-----------------------------------------

            seainterface.c

-----------------------------------------

#include "samlib.h"
#include <sys/types.h>


void    seainit(sync,a,eps,cth,sth,hs,tz,n,m,maxfr,jran,tmax,dt,frmax)


REF a,eps,cth,sth;
double  hs,tz,tmax,dt,*frmax;
int *sync,n,m,maxfr,jran;


{   if (IsUser(a)&&IsUser(eps)&&IsUser(cth)&&IsUser(sth))

seainit_(sync,Data(a),Data(eps),Data(cth),Data(sth),&hs,&tz,&n,&m,&maxfr,&jran,&tmax,&dt,frmax
);
    else
        Put(sync,MakeError(4,seainit));
}


void    seaslv(sync,x,y,z,t,frmax,n,m,a,eps,cth,sth,u,v,w,ax,ay,az)


REF a,eps,cth,sth;
double  x,y,z,t,frmax,*u,*v,*w,*ax,*ay,*az;
int *sync,n,m;


{   if (IsUser(a)&&IsUser(eps)&&IsUser(cth)&&IsUser(sth))

seaslv_(sync,&x,&y,&z,&t,&frmax,&n,&m,Data(a),Data(eps),Data(cth),Data(sth),u,v,w,ax,ay,az);
    else
        Put(sync,MakeError(4,seaslv));
}


void    iclock_(jp)


int *jp;


{   (void)time(jp);
}
```

```
----------------------------------------
          seaparams.c
----------------------------------------
#include "stdio.h"
#include "samlib.h"


void seaparams(sync,ps,nodes,hs,tz,n,m,maxfr,jran,tmax,dt)

REF sync,ps;
int *n,*m,*nodes,*maxfr;
double *hs,*tz,*dt,*tmax;


{FILE   *f1,*f2;
int ns;
double x,y,z;
REF tup;

    f1 = fopen("jonswap.dat","r");
    f2 = fopen("jacket.dat","r");

    fscanf(f1,"%lg%lg%d%d%d%d%lg%lg",
           hs,tz,n,m,maxfr,jran,tmax,dt);
    fclose(f1);
    fscanf(f2,"%d",&ns);
    *nodes = ns;
    for(;ns > 0; ns--){
        fscanf(f2,"%lg%lg%lg",&x,&y,&z);
        tup = MakeTuple(3);
        SetArg(tup,1,MakeReal(x));
        SetArg(tup,2,MakeReal(y));
        SetArg(tup,3,MakeReal(z));
        Put(ps,MakeList());
        SetHead(ps,tup);
        ps=GetTail(ps);
    }

    Put(ps,Empty_List());

    Put(sync,Empty_List());
```

19 Configuration programming: exploiting component reuse in distributed systems

Imperial College of Science, Technology and Medicine

19.1 INTRODUCTION

In 1968, the historic NATO Conference at Garmisch recognized the need for a discipline of software engineering. A vision of software construction from reusable software components was proposed by McIlroy [23]. Although this view is extremely appealing, it has unfortunately proved rather elusive. Other than the provision of libraries of mathematical functions, software component reuse is still essentially ad hoc, with no widescale or comprehensive support.

Some of the key issues in the provision of support for the reuse of software components (Hall [10]) are as follows:

(i)   identification and provision of general reusable software components,

(ii)   storage and retrieval of components using some form of abstract characterization for cataloguing,

(iii)   use of a development method which recognizes and supports reuse, and

(iv)   provision of a software architecture which supports component specialization, instantiation and interconnection to form the required software system.

Each of these issues is in itself important, in need of continuing research into techniques and tools. However, the issues are not orthogonal, and particularly depend on the approach taken in the last one: that of the software architecture. This provides the framework which determines both the form of the software components and the methods of use and reuse. This in turn has a major impact on the component identification and library management facilities. In this paper, we concentrate on the software architecture issue, and describe an approach which is being widely used for the development of distributed systems. This approach adopts the use of a separate configuration language (cf. module interconnection language) as the means for composing systems from their constituent components.

The configuration language provides the means for explicitly specializing, instantiating and interconnecting components which have been selected as useful building blocks for the application at hand. The components are required to be general, context independent types, suitable for use (and reuse) in different environments. Specialization is through actual parameters, instantiation creates an object instance, and interconnection fixes the context by linking instances to permit interaction. An associated development method provides excellent opportunities for reuse. These general notions are more explicitly motivated and described in the next section.

19.2   CONFIGURATION PROGRAMMING

19.2.1   Background Motivation

Practical experience in software engineering has taught us that complex systems can be built and managed provided we adhere to established principles. Software modularity is essential to encapsulate functionality behind clearly defined interfaces through which components can interact with their environment. Descriptions of the constituent software components and their interconnection patterns provide a clear and concise level at which to specify and design systems, and can be used directly by construction tools to generate the system itself. In many cases – particularly embedded applications – it is the structure of the application itself which is used to dictate the structure of the resultant system. This approach has been referred to as 'programming-in-the-large' [6], and component-based system building using module interconnection languages [9,20], 'processor-memory-switch level' programming [1] and 'configuration programming' [15,18]. Furthermore, evolution of the system can be achieved by making extensions or changes to the system configuration by the addition or replacement of components [16]. Since it seems that many 'new' systems are created by modifying or evolving previous versions rather than by design and construction *ab initio,* there is a need to recognize system evolution as a major portion of the development process.

This architecture thus offers the potential for software reuse both at the component level (by component selection and configuration) and by the reuse of previous versions (by component modification and reconfiguration).

The associated design and construction method emphasises the use of a separate, explicit structural (configuration) description during all phases in the software development process, from system specification as a configuration of component specifications (e.g. as in Inscape [30], GRID [28] and PAISLEY [36]), to evolution as changes to a system configuration [13,16]. This description is initially informal but tends to guide the process of initial component identification. However, emphasis is placed on the validation process viewed as construction of the system from components [17]. This is the means by which we gain confidence that our design is satisfactory. This approach thus emphasizes bottom-up composition as a basic operation of configuration.

Although the configuration descriptions vary from one system to another, many of the basic component types pertaining to an application domain tend to be the same. System variation is directed mainly at the configuration level, with some variation being embedded in particular components. Thus the opportunities for the employment of reusable components within an application domain are excellent, with the configuration language providing the means to select and tailor their use to the particular task at hand (cf. program families from information hiding modules [29]).

19.2.2 Basic Principles of Configuration Programming

The basic principles of the configuration programming approach can be summarized as follows:

1. *The configuration language used for structural description should be separate from the programming language used for basic component programming.*

    This separation of concerns facilitates the description, comprehension and manipulation, both by man and machine, of the system in terms of its structure. This is achieved by abstracting away from the component programming concerns. The structural nature of the configuration specification makes it amenable to both textual and graphical description. System construction can be performed by translation of the structural configuration description by component creation and interconnection. Furthermore, the configuration language should be declarative, describing what the structure is, not how it is to be constructed. Declarative descriptions tend to be more concise and amenable to analysis, interpretation and manipulation than their imperative equivalents.

2. *Components should be defined as context independent types with well-defined interfaces.*

Context independence [13] means that the component makes no direct reference to any non-local entities, but can be integrated into any compatible context without redefining or recompiling it. We therefore require that components access only local data and use indirect naming (such as local ports) to refer to connected components. Definition as a type permits instantiation and reuse in different contexts. The component interface should describe the interaction points with other components and permits validation of interconnections at configuration time.

3. *Using the configuration language, complex components should be definable as a composition of instances of component types.*

Hierarchies are a natural and convenient means for the support of subcomponent encapsulation and information hiding. Interconnected instances of more basic component types can be composed to form more complex components (i.e. an instance hierarchy). These composite components should themselves be component types, available for use in further definitions. Such an approach also permits the definition and construction of recursive structures.

4. *Change should be expressed at the configuration level, as changes of the component instances and/or their interconnections.*

This follows from the first principle. Given that it is beneficial to utilize a structural description to comprehend and manipulate the system, then change can also be beneficially expressed as structural change. Changes can be made to component instances, which are then of a new and different type. Change at the programming level can be reflected as a change to the component type if all instances are affected.

For a number of years, the Conic environment [13,22] has supported the use of a configuration language based on these principles. This has been especially successful with respect to ease-of-use and flexibility in system design, construction and evolution. Standard design methods such as JSD [11] and Structured Analysis (Data Flow Diagrams) [35,5] produce designs as system configurations but then fail to make more effort at supporting reuse or to carry these notions through to distributable implementations with explicit configurations. A number of other research projects make use of a separate configuration (or module interconnection) language (DICON [21], Durra [1], Garp [12], Lady [27], C/Mesa [24], Muppet [25], NETSLA [19], RNet [4], Polylith [31], STILE [33], and Linda as a coordination language [2]) but few are as widely distributed and used, and as simple yet versatile as the Conic configuration language. The Conic configuration language includes facilities for hierarchic definition of composite components, for parametrization of components, for replication of both component instances and interface ports, for conditional configurations with evaluation of guards at component instantiation, and even for recursive definition of components [7].

The Configuration Programming approach has much in common with Object-Oriented Programming. Component instances are analogous to objects, component types to classes. One of the main differences is in our use of an explicit configuration language to describe system structure as interconnected instances. In OOP, the calls to other objects are embedded in the objects themselves, thereby making them less context independent. Also, although OOP languages identify a type (class) inheritance hierarchy for objects, they do not provide explicit information on the object instance structure. We believe that the definition of component types as a hierarchy of subcomponent instances provides a clearer and more easily distributable system structure than is provided by extending types (classes) by inheritance, particularly where class variables are used.

In the rest of this paper we briefly describe our experience using 'configuration programming' in the Conic Environment, and assess the benefits of such an approach together with the opportunities for exploiting software reuse. The configuration programming framework has also been adopted as the basis of a recent ESPRIT II Project, REX, on 'Reconfigurable and Extensible Parallel and Distributed Systems'. This major project, which involves 10 industrial and university research groups, is using two large demonstrators in the telecommunications and CIM areas to act as a focus for the work and as a means for demonstrating the techniques and tools developed.

19.3 SUPPORT FOR CONFIGURATION PROGRAMMING

19.3.1 The Conic Environment

The Conic environment [13,22], developed by the Distributed Computing Group at Imperial College, provides support for configuration programming for distributed and concurrent programs. The environment provides support for two languages, one for programming individual components (processes) with explicitly defined interfaces, and one for the configuration of programs from groups of components. In addition, the environment provides support for the reuse of components in different contexts and support for dynamic configuration. This latter facility is achieved using on-line management tools which permit dynamic creation, control and modification of application programs. The Conic environment has been in use for over 5 years, with dynamic configuration as a more recent facility. It has amply demonstrated the utility of configuration level programming and the need for the separate configuration perspective.

We now briefly illustrate some of the features of the Conic structural (configuration) language for describing, constructing, monitoring and changing distributable systems. In order to provide a feel for the approach, we use a simple example: a patient-monitoring system [26]. The intensive care ward in a hospital consists of a number of beds. Patients in each bed are continuously monitored for a number of factors, such as pulse, temperature and blood pressure. For each patient the current readings can be displayed both at the bedside and at the nurse unit. If any of the factor readings of a patient are outside preset limits, then an alarm is sent to the central nurse station.

19.3.2   Configuration Design Descriptions in Conic

(a)   Component types: Provision of context-independent, reusable components (principle 2)

The patient-monitoring system is constructed from the two context-independent component types (referred to as modules in Conic) defined both graphically and textually below in Figs 19.1 and 19.2. The interface to a component is defined by typed exit- and entryports. Messages are sent out via exitports and received from entryports. Messages can be of any standard Pascal datatype (except pointer and file types). The type definitions are imported from definition modules by the use clause.

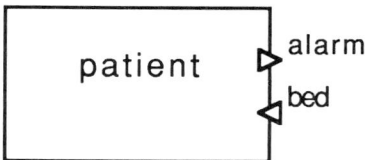

```
group module patient;
        use monmsg: bedtype, alarmstype;
        exitport  alarm:alarmstype;
        entryport  bed:signaltype reply bedtype;

        - The module periodically reads sensors attached to a patient.
        Readings outside preset ranges cause alarm messages to be
        sent to the exitport alarm.
        A request message received on the entryport bed returns the
        current readings and ranges.
    end.
```

Fig. 19.1   The patient component.

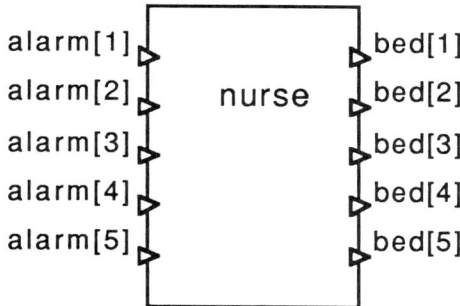

```
groupmodule nurse (maxbed:integer=5);
    use monmsg: bedtype, alarmstype;
    entryport  alarm[1..maxbed]:alarmstype;
    exitport  bed[1..maxbed]:signaltype reply bedtype;

        - the module displays alarms received from alarm[]
        and requests the display of a particular patient via bed[].
end.
```

Fig. 19.2   The nurse component.

(b) Component hierarchies: Composition of component instances to form complex, context-independent, reusable components (principle 3)

In the above, we have described the main component types to be used to construct the patient-monitoring system. In fact, each of the two component types used are themselves configurations of components. For example, the internal structure of the patient component is depicted in Fig. 19.3. It is defined by instantiating an instance of each of a scanner and monitor component types and interconnecting their exit- and entryports. The links between exitports and entryports allow components to communicate by message passing. The Conic environment permits only ports of the same type to be connected.

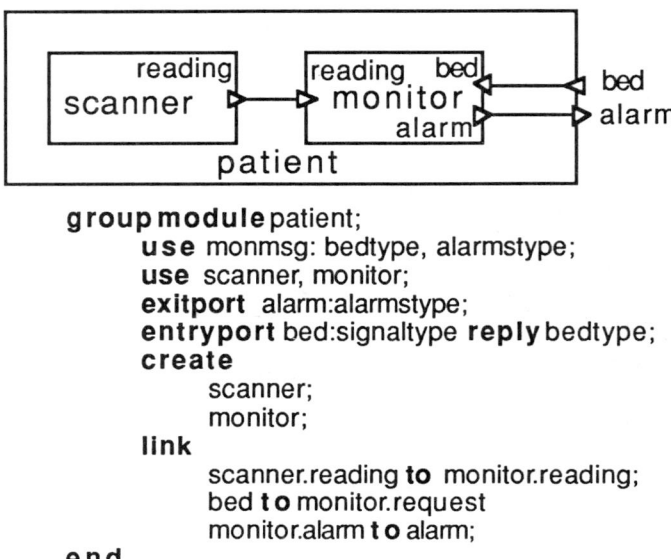

```
group module patient;
        use monmsg: bedtype, alarmstype;
        use scanner, monitor;
        exitport alarm:alarmstype;
        entryport bed:signaltype reply bedtype;
        create
                scanner;
                monitor;
        link
                scanner.reading to monitor.reading;
                bed to monitor.request
                monitor.alarm to alarm;
end.
```

Fig. 19.3 Internal structure of patient module.

A system in Conic is thus an hierarchic structure of component instances. The components at the bottom of the hierarchy are sequential tasks, implemented in a programming language. In Conic, the internal programming language is Pascal extended to support message passing for the distributed environment. Instances of these task modules execute concurrently.

19.3.3 Constructing Systems in Conic

(a) Component selection, specialization, instantiation and inter-connection using a separate configuration language (principle 1)

Given the hardware depicted in Fig. 19.4, we can construct an initial patient-monitoring system consisting of one nurse and one patient by instantiating one instance of each of the above component types and interconnecting their exit- and entryports. Again, the Conic environment permits only ports of the same type to be connected. The configuration description for this initial system is again shown both textually and graphically in Fig. 19.5.

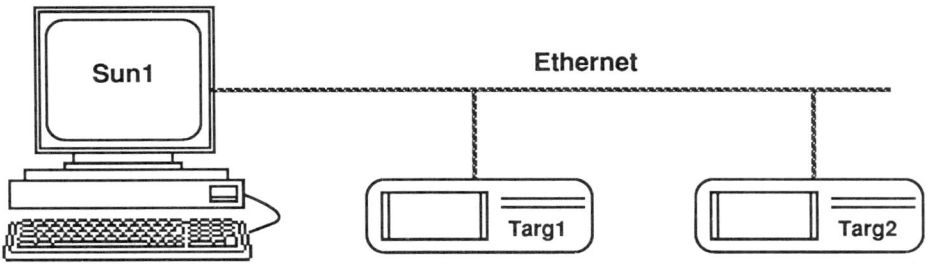

Fig. 19.4   Hardware environment.

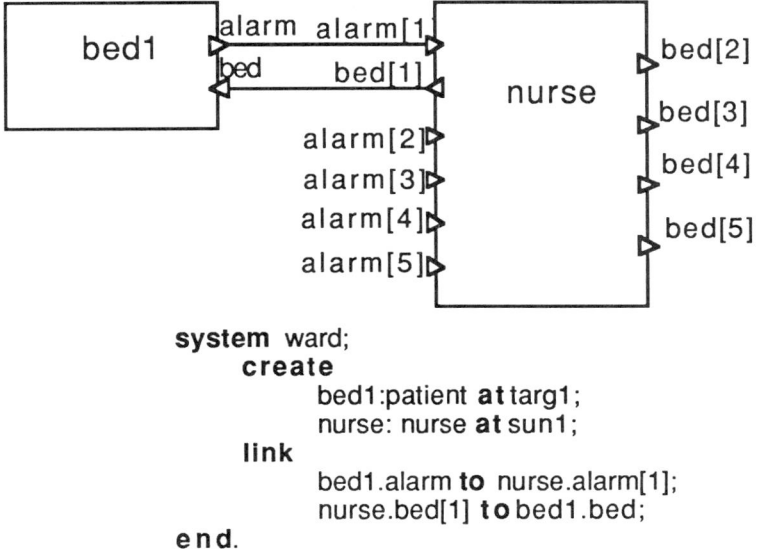

```
system ward;
     create
          bed1:patient at targ1;
          nurse: nurse at sun1;
     link
          bed1.alarm to nurse.alarm[1];
          nurse.bed[1] to bed1.bed;
end.
```

Fig. 19.5   Initial patient monitoring system.

The system is created by submitting the configuration description to a configuration manager tool which downloads component code into target processors or instantiates processes under Unix as appropriate (Fig. 19.6). The configuration management tool and its supporting environment is described in [22]. The configuration description may be submitted directly as text to the configuration management tool or indirectly using a graphical editor described in more detail in [15]. Note that, in addition to instance creation and linking (interconnection), the configuration description includes component location (the at clause) and parameters. For example the nurse has a default parameter setting to the value 5 (Fig. 19.2); however, this could have been changed when the instance was specified, e.g. create nurse:nurse (3) at sun1.

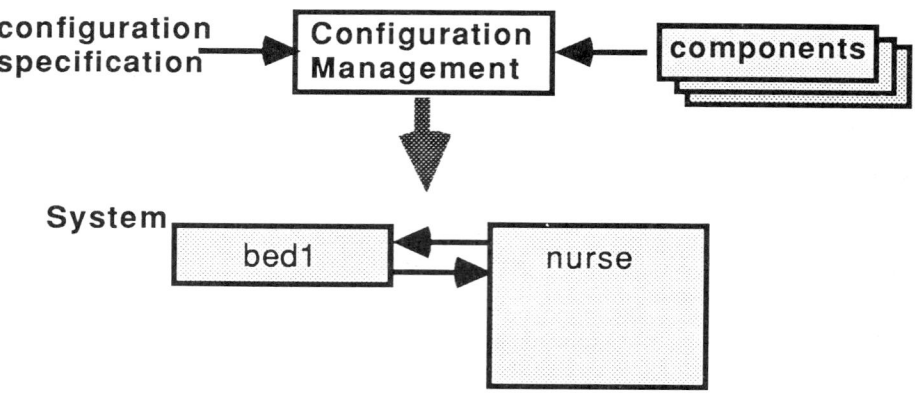

Fig. 19.6 System configuration using configuration management.

Note that the configuration language is declarative. This is more amenable to analysis and validation, and leaves the actual order in which configuration operations are performed to the underlying support system. It can then exploit the inherent parallelism of the underlying architecture where appropriate. If the configuration statements were embedded in a procedural language, the current state of the system configuration would depend on the state of the configuration program (for instance, see [19]). This would complicate the user view of the system and the provision of support for system evolution and dynamic configuration.

19.3.4 Dynamic Configuration for System Evolution

(a) Program families by dynamic reconfiguration (principle 4)

In addition to programming initial configurations, the Conic toolkit permits dynamic configuration: changes to running systems. For example, extending the above system to include an additional patient unit can be performed by submitting the following configuration change of the system 'ward' to a configuration manager:

```
change ward;

  create
  bed2:patient at targ2;
  link
  bed2.alarm to nurse.alarm[2];
  nurse.bed[2] to bed2.bed;

end
```

The resulting system is depicted graphically in Fig. 19.7.

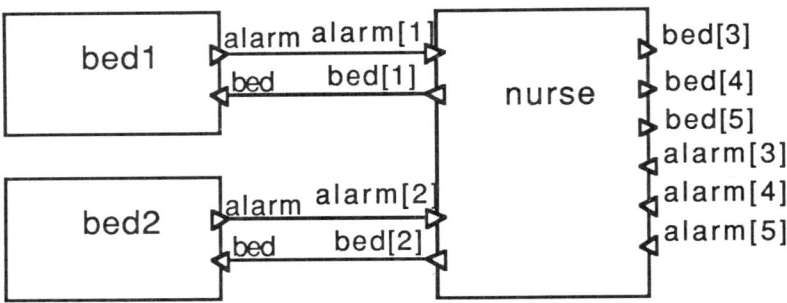

Fig. 19.7   Extended patient-monitoring system.

The change can be thought of as an edit, in configuration terms, of the configuration specification and the system itself. As shown in Fig. 19.8 it results in both a new specification and a correspondingly changed system. Thus the system itself evolves rather than the traditional approach of regenerating the system *ab initio*.

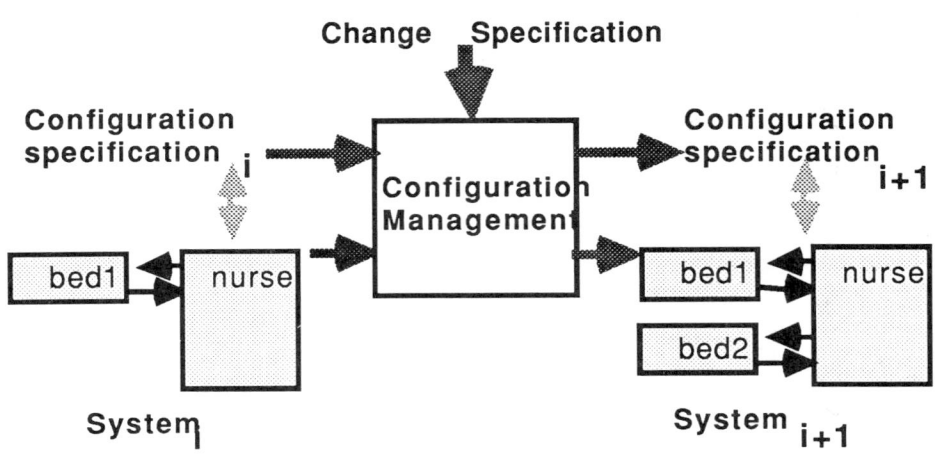

Fig. 19.8   Correspondence between system specification and actual system.

(b) Dynamic change management

As mentioned, changes are specified declaratively at the configuration level in terms of structure. However, these changes must be applied to the system in such a way that the application consistency is preserved. In addition, we would like to minimize the disruption to the application during the change.

Recent work [16] has provided a sound basis for performing change while preserving consistency and without disrupting the unaffected components. The structural concerns are again separated from those at the application (component) level. Changes are specified purely structurally, in the declarative configuration language. Using a set of change rules, it is possible to derive a procedural change transaction which identifies those nodes in a system affected by the particular change, and includes the control operations and ordering decisions necessary to apply the change transaction to the system itself. This change transaction puts the affected part of the system into a quiescent state in order to ensure that it does not contain the results of partial application transactions. Disconnecting nodes are given the opportunity to execute finalisation actions to leave the environment in a consistent state, and newly connected nodes the opportunity to execute initialization actions to make the node consistent with its environment.

Note that this approach to dynamic reconfiguration supports the provision of reusable, context-independent components. Component (dis)connection actions are part of the component type, and are designed to be general and independent of the particular reconfiguration in which the component instance is involved.

(c) Graphical configuration monitoring and programming

In practice, we have found it convenient to create initial systems from the configuration specification. Once created, a graphics tool, ConicDraw, can be used to display and manage the system. As depicted in Fig. 19.9, ConicDraw maintains a graphic representation of executing Conic systems in terms of the component instances which exist in the system, their interconnections and their execution state. It gathers this information directly from the executing system by communicating with a configuration manager. Thus the graphics tool can be used in a monitoring mode to provide users with an up-to-date view of the system configuration.

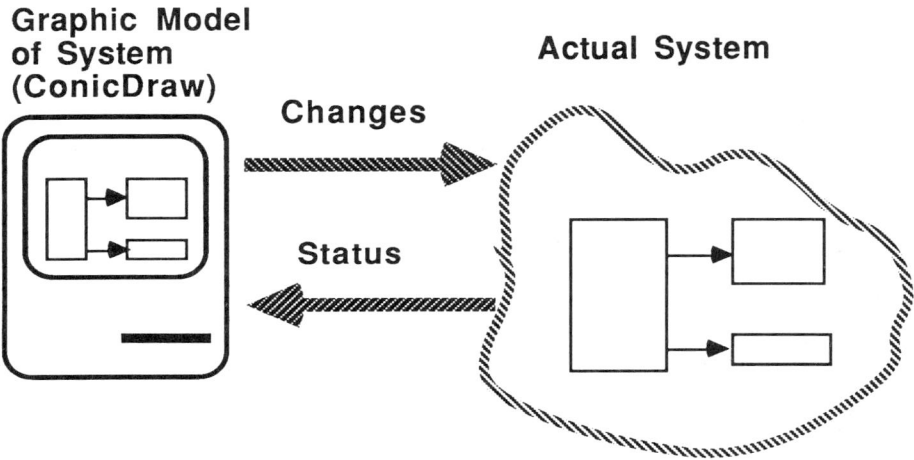

Fig. 19.9 Relationship between ConicDraw and system.

Changes to the system are reported to ConicDraw by configuration management to enable it to maintain an up-to-date view of the system. ConicDraw can itself instigate changes to the system as a result of edits to the graphic representation. A change which has been performed graphically can be saved in its text form for later reuse. The patient-monitoring system was extended by editing the diagram directly to create Fig. 19.10. These edits caused the tool to send the extension configuration text to a configuration manager to change the actual system accordingly. Figure 19.10 shows a further bed, bed3, being linked into the existing system using the link tool in the tool palette. The link instruction generated by this graphic operation (link nurse.bed3 to bed3.bed) is shown at the bottom of the figure.

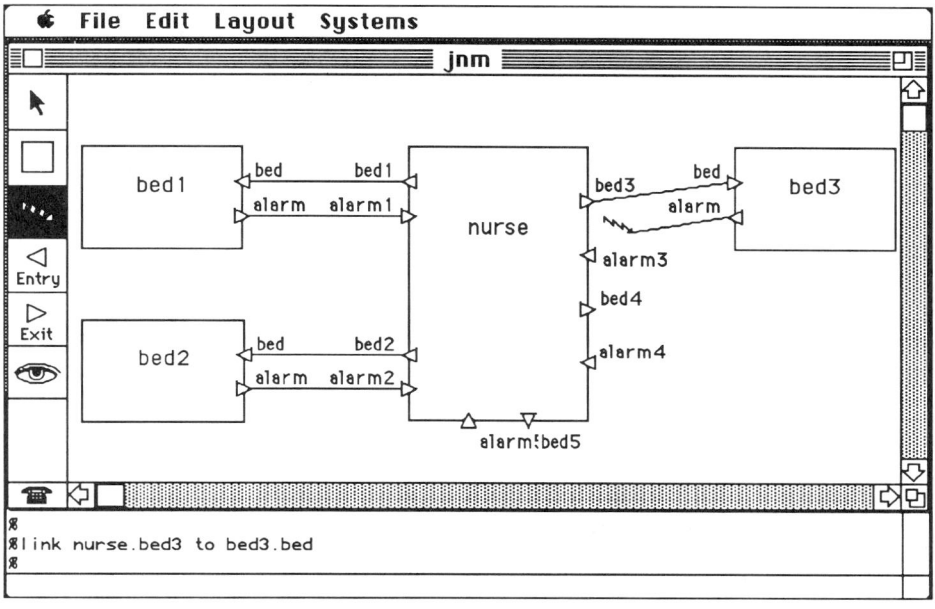

Fig. 19.10 System linking via ConicDraw.

Since ConicDraw always maintains a representation of the actual system, one or more workstations can be connected to the distributed system to allow a number of users to cooperatively manage and monitor the system. ConicDraw contains a comprehensive set of tools for creating and editing Conic configuration diagrams. As such, it can also be used as a standalone diagram editor. A full description of ConicDraw is given in [15].

19.3.5 Summary and Experience

This section has briefly outlined how configuration programming is used and supported in the Conic environment. The configuration language and components both conform to the basic principles described earlier in the paper. The interested reader can find a detailed description of the Conic configuration language in [7] and the Conic environment in [22].

Users of the Conic environment include a number of universities and industrial research centres in the UK, Belgium, Germany, France, Greece, Sweden, Finland, Canada, Korea, Hong Kong and Japan. Their use of configuration programming has included underground monitoring and communications in mines, plant automation, image processing, an object-oriented system manager, and multi-loop self-tuning adaptive controllers. Our experience at Imperial College has been very positive and confirms our belief that the structural configuration level is a useful level of abstraction for system description, construction and evolution. The provision of software tool support has been essential in the successful use of Conic.

This success has encouraged us to embark on a broader and more ambitious project, based on the same principles but incorporating many more of the aspects of the development process. This project, REX [32], includes work on formal specification techniques and tools for analysis and verification, on design methods and tools for recording and aiding the design process, and on configuration and dynamic reconfiguration and tools for performing the construction, reconfiguration and extension of distributed systems. The opportunities for exploiting component reuse are excellent.

19.4   SYSTEM DEVELOPMENT METHODS

The development method we advocate is based on the principles of configuration programming, i.e. early identification of an explicit structural specification, context-independent component types and hierarchical composition of component instances. This has led to our constructive design approach [17] which emphasizes the bottom-up constructive aspect rather than decomposition. The approach (which is recursive) is shown diagrammatically in Fig. 19.11 and consists of the following steps:

1. **Structure and Component Identification:** Initial design aims to identify the main processing components and produce a structural description indicating the main data flows. This step provides an initial identification of component types. Furthermore, hierarchical decomposition of any of the component types into a configuration of subcomponents may be performed at this stage, or left for later refinement.

2. **Interface Specification:** Introduce control (synchronization) between components and refine the configuration, component interface specifications (intercommunication) and component descriptions accordingly. The formulation of precise interface specifications permits the detailed design, implementation and testing of a component type to proceed independently from the rest of the system design.

3. **Component Elaboration** consists of elaboration of the component types, either by hierarchical decomposition of composite component types into a configuration of subcomponents (as in steps 1 and 2), or by detailed functional description of behaviour for primitive process components. As before, the identification of common component types is emphasized.

4. **Construction** is by instantiation and interconnection of components to form distributable components (logical nodes), followed by system configuration by allocation and interconnection of distributed components.

5. **Modification and Evolution** of the system is performed by the replacement or addition of components and connection changes.

As in all realistic development processes, the steps tend not to be followed purely sequentially, but include both iteration (and recursion) and the opportunity to advance in the process on one part of the system while lagging behind on another. This design approach has been extensively used, though there is still little experience of what effect change exerts on the design process. Nevertheless, we do believe that components can and should be designed to accommodate change.

Although component reuse is not explicitly mentioned in the above description of the method, the opportunities for reuse are obvious. Steps 1 and 3 on component identification and elaboration can both be directed towards identifying and selecting standard sets of components applicable to the application domain. It is the configuration facilities which provide the principal means for varying the system design. Component reusability is facilitated by making them independent of the system structure in which they may be instantiated. Furthermore, in application domains where libraries of components do not exist, the basic method can be used to produce such standard reusable components.

We are currently involved in developing a separate CASE tool for the design process based on ConicDraw, the tool used for graphical monitoring and change of the operational system [15]. ConicDraw already provides the required graphical support, but needs to be enhanced to support the duality we preserve between textual and graphical configuration descriptions. In addition, it should include method advice based on heuristics (such as was used in the TARA project [14]), recording of the designer's status and progress in the method, and calls to the component programming and configuration building tools for editing, compiling, constructing and loading the distributable components. Such a tool could be extended to include (or use) facilities for cataloguing and retrieving components from an information store. For instance, we could make use of a simpler form of the approach described in [34] which attempts to handle a greater variety of entities, from functions to abstract data types.

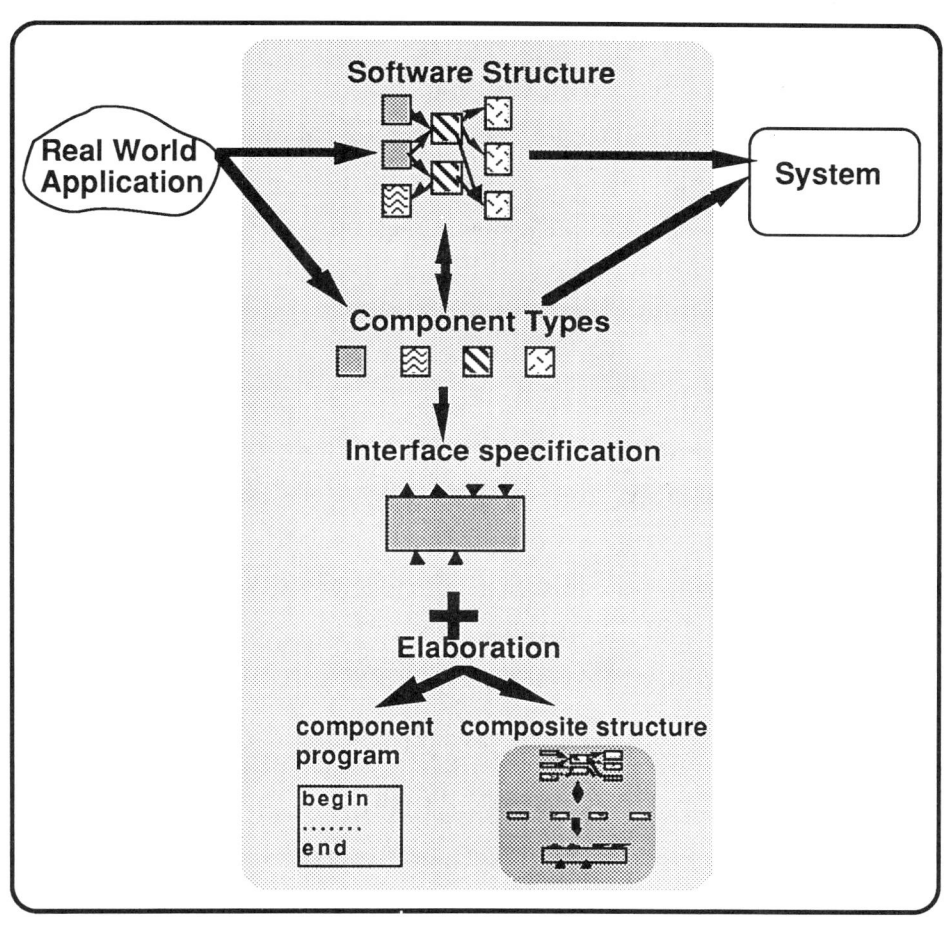

Fig. 19.11 A diagrammatic representation of the design approach.

19.5   CONCLUSIONS

The most crucial issue in the provision of support for software component reuse is the software architecture. In this paper, we have argued that configuration programming, with its use of a separate configuration language, provides a sound environment which supports the required facilities for component specialization, instantiation and interconnection. In a single application domain, variations in systems are principally reflected in their structure. The configuration language provides an excellent means for expressing that structure rather than embedding structural decisions in the software components themselves.

Components are designed to be general, context-independent types, suitable for use (and reuse) in different configurations. Their independence is facilitated by the use of local data and processing, and by the definition of strict interfaces. These interfaces describe not only the services provided (cf. Conic entryports) but also those required (cf. exitports). Furthermore, component definition as parameterized types permits multiple instantiation and specialization. Thus, by making components independent of their context, one is facilitating reusability. The facilities for supporting dynamic configuration provide yet another level of reuse.

Another important issue is the availability of a development method which recognizes and supports reuse. The current method can be used to produce standard reusable components for particular application domains. The component identification and elaboration steps can be easily tailored to exploit reuse by matching and selection where component libraries do exist. Further work is necessary to provide the necessary facilities for setting up, cataloguing, searching and matching in component libraries.

Finally, some more speculative research into reuse has been directed at the earlier phases in the software process, such as requirements specification [8]. Although innovative in its use of analogy for searching and matching specification fragments, that effort suffered from use within an environment (cf. architecture) which did not support an adequate form of specification modularization or reuse in its method. Current work in the REX project is extending the use of a configuration language to the specifications level, and hopes to configure specification components. The approach is analogous to system design description and construction except that the entities being manipulated are not software components but their specifications. Composition rules could be used to derive composite group behaviour from constituent component behaviours. Should this work prove successful, configuring specifications would provide a promising environment for specifications reuse.

ACKNOWLEDGEMENTS

This paper is based on an earlier paper [18] which describes the configuration programming approach more fully. Acknowledgement is made to my colleagues at Imperial College, Naranker Dulay, Anthony Finkelstein, Jeff Magee, Keng Ng, Morris Sloman and Kevin Twidle for their contribution to the work described in this paper. Finally, I gratefully acknowledge the SERC ACME Directorate under grant GE/E/62394, the SERC under grant GE/F/04605 and the CEC in the REX Project (2080) for their financial support.

REFERENCES

1. M.R. Barbacci, C.B. Weinstock, and J.M. Wing, 'Programming at the Processor – Memory – Switch Level', Proc. of 10th IEEE Int. Conf. on Software Engineering, Singapore, April 1988.

2. N. Carreiro, D. Gelernter, Technical Correspondence, Comm.ACM, Vol. 32, 10, October 1989.

3.   J. Castro, R. Kramer,   Temporal-Causal System Specification, Proc. of IEEE Int. Conf. on Computer Systems and Software Engineering (CompEuro 90), Israel, May 1990.

4.   M. Coulas, G. MacEwen, G. Marquis, 'Net: A Hard Real-Time Distributed Programming System', IEEE Transactions on Computers, C-36 (8), August 1987.

5.   T. De Marco, 'Structured Analysis and Structured Specifications', Prentice-Hall, 1979.

6.   F. DeRemer, H.H. Kron. 'Programming-in-the-large Versus Programming-in-the-small', IEEE Trans. Software Engineering, Vol. SE-2, 2, June 1976.

7.   N. Dulay, A Configuration Language for Distributed Programming, Ph.D. Thesis, Imperial College, London University, 1990.

8.   A.C.W. Finkelstein, Reuse of Formatted Requirements Specifications, IEE Software Engineering Journal, Vol. 3, 5, September 1988.

9.   J.A. Goguen. 'Reusing and Interconnecting Software Components', IEEE Computer (Designing for Adaptability), Vol. 19, 2, February 1986.

10.   P.A.V. Hall, Software Components and Reuse, IEE Software Engineering Journal, Vol. 3, 5, September 1988.

11.   M.A. Jackson, 'System Development', Prentice-Hall, 1983.

12. S. Kaplan, G. Kaiser, Garp: Graph Abstractions for Concurrent Programming, ESOP '88, Nancy, France, March 1988, Springer-Verlag, pp. 191-205.

13. J. Kramer, J. Magee, 'Dynamic Configuration for Distributed Systems', IEEE Transactions on Software Engineering, SE-11 (4), April 1985, pp. 424-436.

14. J. Kramer, K. Ng, C. Potts, K. Whitehead, Tool Support for Requirements Analysis, IEE Software Engineering Journal, Vol. 3, 3, May 1988.

15. J. Kramer, J. Magee, K. Ng, 'Graphical Configuration Programming', IEEE Computer, 22(10), October 1989, pp. 53-65.

16. J. Kramer, J. Magee, 'The Evolving Philosophers' Problem: Dynamic Change Management', to appear in IEEE Trans. on Software Eng., November 1990.

17. J. Kramer, J. Magee, A. Finkelstein, A Constructive Approach to the Design of Distributed Systems, to be presented at the 10th Int. Conf. on Distributed Computing Systems, May 1990.

18. J. Kramer, Configuration Programming – A Framework for the Development of Distributable Systems, Proc. of IEEE Int. Conf. on Computer Systems and Software Engineering (CompEuro 90), Israel, May 1990.

19. R.J. Leblanc and A.B. MacCabe, The Design of a Programming Language based on a Connectivity Network, Proc. 3rd Int. Conf. on Distributed Computing Systems, 1982.

20. T. LeBlanc and S. Friedberg. 'HPC: A model of structure and change in distributed systems'. IEEE Trans. on Computers, Vol. C-34, 12, December 1985.

21.   I. Lee, N. Prywes, B. Szymanski, Partitioning of Massive/Real-Time Programs for Parallel Processings, in Advances in Computers, ed. M.C. Yovits, Vol. 25, Academic Press 1986.

22.   J. Magee, J. Kramer, and M. Sloman, 'Constructing Distributed Systems in Conic' IEEE Transactions on Software Engineering, SE-15 (6), June 1989.

23.   M.D. McIlroy, 'Mass Produced Software Components', Proc. of NATO Conf. on Software Engineering, Garmisch, Germany, 1968.

24.   J. Mitchell, W. Maybury, R. Sweet, 'Mesa Language Manual, Version 5.0', Xerox Parc Report CSL-79-3, Palo Alto Research Center, April 1979.

25.   H. Muhlenbein, T. Scheider, S. Streitz, Network Programming with MUPPET, Journal of Parallel and Distributed Computing, Vol. 5, 1988.

26.   W.P. Myers, G.F. Myers and L.C. Constantine. 'Structured design', IBM Syst. J., vol. 13, no. 2, pp. 115-139, 1974.

27.   J. Nehmer, D. Haban, F. Mattern, D. Wybranietz, D. Rombach, 'Key Concepts of the INCAS Multicomputer Project', IEEE Transactions on Software Engineering, SE-13 (8), August 1987.

28.   H. Ossher, 'A Case Study in Structure Specification: A Grid Description of Scribe', IEEE Transactions on Software Engineering, Vol. 15, 11, November 1989.

29.   D.L. Parnas, 'On the Design and Development of Program Families', IEEE Transactions on Software Engineering, SE-2 (1), March 1976, pp. 1-9.

30. D.E. Perry, 'The Inscape Environment', Proc. of 11th IEEE Int. Conf. on Software Engineering, Pittsburgh, May 1989.

31. J. Purtilo, A Software Interconnection Technology, Computer Science Dept., University of Maryland, TR-2139, 1988.

32. REX Technical Annexe, ESPRIT Project 2080, European Economic Commission, March 1989.

33. M. Stovsky, B. Weide, STILE: A Graphical Design and Development Environment, Digest Compcon Spring 87, CS Press, California.

34. M.Wood, I. Sommerville, An Information Retrieval System for Software Components, IEE Software Engineering Journal, Vol. 3, 5, September 1988.

35. E.Yourdon, L.Constantine, 'Structured Design', Yourdon Press, 1978.

36. P. Zave, 'An Operational Approach to Requirements Specification for Embedded Systems', IEEE Trans. on Software Engineering, SE-8 (3), 1982.

Part Six

Support for Maintenance

20 Introduction of maintenance concepts at the requirement stage and their relationship to re-engineering strategy

P.D. Carroll

Royal Air Force

20.1 INTRODUCTION

The growth of organizations such as the University of Durham Centre for Software Maintenance and the increasing number of industrial/academic seminars on the subject indicate that software maintenance is developing into a recognized academic and commercial discipline.

This paper argues that software maintenance problems are inextricably linked with procurement and development practices. Furthermore, it outlines practical steps that can ensure previous software maintenance experience, often unfortunate, is 'fed-back' into the procurement and development of new systems. This paper identifies the importance of according software maintenance considerations a prime input at requirement definition, specification production, design reviews and project management.

20.2   AIM

The aim of the paper is to argue the case for software maintenance being regarded as a prime design driver on new software intensive systems.

20.3   MAIN DISCUSSION

20.3.1   Introduction

The fact that software maintenance costs can dominate software development costs by the ratio of 4:1 for DP systems and by up to 10:1 for real-time systems is widely accepted. However, very few organizations seem to react to these startling figures and change their perception and treatment of software systems to a lifecycle cost approach.

First, let's look at a few typical examples that characterize software maintenance problems on current systems:

* Documentation which is not complete or does not reflect the system as coded.

* Failed configuration control.

* An architecture and design which does not facilitate expansion or enhancement.

* Lack of software engineering principles and quality assurance.

There is a school of thought which believes that many of our maintenance problems will go away as a natural consequence of our using more and more sophisticated tools and methods to develop our new systems. Is it not the case, that this view was aired each time we have had an advance in language generation? The argument is invalid! Why? Because as each time we discover a new technique which increases our capability to control the complexity and size of our software we immediately exploit it to the limit by attempting to develop systems which are more complex than the last generation. The user demand for complexity and scale escalates as fast as our attempts to control that complexity, and hence our maintenance problems will not disappear as a natural consequence of more powerful languages, support environments and methods.

The common area for our list of typical software maintenance problems is that they are rooted in the original development and procurement process. Someone, knowingly or not, accepted incomplete documentation, someone accepted the restrictive design.

It is not the intention of this paper to argue, with the benefit of hindsight, that the problems we have today could have been avoided if our predecessors had identified and acted upon what we might now think of as obvious. However, it contends that maintenance problems will only ease when we consciously apply new techniques and methods with software maintenance as a prime consideration.

Having argued that software maintenance should be a prime procurement and project management consideration it is essential to identify practical steps that can be taken realize this grand, but potentially vague, notion. These practical steps are identified under the following headings.

* Requirement Definition

* Project Design Reviews

* Software Maintenance Strategies.

20.3.2   Requirement Definition

For many individuals and organizations the notion that software maintenance considerations should figure in a system requirement definition seems odd! In fact, many experienced procurers and project managers would actively argue against this view as they regard their objective to be the acquisition of a system which meets the as defined CURRENT business needs, within budget and on time.

However, if approached with the following question, without revealing that software maintenance is the hidden factor, there is usually at least some reaction.

'There is a factor in your project which in cost terms will account for about 4 times the initial procurement cost – are you worried?'

The danger in using this approach is that if the answer to the above is 'Yes' and there is a genuine desire to integrate software maintenance considerations into the requirement definition stage, there has to be some practical way of ensuring that the maintenance requirements can be generated. An example may help.

The example system, one with which the author was personally involved, will, for the sake of anonymity, be called the Costs a Fortune To Maintain System which controlled expensive machinery. Experience on previous generations of similar systems had indicated that a significant proportion of maintenance activity had arisen out of changes to the characteristics of the machinery under control. In that case, why not make the parameters which are likely to change data parameters, changeable easily offline by a change to a data file? This, particularly when described at a superficial level, seems obvious! However, the incorporation of this cost-effective design feature only came about because someone consciously identified that similar parameter changes had been a major source of maintenance work on previous equipments. Once identified, the requirement definition team made it a formal requirement that these parameters be stored in a table; it was not left to the system developer's discretion.

Indeed, the system developer would have found it easier to opt for hard-coding these parameters in the absence of our additional 'requirement for maintenance'.

In large systems it is difficult to identify areas where introducing requirements aimed at assisting maintenance is both possible and effective. However, the key point is that dedicating part of our requirement definition effort to identifying maintenance scenarios in the context of the business/operational role is a practical step. At the very least it affords an opportunity to identify the more significant scenarios.

Another example may help illustrate this theme. It is common on military systems to specify to development contractors that the delivered system will have at least 50% spare capacity in terms of processor, disk and communication performance. This is in itself a recognition at the requirement stage of the inevitable future expansion due to maintenance. However, even this commonsense measure can be improved. It is very little use specifying the extra capacity if the selected application software architecture by its very nature hinders the use of that spare capacity. The details of a design architecture are not easy to specify as a requirement. Furthermore, it could be argued that such implementation detail has no place in a requirement document. However, such implementation features can be greatly influenced by the use of design reviews conducted throughout the development process with software maintenance as a key agenda item.

Before leaving this area it is essential to consider how management structures can be used to motivate our project staff to take account of software maintenance costs. The key issue is that if our management view of success on a project is based on its meeting initial requirements and procurement budgets we are unlikely to reduce future maintenance bills, and hence the full lifecycle costs, as many of the measures required to do this need more investment at the earlier stages of the project. Such 'up-front' extra costs tend to threaten our ability to meet the initial requirement within budget. Changing our management structure to one which assesses success from a lifecycle cost viewpoint is likely to be difficult. Why? Because to achieve this change successfully can only be done by making our financiers aware of software maintenance issues. This is difficult as it involves ourselves, the software maintenance community, translating our arguments into financial terms.

20.3.3   Project Design Reviews

It is necessary to define exactly what constitutes a design review in the context of this paper. A design review is the discussion of the proposed design between the system developer and the customer in open forum. The aim of the review is to give the customer confidence that the design is feasible and that the employed project management techniques and standards will lead to successful completion of the project on time and to budget. There is now a move in the defence community to formally consider the impact of software maintenance at design reviews.

In addition to the impact of the proposed software architecture on future maintenance costs the design reviews are an invaluable opportunity to assess the software maintenance impact of the developer's project management practice on such issues as the use of support tools, of quality procedures, coding standards and configuration control systems. For example, on a particular real-time system the developer decided to use a design method which was supported by a powerful development environment, which we will call TOOLSET-X. The developer admitted to using this method (and the tool) for the first time. As they were particularly experienced in using another tool, TOOL-Y, for functions such as configuration control and test management, they proposed to use both TOOL-X and TOOL-Y on the project. TOOL-X to support the design, and TOOL-Y for the configuration control with manual porting of software elements from TOOL-X to TOOL-Y. It is essential to note that TOOL-X could in fact perform all the functions of TOOL-Y. However, the developer was, sensibly from the development point of view, reluctant to become completely dependent on the unfamiliar TOOL-X and was, from his contractual point of view, reluctant to take on the increased licensing costs associated with using TOOL-X in its all encompassing role. However, by devoting a design review agenda item to software maintenance issues this design decision was critically questioned from a different viewpoint. What would be the licence cost consideration of using both tools throughout the lifecycle? What of the cost of having to train software maintainers in each of the two toolsets? What software maintenance problems would arise from using two toolsets when one would suffice? What would be the cost of continuing with the two toolset approach and then taking the software and hosting it in one support environment? Once again, this important lifecycle issue would not have been aired unless formally raised from the software maintenance perspective.

Another invaluable area in which design reviews can assist future maintenance is in the estimation of future support personnel resources. At an initial design review, only vague estimates of the size and complexity of the proposed system will be available. However, using a proven cost estimation model with these preliminary figures can provide up-front planning information for the maintenance team allowing them to plan and resource the maintenance effort. The figures can be refined at later design reviews.

Furthermore, software maintainers have a legitimate role in design review considerations of language selection, software deliverables, programming standards, quality assurance measures and critical review of documentation.

Let's consider in more detail the matter of software deliverables. The concept that we aim to take delivery of the software at successful completion of the project seems almost too obvious to be worthy of comment! However, on many projects there is dispute as to what constitutes a deliverable software item. For example, is the source code deliverable? Are test scenario files and their associated result files generated for use during development deliverable? Has an assessment been carried out to determine their usefulness during the maintenance phase? Are command build files and installation files deliverable? If so, with what documentation? Exploring these questions in a design review can achieve significant lifecycle cost savings.

Research indicates that software maintainers can spend up to 60% of their working time studying software documentation. Obviously, any reduction in this percentage will have a significant impact on maintenance costs. Therefore it is essential that software documentation features prominently in design review proceedings. For instance, to what standard will the documentation be produced? Will test and support software be produced to the same standard? Will design decisions be documented and explained in addition to the application design? What QA tests will be carried out to ensure that the delivered documentation accurately reflects the delivered system?

On so many projects these questions are not asked during development and procurement. Instead maintainers are faced with accepting a *fait accompli* and making the best of a bad job in almost complete isolation from the area where most of their problems originated, requirement and procurement.

20.3.4 Software Maintenance Strategies

If we are successful in integrating software maintenance considerations into our procurement and development practices we need something against which we can measure the acceptability of features incorporated to facilitate maintenance. An effective option is to identify, during the requirement definition stage, how we wish to maintain our system and record this as a statement of our software maintenance strategy. The strategy should cover such issues as:

  *   Will the maintenance be carried out in-house, by the original vendor
      or by a third party?

* Are there security features which constrain our maintenance options?

* How does our strategy for this system relate to our corporate strategy and maintenance capabilities?

* Is there a need for extra hardware for maintenance activity?

* Will we need to provide extra training?

* What configuration controls and organization will be required for the new system and how will they relate to existing practices?

During the earlier stages the strategy will be vague in areas of detail due to the lack of design information. However, it should be firm on the key issues of which agency will carry out the maintenance work and how much we will be constrained by security considerations.

Armed with such a software maintenance strategy we can participate in design reviews from a maintenance viewpoint. Detail can be added to the strategy throughout the development process. Indeed, our participation in the design reviews may reveal information or problems which require us to change our strategy. If this happens, we are far better placed to effect the change in an efficient way than we would be if we had accepted delivery into the maintenance phase without visibility of the problem. Evolutionary development of our strategy gives maintainers visibility of potential problems.

20.4 CONCLUSION

This paper has contended that most software maintenance problems result from our procurement and project management practices. It has contended that software maintenance problems will not reduce as a result of the use of sophisticated development tools and that the problems will ease only if software maintenance considerations become a fully integrated feature of requirement definition and software project management practice. In addition the paper has outlined some practical measures which can be applied to new systems with a view to reducing maintenance costs.

21   Re-engineering as an opportunity to reduce the maintenance workload

D. Francis

Programmes Know How

21.1   INTRODUCTION

A reduction in the resources allocated to software maintenance is an objective of most commercial organizations and my own, Programmes Know How, is no exception. I should like to describe today the circumstances leading to a decision to rewrite a major application using some of the techniques of software engineering, and the development itself. Since this software has been in daily use for nearly two years now, I am able to judge the effect on the maintenance workload and I intend to show that, with planning, there are benefits to be gained in this area. Whenever possible I will attempt to quantify these benefits but I want to stress that I have approached this subject from the point of view of a commercial user of software tools, whose primary objective is the profitability of the company and not the elegance of the applications software used to support this objective. I should like share the experience of being a user rather than a technical authority on the subject and hope you will find this valuable.

21.2 THE BUSINESS ENVIRONMENT

Programmes Know How is part of the Programmes Network, a group of direct marketing for those who may not be familiar with it. Whilst there is probably even more disagreement about what marketing is than there is about what Information Technology is, it can be considered to be simply the interface between, on the one hand, what a business is capable of delivering and on the other what people want. This is described in Fig. 21.1.

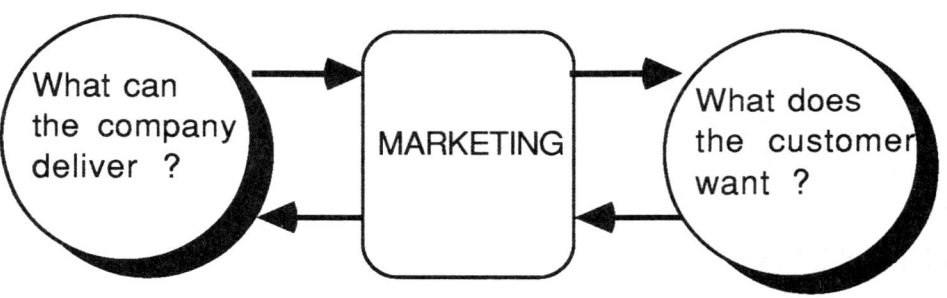

Fig. 21.1 The role of marketing.

The more effectively this interface is built and maintained the better an organization is equipped to achieve its goals. Most of you will remember that Clive Sinclair once ran a business that was capable of delivering a three-wheeled, electric powered vehicle but, in failing to recognize that very few people wanted such a device he demonstrated a profound misunderstanding of marketing and its importance in business.

21.2.1 The Changes Taking Place

Like so many other aspects of business life the process of marketing, i.e. the way in which this interface is built and maintained, is currently undergoing radical change, due in no small part to developments in information technology. This change involves a move away from the general broadcasting (through advertising for example) of a marketing message to vaguely defined, and often quite large target market, e.g. teenagers, car drivers, computer users; to the delivery (in person, by mail, telephone etc.) of a specific personalized message to a highly defined and often quite small target market (IBM mainframe users running CICS with more than 100,000 lines of live Cobol code for example) and then eliciting a response of some sort which influences the next marketing action.

This 'direct' marketing attempts to address the problem of getting the marketing message to the right person, that is the one who actually wants to buy your product or service – if only he knew about it. So what has all this got to do with IT? Direct marketing depends for its success on the intelligent use of information about markets and nowhere in an organization does the IT message about the value of information find more willing listeners or more practical applications than within the marketing department.

So for some time now companies have been building so-called marketing databases, large volumes of data managed by software which is designed to distil the information that is a natural by-product of the daily activities of sales, production and finance departments and presenting it in a way which enhances and supports the marketing process.

21.2.2 Direct Marketing within the IT Sector

The computer industry of course was the first to recognize the advantages to be gained by applying the very technology it was supplying to its customers to its own process of direct marketing, but early attempts to build the databases provided me with varied degrees of success. Partly this was due to the trial and error associated with any innovation but also because the established software development methods simply could not keep up with the speed of change, and what started out as an innovative and exciting idea became yet another contributor to the maintenance backlog. IT was once again criticized for failing to meet the business need.

In 1984 the Programmes Network, encouraged by this perceived need, decided to build a comprehensive and detailed database of computer users in the UK and to offer this information to the suppliers of IT products and services as the basis for their own marketing databases.

21.3. THE MAINTENANCE BACKLOG

We chose an IBM System/38 as the database host and wrote the application software in RPG3. At this time Programmes Know How was a new company, employing 15 people, only one of which was an RPG programmer, and so we relied heavily on the software house we chose to assist us. The degree of sophistication of the development process was commensurate with our size. Some information needs were, documentation was not comprehensive and there was little if any gap between the completion of the initial development and the beginning of the enhancement /maintenance phase. We relied increasingly on the knowledge stored in the heads of the programming team (now increased to two people), and began to muddle through in a way which may be familiar to many of you here. Whilst we didn't realize it, we were already on the downward spiral which inevitably leads to a maintenance backlog, increased pressure to expand the size of the DP department and eventual crisis, as shown in Fig. 21.2.

The software engineering approach to solving the problem of Fig. 21.2 is to recognize that the volume of software maintenance is not going to reduce and to seek to use the available resource more efficiently. This was the approach we were to take two years after our own implementation.

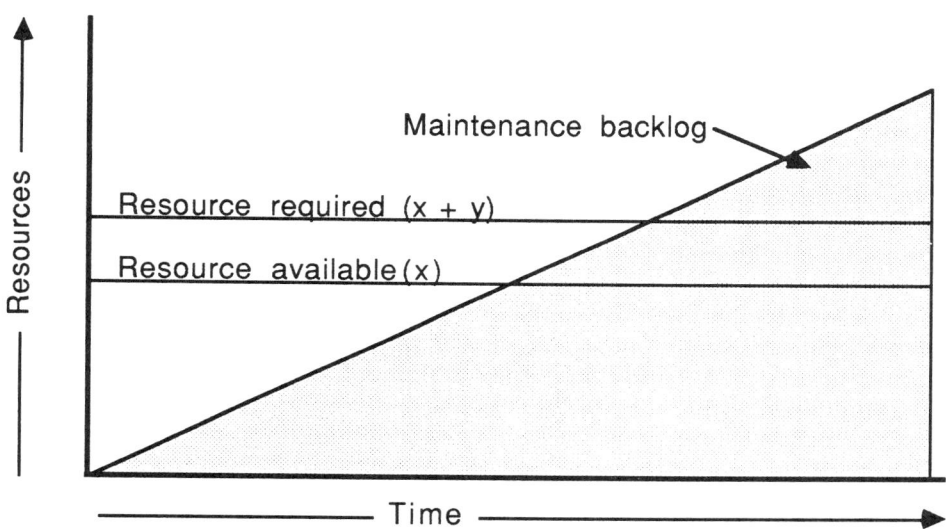

Fig. 21.2 The building of a maintenance backlog.

21.3.1 The Crisis

Meanwhile, however, things were not all bad. Our original business idea proved to be sound, there was a demand for the information base we were building, we traded profitably and built the business to a turnover of over one million pounds within two years. We also learnt a great deal about the practical difficulties of building and managing a databases of this kind, which was to prove valuable later on.

Our success, however, led to a crisis in terms of our computer systems. Our original guess was that our database should be able to provide a breadth of information across many different markets and we built this into the design. In fact we found that many of the real demand was for a great depth of information in just one market sector, the computer industry. The data structures necessary to support this were quite different from those originally envisaged and the enhancements necessary resulted in a system maintenance problem. In June 1987 the management team of the company proposed an expansion into Europe and this was the straw as far as the systems were concerned. The changes necessary to support this initiative were considerable and to our DP minds, unthinkable. In searching for a solution to this problem the necessity to redesign the database and rewrite the applications software became apparent. We estimated this to be at least a six-month project and very expensive, but to my mind what was worse was that there was no guarantee that, even if we went ahead, we would not find ourselves in exactly the same situation in two years' time.

21.4   THE SOFTWARE ENGINEERING APPROACH

At this time we were approached by a software house we had known for some time, with an offer to become a beta test site for a new product, Genesis. Variously described as a program generator, a fourth-generation language and an expert system. Encouraged by an initial demonstration of the product we installed it and began an evaluation.

21.4.1   Description of the Product

We found Genesis V to be a programmer's productivity tool.   That is, it required a good understanding of both the architecture of the System/38 and RPG to be used effectively.   It was capable of producing interactive rather than batch processing programs and it produced RPG code, which was subsequently compiled, rather than inaccessible machine code.   It also permitted changes to the generated code to be learnt by the generator and included in subsequent generations.   It appealed to us because in practice we never wrote a program from scratch (I suspect that very few people do). Given a specification we would cut and paste sections of code from earlier programs and tailor them to the new needs. After all, why reinvent the wheel when a similar one is already tested and sitting in a system library? Genesis did no more than automate this process for us, allowing us to customize a skeleton program through a well ordered process of parameterization, and it was therefore understandable, the mystery of the 4GL was removed. A decision was taken to rewrite our software using Genesis V.

21.4.2 Designing in Reduced Maintenance

In setting our objectives for the redevelopment we naturally included reduced development time and reduced costs since these were the standard benefits being offered by the suppliers of 4GLs; however, we also specifically targeted a reduced maintenance workload. Now it can be argued that if it was possible to predict how, why and when system enhancements are going to be needed in the future, life for the systems developer would be much easier, and that it is the very unpredictability of these requirements that makes it so difficult to accommodate them when they occur. In the light of my own experience I have to question this assumption of unpredictability. I do not know of any studies that have been done into the nature of system enhancements but I suspect that, if they exist, they show that there are some definite trends that can be exploited. Perhaps somebody here today can point me in the direction of this research. Our approach was to make our best guesses about the future and then, by examining the 'worst case' of all eventualities and assuming that Murphy's Law would operate (e.g. that the likelihood of an enhancement being required is directly proportional to the degree of difficulty of incorporating it into the system), then the parameters within which the system had to be constructed to meet the reduced maintenance objective became clearer.

21.4.3 An Example of a Design Feature

Our database contains details of products used by commercial organizations. Each of these products is described by a number of elements (make, model, size etc.) and in the original database design a field is defined for each of these data items. We knew from experience that new elements would be needed in the future and we wanted to avoid having to add new fields to the redesigned database. The trick of adding a few blank fields would not work because Murphy's Law would ensure that they would not be big enough or be needed more than once for any actual change. Even if it was possible to use a 'spare' field there was still the problem of cross-referencing all the programs that used it, changing screen layouts and redesigning reports. In the light of this we chose to hold only three fields for all this data. For the purposes of this description I will call them 'Parameter ID', 'Parameter Question' and 'Parameter Answer'. So a selection of the file appeared as shown in Fig. 21.3.

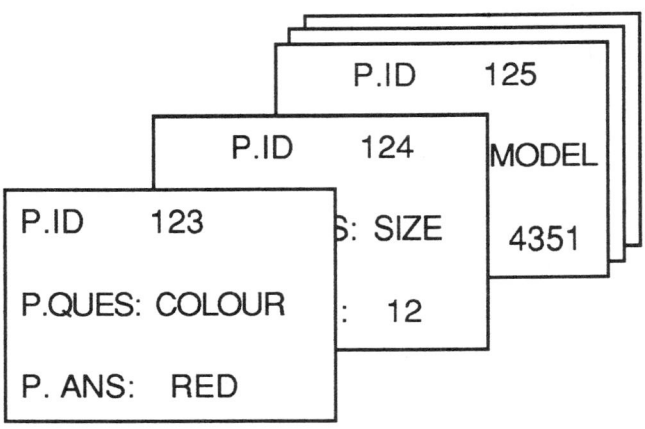

Fig. 21.3   The product information file.

This has been oversimplified to make the point but I hope you can see that if the user decides to hold information about a completely new product where it is necessary to hold information about, say, its weight, the system enhancements are reduced to:

- adding a new Parameter ID to a table of permitted PIDs,

- adding a new Parameter Question 'What is the weight of product X?' to the parameter question table,

- adding a new Parameter Answer table containing allowable responses to the question.

Since both the on-line update programs and the report generator that we wrote are both table-driven, making these table changes automatically updates these programs, without recompilation or debugging.

So this is an example of applying the same sort of logic that exists within program generators to the programs they are used to generate in order to reduce quite complex program changes to simple table changes that are within the technical abilities of the users themselves.

21.5 CONCLUSIONS

Re-engineering can be a daunting task. It often represents a large investment and the benefits are difficult to quantify beforehand. However, we have come a long way since the days of the creative programmer producing reams of clever but unintelligible code before moving on to his (or her) next victim. The tools are available and if we are ever to be free of the maintenance 'problem' I believe that we owe it to ourselves, if not to the companies that employ us, to make full use of them. I would encourage you to do so.

22 SMS – a software management system

M. Lamb and J. Barchan

Intasoft Limited

22.1 SOFTWARE MANAGEMENT

It is generally accepted that a piece of software, or indeed any computer project, undergoes various phases during its lifetime, generally referred to as the life-cycle .

A typical life-cycle might be as shown in Fig. 22.1.

Each of these phases will involve the generation of documents, design diagrams, source code or other data. Most, if not all, of this information is likely to be held on computer. Furthermore, all of the information must be maintained as the software undergoes various revisions for bug fixes and upgrades to the facilities offered. Maintenance is often associated with source code alone, and the other parts of the life-cycle are not considered to be important to the maintenance issue. It is, however, essential that requirements, specifications, and so on are maintained as rigidly and in parallel with developments to the source code. If this is not adhered to then the system's requirements specification will not necessarily relate to any particular version of the source code, for example, and hence may become increasingly unrelated to the software, negating the effectiveness of having such documents at all.

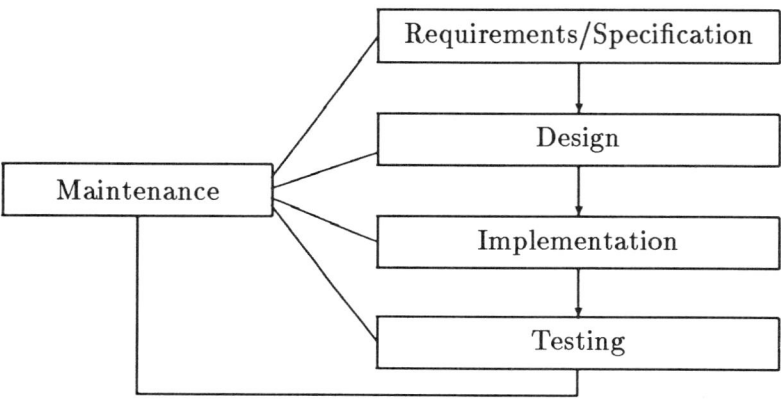

Fig. 22.1 Life-cycle.

Maintenance is accepted as being the most expensive element of a software project: the proportion of the cost of maintenance of a project is generally agreed to be between 50 and 80. Given the high cost of maintenance, tools which assist in the automation of maintenance procedures are extremely important and cost-effective.

There are several related tasks which can be automated to assist in software management and maintenance:

● Version Control

● Configuration Management Modification

- Request Management

SMS is a software management system which addresses the problem of automating maintenance procedures. It provides tools to assist in all the above tasks.

Each organization has its own existing procedures for Version Control, Configuration Management and Modification Request Management: any tools which are to assist in the automation of these tasks must therefore be flexible enough to fit in with existing procedures.

SMS achieves this flexibility by allowing users to set up their own default parameters for all aspects of the system on a project-by-project, or even file-by-file, basis.

22.2 VERSION CONTROL

Throughout the life-cycle of a software project, documents and source code undergo a number of revisions as the requirements change or the software is developed and updated to incorporate new facilities and correct bugs.

Version Control is the process of maintaining a history of these revisions. Given this revision history such vital questions as:

- What changes were made?

- Who made the changes?

- When were the changes made?

- Why were the changes made?

can all be answered.

A manual Version Control System can probably answer some of these questions, but the information may not be readily available. All too often the manual Version Control procedures are not enforced, since it is a time-consuming and tedious process, so the information available may not be accurate or up-to-date. Furthermore, to maintain manually all revisions of a file or number of files involves keeping complete copies of the files, which is very expensive in storage space.

An automated Version Control system should maintain a revision history of a text file by storing only the changes between one revision and the next. This is extremely efficient in terms of storage space, and also enables the Version Control system to show exactly what lines of code changed between one revision and another.

An automated Version Control system should have the capability to maintain not only text files but also data or object files, such as diagram files, requirements documents, test sets and even entities such as the compiler used to compile a particular version of the source code.

If Version Control is maintained across all aspects of the system at all times during the life-cycle, then at any point in the future you can go back to a complete old version of the system. If, for example, Version Control is only performed on the source code, and at some later date it is desired to go back to an old version of the software then the old version of the source code may be retrieved. However, if the compiler has changed then the old source may not compile, or perhaps simply behave in a different or unexpected fashion. If the compiler used for a particular version of the software is also maintained under Version Control then this problem will not arise.

The main principle of Version Control is the storage and retrieval of revisions in a revision tree, allowing any old version (back to the very original one) to be retrieved at any time.

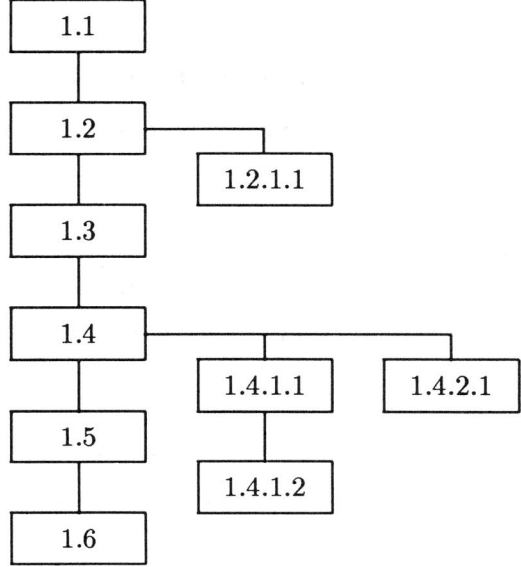

Fig. 22.2   Revision tree

Other essential features of a Version Control system include:

Access Control
　　Access to the revision history of a file should be restricted to only certain authorized users. SMS provides 3 levels of access control (Manager/Admin users, Write users and Read users): this therefore allows a high degree of control over access to file revisions.

Edit Control
　　Control of the editing of a file to ensure that two programmers do not make changes to the same file corrupting each other's changes.

Tree of Revisions
　　Enables separate lines of development to be pursued in parallel. Figure 22.2 illustrates a revision tree. SMS allows arbitrarily complex revision trees to be created if so desired, with branches from the main line of development and further branching from the branches.

Merging

SMS provides a tool for the automatic merging of separate lines of development into the main line of development, reporting any conflicts that may be encountered.

Revision Identification

Automatic revision identification with name, revision number, date etc. This allows the retrieval and reporting of revisions via a number of useful selections.

Report Generation

SMS provides a flexible and powerful report generator enabling the production of user-defined reports containing the information required in whatever format is required.

SMS provides all of the above essential features, plus a number of further facilities.

22.3   CONFIGURATION MANAGEMENT

Configuration Management is the process of managing what makes up a configuration of a piece of software.

This incorporates Version Control for the management of the versions of the modules programs making up a configuration of a software package (as well as associated documentation, specifications, designs etc.).

A Configuration of a software package could be regarded as a slice across the versions of the modules making up the software. A particular configuration (CONFIG) may consist of version 1.4 of module 1, version 1.7 of module 2 and version 1.2 of module 3 , as illustrated in Fig. 22.3.

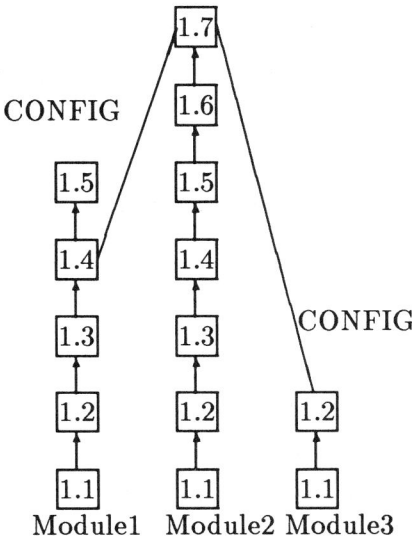

Fig. 22.3 A configuration as a slice across versions.

In order to automate Configuration Management, Version Control tools are required, and these must allow a configuration to be described as a slice across the versions. A tool should also be provided to allow a configuration to be automatically retrieved and built.

SMS provides methods of managing configurations by the use of symbolic names to describe a configuration and a build utility to generate configurations, maintain them up-to-date and ensure data integrity during development or maintenance tasks.

22.3.1 Symbolic Names

A Symbolic Name is the user-specified name to be associated with a particular revision. In the above diagram the name CONFIG is associated with version 1.4 of module 1, 1.7 of module 2 and 1.2 of module 3. In this way a configuration can be easily identified, retrieved etc.

In SMS a symbolic name may be used to represent any part of a revision number. A revision may then be specified by any combination of symbolic names and numbers. Thus if were a symbolic name for 2 and were a symbolic name for 1.1 then centre would be equivalent to version 2.1.1.1.

This method provides a powerful mechanism for specifying the constituents of a configuration over a number of files.

22.3.2 Build

The build utility provided by the SMS system is used to automatically build a software system. It ensures that only those modules that have changed since the last compilation are recompiled (and that all those modules that have changed are recompiled).

It is integrated with the Version Control enabling a complete configuration to be retrieved and built automatically.

A utility is provided to automatically scan files to find what files depend on other files and creates a dependency description for use with the build utility. This provides a valuable document describing the constituents of a program and how the software is made up, as well as allowing build to know what modules to compile when others are changed.

22.4 MODIFICATION REQUEST MANAGEMENT

Modification (or Change) Requests are bug reports or upgrade requests. Managing these is of great importance in the maintenance process: managers need to know what requests are outstanding, what stage they have reached etc.

Furthermore, there is a direct relationship between the versions of software and the Modification Requests: new versions are in response to Modification Requests.

Most organizations have manual bug reporting and upgrade request procedures which, as with manual version control systems, may not be accurately maintained or kept up-to-date. If they are, then automating the process would save considerable time and probably provide facilities information difficult to obtain with a manual system.

Every organization has a different Modification Request system, so an automated system should be flexible to allow it to fit in with existing procedures.

SMS provides a Modification request system which is extremely flexible and fully integrated with the Version Control System.

Modification Request management involves:

- the assignment of Modification Requests to programmers and notifying them that they have been assigned the task of dealing with an MR

- the movement of MRs through various statuses, for example:

  accepted - > fixing < - > testing - > completed - > released

- the notification of appropriate personnel on status changes and the reporting of information about MRs itemized.

SMS provides all these facilities while still maintaining flexibility and allowing precise statuses used, their names, notifications and so on to be determined by each organization.

22.5 CONCLUSION

SMS provides a fully integrated Software Management environment, providing facilities for Version Control, Configuration Management and Modification Request Management.

It also provides a menu-driven front-end with full context-sensitive on-line help to allow the benefits of using the system to be achieved with a minimal learning curve.

Version Control, Configuration Management and Modification Request management are central to the management of any software development project. Typically, however, version control/configuration management tools are not widely adopted by software developers because they are difficult to use or it is felt that they will interfere with current working practices. It is therefore essential for an automated system to be easy to use and highly flexible.

SMS has achieved this by providing a suite of tools which may be used as commands (since some users prefer this) or may be used from a front-end. SMS provides a large number of tools, all with several options which allow the user to select the exact functionality required. To learn all these options is a time-consuming and tedious process: the front-end therefore shows for each tool the options that are available in an easily comprehensible manner, together with on-line help for clarification if required. The user simply 'ticks off' those options required and then tells the system to perform the desired function.

Flexibility is achieved by providing a wide variety of options to each tool, together with facilities for default actions/option selections which may be set up on a file-by-file or project-by-project basis as required.

23 Analysis tools to support software maintenance

A. Tilbury

Yard Software Systems

23.1 INTRODUCTION

Useful analyses require that the software is in some form of recognizable order.

This paper advocates that the most valuable maintenance analysis tool is in constant use throughout development to ensure that the software is passed over to maintenance in good order. The maintainers will hopefully continue to use the tool to retain this good order.

23.2 THE HEART OF THE MAINTENANCE PROBLEM

23.2.1 Change

If the original design concept of a software product were to be carried through the entire development phase then the task of the eventual maintainers would be comparatively easy. If the design was itself bad, it would at least be uniformly bad.

Even when ease of maintenance is ranked with functional compliance as a major design and manufacturing goal for long-lived systems, and great care is taken with design, a number of conflicting practical factors conspire to confound the maintainers.

- **Early Planning.** The basis for efficient and effective maintenance is good 'forward engineering' from the outset of the project (as opposed to 'reverse engineering' applied at the end of the project). But...

- **Requirement Creep and Revision.** These make it hard to predict (and hence hard to plan) where the major maintenance effort will be concentrated.

- **Information Hiding.** While this design technique yields high reliability software it can present maintainers with a major problem since introductory descriptive documentation is a threat to the design integrity and should have been omitted.

- **Design Sensitivity.** Since design is usually a compromise between performance, cost and time it will generally be predicated upon a number of assumptions; the most dangerous of which are the implicit ones (and which are also probably undocumented). Small changes affecting these assumptions may have large deleterious consequences.

- **Bad Design and Implementation Practice.** Past howlers may be well known (e.g. using FORTRAN COMMON blocks to store 'real time' flags), but it must also be borne in mind that our modern tools and techniques also embody howlers that will not be perceived until major projects are well into their maintenance phases.

These factors make design change and modification certain; but when and in what form is uncertain.

The analysis tool of most value to the maintainers is one which will be integrated into the development process and which is routinely used to control the inevitable process of change.

23.2.2   Coping with Change

The significance of change is hard to determine analytically solely by means of automated tools operating upon the design and implementation documentation. For the present and probably the immediate future the detection mechanism must therefore be a human activity, or more accurately for large projects, a collective human activity.

Consequently the basic requirement at the maintenance phase is a tool, or a set of tools, that successfully engage the necessary human participation to detect and log the semantic problems so that they are subsequently available at maintenance time. This base tool is, of course, the Configuration Management and Control tool.

23.2.3   Participative Configuration Control

The term 'participative' is here used to distinguish between 'track and report' (non participative) tools and those that more closely follow the EEA 'Software Configuration Management' definition:

CONFIGURATION CONTROL. The discipline which ensures that any proposed change (modification or amendment) to a baseline shall be prepared, accepted and controlled in accordance with set procedures.

Note the position of the word 'accepted' which is the key word concerned with the impact of change analysis. In other words the guidelines are specifying that the semantics of the change must be examined and approved before the change takes place.

This approach has its roots in long established hardware practice in which this prior acceptance is provided by a Configuration Control Board(s) set up to review the submitted (paper) Engineering Change Notes and also possibly any Fault Reports to which they are a response. It is also the duty of the board to consider the technical aspects of the proposed changes and to attempt some form of Impact Analysis.

CCBs are often used for software, but suffer from two particular problems:

1.   **Rate of change.** For software this is generally very high at all points in the lifecycle, so that a board, and even a set of delegated boards, is easily swamped with proposals.

2.   **Software complexity.** Sensitivity to small changes, particularly the accretion of small changes, is such that the impact analysis is exceedingly difficult to carry out for a relatively small number of people to conduct; no matter how expert they they may be individually.

The role of a 'participative' configuration control system is to handle both. To do so realistically it must be very extensively automated.

One of the very few automated configuration control tools able to provide adequate facilities is LIFESPAN. How it automatically handles impact analysis as a built-in facility is the subject for the remainder of this paper.

23.3 LIFESPAN'S AUTOMATED CONFIGURATION CONTROL

LIFESPAN provides a 'database' for storing modules and sets of modules (packages) and their updates. Entry to the database is only permitted if the rules for handling changes are exactly obeyed. No privileges are provided for overriding these rules, so that the integrity of LIFESPAN as a control system is guaranteed.

Contained within those rules are Quality Control (QC) procedures for formally closing-off changes made to modules and packages. Until closed-off, a change may cause interlocks on other overlapping changes and thus hold up development: which provides pressure for inspection during manufacture. Proper QC therefore plays the key role in the control process (thereby supporting compliance with BS 5750).

For the purpose of this paper we are only interested in three LIFESPAN objects (Module, Package and Design Change) and the general rule concerning change control. Figure 23.1 shows the pictograms used in this paper.

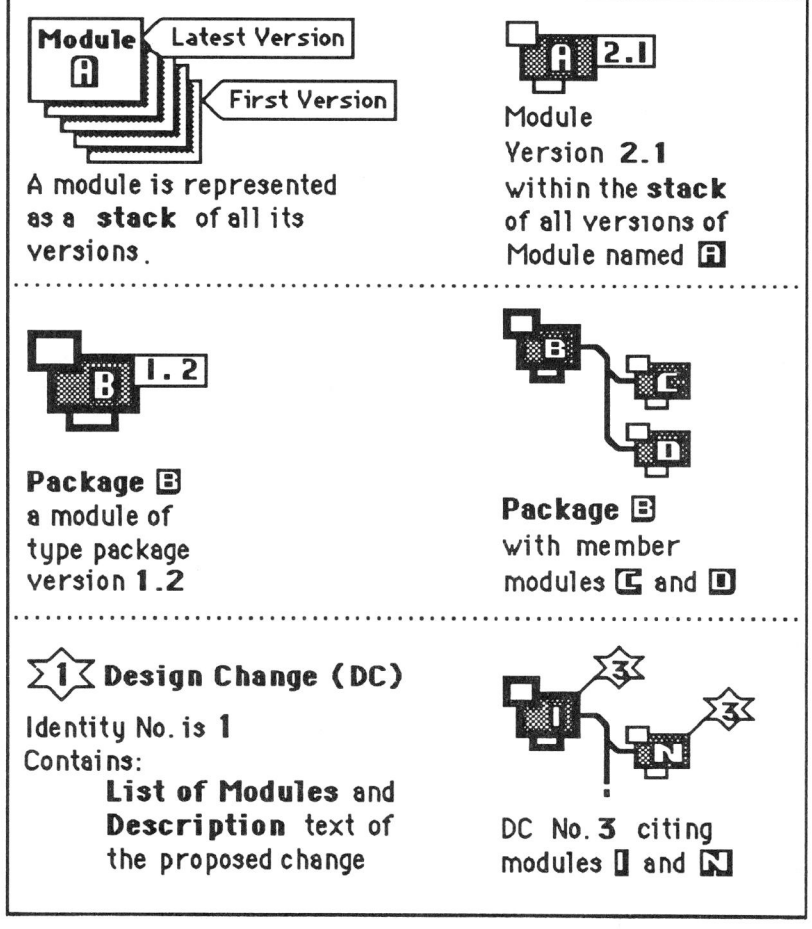

Fig. 23.1

A LIFESPAN 'Module' may be any file of any kind that contains, or that is explicitly associated with, a header that defines the module's unique name (usually different from the file name) and successor version number. Thus any information that can be held on the computer is a candidate to become a LIFESPAN module.

Configurations are defined using 'Packages' of modules. In fact, packages are the basic unit of control, so that the module must be a member of at least one package, and of course may be a member many.

A Design Change (DC) is a control document defining the substance of the change together with the exact list of modules that will be involved. To permit change to take place a DC is attached to a package that contains the modules in the list, usually plus many other modules necessary to define the context of the change.

The feature of LIFESPAN that gives control over development and change propagates the representation of a package as a module that describes the package membership. Thus,

- a package is a configuration object which must be 'up versioned' when the package contents are changed,

- a package may be a module member of any other package, and hence it is possible to form hierarchies of any depth and complexity, and,

- changes to the member list of a package are controlled in exactly the same way as a change to a module's contents.

An organization of packages is often, and herein is, termed a configuration control structure: since the exact arrangement of packages controls the environment in which changes are made, and subsequently in the way that those changes propagate from development through to a released product.

The configuration control structures are the basis for LIFESPAN's automatic impact of change analysis.

23.4   BASIS FOR IMPACT ANALYSIS

23.4.1   Modelling Software Production

The configuration control structure and their DC controls in LIFESPAN provide a powerful modelling medium with which to plan an orderly development environment that is a prerequisite for those evaluating the analysis.

The traditional representation of a software system is the software structure that embodies the design; i.e. the design syntax. However, the real impact of change is often more concerned with the design semantics which will often be a different logical configuration from the software structure. Thus the configuration control structure should incorporate both these aspects of design.

It turns out that a good starting point for bringing both aspects together is to consider both the low-level and high-level manufacturing process for the product.

23.4.2   Low-Level Manufacture

A principal LIFESPAN design intention was that of all documentation control: e.g. specifications, designs in graphical form, program code on any language etc. Moreover, the choice of a package as the unit of control is the means of ensuring that quality approval is defined with regard to a very specific context. A module that has undergone a change will necessarily have been changed in a package, and it is in the context of that package that the quality of the work done is approved. (A module cannot sensibly be 'universally' approved.)

Thus Fig. 23.2 shows a development configuration that contains design requirements as well as test requirements and a test harness. Such a configuration can be thought of as a special workshop in a software factory. Other documentation that might be included is the appropriate quality standards to be achieved and the tools to be used, e.g. compiler and its exact version.

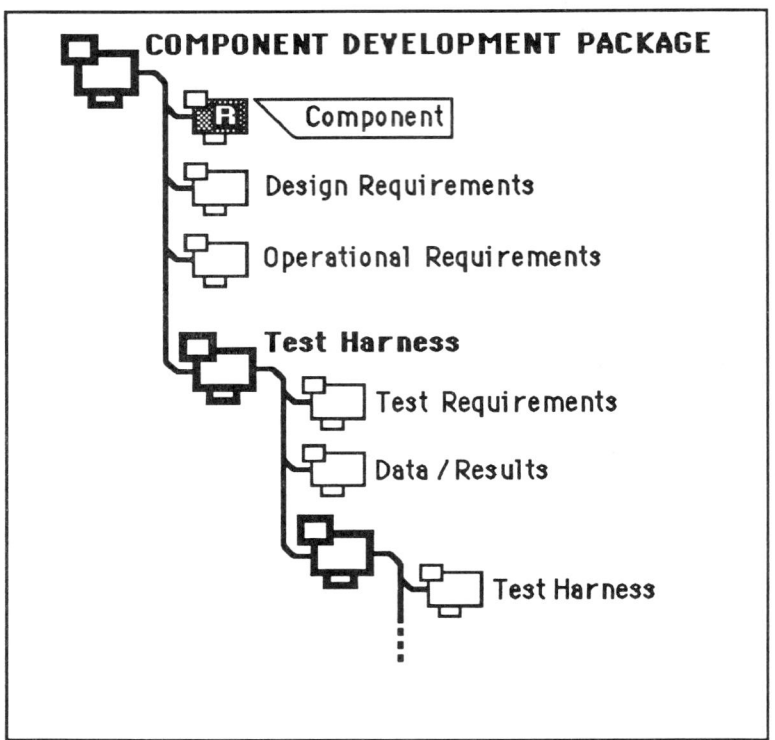

Fig. 23.2 Component development package.

Continuing with the manufacturing simile the top-down approach is equivalent to the task of designing the particular factory that will produce the required software product. In LIFESPAN this is handled as a hierarchical Configuration Framework of packages into which the 'output' from the development packages (workshops) are entered into configuration (assembly shops) for the purposes of integration and test. The principle is illustrated in Fig. 23.3.

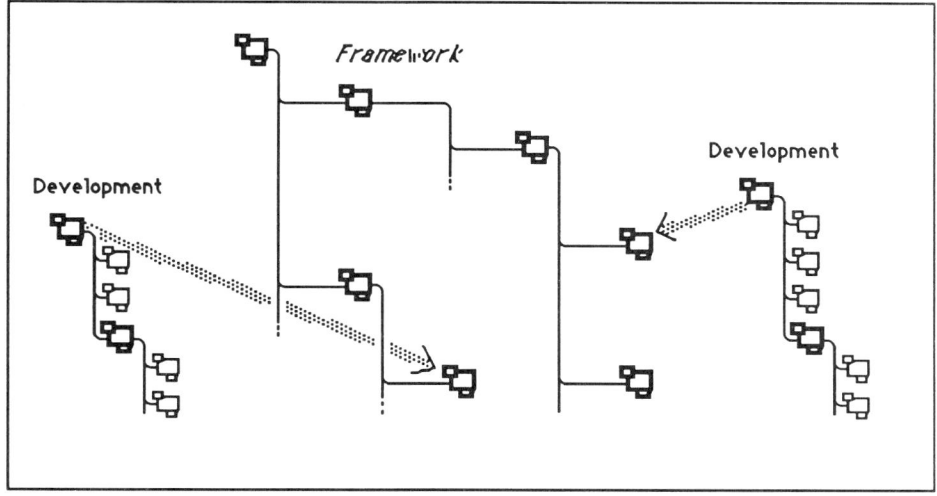

Fig. 23.3

To illustrate how this framework should be used to provide the required orderly development consider the problems created by 'requirement creep' imposed by the customer during the later stages of development and, of course, during maintenance.

The key to handling this problem is that it is really a new product that is being requested. Although it is tempting and indeed logical to think of a modified product rather than a strictly new product, the probable outcome will be confusion in the minds of all concerned: particularly if modifications to modified products (and so on) are permitted.

The technique is illustrated in Fig. 23.4. When the customer requirements creep from those satisfied by the original framework configuration structure shown on the left, a new framework structure (using separate package identity names) should be formed. The new framework may differ from the old, as is shown in the right-hand structure.

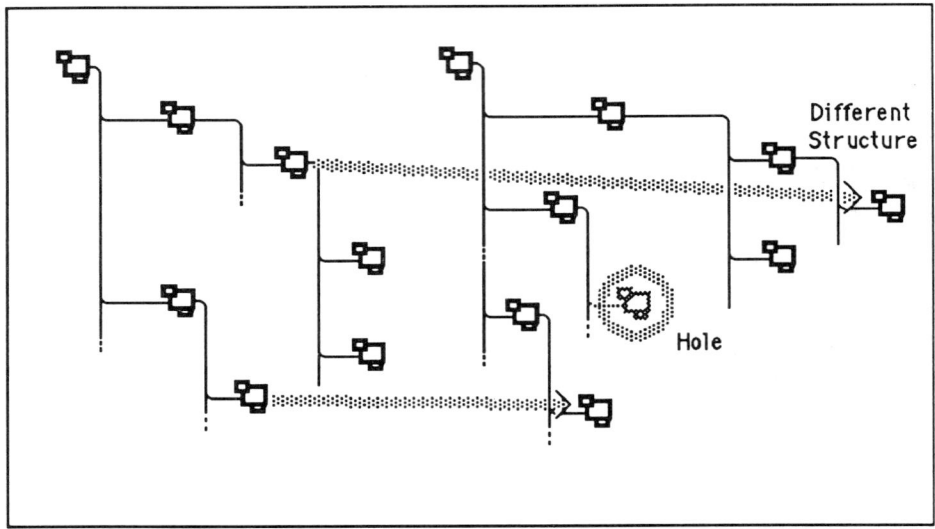

Fig. 23.4

As the new framework structure is built up it can be populated with the software configuration from the 'old' product that will remain the same in the new.

Where the 'old' software had to be changed or replaced to satisfy the creeped (sic) requirements a hole is left in the new structure. A hole is represented as an empty package, and it is likely some local restructuring of the affected area of the 'old' configuration may be necessary to achieve this representation as it is passed into the new configuration.

The clarity of this approach greatly simplifies the meaning of the impact analysis that LIFESPAN will automatically carry out as each change is proposed.

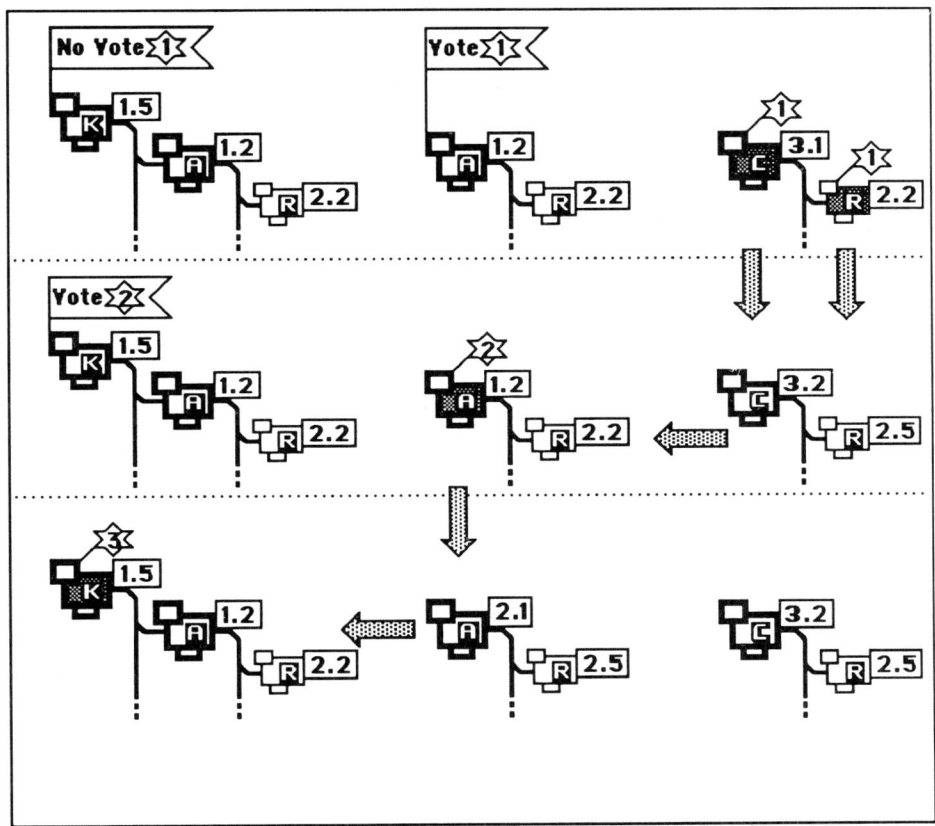

Fig. 23.5

23.5 AUTOMATED IMPACT ANALYSIS

23.5.1 Scope

Once the low-level and high-level framework configuration control structures have been set up, LIFESPAN will automatically use these structures to carry out an impact analysis for each change submitted for acceptance. When the change(s) are to low-level modules (and packages) LIFESPAN provides automated facilities to support controlled and progressive impact analyses to higher levels until the changes reach the product level for incorporation in a product release. However, some low-level modules will be incorporated into several different products which may lead to conflicting development requirements. In this case LIFESPAN will automatically find the products and extend the acceptance process accordingly.

23.5.2 Acceptance Procedure – An Example

The acceptance procedure is most quickly understood by means of an example. The configuration control structures for example are shown in Fig. 23.5.

It concerns the progressive impact analyses that take place when a change (DC1) is proposed for Module R in Package C. DC1 cites changes to both Module R and Package C since when a new version of R is produced a new version of package C will also be required to reflect that change.

When DC1 is submitted for acceptance LIFESPAN automatically carries out an impact analysis to discover which other packages will be directly affected by the change. In this example it finds package A which also has module R as a member.

The acceptance procedure itself is a voting process. LIFESPAN mails the owner of package A a request to inspect DC1 and to vote YES or NO for its acceptance. In order to encourage proper consideration of the change the vote is mandatory and each voter has an absolute right of veto. This is the mechanism for obtaining active involvement in the change process and thereby proper consideration of the semantics of the proposed change. Only when all the voters agree that the change is individually acceptable to them in their particular circumstances will LIFESPAN allow the change to proceed.

Once the change has been implemented and module R has become version R(2.2), the owner of package A is informed. If he wishes to incorporate this new version in A then he raises a DC(DC2) to change A accordingly. When this is submitted for acceptance to LIFESPAN, another impact analysis is performed to discover that package A is directly used in package K and accordingly the owner of K is requested to vote on the acceptance of DC2. Assuming it is acceptable then in due course DC3 is submitted to incorporate the up-versioned package A in package K.

The decision to limit the automatic impact analysis to one level of a package at a time is a pragmatic one taken to prevent the owners of the higher levels of package from being saturated by requests to vote on a mass of detailed low-level changes which individuals say they have little chance of sufficiently understanding.

23.5.3   Forward Planning and Monitoring

The maximum benefit from the automatic impact assessment in LIFESPAN is achieved by carefully planning the configuration control structures with the impact analysis procedure in mind.   Generally this leads to multiple structures each handling a different aspect of the impact of change, many of which primarily reflect the semantics of the software rather than its procedural structure.

As the project proceeds it is important to monitor the effectiveness of the automatic impact analysis. If necessary it is not difficult in LIFESPAN to adjust existing configuration control structures or to create new ones.

23.5.4   Additional Analysis

As changes progress in the manner described they are retained in LIFESPAN's database (online or offline). This information can be recovered by the reporting system and subjected to additional analysis. For example, the distribution of changes across the product will highlight the areas of the software design that gave most trouble during development, and are therefore likely to be areas where maintainers proceed with great caution.

A particular interest during maintenance is the overall impact of a planned series of changes. To assist this analysis LIFESPAN produces a 'where used' report which can be processed to trace all the areas of the software that might be affected as the changes spread into the higher levels of subsystem.

23.6 CONCLUSION

This paper has sought to show that a major contribution to ease the task of software maintenance is routine, even mundane, application of relative minor impact analysis to ensure that a reasonable degree of good order is maintained throughout the twists and turns of software development. Better the little and often approach than the grand analysis.

24 PISCES – an inverse configuration management system

R. Kenning and M. Munro

University of Durham

24.1 INTRODUCTION

Software maintenance, defined as the modification of a software product after delivery to correct faults, to improve performance or other attributes, or to adapt the product to a changed environment [6] accounts for between 40% and 70% of all software expenditure [8]. For systems that have been in operation for some time it is likely that the costs of maintenance will be at the upper end of this scale. This can be largely attributed to the high costs incurred in identifying and understanding the affected parts of the system [1, 9]. In operational systems the process of identification and understanding is compounded by several time-related factors which act individually or in combination to increase the cost of maintaining the system. Examples of these factors are:

- Increased complexity over time – as a project increases in size, its complexity increases in a manner which is based on more than just lines of code. Large software projects are invariably complex both in terms of the number and diversity of components, and the relationships existing between them.

- **System version explosion** – as a system evolves, new versions of components arise for reasons of adaptation to new hardware or operating systems, tailoring for individual customers, enhanced functionality, or to correct bugs. It can be argued therefore that software does not exist as a single monolith but as families of systems each catering for slightly different requirements [13, 14].

- **Lack of useful documentation** – as the system ages, there is a tendency for the documentation to fall out of step with the code changes. This means that even if documentation is available it is highly probable that it is incorrect or misleading.

- **Personnel changes** – in all software projects there is the inevitable turnover of staff. For systems with a long operational lifetime it is highly likely that many of the original development personnel will have left taking with them much of the knowledge about the system.

- **Maintenance-induced errors** – as system complexity increases so does the probability of new errors being introduced as the system is maintained [3]. This results in system degradation.

- **Loss of control** – in operational systems the above factors act in combination to result in poor management visibility and a loss of control over the system.

Software Configuration Management, a discipline for controlling the evolution of complex software systems, has been successful in reducing costs for systems under development. For operational systems, it follows that control must be regained if cost-effective further development and maintenance is to be achieved. At the Centre for Software Maintenance, Inverse Software Configuration Management has been identified as the process of bringing existing (operational) software systems under configuration control.

24.2 INVERSE SOFTWARE CONFIGURATION MANAGEMENT

Like Software Configuration Management (SCM), Inverse Software Configuration Management (ISCM) encompasses the four basic elements of:

- **Identification** – defining and uniquely identifying the baselines and corresponding components of a system, and any changes made to the components of the baselines.

- **Control** – controlling through defined procedures any changes made to components and baselines of a system.

- **Status accounting** – providing an administrative history and current status of how the system has evolved.

- **Audit** – determining that defined baselines meet their requirements and that the control, identification and accounting procedures are being correctly adhered to.

The major difference between ISCM and SCM lies in ISCM's more comprehensive treatment of the identification phase of the process. The increased importance of this phase for existing systems may be attributed to the increased complexity of a system through its evolution over time, linked to a general lack of knowledge regarding the system and the probability of poor associated documentation.

- Inverse Software Configuration Identification

Inverse Software Configuration Identification (ISCI) encompasses component identification, component relationship understanding, component location mapping and incremental documentation.

There is therefore a need to identify components of a system at several levels and related to several areas:

- **Application components** – these are the components that comprise the actual running version of the system.

- **Associated versions** – these are components which have arisen from changes to components of the system, they include both variants and revisions, and collectively form the program family.

- **Redundant components** – these are components that are never referenced by the system.

- **Missing components** – these are components that are referenced by the system but which have been destroyed, lost or misplaced.

- **Allied (environmental) components** – these are components that make up the operational environment for the application. Examples are compilers, linkers, editors, other system software, JCL, hardware etc.

As systems become more complex in terms of the number and diversity of components so do the relationships between the components and the way they interact with the operational environment. Consequently there is a need to identify and understand:

- **Intra-specific relationships** – those existing between the components within an application.

- **Inter-specific relationships** – those existing between the components of an application and the components of the operational environment.

Another feature of ISCM is determination of the location of identified components within the file structure imposed by the operational environment. This will result in the production of location maps which will aid component retrieval for maintenance purposes.

Also associated with ISCM is the concept of incremental documentation [7]. This enables information obtained during the maintenance process to be documented with little extra effort or overhead. As a result accurate up-to-date documentation is produced as a by-product of the maintenance process which enables the knowledge of one maintainer to be available to subsequent maintainers. Adopting incremental documentation techniques ensures that only the affected parts of the system are documented. This realizes cost benefits in accordance of the 80:20 maintenance rule: 80% of time spent on maintenance is spent on 20% of the code.

24.3 PISCES – AN ISCM SYSTEM

In order to address the issues of ISCM and regain control of existing software systems a tool, PISCES [10], is being developed at the Centre for Software Maintenance. PISCES (Proforma Identification Scheme for Configurations of Existing Systems) is an interactive computer-based system that enables the identification and documentation of system configurations. The principal functions of the tool are:

- **Genericity** – the tool will be as generic as possible, both in terms of its operation and in terms of the applications it can support.

- **Identification** – the tool will identify the components of an application, and any family components, together with their location maps. Listings will be produced of any missing components and of any components that are redundant. Intra-application and inter-application relationships will be identified.

- **Reporting** – the information obtained regarding an application will be reported both textually and graphically.

- **Incremental documentation** – any information gained about a system will be documented incrementally using hypertext technology.

- **Interfacing** – mechanisms will developed which will allow the tool to interface with other documentation and configuration management tools.

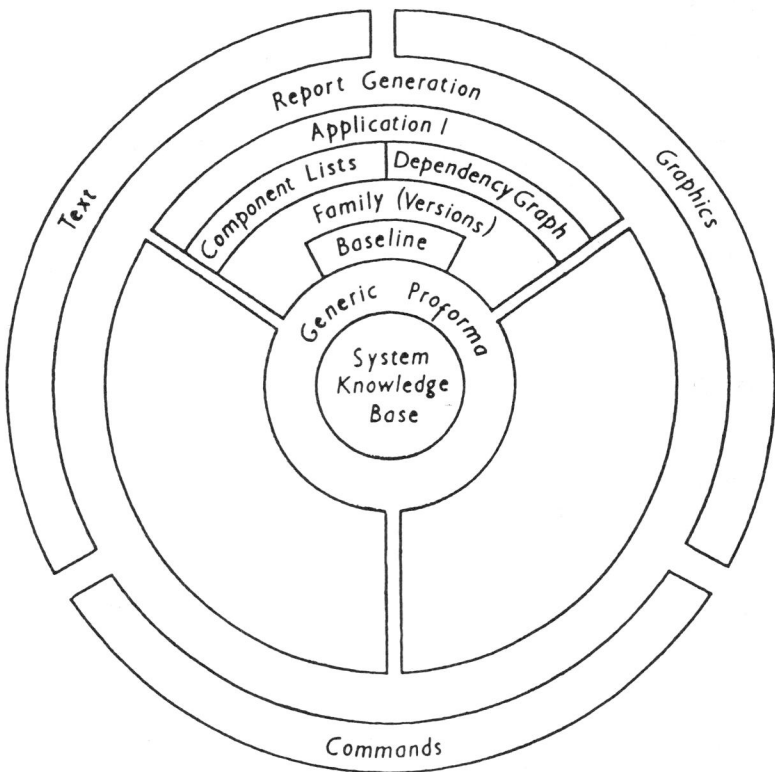

Proforma Identification Scheme for Configurations
of Existing Systems

Fig. 24.1 Structure of PISCES.

PISCES consists of a system information knowledge base, an application mapping facility, and a report generation and interface facility. The structure of the tool is shown in Fig. 24.1.

- **Knowledge base** – the system knowledge base provides the foundation of the tool. It contains information regarding key features of operational environments, operating systems, system architectures, application types and programming languages etc. This information is held at two levels:

  Generic – this contains information about systems and programs which assists in the construction of a generic proforma or template.

  Tailored – this contains more specific information that is used to tailor the generic proforma for a particular class of system and application type, for example, a COBOL application on an IBM mainframe, or a C application on a Unix system.

- **Application Mapping** – application mapping is the process of inserting information into the tailored proforma. This is achieved by extracting the information as defined in the tailored proforma, using tools defined by the proforma, and inserting the results into the proforma. Information will be gathered first at baseline (running application) level, and then at the family level in order to generate information about the associated versions of the application. The product of application mapping is a completed proforma, now specific to the application. It will define the component lists of an application at baseline and family levels, hold information regarding the dependencies between the components, list redundant components, and any that appear to be missing.

- **Report generation and incremental documentation** – the PISCES reporting, documentation and interfacing facility displays graphically the information contained in the application-specific proforma. In response to requests from the user it produces a report on the composition of the application in the form of baseline dependency networks, program family diagrams and file location diagrams. Figures 24.2-24.4 give examples of the types of pictorial reports generated by PISCES.

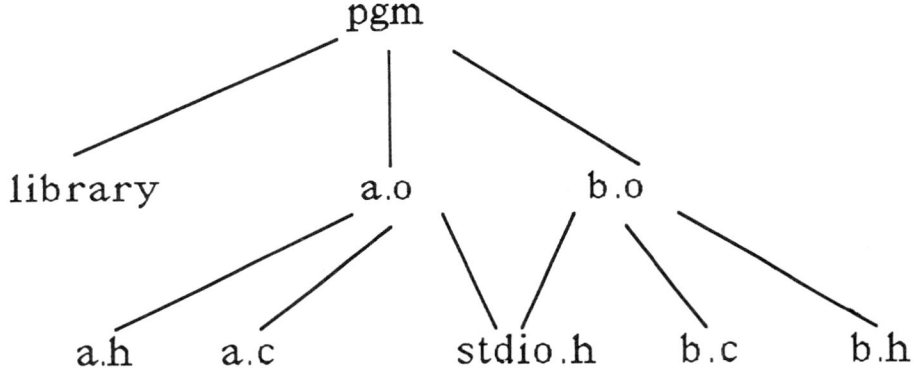

Fig. 24.2   PISCES dependency graph report.

Hypertext principles are being used to support the production and storage of these reports [4]. Hypertext supports links between related documents and enables the user to browse the document and traverse the links. In this way configurations of large systems can be identified and documented usefully as the user can view as much or as little of the system configuration as is required. By including the incremental documentation facility annotations may be made to the output as and when required. The PISCES hypertext facility is currently being developed using Windows 3 Development Kit [12].

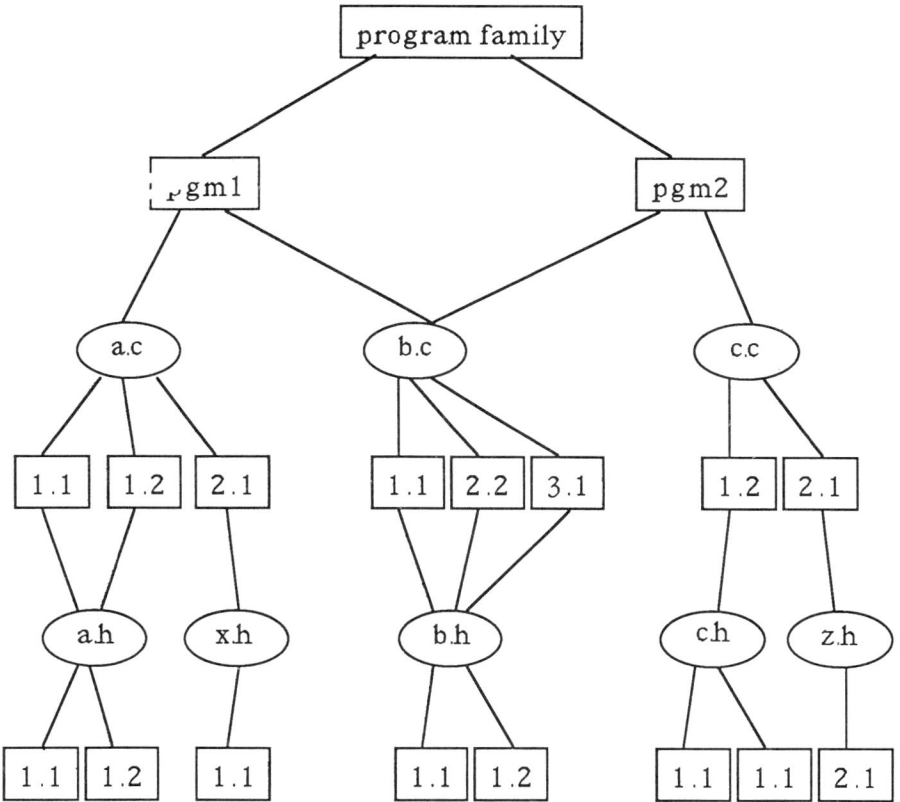

Fig. 24.3 PISCES program family report.

Interfaces within the hypertext system will allow integration with other documentation and configuration management tools. It is intended that PISCES will be integrated with the DOCMAN source code documentation tools to produce another level of documentation [7]. The output of the PISCES tool will form the input to another tool being developed at the Centre for Software Maintenance concerned with the restructuring of the system at system level. Additionally further developments will link PISCES with the SCIMM system for configuration and change metrics [5]. In this way it is envisaged that a complete configuration management environment will be established.

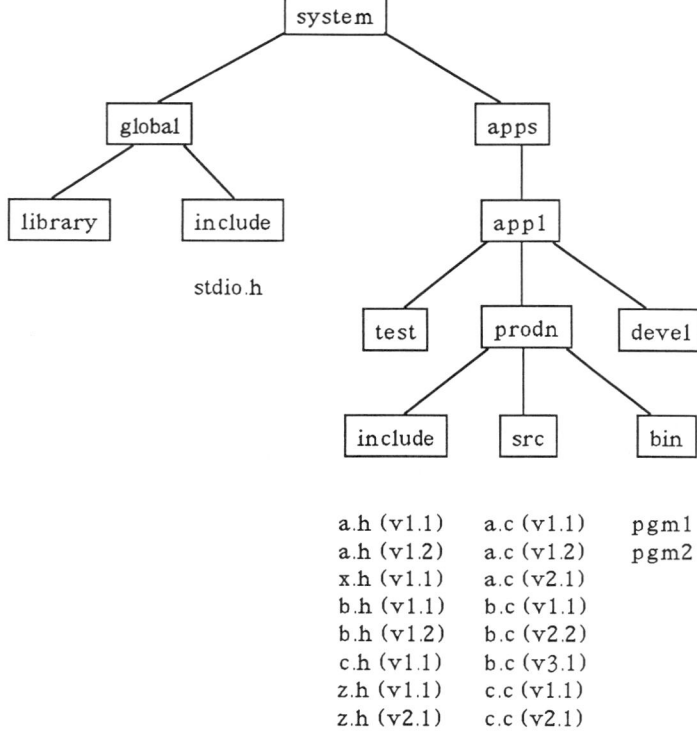

Figure 24.4   PISCES file location report.

24.4   BENEFITS

The benefits of adopting ISCM procedures and using the PISCES tool are:

- **Identification** – system configuration part lists and the relationships existing between these components will be identified, along with any that are missing or redundant. The interrelationships existing between components of an application and its operational environment will be established.

- **Documentation** – system level documentation will be produced. The use of graphical representation will provide a more coherent method of describing system configurations. The annotation facility will enable descriptive information about a particular module being investigated by the maintainer to be recorded. In this way the knowledge of the maintainer may be incrementally documented with little extra effort and this information will be readily accessible.

- **Maintenance indicators** – regular use of the tool over the system lifetime, will cumulatively provide a configuration level history of the system. It will afford a basis on which to measure system degradation and complexity at a configuration level, and can be used to confirm that an orderly software project structure is being adhered to.

- **Framework for control** – the tool will provide a sound basis on which subsequent control of development and maintenance may be based, or could be used as the initial step in the re-engineering of a system [11].

- **Cost effective** – by allowing maintainers to identify and understand a system more easily, and record their knowledge about a system with very little effort it will assist in the reduction of maintenance costs.

24.5 SUMMARY

In order to reduce the costs of maintaining operational systems there is a need to regain control of the system and minimize the time spent trying to understand and identify the affected parts of the system. It is also important to document this understanding of the system in a cost-effective manner. The PISCES inverse software configuration management tool, through its identification procedures and preservation of system level documentation, will reduce maintenance costs by enabling the maintainer to locate and understand the problem more rapidly. Additionally, by presenting a clearer representation of the dependencies between components the number of maintenance-induced errors will be reduced. Management visibility into the current state of the system will be increased and an infrastructure provided onto which full change control can be built.

ACKNOWLEDGEMENTS

Rachel Kenning is sponsored by British Telecom Research Laboratories, Martlesham Heath, and K3 Group Limited, Worcester and would like to thank them for their support. The authors would also like to thank Fred McCrindle for his valuable comments on earlier versions of this paper.

REFERENCES

1.   Babich, W.A., 'Software Configuration Management: Coordination for Team Productivity', Addison-Wesley, Reading, Massachusetts, 1986.

2.   Bersoff, E.H., Henderson, V.D. and Siegel, S.G., 'Software Configuration Management: An Investment in Product Integrity', Prentice-Hall, Englewood Cliffs, 1980.

3.   Collofello, J.S. and Buck, J.J., 'Software Quality Assurance for Maintenance', IEEE Software, pp. 46-51, September 1987.

4.   Conklin, J., 'Hypertext: An Introduction and Survey', IEEE Computer Vol. 20, No. 9, September 1987, pp. 17-41.

5.   Cooper, S.D. and Munro, M., 'Software Change Information for Maintenance Management', Proceedings Conference on Software Maintenance 1989, Miami, Florida, pp. 279-287.

6.   IEEE, IEEE Standard Glossary of Software Engineering Terminology, ANSI/IEEE Std 729, 1983.

7.   Fletton, N.T., and Munro, M., 'Redocumenting Software Systems using Hypertext Technology', Conference on Software Maintenance 1988, Phoenix, Arizona, pp. 54-59.

8. Foster, J.R., Jolly, A.E.P. and Norris, M.T., 'An Overview of Software Maintenance', British Telecom Technology Journal, Vol. 7, No. 4, pp. 37-46, October 1989.

9. Freeman, R.M. and Munro, M., 'XEBRA – Xerox Based Redocumentation Aid', Proceedings Annual Meeting and Conference of the Software Maintenance Association, Vancouver, Canada, pp. 4.35-4.47, April 1990.

10. Kenning, R.J. and Munro, M., 'Understanding the Configurations of Operational Systems', to appear in Proceedings IEEE Conference on Software Maintenance 1990, San Diego, California, November 1990.

11. Kenning, R.J. and Munro, M., 'Inverse Software Configuration Management – A Stepping Stone in the Reverse Engineering Process', Technical Report in preparation, October 1990.

12. Microsoft Corporation, 'Microsoft Windows Software Development Kit Version 3.0', 1990.

13. Narayanaswamy, K., 'Version Control in the Common Lisp Framework', International Workshop on Software Version and Configuration Control, Grassau, pp. 83-97, January 1988.

14. Parnas, D.L., 'On the Design and Development of Program Families', IEEE Transactions on Software Engineering, Vol. SE-2, pp. 1-9, March 1976.

Part Seven

Management and
Business Issues

25 The management of reuse

P. Walton

Logica, CES Ltd

25.1 INTRODUCTION

Software reuse is becoming a major topic in the IT industry, and with good reason. Many organizations are finding themselves under increased pressure from their markets to respond ever faster, and this pressure reflects directly on IT development. Major changes are required to handle this problem, and, among the techniques available, software reuse looks very promising.

But it is wrong to think of software reuse as a modern idea. Many companies (including Logica) have been reusing software successfully in a variety of forms for more than a decade; so there is clear evidence that it works and can provide greater organizational responsiveness. This poses a question: if it is so useful, why doesn't everyone do it?

This is the question addressed by this paper. The answer we give, based on work carried out in Logica over the last two years, is that the management of reuse is the key issue. In other words, reuse works when, and only when, it is supported by the structure and culture of the organization. We have developed a technique, called reuse analysis, which can be used to define the correct forms of reuse for any organization.

25.2   THE CONTEXT OF REUSE

There are many reasons for believing that now is the correct time to be thinking about reuse, and planning for it. The pressure for increased responsiveness is the predominant external factor, but several processes within the industry are now converging to provide a much clearer view of reuse, and a consequent growth in its importance.

The most important reason for this growth is that there is now a much better understanding of the fundamental ideas and processes involved (many of these ideas are outlined in this paper). This understanding is matched by the emergence of important technologies, but the main driving force is the new understanding that software represents an expensive organizational resource which must be managed effectively, not just on individual projects, but throughout entire organizations.

The analogy with other industries has always been a strong motivation. They pay considerable attention to extracting the greatest value from their assets and resources. In practice this means that they are geared up for reuse, and new products and techniques are based on old ones.

For many years data management has been practised and developed. The data belonging to organizations plays a major part in their success or failure, so it is important to manage it effectively. The management of reuse extends this concept. Managing the resources that use and change the data (that is, the software), will provide an improved response to changes, and improvements in handling the data in the future. This will allow organizations to repond more rapidly to their environment, and give them a better chance to move ahead or stay ahead.

Technology is also driving the process. One of the main current developments, the object-oriented approach, binds data and processing closer together. So the use of object-oriented analysis, languages or databases will generate a requirement for the management of reuse. Other recent developments, including domain analysis, reverse engineering and CASE tools, all provide the means to support some aspects of reuse and its management.

However, the technology is a secondary consideration. Much more important is for management to realize the importance of reuse: to realize that software is an asset which must be managed. Without management commitment to this principle, from the top downwards, reuse initiatives have little chance of succeeding.

The aim of this paper is to show why this is true, and to demonstrate the large number of management issues that must be addressed. The implementation of reuse provides a very large number of pitfalls at a variety of levels (organizational, managerial, technical and personal), any of which can successfully defeat it. It is not a straightforward extension of existing software development practice (which is what object-oriented technicians, among others, claim). Instead, software development projects must take place in an environment which provides support for reuse. The environment will not grow out of single projects; it must be put in place at a much higher level.

To create the correct environment (which will be different for different organizations) it is important to understand the fundamental ideas which lie behind reuse. This paper outlines these ideas and introduces the subject of reuse analysis which has been developed by a software reuse working party within Logica. Reuse analysis uses these ideas to determine the style of reuse which is most suitable to any organization, and the environment required.

With a suitable environment in place, organizations will be well placed to tackle the future with confidence. The major benefit which reuse holds out is greater responsiveness. This may be expressed in terms of increased profit, greater market share, reduced overheads or in other ways, but one thing is certain. The rewards provided by adopting sensible reuse practices will increase, both as organizations come to terms with it, and as technology provides greater support. Organizations which delay may find themselves further and further behind.

25.3 WHAT IS REUSE?

Before discussing the management of reuse it is important to define clearly what software reuse is, and what can be reused. This discussion will start to indicate the complexity of reuse, and show that a large number of major decisions must be made to achieve success.

If we are considering software as an asset, then anything which contributes to the development of software, and which can make that development more efficient, is worth reusing. We can call this organizational knowledge about software, and it is normally held in three forms:

in people's heads;

as part of the documentation for systems, and in the systems themselves (this is the product of software development);

in the processes and procedures used to develop the systems (which we can call the process of software development).

Traditionally, reuse of people has been the standard form of reuse within organizations. This will still happen in the future, of course, but skill shortages and the need to provide greater organizational responsiveness mean that the other two (which we call tangible reuse) will become more and more important. We define software reuse as the subject which is concerned with maximizing the use of tangible organizational knowledge.

Within this overall framework many approaches are possible. For example, each of the following could be reused:

- specifications, designs or code

- quality plans and standards

- test tools and test data

- development tools (e.g. CASE tools)

- methodologies

- project planning techniques and tools.

Each can be reused in a variety of ways, for example:

- reuse with no change

- reuse with some modification

- reuse in the form of a template, with gaps which must be completed according to the circumstances of each use

- reuse by example

- reuse with the help of notes.

Purists consider only the first (and sometimes the second) of these, but they are not applying the correct business criteria. Each can be useful in its own way, because each can embody useful organizational knowledge. Indeed, in some cases "impure" reuse may provide a low-risk, low-cost starting point. The purer forms, which are likely to provide greater benefits, will be more costly and riskier.

Some of the most impressive examples of reuse use templates, which remove the need to consider unnecessary, repetitive detail, and focus attention on application-specific parts. Examples can also be useful to show how to tackle a particular problem. The advantage of these lowtech approaches is that they can be achieved easily using proven technology.

In Logica, for example, as well as the well-known reuse of systems kernels, several lower-tech ideas are employed. These include templates and examples to support software engineering ideas, methods and principles. Configuration management, quality management, the use of methodologies and the use of project management tools are all included in this approach.

To encompass all of these cases (and to avoid the term software component, which has a more specialized meaning) we call any tangible form of organizational knowledge which can be reused a REO (REusable Object).

A number of technologies are now available to help with software reuse, including:

-   re-engineering and reverse engineering products, which can generate REOs

-   CASE tools, which provide a better basis for reusable designs and specifications

- object-oriented languages, which make code reuse easier and more effective

- configuration management tools, which help solve one of the difficult areas associated with reuse

- systems kernels (such as those provided by Logica), which provide a reusable core for systems, and which are designed to be tailored to individual requirements

- libraries and templates, especially to support popular PC-based products.

All of these can help effective reuse now, and over the next few years they will develop further.

On the horizon there are a number of technologies which will become available in the 1990s. These include:

- sophisticated cataloguing products which will be able to support very large libraries

- domain analysis, which provides analysis techniques, not just for a particular application, but for a particular type of application

- very high-level languages, which will embody domain-specific knowledge and allow the fast generation of applications

- object-oriented databases.

The sheer range and variety of the options available provide the first clue to the difficulty of reuse, and why careful consideration of management issues is so important.

25.4 PROBLEMS WITH REUSE

Before looking at the other problems which must be managed, it is important to understand the principles of reuse.

25.4.1 Fundamental Principles of Reuse

In the most general possible case each REO (REusable Object) will have an owner and a supplier (not necessarily the same). Each instance of reuse will also have a user and a buyer (there may be several users, but we can assume that someone will be in charge).

The supplier and the user may be in different organizations, the same organisation, the same part of the organization, or, in the most extreme case, they may be the same person.

We cannot assume (as many people do) that REOs will be free. More generally, we must assume (in the most general case) that commercial considerations must apply to each use of the REO. In fact each use forms an exchange between owner and buyer to which terms and conditions must apply. The sum of these exchanges forms a market in REOs. Within this market each REO (or possibly a group of REOs) forms a product. This idea of the REO market is explored later in this paper.

There are, in general, four stages in each instance of reuse:

– creating one or more suitable REOs

– retrieving information to allow the user to find those which might be applicable

– choosing between them

–   extracting and using the one selected.

Apart from the first, these all place great demands on the availability of information.

25.4.2   Choices

These stages present some of the previous options in a clearer light. For the first stage, REOs have to be created, which throws up a list of new questions.

Where will they come from?

How big should they be?

Who will decide what they should be?

Should they relate to the development process or the software product?

What technologies should be used?

For the second and subsequent stages, some information will be required about each REO.

Who will produce it?

What form should it take?

Where will be it stored?

How will users have access to it?

It doesn't take too much thought to extend this list of questions almost indefinitely.

25.4.3 Difficulties of Reuse

The reason that there are so many questions is that there are many difficulties placed in the way of reuse, at many different levels. The different types of REO incur the difficulties in differing degrees, but the greatest difficulties apply to the reuse of code.

To begin with there are organizational difficulties. If the supplier and user (or owner and buyer) are in different parts of an organization, or even just on different projects, there are clear organizational barriers to reuse. The different parts will in general have different objectives and plans, and exchanging REOs will not be included, unless someone makes an effort to include it. Unless a special effort is made, one project will have no incentive to produce REOs for other projects. In the worst case (but it is extremely common!) the supplier and user may not know of each other's existence, or there may be no appropriate information about the REO. If no-one thinks about it, any instance of reuse will probably fail because all of the commercial terms and conditions are not decided or agreed in time.

The nature of the technical difficulties are probably clearer and more widely understood. Any differences between machines, development environments, development methods and storage formats may be insurmountable, or not cost-effective. For large code REOs, any differences between the applications of the supplier and user may be a problem, because application-specific details may well be embedded in the code.

Much of the literature has been concerned with personal factors, including the Not Invented Here syndrome (in which the user does not want to use the REO because (s)he did not create it). The capability of the user is important: is (s)he capable of using the REO? will the supplier be available to help out if necessary?

Finally there are many factors which are specific to each REO. Some of these are just administrative: where is it? is it (including the documentation) in the correct (human) language? Others are more fundamental: was it created for reuse? how many modifications would it need? if it is changed will it be useful in the future?

These are only some of the many factors which will inhibit reuse. In most organizations their impact will boil down eventually to money. But providing detailed estimates is difficult. A more useful metaphor to use is that of distance. The combined distance caused by all of these factors provides a general indication of the difficulty of reuse in any single case, called the reuse distance. Over time, this distance may be calibrated within an organization.

25.4.4   Benefits and Measures

The reuse distance is not the sole measure of importance. On the other side is the benefit distance, which describes the benefit to the organization. Again this is a complex factor which should be linked directly to the overall objectives of the reuse programme.

25.4.5   Important Reuse Concepts

The number of choices to be made, and the difficulties at many levels, imply very strongly that reuse can only be implemented successfully if considerable thought is given to its management. The rest of the paper looks in more detail at this question. The approach (which we call reuse analysis) rests firmly on some fundamental ideas which we have already touched on, but which will be developed further before describing the approach.

25.4.6   When Will Reuse Happen?

The starting point is the decision to use a REO. It is clear that suitable REOs must be created, and that the correct information must be made available to the user. From that point the decision to use a REO will rest on three points:

- the reuse distance (i.e. how easy the REO is to use)

- the benefit distance (i.e. the benefit derived from using it)

- the uncertainty of the two measures.

Crudely speaking the user will decide to use a REO if the benefit distance is greater than the reuse distance plus the uncertainty. This provides the key to successful reuse. The benefit distance must be maximized through the availability of the correct, easily used REOs. The reuse distance must be minimized by introducing the correct organizational structures and by integrating reuse with the IT strategy. And any uncertainty surrounding the process must be clarified.

In most large organizations it is easy to think of numerous examples which violate one or more of these conditions. For example:

- although a good REO exists, the commercial difficulties cannot be resolved in time (e.g. who provides support? what about warranty?)

- although a good REO exists, no-one knows about it

- the correct documentation is not available

- the user does not have enough time to establish the benefits to be gained

or more fundamentally:

- there is no process for trying to find REOs which can be used.

While problems like this occur, reuse will not be successful.

25.5 REUSE ANALYSIS

Reuse analysis tackles the difficulties head on. The main principle is that the type of reuse proposed should match the structure and culture of an organization, to reduce the reuse distance and uncertainty for any instance of reuse, and increase the benefit distance.

This matching defines one or more reuse markets which are firmly based on the needs of a part of the organization or a set of users. Each market must be supported by organizational systems, related, wherever possible, to existing systems. There are three main steps in the process, containing increasing levels of detail:

- definition of the reuse strategy

- definition of the reuse markets

- definition of the support systems.

It is extremely important that the whole process is based firmly on the objectives of the whole organization.

25.5.1 Strategy

The first stage produces a reuse strategy. This idea follows from a close examination of successful types of reuse in industry. In these examples organizations side-step many of the problems by defining company structures and systems to circumvent them. The reuse strategy has two main parts.

The first is a division of the organization into different parts for which different types of reuse are appropriate. The division may well follow the company structure (with, say, the DP and production departments in different parts); or it may be horizontal, with programmers in one part, and analysts in another; or it may be completely different. The choice depends on the company structure and culture, the IT strategy and potential REOs which can be identified. The aim of the choice is to constrain reuse to reduce reuse distance.

The second part of the strategy defines the type of REO which will provide most benefit to each part.

25.5.2   Reuse Market (Internal and External)

The next stage of reuse analysis defines the market for each part of the organization as defined in the first stage. Company culture plays a large part in this as well, because there are a wide range of possibilities. At one extreme is the totally controlled market, in which the production, quality, and commercial terms and conditions (including price) are controlled by a central department, and the REOs are fed out to users. This style might suit some DP departments, for example.

At the other extreme is the free market in which nothing is controlled. In this case, the market would provide a conduit optimized for the flow of information. Production, quality and other issues concerned with REOs would be defined by suppliers (or owners), and the market would react according to their suitability. It would be up to the suppliers and users (or owners and buyers) to negotiate mutually favourable terms and conditions. This style would place much greater emphasis on an entrepreneurial spirit amongst suppliers, but it might suit organizations with a large number of small, highly devolved, profit centres. Most examples would lie between these two extremes.

This stage of reuse analysis will define appropriate market conditions for the part of the organization. This will include identifying the users, suppliers, owners and buyers. It is also important to consider whether an internal or external source for (some of the) REOs is more appropriate.

25.5.3 Systems

The third main stage of reuse analysis defines the new or altered systems that the organization should introduce to support reuse. In the most general case several may be required (and each must be considered). The particular systems chosen will depend on the existing systems within the organization. (System in this case does not necessarily mean computer system, although that may well be the case.)

Support will be required for the following:

- storing, retrieving, and updating REOs

- educating and training users and suppliers to create and use REOs

- educating users in the reuse system itself

- promoting new and existing REOs

- storing and disseminating information about REOs

- managing the whole process.

25.6 SUMMARY

Increased software reuse can provide important benefits and, in the future, reuse will contribute greatly to increased organizational responsiveness. But there are a number of pitfalls which must be avoided to achieve these benefits. The fact that a number of companies have managed to avoid the problems provides the answer.

To provide the correct form of reuse and set up the correct structures and systems to support it, reuse analysis uses three fundamental ideas:

- a reuse strategy, which defines the correct type of reuse for each part of an organization

- reuse markets

- systems to support reuse.

Together, these provide the key to successful reuse, and the important long-term benefits it will provide.

26 Human aspects and organizational issues of software reuse

I. Kruzela and M. Brorsson

Telesoft AB

26.1 INTRODUCTION

Most people would agree that reuse in general is something 'good'. In the field of software engineering there are numerous papers praising advantages of reuse. Reuse can make production of software cheaper, faster, of higher quality, more predictable, more maintainable etc. The list of advantages can be made long.

Other papers demonstrate in a convincing way that reuse can be applied to all stages of the software lifecycle. It is possible to reuse specifications, designs, test programs, all kinds of documents, the development process itself, knowledge, code etc. The potential for reuse of information of different kinds seems to be unlimited.

Good collections of papers on reuse supporting these claims are [Fre87, Tra88, Big89].

One of the great minds in the computing science field, P. Wegner [Weg83], goes as far as to say the following: 'Our desire to create reusable rather than transitory artifacts has aesthetic and intellectual as well as economic motivations and is part of man's desire for immortality. The drive to discover and exploit reusable patterns distinguishes man from other creatures and civilized from primitive societies'.

After such an overwhelming introduction, we must return to reality. If reuse is so great and so advantageous, why is it actually used so little in software production? If we honestly look around at the software developing companies we will see that reuse is done mostly in a spontaneous and often undisciplined way. Most of the time, reuse just happens, somebody simply remembers that he has earlier created something similar to what he is doing today and reuses it. Systematic reuse is still rare, except for reuse of large standardized components like, e.g. window management systems or reuse in limited and well understood domains, e.g. mathematical routines.

The reason for the not yet fulfilled promises of reuse is simple: planned and systematic reuse is difficult! The main advantage of reuse is that it reduces the complexity of the development process. But this reduction is not for free. Reuse has created many new complex problems that must be solved.

In the next section, we will list some problem areas associated with reuse. In each area, there is a need for more research and also more knowledge about practical experiences.

In section 26.3, we will look more specifically into one of the areas. We will present a number of examples of human resistance to reuse. It seems to be odd, but this resistance is quite common and natural.

In section 26.4, we will briefly describe two software developing organizations, one Japanese and one American. Both of them are claiming to be very successful. In section 26.5 we will extract some common features of those organizations. We claim that the key to overcoming the natural human resistance to reuse is a well planned organization.

26.2 PROBLEM AREAS IN REUSE

In a typical non-reuse based software production, requirements for certain deliverables, e.g. design, code or documents, are submitted to a development process which after a while, without regard for previous similar work, delivers a result.

In a reuse-oriented software production a useful and suitable piece of information developed in some previous activity is recognized and reused in the development process. It is as simple as that. The reuse leads to all the advantages which we mentioned in the introduction. But even though reuse simplifies the development process in many ways it creates new tasks and problems.

The simple model in Fig. 26.1 provides a framework for identification of problem areas of reuse. Six general interdependent areas which include problems of both technical and non-technical nature are shown.

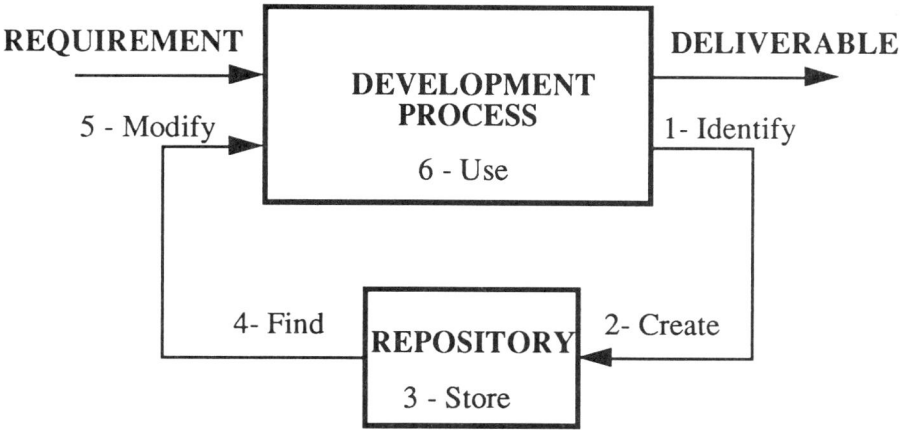

Fig. 26.1 Problem areas in reuse.

In principle, any kind of information occurring in the software development process at any place in a software-producing organization could be reused. But there are many trade-offs; it is not always true that everything that is reusable should also be reused. In the area (1) there are problems of identifying suitable reusable information.

The area (2) covers problems of how to transform reusable information into components. What is the proper size and form of reusable components and how should they be classified? What are proper techniques and languages for describing certain aspects of components, how to guarantee the quality of components? Formal methods will play an increasingly important role in the future.

The reusable components will be stored in a repository. Suitable types of repositories, which is the next important problem area (3). Is a relational database enough or is there a need for more powerful object-oriented databases with maybe some hypertext features? There are also some important non-technical problems in this area, e.g. the role of a librarian.

The future user of components does not have a complete knowledge about all the components in the repository and probably not even an exact understanding of what component he is looking for. So he needs tools for navigation in the repository and for retrieval and examination of selected subsets of components (4).

After obtaining a set of potentially useful components from the repository, the user must be able to understand, modify and use them (5). There is a need for tools and methods for evaluation and modification of components.

The area (6) is related to the development process which must support reuse. This area includes non-technical aspects, e.g. organizational, legal (copyrights, liability) and economical ones. The poorly understood domain of human aspects, which we will look at in the next section, can be referred to this area.

26.3   HUMAN RESISTANCE TO REUSE

Software production in large projects is a highly cooperative intellectual activity. Many persons with different roles are involved.

To simplify the discussion, we will consider only two roles in the software development process, a programmer and a manager. Both of them may be involved in two complementary activities related to reuse. The first activity is about reusing something and the other is producing something reusable. We will see that in both activities, the programmer and the manager, can have quite natural and legitimate reasons against reuse.

We will present attitudes of programmers and managers in the form of statements. Some of them were found in the literature but most were extracted from discussions with a large number of programmers and managers from different companies in different countries. There is no ranking between attitudes, some are more important than others. Some are probably more common in certain cultures and organizations.

26.3.1   Programmer's Point of View

(a)   Using reusable components

* I prefer to do it myself because it is more fun to write it than to just use another person's work.

Programmers have been trained to write programs and to be creative in finding algorithms, not in reusing other people's results. As students, they were even forbidden to actively reuse work of their friends. In addition, it is intellectually more rewarding to create program components instead of trying to find, evaluate and to modify them.

● I will be showing weakness to my colleagues and to my boss if I cannot do it myself.

This is quite a surprising attitude. It has been described by an American, in (Tra87). This attitude may be culture dependent since a quick survey among some Swedish programmers showed that this attitude probably does not exist in Sweden.

● It is not my code! I will do better.

This is a private version of the NIH (Not Invented Here) syndrome.

● It is easier for me to rewrite it than to modify it.

In order to rewrite a piece of software, the programmer only needs to understand its specification. To modify it feels for him sometimes more difficult since he must understand the implementation as well.

● It is difficult for me to maintain other people's work.

If the programmer will be responsible in the future for what he has produced he will surely prefer to update and modify his own software.

● I don't like the colleague who made this component and that is why I do not want to use it.

This is very human but also a very destructive attitude. The first thing this programmer will do is to start looking for deficiencies of a component produced by the antagonist. A lot of time will be used to demonstrate that this component is too large, inefficient, poorly documented and, in general, not to be trusted.

● I don't trust that person's components, he's always writing poor programs.

Also very human and common attitude.

(b) Producing reusable components for others

- I do not want to maintain my components used in a contest I did not intend it for, which will be the case if they are used in another project.

Maintenance is often the largest and most costly activity in the software lifecycle. Many programs live their own life independently of what was the initial intention. If this programmer gives away something to another project, he may expect that they will sooner or later call him asking for help or explanation. Why should he bother?

- If somebody outside my project will use my component, he might discover its poor quality or poor quality of its documentation.

This is something that most programmers know but do not talk about. They are well aware of the weaknesses of their programs, which may not be of importance in their own project, and do not want others to reveal them. It may also be that the programmer delivers a component fulfilling the required functionality but produced quick-and-dirty which he does not want anyone to see.

- Software reuse is software socialism! Why let anyone else benefit from my work and put my job security at risk?

The programmer sometimes has his own set of useful components, of a well-known quality, which (due to benefits of reuse) makes him a better programmer. If they are shared with his colleagues or given to the company, the relative value of him as a programmer decreases. Again this attitude is likely to be culture dependent.

26.3.2 Manager's Point of View

(a) Using reusable components

- The more lines of code that are produced the more impressive will my project be.

It is unfortunately true that the size of projects is often measured in the number of produced lines of code. If a manager is boasting about his past projects, he would rather say that his staff had produced 200 000 lines of code instead of only 20 000 and that they have reused many components produced by someone else.

- A smaller staff can make my project more vulnerable.

Many managers feel that there has to be a certain number of programmers, a critical mass, in order to guarantee the result. Programmers do not only produce code but are also an intellectual resource of the project sharing among them the domain knowledge. If they are only a few and some of them leave the project taking with them their understanding of problems it might create big problems for the manager.

- I do not have the full control of the quality of the components.

It is not a question whether the components do have the proper quality. The problem is that the manager might feel that by allowing reuse he might be responsible for something he cannot influence.

- The customer is my only friend, everyone else is a potential problem. I want to have full control of what is going on in my project and not waste time discussing with subcontractors.

This rather paranoid attitude really exists! There is a certain trade-off between the total production of the project group and the burden on the manager with additional meetings with other groups.

- Reuse may make my project look too simple.

Personal career motivations induce managers to make more out of the project results than they are really worth.

(b) Producing reusable components for others

- If somebody else will use the results of my project, he might discover their poor quality.

This attitude is similar to that of the programmer. Both want to hide the possible deficiencies of the result.

- As a manager of my project I do not have any gains from long-term pay-offs of producing reusable components. Why bother wasting project resources with something that's not in the budget?

This is actually a more economic aspect than human; however, managers tend to be sensitive to these since they do not like activities that do not directly contribute to the project.

26.4 REMEDY: ORGANIZATION FOR REUSE

We present two organization forms that are successfully practicing reuse. They have both in common strong organizational commitment to reuse and an effective management structure. Both are promoting reuse from the start of projects and reuse is an organic part of the software development lifecycle.

26.4.1 Fuchu Software Factory

- The Fuchu Software Factory (FSF), [Mat87], manufactures application software for industrial process control systems in the Toshiba Fuchu works of the Toshiba

Corporation in Japan. FSF claims that the following impressive figures of reuse rate are achieved: 32% of reuse in the design phase and 48% at the coding level. High reuse rates are achieved also for other reusable items such as test programs and documentation.

The reason behind this successful reuse practice is mostly due to the organization depicted in Fig. 26.2.

The three main components of the organization are the following:

● Software parts steering committee

● Software parts manufacturing department

● Software parts centre.

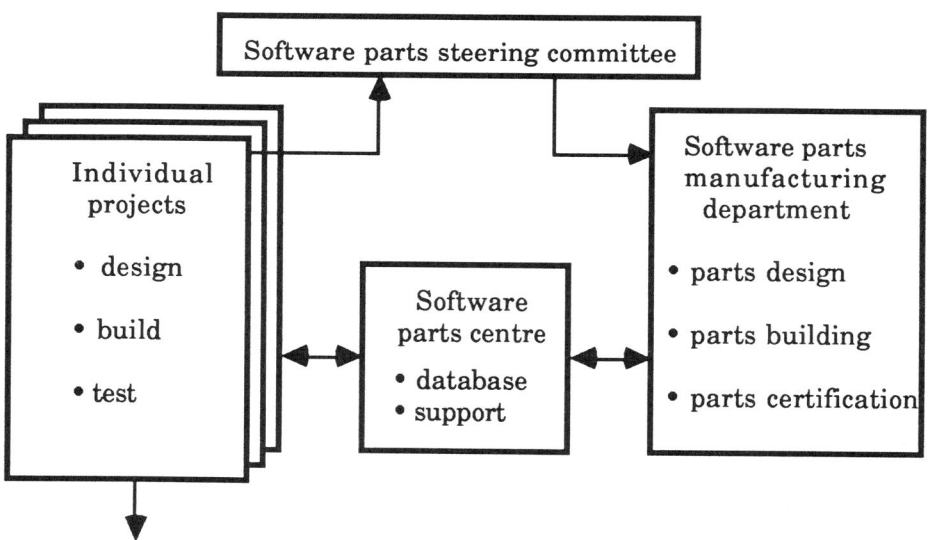

Fig. 26.2 Organization of Fuchu Software Factory.

The steering committee gathers, selects and authorizes the needs concerning creating, updating and discarding reusable parts. The reusable objects may be modularized documents, specifications and code. Different software tools, e.g. application generators, are also reusable objects.

Parts are produced upon request by the manufacturing department. After thorough tests and evaluation the part is taken over by the software parts centre. To every authorized reusable part a check-list is attached which contains different evaluations of it. The software parts centre is responsible not only for the storage and registration, but also provides services such as retrieval, maintenance and publication of reusable modules.

Software projects try to determine their need of modules as early as possible, preferably during the requirements capture phase. This early feedback from the software module centre provides a possibility for the project to influence the customer's requirement specification in order to take advantage of the use of existing parts.

A very important factor for promoting reuse at FSF is the regular training of programmers and designers in reuse and familiarization with the content of software parts centre.

26.4.2   GTE Organization

- GTE Data Services in the USA have achieved code reuse rate of 14% in the first year (1987) after introducing reuse in the organization [Pri90]. The ambitious goal is to reach 50% code reuse by the fifth year. The increase of reuse will be achieved by the growing population of reusable components in the library.

An organizational infrastructure at GTE Data Services supporting reuse consists of the following components:

- Management support group to provide initiative, funding and policies for reuse

- An accessible, densely populated, fully supported, and easy to use library system

- An identification and qualification group responsible for the quality of the repository that identifies potential reusability areas and collects procures and certifies new additions to the repository

- A maintenance group that maintains and updates reusable components

- A development group that creates new reusable components

- A reuser support group that assists and trains reusers and run tests and evaluations of reusable components.

An interesting feature of the GTE method is that the company is giving very popular economical awards to inventors and developers of useful components. Maybe the greed as a motivator, which is so typical for western society, may compensate for the lack of loyalty to collective which is inherent in the Japanese society.

26.5 DISCUSSION

To make reuse a successful ingredient of the software development process it is important to consider both associated technical and non-technical problem areas. Problems having to do with human related aspects are often overlooked. In section 26.3 we have listed a number of attitudes, some of which are perfectly natural, among actors in the software development field which make them less inclined to practise reuse. The sample of statements presented was about what is going on in people's minds. It is not important whether what people believe is true, false, right or wrong. Important is that they believe it, which has consequences for their behaviour. It is a problem that must be dealt with.

We have briefly presented two successful reuse practising organizations. Though they are from different parts of the world and from different cultures they have very much in common:

- Reuse is planned from the start of projects.

- Production of reusable components is separated from their use.

- Strong management support.

- Strong emphasis on quality of components.

- Repository of components with a dedicated support staff.

- Training of programmers in the use of repository.

It is well known that it is sometimes difficult to change people's attitudes. Instead of changing the people it is much easier to change the environment so that negative attitudes will disappear.

If we now study the negative statements in section 26.3, we can see that most of them do not apply to either Fuchu or GTE organizations. Users are not worried about the quality of components since components do have high and certified quality. Producers of components know that making components for others is their job and not an extra burden.

Our conclusion is that the solution to the problem of people's reluctance to reuse is a proper organization of the software developing process.

ACKNOWLEDGEMENT

This work was partly done with the ARISE Project in the European Community Research Programme RACE.

REFERENCES

[Big89] Biggerstaff, T.J. and Perlis, A.J., editors, Software Reusability, Vols. I and II, ACM Press, 1989.

[Fre87] Freeman, P., editor, Tutorial: Software Reusability, IEEE Computer Society Press, 1987.

[Mat87] Matsumoto, Y., A Software Factory: An Overall Approach to Software Production, Tutorial: Software Reusability, ed. Freeman, P., IEEE, 1987.

[Pri90] Prieto-Diaz, R., Implementing Faceted Classification for Software Reuse, Proceedings of the 12th International Conference on Software Engineering, IEEE, 1990.

[Tra87] Tracz, W., Software Reuse: Motivators and Inhibitors, Proceedings of COPCOM S'87, IEEE, 1987.

[Tra88] Tracz, W., editor, Tutorial: Software Reuse; Emerging Technology, IEEE Computer Society Press, 1988.

[Weg83] Wegner, P., Varieties of Reusability, ITT Proceedings of the Workshop on Reusability in Programming, 1983.

27 Reuse directions in British Telecom

S. Whalley

Reuse Group BTRL

27.1 INTRODUCTION

The Design Reuse Group of BTRL was set up to transfer the 'best practice' in reuse into BT software developments. During its first year, it has looked at the state-of-the-art in reuse and the successes and problems of the various approaches identified in that work. In addition to this, it has conducted a survey of existing reuse practices and possibilities within BT. This has the aim of finding those BT development units which could benefit from the introduction of reuse techniques or those who could enhance their current approach to this subject.

There are a number of examples of current practice in reuse, outside of BT, which achieve the incorporation of a high degree of previously developed reusable components into new software products, between 30% and 55% being attainable on average [1] [2]. These are attractively large figures, although it should be kept in mind that such savings mostly apply to the design and implementation parts of the complete development cycle. The contribution of reuse techniques to overall annual improvement in productivity is quoted at about 9% [2]. The figures are the stated results of successful reuse ventures and are considered a target to aim at for BT, whilst not being expected to be achieved in the short term.

A number of significant themes have emerged from the studies of the available literature, including the importance of attending to the organizational and managerial aspects of introducing reuse, before attempting the downstreaming of the technical issues. Accordingly, this forms the main basis of the strategy of the group within BT. This does not mean that the technicalities of reuse are to be neglected – there are key technical issues which will be be addressed in the areas of classification and retrieval, library management and reuse related toolsets. It is likely that in the first instance, the specific organizational matters will be dealt with by the group, with some of the technical issues jointly addressed with related groups.

The downstreaming of reuse, as with any other technology, faces problems on the path to general acceptance. Some of these relate to technical issues, but others relate to an (understandable) reluctance on the part of many to take up something new unless well proven. Generating confidence in new trends in software takes time, but is crucial to their success. A small number of enthusiasts for a cause will not be enough to establish a technology, when what is required is the proving of that technology in real developments over a period of time.

27.2 THE MANAGEMENT OF REUSE

Reuse techniques and toolsets by themselves will not guarantee the expected benefits of reuse. It is also necessary to attend to the organizational and motivational aspects of reuse. The management procedures of a reusable component library are important, to ensure full utilization and to maintain the quality of the contents of the library. Procedures which identify responsibilities and rights pertaining to the library have to be in place before the library is exposed to users.

The component library must have at least the following factors, to instil confidence in users and contributors alike:

- components are entered into the library only if they have passed appropriate quality criteria standards

- there must be a meaningful description scheme for the components

- code components used in the library must be accompanied by adequate documentation and test scripts or evidence that they have been tested

- procedures to track usage of the components should be in place, so that problems found, or modifications made by one user, can be indicated to all users

- a clear definition of responsibilities for the maintenance of the items in the library

- copyright and ownership of the components to be unambiguous

- a policy for the removal of unused or superseded items in the library.

Figure 27.1 shows where such factors may be applied to the introduction of a component to a library and its subsequent use in a product design. The entry of a candidate component to a library can be subject to a number of processes. They can include classifying it according to the required library scheme, verifying and testing it to ensure that its function corresponds to the support documentation and finally submitting it to the insertion process. Other insertion criteria may be applicable, such as the requirement that no items in the library possess duplicate function, unless a good reason can be found for keeping them both. The insertion process itself may be accompanied by notification of acceptance to the component owner and indication of its presence in the library to potential users. Library statistics will be updated and reports generated for management purposes, also.

The designer obtains items from the library for inclusion in new products, by searching for components using the component classification scheme, this may be a simple keyword search or a many-faceted approach [3]. Upon finding a component which could fulfil a requirement, the designer can retrieve the item from the library and evaluate it with other components already selected for the partial or final design.

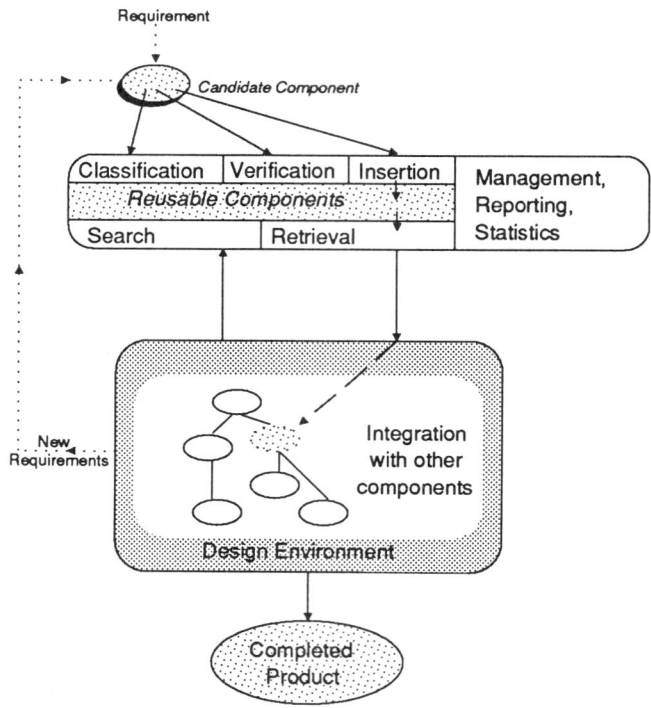

Fig. 27.1 Use of a component library for design.

If the component under evaluation is acceptable, the designer can proceed further with the next stage of the development of the product. However, the designer may not be able to find a component which meets the requirement, in which case, either a specification for a new candidate component to fulfil that role can be generated, or the designer can elect to generate product-specific code equivalent to the role requirement.

27.3 ARCHITECTURAL AND STANDARDS DRIVEN REUSE

Reuse techniques have a very practical purpose in facilitating the development of software products and improving quality, but there are other reasons why reuse and reusability are desirable. They are mainly in the area of control over the software in related or generic products and in the issuing of software for products where adherence to standards is mandatory. This chapter shows where the key reuse techniques above can be used to support generic and standards-based product policies.

27.3.1 Architectural

In layered architectures, where functions contained in one layer of an architecture provide services for the layer above, there are opportunities for reuse in the software implementations of the architecture. For different products, the same sets of layer components can be (re)used in different ways.

Applications based on the architecture incorporate the layer components in their designs. The components will be kept in reuse libraries, possibly with refinements such as classifying the components in the library to reflect the structure of the architecture.

27.3.2 Standards

A large number of product developments in telecommunications use common standards and are required to ensure conformance to those standards. It is advantageous if all product developers have available to them the same implementation of the standard, for the following reasons:

- the standards software can be centrally maintained

- control over the issuing and the tracking of the components of the standards software is made easier

- the implementation of the standard can be subjected to validation procedures centrally, instead of the developers being individually responsible.

Motivation for conformance is the prime consideration here. However, it can be seen that the management of the standards components contains many of the same issues which apply to more general reuse libraries and the same reuse techniques are applicable.

Keeping the standards domain-related software in a centrally held library, controlled by a team who have expertise in its application, indirectly promotes reuse. It can serve to illustrate possibilities for the reuse of components outside of the mandatory fields of standards related or generic product sets. Much software which is ostensibly connected with a particular standard can be used in areas where conformance is not an issue, but which nevertheless has similar functions to the standard.

27.4 STRATEGY FOR THE DOWNSTREAMING OF REUSE

The longer term aim is for acceptance of reuse as a regular part of software development, with reuse possibilities exploited at different stages of the development cycle. It should be the aim of reuse techniques to give benefits in the areas of productivity, quality of delivered product, control over the issuing of software and maintenance aspects.

Some of the characteristics of reuse, which lead from the aims, to a strategy for achieving those aims are:

- organizing for reuse and being committed to reuse are as essential to success as the technical considerations

- reuse techniques are applicable to different aspects of software development, not just the coding phase

- the working practices of developers and their domains of interest need to be taken into account.

The basis of the strategy is to proceed by a succession of relatively small case studies, targeted on particular developers, each addressing some aspect of reuse. The case studies will consist of three parts:

- a study of the working environment and domain of interest of the developer

- selection of an area of working practice which could benefit from reuse, initially this will focus on organizational and managerial issues before the more detailed issues such as identifying reusable components

- field trial or introduction of the selected techniques and follow-up.

The benefit of the smaller case study is that results can be fed back to the reuse group more quickly and also disseminated back out to the same or other case studies, without delay.

The intention is that the reuse group team members work closely with the developers on the case study to ensure rapid and effective uptake of the selected techniques. Further, it is hoped that the developers themselves will be encouraged to contribute ideas and observations to the reuse group team as equal partners. Neither of the above would be practical with a large and singular field trial.

The introduction of reuse should proceed through such a series of case studies, all cross-feeding useful results or advice. The relatively close working of the reuse group teams with developers will ensure that reuse technology is tailored to the developer's requirements, but in such a way that it does not inhibit subsequent upgrade or expansion.

The reuse group will be addressing research topics in parallel with the case studies, particularly regarding toolsets for reuse (Fig. 26.2). This is an essential part of the strategy, but being more applicable after the first wave of case studies is completed.

As part of the strategy, the reuse group is continuing to review reuse research and achievements outside of BT, where there are areas of common interest, such as component classification schemes and toolsets offering library management, search and retrieval.

Some other work of the group, performed as a part of a contribution to the Telstar programme [4], will assist reuse introduction. Telstar is a set of procedures for harmonizing the approach to software development within BT and as such it forms a good basis for reuse. The spread of reuse is greatly aided by the uniformity of methods used by developers.

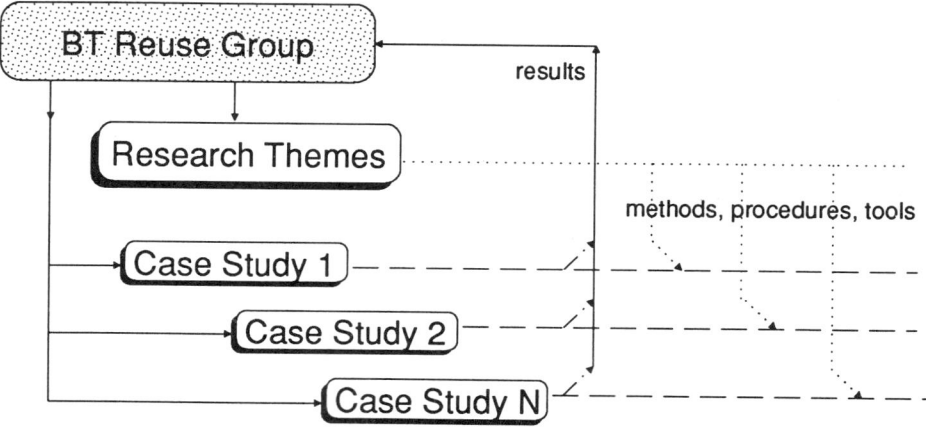

Fig. 27.2   Reuse downstreaming.

The reuse group is due to start the first case study shortly. The requirement at the technical level is for a managed component library, accompanied by the necessary organizational procedures. This first study will allow the group to hone its skill at the downstreaming of reuse and allow an initial assessment of the impact of reuse techniques. There will then follow a series of such studies with introduction of the reuse specific toolsets and ideas from the parallel research themes of the group when appropriate. Having refined the techniques for downstreaming reuse, later case studies will also pursue the quantification of the benefits of reuse, through the development of suitable metrics for reuse.

27.5 CONCLUSIONS

There are a number of benefits which could be achieved through the widespread introduction of reuse techniques, but these are only likely to be realized upon certain conditions. The introduction of the technical aspects such as component classification schema and library search and retrieval tools must be accompanied by proper management of reuse into a receptive organizational structure. The case studies and close inter-working with developers, proposed above, will seek to create the necessary conditions for reuse to be appropriately embedded and to flourish without intervention.

REFERENCES

1. Quantitative Studies of Software Reuse, R.W. Selby, in T.J. Biggerstaff and A.J. Perlis, editors, Software Reusability: Application and Experience, volume 2, ACM 1989.

2. An Overview of Japanese Software Factories, in Japanese Perspectives in Software Engineering. Addison-Wesley 1989.

3.   Towards a Generic and Extensible Reuse Environment, T. Moineau, J. Abadir and E. Rames. Proceedings of Software Engineering '90, BCS Conference Series.

4.   The Systems Engineering Approach within British Telecom, A. Fawthrop. Proceedings of Software Engineering '90, BCS Conference Series.

28 The business case for re-engineering

R. Warden

K3 Group Limited

28.1 INTRODUCTION

'The survival of the species depends upon the effectiveness of the nervous system.'

Whilst taken from natural history, this principle of evolution is equally applicable to industry in the 1990s.

With growing national, and international, competition in so many sectors of industry, business survival depends upon the ability to react to a changing world. In order to respond effectively, a company depends upon the information it receives through the corporate nervous system. For most companies, this system is fed by Information Technology.

When IT is installed to support business functions, it may be the end of a relatively short software development process, but it is only the beginning of a much longer operational phase. Inevitably, as business changes, so the information systems need to be modified.

However, it is well documented that systems become more complex and difficult to maintain as they are changed during their operational life. They may be required to perform tasks which fall well beyond their original design criteria.

Consequently IT has great difficulty following the speed and direction of change. If systems cannot meet new requirements then they will lag behind business. Whereas IT was once seen as the agent of change, it can now become the cause of stagnation.

This situation is summarized in Fig. 28.1, the lifecycle costs and benefits graph. The graph shows two main phases. The first is the initial development, when costs are high and benefits are nil or low. The second phase shows the operational life when a system should be providing benefits which are much greater than the support costs. The end of the second phase is marked by the point where costs are rising sharply in relation to any increase in benefits, and where the new requirements are outpacing the rate of delivery. It is at this point that a system loses viability.

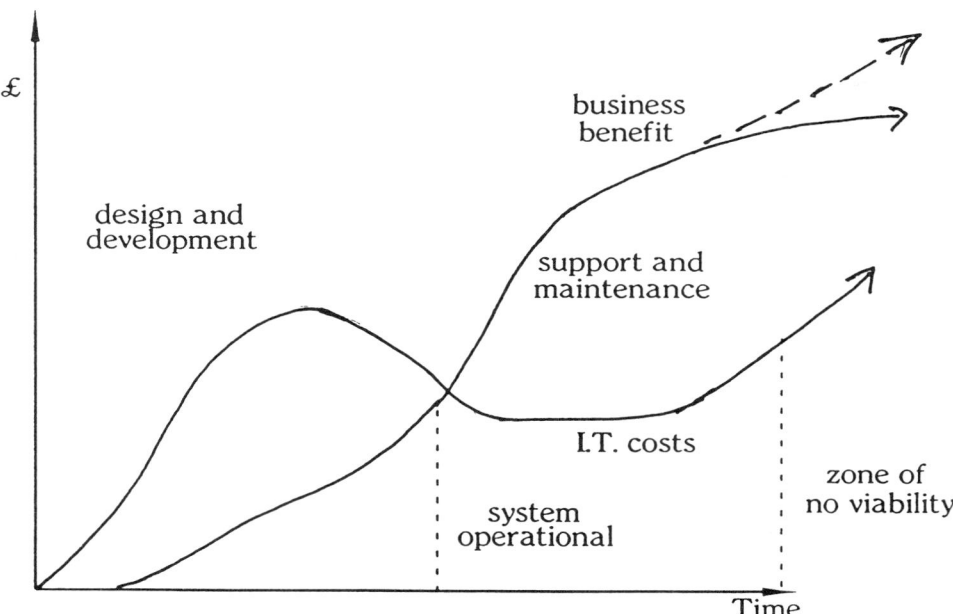

Fig. 28.1 Lifecycle costs and benefits.

Keeping systems viable, that is aligned with the business, is one of the biggest challenges facing IT managers. Any strategies must address the underlying user, operational and financial issues.

For many companies strategies such as total redevelopment or the use of software packages are either too costly, or impractical, or too disruptive to the business. This may leave re-engineering as the only possible solution, or as the first part of a long-term strategy. Either way, the key issue is to determine how re-engineering can be used successfully in a given situation.

The most important single condition for successful re-engineering is to start with a sound business case. This case must link a re-engineering strategy to the business objectives. In this way the application of these techniques can be seen by user and financial groups within an organization as an appropriate solution.

This paper will describe the main considerations of building a business case for re-engineering under the following headings:

● When to consider re-engineering?

● What makes a business case?

● Developing the case for re-engineering.

28.2 WHEN TO CONSIDER RE-ENGINEERING?

The economic lifecycle in Fig. 28.1 shows the point when systems lose viability. There are a number of conditions which may indicate that this point has been reached, or is approaching, and that re-engineering should be considered.

The most important ones are those concerning user and financial issues, such as:

- high operational and maintenance costs

- untimely responses to business change

- inadequate service to the users

- no capacity for systems replacement

However, there are also technical issues where re-engineering may be part of a solution, such as:

- poor productivity within IT

- a need to migrate to a different environment

- a need to use IT staff more effectively

One of the important principles behind any re-engineering project is that re-engineering is driven by the types of problem to be solved, e.g. enabling business change. It is not driven by technology, or the abilities of a particular tool. It is essential that the use of technology does not obscure the objectives.

28.3 WHAT MAKES A BUSINESS CASE?

This section introduces the main elements of a business case, which are discussed in more detail later.

There are three main steps in producing a case:

- to determine a set of objectives

- to identify options available

- to evaluate the options

Executing them may be an iterative process, where the options available and their cost/benefit implications may affect the original objectives.

28.4 OBJECTIVES

The starting point of any case is to examine the business plan against the current position and identify a set of objectives which, if achieved, move the business towards completion of the plan.

Objectives may be quantifiable, e.g. to reduce maintenance costs by a specified amount over a given period of time. Such objectives can, clearly, be of a variable nature, and a partial solution may still offer very significant benefits. Objectives may also be absolute. For example, an objective may be to enable a particular change to be made. In this instance re-engineering may be concerned with removing a specific design limitation which enables that change. This objective is either met or it is not. There may be no room for partial solutions.

Objectives may also be unquantifiable, e.g. to ensure a system can meet future business requirements, even though the exact nature of change is unknown. In this instance the objective may need to be translated into more tangible items, e.g. to reduce complexity or to improve design characteristics which will ease future change.

28.5 OPTIONS

Within any business case there are likely to be many options, and they may be considered individually or in a composite fashion. For example, re-engineering may focus on data, program code, complexity, design and other types of problem.

The options need to be described in some detail. They must be specified in such a way that they can be:

- sized and costed

- evaluated against the objectives

- considered for feasibility and risk

28.6 EVALUATION

The third element is to evaluate the options so that a decision can be taken on which ones to implement. In order to assess the ability of each option to meet the objectives, there are a number of considerations. Examples are as follows.

Situations are often complex, with many objectives derived from the business plan. The business case must evaluate options against multiple objectives.

Any cost savings must be calculated from true costs and expenditure for the remaining life of systems.

Advantage should be taken of economies of scale, e.g. how to maximize the return on building a re-engineering environment. It is necessary to avoid diseconomies of scale, e.g. do not unnecessarily re-engineer an entire system when only a part of it is a problem.

The degree of risk associated with the options must be assessed and shown in the business case. Risks in re-engineering may come from estimating inaccuracies, leading to unreliable project costing, through to difficulties in translating the abilities of re-engineering technology into benefits to the business. Areas of uncertainty must be highlighted in the business case.

Following evaluation of the options, it may be necessary to revise the objectives and go through the process again.

28.7 DEVELOPING THE CASE FOR RE-ENGINEERING

In order to develop a business case for re-engineering it is necessary to deal with a traditional problem within the IT industry, that of justifying investment in technology on business grounds. The major problem is presenting benefits in a tangible form so that they can be considered objectively against the costs. This problem raises several implications for re-engineering:

● the case must start by analysing how the business has changed since the system was developed

● a method is needed to translate technical re-engineering work into business benefit

● that if the reasons for re-engineering are largely technical, i.e. they are not aimed at solving user or financial problems, then the level of benefits will probably not be acceptable

For re-engineering to succeed, in addition to a sound business case there must be disciplines and methods for managing the project and controlling costs.

The K3 Group has developed methods based upon the following re-engineering cycle. This cycle is contained within the MAINSTREAM software maintenance framework.

28.8 THE RE-ENGINEERING CYCLE

initial study	pilot project	reverse engineering	re-eng analysis	forward engineer	system test	release out	evaluate

The re-engineering cycle.

28.8.1   Initial Study

The Initial Study is the process which will build the case for re-engineering. This is the most important stage for discussion in this paper and it is described in more detail under the headings of:

- objective setting

- initial plan

- option evaluation

Some case history information is used to provide examples of the different phases of a study.

28.8.2   Pilot Project

Following the Initial Study is an optional stage for a pilot project, which is not discussed further. It is only mentioned here because it is the means of containing risks which may be identified in the Initial Study.

28.8.3   Objective Setting

The first phase of an Initial Study examines the current state of a system against the business objectives. The purpose is to define a set of objectives which, if achieved, will enable the system to remain aligned with the business. This is done by both business and technical analyses of a system.

The business analysis task seeks to determine:

- the current business requirements

- how well the system services them

- how the business is evolving and future requirements

- how well the system meets user service levels

- the degree of support that users receive from IT

- the cost to users of the service

The technical analysis work determines:

- the maintainability of a system

- planning and management of change to the system

- system design and complexity

- the current ability of staff to support the system

- the availability of support staff for the remaining life of the system

- the documented knowledge of the system

- the technical support environment

By combining these two views a picture is obtained of where and how a system is failing to meet business objectives. By identifying the problems associated with a system in this way, a comprehensive set of objectives can be determined.

As an example, an Initial Study was performed in a financial services company where this phase led to the following conclusions:

- a change in business plan would require existing systems to cope with many new products

- these systems would be expected to grow at a rate of 30% a year

- the systems were not well matched to current business needs

- the systems needed 80% of IT resource to maintain

- internally the systems, although only five years old, had undergone one migration to a new hardware vendor, and many functional changes

- the systems lacked the internal flexibility required to meet the new business demands

A medium-term strategy, 3-5 years, was needed for systems redevelopment. However in the short term, 1-3 years, the existing systems would reach a point of unmaintainability. Therefore re-engineering was considered in order to:

- extend the life of the systems

- free IT resources for the redevelopment programme

- improve productivity

- improve maintainability

- service the 1-3-year business needs

- document for future business understanding .

28.8.4 Initial Plan

The second phase of the Initial Study is to identify the options available and represent them in an initial plan.

Options may include the following types of re-engineering:

- procedure code restructuring

- program redesign

- systems redesign

- data normalization

- database re-engineering

- re-implementation of business rules

With almost any form of re-engineering there will be a need for retro-documentation to support the work. Some procedural information may be recaptured by automated tools and stored in a repository. Functional and non-procedural information may have to be recreated by analysts and others with knowledge of a system.

Specifications of the work involved in each option and the likely benefits are raised, sized and estimated. To do this metrics are essential to describe the nature and frequency of problems to be removed during re-engineering. Some standard sizing metrics may be applicable to a project, which may be input to formal estimating methods. For example, the number of lines of code (COCOMO) or the number of program functions (function point analysis) to be re-engineered.

However, sizing may require totally different types of metrics such as:

- number and severity of design errors

- level of data complexity and degree of normalization required

- types and frequency of control flow knots

A system may contain very specific problems which need to be addressed. In this case, new measures may be required to describe these problems, and code and data analysers modified to find them.

At this point the plan can be drafted showing the current problems, objectives, and the options available to achieve the objectives.

In the case history, the technical analysis had indicated that about 10% of the systems, 40,000 of 420,000 lines of code, were the major problem. The options proposed to deal with these parts of the systems were:

- cosmetic re-engineering, standardization of data names and other improvements to readability .

- data re-engineering, the removal of duplicate data structures and other data anomalies which had led to high data complexity

- programs redesign, the removal of design faults at a higher level and of knotted code at a procedure level

- detailed functional documentation of the code being re-engineered

Soft estimates were made at this stage based upon the number and size of the programs in conjunction with the types of re-engineering to be performed.

28.8.5 Option Evaluation

The final phase of the Initial Study is to evaluate the options and identify those which give the best cost/benefit commensurate with the risk factors involved.

The costs of the options can be determined from the sizing and estimation process. There are a number of cost drivers for re-engineering, just as there are for other type of software engineering. They include the skill levels required for the work, and the degree of automation available.

The benefits of each option have to be assessed by comparing the expected deliverables against the objectives. Making such judgements, which link the technical improvements defined in a re-engineering specification to achieving the business objectives, is of crucial importance in the business case. As most situations will involve multiple objectives, it will be necessary to consider how far each option meets each objective, and where compromises can be made.

It is also necessary to evaluate the effects of composite options. For example, if data normalization precedes program redesign, the latter may take significantly less effort than if it was performed alone. The reason is that data normalization reduces data complexity, which in turn may make programs easier to redesign.

At this point risk assessment may be considered. Some common rules which can be applied are:

- identify the 'play safe' option, which gives the highest minimum benefit of all options and has low risk

- identify the 'optimist's' option, which gives the highest maximum benefit of all options but with higher risk

- assume all options have an equal chance of success, and choose the one which which gives the maximum expected value

A characteristic of re-engineering is that it is amenable to pilot work and small-scale projects. Benefits can more easily be assessed with low cost and risk, unlike large redevelopments where any benefits will not be visible until very significant costs have been incurred. In the case history, there was some uncertainty over the estimates and the likely benefits. However, the difficulty of working with the current code, and detailed measures and reports from code analysis, had indicated a very large potential for improvement.

In general terms, it appeared feasible that a re-engineering project could be completed in about six months' elapsed time, which would fit in with the mid-term strategy. Furthermore, the benefits could start as soon as the first re-engineered programs were released, i.e. within weeks.

28.9 CONCLUSION

In the case history, a post re-engineering review was performed which identified a number of specific benefits. The most important of them, and the one which had the greatest contribution to meeting the original objectives, was that productivity on the re-engineered parts of the systems was doubled. This could be translated into a number of other benefits such as reduced support staffing and acceptable response to change.

One of the main virtues of the approach described here is the involvement of all affected groups within a company. In this respect, business managers and system users can be presented with a case for re-engineering which meets their needs. This will help to ensure that re-engineering is not seen as an isolated technology, but as a genuine solution to the business problem of coping with change.

Overall, the business case will acknowledge that whilst IT feeds the corporate nervous system, the emphasis is on delivering benefits to the main business organs attached to this system.

29 The legal position of reverse software engineering in the UK

M.K.O. Lee

BP International Ltd

29.1 INTRODUCTION

Reverse engineering is an important concept in software engineering. In a very broad sense a significant proportion of effort in real-life software engineering is concerned with reverse engineering. Reverse engineering of one kind or another occurs in a whole spectrum of activities ranging from software maintenance to the design and development of competing or inter-operable products. It is essentially a powerful way to gain intimate information on a piece of software. However, such an apparently innocuous activity may be actually illegal because it could infringe on the intellectual property rights of someone who owns these rights in relation to a piece of software. Copyright is particularly relevant in this context. In the following section UK copyright law in relation to software is briefly outlined. Then the legality of some typical reverse engineering activities are examined in the light of copyright law in the UK. The law in this area is changing fast. In particular, the forthcoming European Directive on Software Protection is going to play a crucial role in setting a uniform European legal framework governing, *inter alia,* the problematic and controversial practice of software engineering. This Directive and its potential impact on reverse engineering will be examined in section 29.4 below.

29.2 COPYRIGHT LAW IN RELATION TO SOFTWARE

Intellectual property is about the protection of[1] information and ideas in a commercial/industrial context. The owner of intellectual property has available to him certain intellectual property rights pertaining to the property (the gist of which is information/ideas). Copyright is an important species of such rights. The other well-known varieties are patents, design, trade marks and confidential information. For computer programs, copyright is the most important kind of intellectual property protection.

In essence, copyright is a property right given to the authors or creators of works such as books, drama, films, and musical scores whose production has involved a reasonable amount of skill, labour and judgement. Much of the current law in this area can be found in the Copyright, Design and Patents Act 1988. Under the 1988 Act, computer programs are specifically protected by copyright as literary work. In theory copyright generally protects only the expression of ideas but not ideas as such. One practical consequence of this theory is that an idea must be recorded (or fixed in some form) and it is the recorded form (which is taken as an expression of the idea) which is given protection.

Copyright is really an entrepreneurial (rather than industrial) right, the main aim of which is to protect the skill, labour and judgement expended in commercial or artistic (rather than purely technical) innovation regardless of novelty or aesthetic

---

[1]   Dr. Lee is a barrister and a computer scientist with BP International Ltd., IT Research Unit, BP Sunbury Research Centre, Chertsey Road, Sunbury-on-Thames, Middlesex, TW16 7LN, email: matthew@bprcsitu.uucp

appeal. The copyright owner is given exclusive control over the reproduction or other exploitation (altogether known as 'restricted acts') of the copyright work. Although copyright is exclusive, it is only quasi-monopolistic in contrast with patents. If two identical pieces of copyright work are created entirely independently by two different authors, then both authors will enjoy their respective copyright independently.

The substantive legal requirements for copyright protection are that the author must be a 'qualified person' at the time when the work is made (or alternatively the work is first published in the UK) and that the work in question must be of a nature in which copyright can subsist. A 'qualified person' basically means that the author is a citizen of, or resident or domiciled in, or a body incorporated in, the UK or some other country to which the 1988 Act extends. As for the subsistence of copyright, the 1988 Act has stipulated that the following kinds of work are copyrightable:

- original literary, dramatic, musical or artistic works

- sound recordings, films, broadcasts or cable programmes

- the typographical arrangement of published editions

In particular, computer programs, tables and compilations are specifically regarded as literary works enjoying all the usual protections afforded to such works plus a few more (e.g. restriction on rental). This would seem to cover databases as well, since they could be regarded as tables or compilations. However, the 1988 Act does not give a definition of computer program, presumably because a concrete definition would probably be too restrictive to cover all the possibilities now and in the future, and an abstract definition would not be in conformance with the usual concrete and detailed style of UK legislative practice. Finally, copyright will not subsist in a piece of work unless the work is original and recorded. Originality refers to the way an idea is expressed in a copyright work and it has nothing to do with the originality or novelty of the idea as such. The standard required is fairly low requiring merely that the work originates from the author and has not been copied. A copyright work must also be recorded. This may be in writing or otherwise, including the use of electronic or magnetic recordings on any medium.

Copyright protection is given to the owner of a copyright work. The author is usually regarded as the first owner except for work done during employment in which case the first owner is taken to be the employer unless there is a written agreement to the contrary. However, a contractor commissioned to do a piece of work is regarded as the first owner. To ensure that the commissioner will own the copyright in the work produced, an explicit written assignment is needed. Problems often arise with multiple-authorship which may not be severable, in which case a single uncooperating author can thwart any attempt on commercial exploitation. To prevent such a situation from arising it is important to agree on future ownership by contract from the very beginning. Interesting issues arise when computers are used creatively in the production of a piece of work. The position with computer-aided work (e.g. work produced using an intelligent syntax-directed editor) is no different to the general copyright position. However, for computer-generated work (e.g. code produced by a fourth-generation language) the 1988 Act provides that the author shall be taken to be the person by whom the arrangements necessary for the creation of the work reundertaken. The user of a computer program that generates the work in question is clearly such a person. However, it is not so clear whether the author of the computer program or indeed the computer is also such a person who will share the copyright.

Once the substantive legal requirements are satisfied copyright protection comes into effect automatically. Unlike patents, copyright does not need to be applied for or registered. The copyright period is generally 50 years from the end of the year in which the author (or the last surviving or known author in case of joint-authorship) dies or, in the case of computer-generated works, 50 years from the end of the year in which the work concerned was made. Copyright notices appearing on copyright works are admissible as evidence and presumed to be correct until the contrary is proved. This piece of evidence can be very useful if copyright is disputed. Although there are no procedural requirements to be satisfied for copyright to come into effect, it is obviously useful if the copyright owner keeps detailed internal records concerning all copyright material in case he has to prove ownership in a disputed situation.

The 1988 Act provides that, *inter alia,* copying, adapting, or issuing copies of a copyright work to the public constitutes primary copyright infringement if done without the consent of the copyright owner. This is so, regardless of whether the infringer knows he is actually infringing. Copying means reproducing the whole or any substantial part (quality-wise or quantity-wise) of the work in any material form, including the storing of the work in any medium by electronic means even if it is done transiently or incidentally. Adaptation includes any translation of the copyright work except in the case of computer programs where the translation is done incidentally in the course of running the program (s21(4) of the 1988 Act). It would probably mean that running a program using an interpreter *per se* is not an infringing act but compiling one without authorization clearly is. In reality, executing a program stored on any permanent secondary storage device (e.g. diskettes or tapes) necessitates copying from the storage device to the random access memory (RAM) of the computer and as such will be regarded as an infringing act whether an interpreter is used (in which case the source code is copied) or otherwise (in which case the compiled object code is copied). The 1988 Act also provides that commercial dealing with infringing copies, providing articles for making specific infringing copies or circumventing specific copy-protection, and facilitating infringement by electronic transmission, all constitute secondary copyright infringement (if done without authorization) if the infringer knows or has reason to believe infringing copies are involved. However, there are certain exceptions based on the notion of 'fair dealing'. For example, 'fair dealing' with a work for the purposes of research or private study is permitted without consent of the copyright owner even though restricted acts may be involved (s29 of the 1988 Act). Both primary and secondary infringements give rise to a cause of civil action against the infringer which the copyright owner can pursue. The usual remedies of injunctions (interlocutory or final), damages, and various orders (as in patent infringement cases) are available to the copyright owner. In addition, criminal sanctions are available if an infringer deliberately infringes copyright for commercial gain. The highest penalty is two years' imprisonment or an unlimited fine on conviction by indictment. More details on UK copyright law can be found in a good many standard intellectual property textbooks.[2]

29.3 COPYRIGHT INFRINGEMENT AND REVERSE ENGINE-ERING

As far as computer programs are concerned, reverse engineering serves two main purposes in practice: (1) to find out interface information (so that compatible products may be produced), (2) to find out the design structure of a program so that a similar program may be reproduced. Interface information includes those between software and software, software and hardware, and software and human. The latter one is the human-interface specification while the others may be regarded as the functional or behavioural specification of software components including those addressing hardware facilities directly. Knowledge of the interface and structure of a piece of software is of course useful in its maintenance. Typical maintenance activities include error-fixing and software modification in response to changing user demands.

Reverse engineering of a software product takes many forms. On the one end of the spectrum it may involve the crude disassembling of object (machine) code and a superficial rewriting of the resulting assembler program to produce a similar product. At the other end of the spectrum it may involve a sophisticated 'clean room'

---

2   For example, a well-known textbook is 'Intellectual Property: Patents, Copyright, Trademarks and Allied Rights' by W.R. Cornish, 2nd edition, Sweet & Maxwell, 1989.

procedure using two separate teams of software engineers. One team analyses the product in question (by examining the code and/or running the program analytically) with the production of its functional specification as the final aim. The other team takes the functional specification and goes through the normal development lifecycle to produce the functionally equivalent product. In between the two extremes there is a wide variety of practices. To see whether and to what extent reverse engineering could infringe copyright it is useful to list out the sorts of activities typically involved in reverse engineering:

1.   disassembling object code, adapting the result and re-assembling to give an equivalent object program,

2.   executing a program, analysing it to find out its structure,

3.   executing a program, analysing it to find out how it interacts with certain hardware/software functions (i.e. interaction protocol),

4.   executing a program, analysing it to find out what it is supposed to do (i.e. its functional specification),

5.   executing a program, finding out the screen layout and user interaction (i.e. user-interface) and mimicking them in another program.

(1) above is very likely to be regarded as a process of translation within the meaning of the 1988 Act and as such constitutes copyright infringement if done without authorization. The results of (2) to (5) are usually the inputs to the writing of compatible or equivalent programs; (2) amounts to indirect copying of the so-called structure, sequence, organization of the original program. This constitutes copyright infringement in the USA but the situation in the UK is unclear. The result of (3) indicates how a compatible or equivalent program should behave when it wants to interface with certain external hardware/software functions (e.g. in order to work with other

programs or hardware devices). This will probably not be regarded as indirect copying of any part of the original program because the program is just one way of achieving the requisite behaviours and the new program may achieve the same in a totally different way. The situation with (4) is similar. (5) may be regarded as indirectly copying the look and feel of the (user interface) of the original program. In the USA, the recent case of Lotus v Paperback Software has confirmed that copying the 'look and feel' of a user interface to a software can constitute copyright infringement. The situation in the UK is still unclear. Given that the crux of the UK approach to copyright has been the protection from misappropriation of any significant skill and labour expended by an author rather than a straight adherence to the doctrine of giving protection only to expression of ideas it may turn out that the scope of copyright protection in the UK is even wider than in the USA. In any case, under the 1988 Act running a program without authorization constitutes copyright infringement. If the program copyright owner does not authorize the reverse engineering of its work then technically performing any of the activities listed in (1) to (5) above constitutes an infringement. The situation will be clarified by the forthcoming European Directive on Software Protection discussed in the following paragraph.

29.4   EUROPEAN DIRECTIVE ON SOFTWARE PROTECTION

Since the early 1980s the European Community has been attempting to formulate standards and regulations in the area of computer law. This is becoming more important and pressing as the Single European Market becomes a close reality. It is clear that in the near future there will be more and more standardization (or at least harmonization) in Computer Law on a European scale. In the area of software protection the current trend is reflected by the proposed EEC Directive on the protection of computer programs. This Directive has its roots in the EEC Green Paper of 7 June 1988 entitled 'Copyright and the Challenge of Technology: Copyright Issues requiring Immediate Action'. The Green Paper has recognized that the most adequate form of legal protection for the majority of software systems is copyright, not least because most software systems are not patentable by current recognized criteria because of the lack of required level of originality and inventiveness. The Green paper has further outlined a number of principles (based on copyright law) which form the basis of the proposed Directive. Essentially, the principles are as follows:

- Copyright protection should apply to computer programs fixed in any form (i.e. firmware, microcode, programs, etc., recorded on any medium).

- The exclusive rights of the author in authorizing restricted acts (the performance of which without consent constitutes infringement) should be clearly defined.

- The level of originality required is simply that the computer programs are the result of the creator's own intellectual effort and that they are not commonplace in the software industry (similar to the standard required regarding design right under UK law).

- All essential aspects of interface specification (including access protocols) and ideas should be excluded from protection.

- Program adaptation by a legitimate user for his own use exclusively should be permitted without explicit authorization. Back-up copies can be made by a legitimate user without authorization but reproduction for any other purpose can only be made with authorization.

- The term of protection shall start with the creation of the program and last for between 20 years and 50 years (to be decided in the Directive).

- The issue of authorship of computer programs should be left to the national law of member States.

- Protection should (at least) apply to all natural andlegal persons domiciled or resident in a State adhering to the Berne Convention or the Universal Copyright Convention.

- In infringement cases the burden of proof on the plaintiff is that he has to show similarity between the right holder's program and the alleged infringement copy and that the alleged infringer has access to that program; once this burden is discharged the onus of proving non-infringement rests on the alleged infringer. The standard of proof (as in all civil cases) is one of balance of probabilities.

Many of these principles have manifested themselves in the first draft of the Directive published in December 1988, although some have been compromised. The issue of criminal sanction is not dealt with under the draft at all. The draft contains 10 Articles the most important of which are Articles 1, 4, 5, 6, 7, 8. Article 1 defines the object of protection confirming that computer programs fixed in any form are to be protected as literary works under copyright. However, ideas and principles underlying user interfaces are not protectable, nor are algorithms, logic, or programming languages underlying the programs. In particular, interface specifications are not protected. The level of originality required is to be the same as for literary works. Article 4 defines the restricted acts constituting infringement if done without the consent of the right holder. Basically, the reproduction, execution and adaptation of a program by any means and in whatever manner are restricted acts. Further, the copyright holder is given exclusive control over the distribution of his programs. Article 5 then lays down the exceptions to Article 4. Essentially, Article 5(1) provides that a legitimate computer program user can adapt and reproduce a program for his own purposes unless the program was distributed under a written licence signed by both parties (i.e. not a 'shrink-wrap' licence). Article 5(2) permits public libraries to lend out programs without explicit authorization of the right holder. Article 6 provides for secondary infringement similar to the provisions in the 1988 Act. Article 7 defines the term of protection as 50 years from the date of creation of a program. Article 8 makes clear that copyright protection on programs can co-exist with other intellectual property protections as well as contractual protections.

Not surprisingly, the draft has received intense European and international attention from many interested parties and pressure groups, not least from the large computer manufacturers and software vendors. The main issues of contention are as follows:

- Standard of Originality required

- Interface Specifications

- Reverse Engineering

- Licence Terms

The standard of originality required for copyright protection as regards literary works is not the same for all EEC countries. The obvious consequence is that some programs will be copyright protected in one country but not in another. This is clearly against the spirit of the draft which is to standardize and harmonize legal protection for computer programs in all member countries. Article 1 of the Directive excludes interface specifications from protection. This is vital if competition in inter-operable products is to be encouraged. However, it is often necessary to reverse engineer a program to obtain its interface specification. Reverse engineering necessarily requires running the program concerned for the purpose of figuring out the interface specification. This is prohibited under Article 4. Since it is almost practically impossible to obtain interface specifications without some sort of reverse engineering (unless, of course, the manufacturer is willing to release the information), the consequence of Article 4 is that interface specifications are protected indirectly despite the provisions under Article 1. The scope of the exceptions under Article 5 relating to licences is also unclear. For instance, the question of what exactly is a written license and how as well as why it is different to a 'shrink-wrap' licence is not addressed. Also, there are references to the term 'sale', the meaning of which is not at all clear in the context of commercial marketing of software in practice (e.g. strictly speakly, in marked contrast with other literary works, software systems are not actually sold but only licensed in most cases). There are also uncertainties regarding the relationships between this draft and other existing EEC Directives and rules (e.g. on European competitive laws).

As expected, there will be some changes to the draft before it becomes final. It can be expected that the Directive will be published in its final form in the near future. The plan is to have the Directive implemented by all the member States (by introducing new national legislation or amending existing legislation) by the end of 1992. However, Articles 1, 4, 8 and especially 5 are likely to be extensively re-drafted before the Directive becomes final. The main emphasis of the re-drafting is to ensure that independent development of inter-operable computer programs will be encouraged and reverse engineering will be allowed in so far as necessary to achieve this aim (overriding contrary contractual provisions if necessary). Also, the scope of exception under Article 5(1) will not be defined by reference to terms such as sale or licence; the legitimate private user will simply enjoy the exception (in particular, the making of back-up copies is allowed) in the absence of specific contrary contractual provisions. Finally, it is to be further clarified under Article 8 that this Directive shall not prejudice other existing requirements of Community law or Directives in the area of information technology.

Recently, the draft has been considered by the European Parliament and various modifications have been recommended. In stark contrast with the original draft, the European Parliament has recommended that logic, algorithms and programming languages should be given copyright protection. Given the increasing level of abstraction and sophistication used in software development, the notions of logic, algorithm and programs are no longer clearly distinguishable. In some cases they can even be seen as isomorphic to each other. It follows that as a matter of consistency copyright protection should be given to all of them. It is more difficult to argue for copyright protection for programming languages though, given that one cannot get copyright protection on natural or mathematical languages. Regarding reverse engineering, it is proposed that Article 4 should be relaxed to enable the construction of inter-operable products. However, the scope of the relaxation is quite narrow. It would permit reverse engineering only on those parts of the original program which are necessary to obtain inter-operability information, and only in circumstances where the relevant information is not available. Furthermore, reverse engineering is permitted only if necessary for building inter-operable products (i.e. those that would work with the original program), and not for developing competing or replacement products. Such a relaxation does not appear to be very useful for potential competitors! Finally, it should be borne in mind that the recommendations of the European Parliament are only advisory in nature; it will be up to the Council of Ministers to decide on the final content of the Directive.

29.5 CONCLUSIONS

Under present UK legislation it is arguable that all forms of reverse engineering *per se* would constitute copyright infringement if done without authorization. If the information obtained from reverse engineering is used in developing competing products then the chances of copyright infringement are even higher since there would be an element of (direct or indirect) copying involved. At one end of the spectrum, copying the functionalities of a program would probably not amount to copyright infringement since ideas *per se* are not copyrightable. On the other hand, copying the structures of a program is likely to amount to copyright infringement. In the US, even copying the 'look and feel' of the user interface to a program would amount to copyright infringement. It is unclear whether the UK will adopt a similar approach.

The forthcoming European Directive on Software Protection is likely to relax the legal position of reverse engineering in the UK to some extent. If the Council of Ministers adopts the European Parliament's proposals then reverse engineering would be allowed for inter-operability but not for building competing products. No doubt a great deal of lobbying will continue to go on in Brussels. There are essentially two groups: (1) the big multinational computer manufacturers and (2) the smaller hardware/software vendors and big IT user organizations. The former (quite understandably) argue for wider copyright protection and restriction on reverse engineering. The latter (equally understandably) lobby for just the opposite. Some sort of compromise will be inevitable. There is little doubt that reverse engineering will be permitted; the question is under what circumstances it will be permitted. Currently, it seems the big computer manufacturers are winning the upper hand and the narrow approach of the European Parliament is in favour. However, nothing is cast in concrete yet and more changes may occur in the near future as lobbying from both camps intensifies. Whatever the end result may be, this Directive is going to be a major legal milestone in relation to reverse engineering not only in the UK but the whole of the EEC.

30 Software maintenance, reuse and reverse engineering

M. Munro

University of Durham

30.1 SOFTWARE MAINTENANCE

Software maintenance has become established as a sub-discipline within the general field of software engineering. This has not always been the case, with software maintenance being given very low status by the software engineering community. In a recent paper, Bennett *et al.* {BENN88} argue that there is an urgent need to address the problems of software maintenance.

Software maintenance has been defined [2] as:

The modification of a software product after delivery to correct faults, to improve performance or other attributes, or to adapt the product to a changed environment.

Thus, maintenance refers to the activities that take place after a software product has been delivered to the customer. Four types of maintenance activity have been identified:

Perfective Maintenance

- improving software function by responding to customer's defined changes
- enhancing the software by adding more functionality
- 60% of the maintenance activity
- requires changes to the requirements, design and code

Adaptive Maintenance

- changing software to adapt to environmental changes
- 18% of the maintenance activity
- requires changes to the design and code

Corrective Maintenance

- bug fixing, correction of software errors
- 17% of the maintenance activity
- requires changes to the code

Preventive Maintenance

- updating software to forestall future problems
- 5% of the maintenance activity

30.1.1 Why is there a Maintenance Problem?

- most existing software was produced prior to significant use of structured programming

- it is difficult to determine whether a change in code will affect something else

- documentation is inadequate, nonexistent, or out of date (or even there is too much of it)

- maintenance is perceived as having a low profile

- software is not seen as a corporate resource

- maintenance programmers have not been involved in the development of a product and find it difficult to map actions to program source code

30.2 REVERSE ENGINEERING

In order to extract reusable components from software systems there must exist a mechanism for identifying them. This identification process implies that there is an intelligent way of understanding existing software systems.

First though a definition of the term {\it software system} must be given. By this is meant all the elements such as the source code, the job control for constructing and running the system, databases, object code, documentation, design information, requirements and specification details. It is all these elements, not just the source/object code of the system that constitute a software system. It is actually more than these tangible elements, it is also the knowledge and expertise of the analysts and programmers who developed the system plus the knowledge and expertise of the maintenance programmers who are carrying out the various maintenance tasks in the continuing evolution of the system.

In order to be able to identify the reusable components in the system, all of the elements that go to make up the system must be used as a source of information and understanding. In other words it is necessary to use more than just the source code of the system to gain an understanding of it. How can this understanding be achieved?

It is easy for machines to perform some operations and humans to perform others. One approach to this problem is to list the important operations that are required for the understanding of software systems on some scale of machine/human ease of achievement. Such a scale could look something like this:

Low-level (Easy for Machine)

> restructuring
>
> verify simple invariants
>
> express data structures as ADTs
>
> discover global invariant
>
> express data structures in terms of problem domains
>
> translate into a specification

High-level (Easy for Human)

From this it can be seen that it is easy for a machine to restructure and easy for humans (and very difficult for machines) to translate into a specification. If this last point were possible by machine then the problems of systems understanding would be near to being solved.

In order to ascertain current state of the art it is necessary to look at reverse engineering to discover what is possible in terms of system understanding.

30.2.1 Definition

There has been a great deal of debate about what is meant by the term reverse engineering. This part of the paper attempts to give a simple definition of the term and then presents a hierarchy of reverse engineering concepts in order to bring perspective to bear on the subject.

Two similar definitions of reverse engineering have been given:

Reverse Engineering is an attempt to bring new and existing (old) software systems under the control of a modern development method.

and

Reverse Engineering is a process to support the analysis and understanding of data and processing in existing computerised systems.

Keith London Associates

These definitions imply that a complete system understanding can be achieved at the source code level together with an overview picture of the system. Both these definitions, however, beg the question of how this can be achieved. The overview picture of the system is important because it well gives the relationship between the elements (and their components) that go to make up the system. It is thus the contention that reverse engineering is not just about source code and data but it is also about complete system understanding.

30.2.2 Levels of Reverse Engineering

In order to put reverse engineering into perspective a hierarchy of reverse engineering has been devised. One of the problems in this area is the proliferation of terms, all with mixed and (sometimes) interchangeable meanings. The proposed levels, together with the point in the simple waterfall model of the software lifecycle to which it is proposed the backward step can be made, are:

	Level	Step back to
1.	Inverse	Engineering Specification
2.	Renovation	Design
3.	Re-engineering	Code
4.	Redocumentation	-

Here Inverse Engineering is at the top level indicating that a specification can be derived from an existing system. This is followed by Renovation that derives design information and Re-engineering that just works at the source code level. Redocumentation is included as a reverse engineering technique because it will allow some degree of overall system understanding without being concerned how the program works.

The important features of these techniques are now discussed.

(a) Redocumentation

Research at the Centre for Software Maintenance indicates that there are two approaches to redocumentation, namely:

Redocumentation of Source Code

The research into redocumentation of source code is described in the papers by Foster and Munro {FOST87} and Fletton and Munro {FLET88}. A summary of this work is presented below.

An old system needs to be redocumented because existing documentation is often:

- Out-of-date

- Incomplete

- Difficult to update

- Difficult to read

- Difficult to extract information from

- Not tailored to the programmer's needs

The research identified three important types of source code documentation:

1. Source code

2. Technical documentation

- Cross-reference

- Control/Data Flow

- Call Graphs

- Metric Information

- etc.

3. Comprehension documentation

The desirable properties of a redocumentation system were identified as:

- Incremental documentation

- Casual update

- Quality Assurance

- Incorporation of Static Analysis data

- Incorporation of Source Code

- Team Use

The important conclusion from this research was the ability to connect these three types of documentation together and the provision of a browser based on hypertext.

Inverse Configuration Management

Inverse Configuration Management is defined to be:

The process of bringing an existing software system under configuration control.

The need for an overview picture of the elements that go to make up a software system is important. There is a relationship between the size of a project and its complexity based on more than just lines of code. Large software systems invariably tend towards a high level of complexity both in terms of the number and diversity of components, and in the complexity of the relationship between the components.

The Inverse Configuration Management research project {KENN89}, worked on at the Centre for Software Maintenance, places great emphasis on the identification phase of the configuration management process. It is clear that the following needs to be identified:

- Application Components

- Associated Versions

- Redundant Components

- Missing Components

- Allied Components

It is also important to be able to understand the relationships and interactions that exist between:

- the components within an application, and

- the components of an application and those of the host environment.

(b) Re-engineering

Re-engineering works at the source code level and has been defined by Richard Warden of K3 Group as {WARD88} (and elsewhere in this publication):

> *The simple modification of existing code and data structures using today's software engineering principles to improve the maintainability and adaptability of systems.*

- Reduce code complexity

- Simplify control flow

- Improve program structure

- Remove standards violations

- Remove redundant code and data

- Simplify file and data usage

The essence of this technique is the use of simple tools to highlight potential problem areas within the code and to make the changes at this level.

(c) Renovation

Renovation is defined to be the process in which an approximation of the design of the system is achieved. It is a set of tools to renovate old software in a semi-automatic way. This definition is based on the work of Harry Sneed and is described fully in {SNEE87}. It achieves its goal by the following processes:

- Static analysis

- Modularization

- Restructuring

- Backwards translation in a design language

- Code regeneration

In this technique, understanding is gained through the use of tools that change the original source by breaking it down into smaller modules then restructuring them. The design can then be extracted in a semi-automatic way from these simpler smaller modules.

(d) Inverse engineering

Inverse Engineering is the basis of a research project being carried out at the Centre for Software Maintenance. Its objectives are complete reverse engineering by the use of formal methods.

The input to the system being developed is:

- source code of the system

- any existing knowledge of the system that can be elicited from human personnel and documentation

- encapsulation of maintenance programmers' expertise

The intelligent understanding of the system is achieved by the use of a set of formal transformations. These transformations are the outcome of research carried out by Martin Ward and are described in the papers {WARD88,CALL88,WARD89}.

An important additional factor in this approach is the construction and use of knowledge bases. The types of knowledge bases required are as follows:

Maintenance Knowledge

The expertise of maintenance programmers.

Program Class Knowledge.

Knowledge about the characteristics of a particular type of program. For example, knowledge about compilers, text editors, report generators.

Program Plan Knowledge

Knowledge about the particular programming language being used and knowledge about programming for that language.

30.3   CONCLUSION

Through the use of reverse engineering techniques the reusable components of a software system can be identified. However, research into reverse engineering techniques is in its infancy and this paper has shown some approaches that are being taken in establishing techniques for full system understanding and complete reverse engineering.

REFERENCES

1.   Bennett, K.H., Cornelius, B.J., Munro, M. and Robson, D.J., 1988, Software Maintenance: A Key Area for Research, University Computing, 10 (4) pp. 184-188.

2.   ANSI/IEEE Standard 729, 1983, IEEE Standard Glossary of Software Engineering Terminology, IEEE.

3.   Foster, J.R. and Munro, M., 1987, A Documentation Method Based on Cross-Referencing, Conference on Software Maintenance, Austin, Texas, IEEE 181-185.

4.   Fletton, N.T. and Munro, M., 1988, Redocumenting Software Systems using Hypertext Technology, Conference on Software Maintenance IEEE.

5.   Kenning, R., 1989, Inverse Configuration Management, Third Software Maintenance Workshop Notes, Centre for Software Maintenance, University of Durham.

6.   Warden, R., 1988, Re-engineering for Business Change, Second Software Maintenance Workshop Notes, Centre for Software Maintenance, University of Durham.

7.   Sneed, H. and Jandrasics, J., 1987, Software Recycling, Proc. Conf. on Software Maintenance.

8.   Callis, F.W., Khalil, M., Munro, M. and Ward, M., 1988, A Knowledge-based System for Software Maintenance, Conference on Software Maintenance, Phoenix, Arizona, IEEE.

9.   Ward, M., Calliss, F.W., and Munro, M., 1989, The Maintainer's Assistant, Conference on Software Maintenance, Miami, IEEE.

10. Ward, M., 1988, Transforming a Programming into a Specification, Centre for Software Maintenance Report 88/1.